True Spirituality
A Study of 1 Corinthians

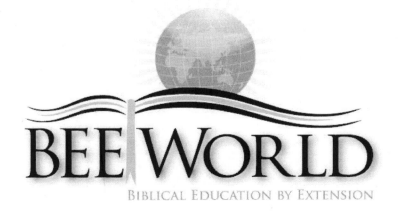

BEE WORLD

BIBLICAL EDUCATION BY EXTENSION

TRUE SPIRITUALITY: A STUDY OF 1 CORINTHIANS

For information regarding permissions or special orders, please contact:

BEE World
International Headquarters
990 Pinon Ranch View, Ste. 100
Colorado Springs, CO 80907

ISBN: 978-1-937324-23-0

First Edition

Printed in the United States of America

1 2 3 4 5 6 7 8 9 10

04152013

Contents

True Spirituality: A Study in 1 Corinthians

Course Introduction

When Paul wrote 1 Corinthians, the church in Corinth was probably not the type of church that most of us would have wanted to join. Many of its problems would have been immediately obvious to the casual attendee: The church was divided; people behaved in selfish, unloving ways; some denied such fundamental doctrine as the resurrection of the dead; the church tolerated gross immorality; worship services were disorderly. Believers were sick—some had died—as discipline from the Lord for unruly behavior. Much emphasis was placed on displays of speaking in tongues and prophesying, but often in unregulated meetings. The church leadership seemed to have abdicated responsibility.

Paul counsels the church to let love and godliness have first place in their assemblies. Their meetings must not be given over to unbridled freedom where anything was allowed. Such an environment promotes arrogance, individuality and the trampling of social sensibilities. The Corinthian believers had lost sight of the focus of the gospel: love God and love one another.

Course Objectives

Lotus loves Jesus, but with all the crazy things happening in her church, sometimes she doesn't know what to think or do.

Five years ago Lotus trusted the Lord when Brother Thomas, an evangelist, came through her village and spoke so movingly. All he talked about was Jesus and how He died on the cross for everybody's sins, and how anyone could be free from his sins and live with God forever just by trusting Him. A number of people in the town became believers during the weeks that Brother Thomas spoke, visited in homes, and prayed over the sick. Brother Lee and his wife, Sister Ruth, hosted Brother Thomas then. After Thomas left, the believers kept meeting weekly in their home. Ruth could play the piano and Lee usually spoke during their meetings. It was better to meet in their house since it was so large.

Things have changed since those early days. The church still meets in the same place, but there are more people now, and the meetings are more confused. People don't seem as unified as they once were. Sometimes traveling speakers come through with strange teachings, and they want the church to give them generous offerings. People get divided over all sorts of issues, such as who gets to speak, sing, pray, and lead the meetings. They struggle with what to do about a church member who has left his wife and has taken up with another woman. They wonder how to handle a group of young women who come to the meetings dressed immodestly or how Christians should behave during the yearly celebrations at the village temple honoring the goddess of blessings, and many more issues.

The Bible is precious to Lotus. With her eighth-grade education, she has no problem reading and writing, but there are many things in the Bible she doesn't understand and needs someone to explain to her. A couple of ladies in the church have told her that their church is going the way of Corinth. Lotus opens her Bible to 1 Corinthians, hoping for insight and direction that will help her and her church spiritually. How can she regain the sense of warmth, acceptance and unity that she so fondly remembers from the early days of her church experience? How can all these disputes and conflicts be resolved? What should she do to improve the situation?

By the end of this course, you will be able to:

- Understand the core issues that lead to disunity, both in the early Corinthian church and in many churches today

- Explain Paul's resolutions to the issues and see his purpose in writing the letter
- Identify the difference in wisdom of man and wisdom of God and how it applies to discernment of false teachings
- Develop an understanding for what "freedom in Christ" is and the importance of exercising those freedoms in love for your fellow brother
- Recognize that the struggles that took place in ancient Corinth also take place in many churches today
- Have practical ways to apply Paul's teachings to your own life and in your church today

Course Information

Units of Study

The lessons are grouped into four units:

Unit 1: Paul Responds to Reported Problems

Lesson 1: Paul's Relationship to Corinth (Acts 18:1-17; 1 Cor 1:1-9; 16:1-24)

Lesson 2: Disunity Problem (1 Cor 1:10-17a)

Lesson 3: True Wisdom (1 Cor 1:17b–2:16)

Unit 2: Applying Wisdom to Solve Problems

Lesson 4: Right Attitude Toward Leaders (1 Cor 3:1–4:21)

Lesson 5: Immorality and Lawsuits (1 Corinthians 5:1–6:20)

Unit 3: Freedom Has Limits in Personal Behavior

Lesson 6: Freedom in Marriage (1 Cor 7:1-40)

Lesson 7: Freedom in Food (1 Cor 8:1-13; 10:1–11:1)

Lesson 8: Freedom and Ministry (1 Cor 9:1-27)

Unit 4: Freedom Has Limits in the Church

Lesson 9: Freedom in Worship: Women and Men (1 Cor 11:2-16)

Lesson 10: Freedom in Worship: The Lord's Supper (1 Cor 11:17-34)

Lesson 11: Freedom in Worship: Spiritual Gifts (1 Cor 12:1-14:40)

Lesson 12: Freedom in Doctrine: Resurrection (1 Cor 15:1-58)

As you plan your study schedule, decide when you want to finish each unit, picking a target date. You can then divide this time into study periods for each lesson.

We suggest that you try to do one lesson per week or three lessons per month. You can do this if you study about one hour each day.

Unit 1: Paul Responds to Reported Problems

The problems at Corinth were so many and mammoth that one must ask: If you had planted the church and maintained a close relationship with them over several years, where would you begin?

More importantly, the church's problems were not entirely separate from their relationship with Paul. This meant that Paul had to take into account their personal reaction to him when dealing with the issues. In his pastoral ministry to them by letter, Paul starts with their disunity problem. In his discussion of their divisions, he argues that their disunity is symptomatic of deeper problems. Somehow, they have missed out on something basic—the wisdom of God. In its place they have substituted the wisdom of man and are reaping the fruits of that error. This is not surprising, for human wisdom was all around them, constantly pressuring them from their own culture. They were falling into the trap of viewing spirituality from invalid human standards, and the results were disastrous.

In this unit we will attempt to follow Paul's thinking and arguments as he begins to address problems in the church at Corinth. We will examine his relationship with those believers, consider how he learned of their problems, and analyze his teaching on true and false wisdom. Lesson 1 focuses on Paul's relationship with Corinth from the founding of the church until the writing of 1 Corinthians. Lesson 2 identifies the first problem that Paul addresses (divisions) and examines the reason for it. Lesson 3 introduces the root of the problem, which is fundamentally anti-Christian. As you study this unit, consider how the truths Paul teaches relate to problems in your own church.

Unit Outline

Lesson 1: Paul's Relationship to Corinth (Acts 18:1-17; 1 Cor 1:1-9; 16:1-24)

Lesson 2: Disunity Problem (1 Cor 1:10-17)

Lesson 3: True Wisdom (1 Cor 1:17–2:16)

Unit Objectives

Lotus highly respects Brother Thomas. She knew that if he were here, he would know what to do. When he first came to the village with his team, he wasn't very impressive. For some reason, his left leg was weak and kept hurting him, so he often sat to speak or when he visited in homes. But he had such wisdom and such love. Even though he spoke with an accent, his messages were full of truth and practical wisdom about life. When he prayed, it was like the Spirit was right there in the room, and everybody was focused on Jesus.

Now things are falling apart. Brothers and sisters are forming cliques and looking down on each other. Lotus admits that there are problems and differences of opinion, but she wonders why the church can't focus on Jesus and solve the issues with the answers that He gives.

She turns to 1 Corinthians to see what Paul did to resolve issues at Corinth. She wonders: Are there principles I can learn and share with church members to help reestablish unity in our church? What is God's wisdom for me and for our congregation? What should I think about the visiting speakers who are so entertaining, but seem to leave things worse after they go?

Lesson 1: Paul's Relationship to Corinth (Acts 18:1-17; 1 Cor 1:1-9; 16:1-24)

One of the first steps to understanding a biblical passage is identifying the historical situation that formed the background for the author's words. In the case of 1 Corinthians the background includes Paul himself, the identity of the Corinthian believers, the circumstances of the establishment of the church, and the events between the founding of the church and Paul's letter to them. Our approach to this part of the study is to concentrate on the record in Acts and the first and last chapters of the letter. From these primary sources we can develop an understanding of Paul's relationship to the church at Corinth.

Topic 1 briefly researches the geography, people, culture, and importance of Corinth in the mid-first century, when the church was founded.

Topic 2 examines Paul's pioneer evangelism and pastoral ministry with the church. Acts records the founding of the church and its early history. From references in the opening and closing chapters of 1 Corinthians, we can discern further information about Paul's continuing contact with the church subsequent to his departure from Corinth.

Topic 3 delves into the main reasons why Paul wrote this letter.

Topic 4 examines the opening content of 1 Corinthians, where Paul greets and offers thanks for those believers.

Topic 5 attempts to discern more of Paul's relationship with Corinth from his closing remarks, which are more personal. He talks about his plans for a future visit to them.

Topic 6 considers the basic question of the application of the teaching of 1 Corinthians for believers today. Since the problems addressed were specific to that church in the first century, why should we study them today, and what can we hope to gain from our study?

Lesson Outline

Topic 1: Location and Importance of Corinth

    Location

    Importance

Topic 2: History of Paul's Relationship With Corinth

    Paul's Arrival at Corinth (Acts 18:1-17)

    Founding of the Church

    Continuing Contacts

    Nature of the Church at Corinth

Topic 3: Purposes for Writing 1 Corinthians

Topic 4: What Paul Was Thankful for at Corinth (1 Cor 1:1-9)

    Greetings (1:1-3)

    Thanksgiving (1:4-9)

Topic 5: Closing Remarks (1 Cor 16:1-24)

Principles for Handling the Collection (16:1-4)

Reasons for Paul's Delay (16:5-24)

Topic 6: Question of Application

Lesson Objectives

When Lotus reads through 1 Corinthians, she is struck by how similar Paul's relationship to the church at Corinth is to Brother Thomas' relationship to her church. Things went crazy at Corinth after Paul left, just like with her church now that Brother Thomas has moved on. Lotus remembers how deeply Brother Thomas loved the church and how sometimes he would stop by for a visit. She wishes he would come now and clear up the confusion.

Wanting to understand as clearly as she can why Paul wrote 1 Corinthians, Lotus finds the record of the founding of the church in Acts 18. Then she rereads the beginning and end of the letter to try to get a feel for how Paul really felt about the church at Corinth. Of course, she knows there are many differences between her church and the church at Corinth two thousand years ago, but she hopes much of Paul's teaching will speak to her situation. She wonders if he outlined any foundational principles that transcended boundaries of culture and time and will help her deal with the division and immorality in her church today.

By the end of this lesson, you will be able to:

- Develop an understanding of the history and the background of the church of Corinth
- Explain the relationship that Paul had to the church of Corinth
- Understand Paul's purpose in writing the letter to the church of Corinth
- Identify some practical ways to apply 1 Corinthians 1 to your life

Topic 1: Location and Importance of Corinth

Since 1 Corinthians was written to a specific church in history, it is valuable to examine the geography, prominence, and culture of the letter's destination. This study will give us clues as to certain influences on the lives of the recipients of the letter.

Do geography, local history, culture and politics affect your church? Every church has its own unique setting, identity, and characteristics. The location of Corinth was one important factor affecting the thinking, vocations, and identity of its members.

Location

Study the maps of the Mediterranean region in the first century and the map of Greece. Locate the city of Corinth. The most notable feature of Corinth's location is its closeness to the Saronic Gulf and to the Corinthian Gulf near an isthmus. This isthmus was about eight kilometers wide.

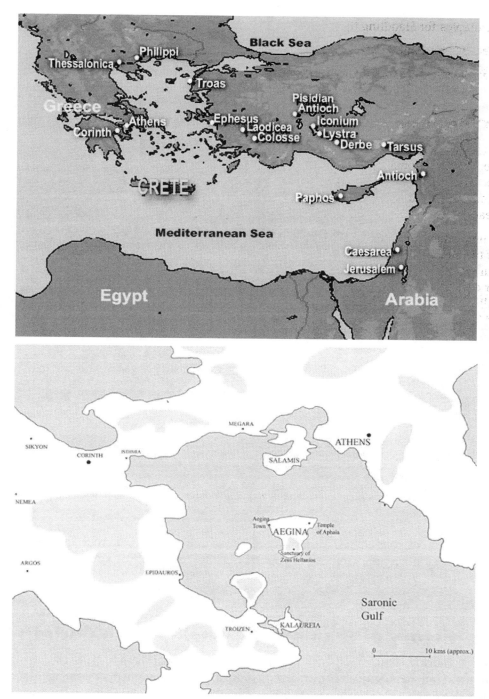

(Map from "Aegina: Contexts for Choral Lyric Poetry: Myth, History, and Identity in the Fifth Century BC" by David Fearn. Oxford Scholarship Online of Oxford University Press, January 2011. Accessed March 2013. www.oxfordscholarship.com)

Importance

Assignment

- Read "Historical Background" in *Constable's Notes on 1 Corinthians* (refer to the Articles section at the end of this lesson).

- Read "Importance."

Importance

Corinth's location was important for trade, since ships were reluctant to venture into the Mediterranean, particularly in winter, because of the danger of storms (Acts 27:9). Many ships would unload their cargoes on either side of this isthmus for transport to the other side, or perhaps the whole boat would be hauled on a platform across the strip of land. The shipping trade was a major source of income for the city.

The Isthmian Games—somewhat similar to the Olympic Games—were held every two years on this isthmus. Paul used athletic imagery in 1 Corinthians 9:24-27, probably alluding to these Games.

Corinth was the capital city of the Roman province of Achaia in the first century. It had been destroyed by the Romans in 146 BC and reestablished one hundred years later by Julius Caesar. When Paul visited, it was the largest city in Greece.

Christians were a small minority in Corinth when Paul wrote this letter. The house churches at that time had no "church" property, and the members faced tremendous pressures from a multi-cultural, materialistic, pagan society.

QUESTION 1

Which aspects of ancient Corinth would make it an attractive target for evangelism by Paul in AD 50? *(Select all that apply.)*

    A. Major city

    B. Good transportation

    C. Jewish synagogue

    D. Unevangelized

    E. Newly rebuilt

QUESTION 2

How does the location of your church or ministry affect its outreach? What criteria might be helpful in determining a future ministry area for you or your church? Record your response in your Life Notebook.

Topic 2: History of Paul's Relationship With Corinth

Paul and his evangelistic team established the church at Corinth near the middle of the first century. After departing from Corinth to continue his evangelistic ministry, he maintained a relationship with the church for some years before he wrote this letter. Many problems had come up in the intervening time, and quite a few have to do with the Corinthians' relationship with Paul and their understanding of his teaching. This topic will give us important information about Paul's relationship with the church at the time he wrote the letter.

Establishing a new church is a faith exercise that is rarely accomplished in only a week or two. The church planter must expend himself over a period of time, exerting himself to communicate the gospel message. In this way, he shows himself and his message to be trustworthy—overcoming obstacles and opposition, and bringing together a unified congregation. By the time Paul wrote 1 Corinthians, he already had quite a history with that church. In this topic we will learn the history of Paul's relationship with the church at Corinth.

Paul's Arrival at Corinth (Acts 18:1-17)

Assignment

- Read "Paul's Arrival at Corinth."

Paul's Arrival at Corinth

Luke gives a brief account in Acts 18:1-17 of the founding of the church at Corinth during Paul's second missionary journey. The mention of the proconsul Gallio in Acts 18:12 is key for the dating of Paul's first visit to Corinth. Paul first arrived at Corinth from Athens, probably late in AD 49 or early AD 50.

In what condition did Paul arrive in Corinth, with what motive and attitude? Paul arrived alone, in an unfamiliar city, where he knew no one. He had received a clear call to preach the gospel in Macedonia and had suffered in this ministry gospel.

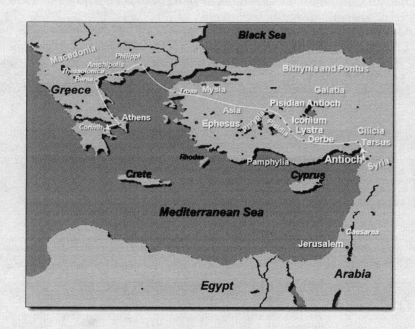

Paul began his second missionary journey following the Jerusalem Council (Acts 15) and the dispute with Barnabas over John Mark (Acts 15:36-41), probably in AD 49. Paul's initial partner was Silas (Acts 15:40), and they set out with the blessing of the church of Antioch in Syria. They went about strengthening the churches planted during the first missionary journey, recruiting Timothy to join their team in Lycaonia (Acts 16:1-3). Desiring to further spread the gospel, they were prevented by the Holy Spirit from preaching in the province of Asia (Acts 16:6). In Troas, by the Aegean Sea, Paul received the famous vision of the Macedonian man and concluded that God was calling them to preach the gospel in Europe (Acts 16:9-10). This begins the first "we" section in Acts, where the author (Luke) implies that he traveled with Paul and Silas.

Crossing the sea to Macedonia, Luke records how Paul and Silas evangelized in Philippi, where they were beaten and imprisoned. Next, they went to Thessalonica, perhaps for as short a time as three weeks (Acts 17:2). Successful evangelism stirred up jealousy from the Jews, so Paul and

Silas were sent to Berea during the night to escape danger. Antagonistic Jews from Thessalonica came to Berea to stir up opposition to Paul, so "the brothers sent Paul away to the coast at once" (Acts 17:14), again to escape danger. Paul was without his support team in Athens, but began to evangelize. In Acts 17:22, he was given the opportunity to speak before the Council of the Areopagus (see Note 2 at the end of this article). Paul then traveled eighty-eight kilometers to the next major city—Corinth.

Even though Paul was clearly called and directed in a vision to evangelize in Macedonia, his short time there (perhaps only two or three months) was filled with persecution and troubles from the Jews. In every city he was beaten, imprisoned, asked to leave by the authorities, forced to flee because of persecution, or denied permission to preach. True, he saw some fruit from his preaching efforts, but this must have been very stressful for Paul.

Note 2: Areopagus: This term refers to the advisory council of Athens known as the *Areopagus*. They dealt with ethical, cultural, and religious matters, including the supervision of education and control of the many visiting lecturers.

On his second missionary journey, Paul traveled extensively and faced heavy persecution. For fifty-year-old Paul arriving alone in Corinth for the first time, he must have been physically drained and felt like a stranger who had been constantly traveling for months.

QUESTION 3

What do you think Paul meant by his statement in 1 Corinthians 2:1-3 that "When I came to you, brothers and sisters…I was with you in weakness and in fear and with much trembling"?

Founding of the Church

The founding of the church at Corinth did not happen without problems! The majority of the Jews did not believe, and Paul had to separate from them because of abuse. Despite that move, the Jews kept up the pressure by bringing a lawsuit against Paul.

Assignment

- Read Acts 18:1-17.
- Read "Founding of the Church."

Founding of the Church

Paul's pattern of ministry at Corinth was typical of his practice in other cities. First he targeted his own people, the Jews, visiting the synagogue on the Sabbath in order to testify about Jesus. As a traveler who had been educated in Jerusalem under Gamaliel (a well-known Jewish scholar and teacher), Paul would be invited to speak at the synagogue. He knew those attendees had already been prepared in many ways to receive the gospel—they believed in one God, and were familiar with the doctrines of sin, the authority of God's Word, and the hope of the Messiah.

Paul continued to focus on the Jews until "they opposed him and reviled him" (Acts 18:6). He then shook out his clothes, left the synagogue, and turned his focus to the Gentiles. Shaking out one's clothes is a symbolic action of protest, similar to the practice of shaking the dust off one's feet (see Acts 13:51). In doing this, Paul was not being nice, gentle, welcoming, affirming, or tolerant! Instead, he was recognizing them as enemies of the gospel and taking a clear step to separate from them.

The decision by Gallio was actually quite significant. In Roman law, certain religions were legal but others did not enjoy this status. The Jews' allegation against Paul was that he was not spreading orthodox Judaism (which enjoyed legal status) but rather an illegal religion. Therefore they wanted the government to stop him from preaching. This was an effort to bring Roman government sanctions against Christianity. When Gallio threw out the case, according to the record of Acts there was no further Roman government imprisonment or court case against Paul until his arrest in Jerusalem (Acts 21:33) perhaps six years later.

QUESTION 4

Paul stayed in Corinth for twelve months on his first visit. *True or False?*

Study how Paul planted the church at Corinth in Acts 18:1-17 and then answer Question 5.

QUESTION 5

Match five ways in which God encouraged Paul during his ministry there with the appropriate Scripture.

Encouragement	*Scripture*
In the temporary absence of his team members, Paul found fellow Jews, Priscilla and Aquila (though they may have not been believers yet), to work and live with.	Acts 18:5 (see Phil 4:15-16)
Paul's team members, Silas and Timothy, arrived in Corinth.	Acts 18:14-15
Silas and Timothy apparently brought a financial gift from the church in Philippi to enable Paul to devote himself completely to preaching.	Acts 18:9
In a vision, the Lord told Paul to continue his ministry at Corinth, for God would protect him from harm.	Acts 18:5
The Roman official Gallio (refer to Notes section at the end of this lesson) refused to hear charges against Paul brought by the Jews.	Acts 18:2-3

QUESTION 6

Answer the following questions in your Life Notebook: Was Paul's action in separating from the Jews justified? Shouldn't he have continued to hold out the Word of life to these people who rejected his message? In your answer, refer to Matthew 7:6; Matthew 10:14; and to Acts 13:51. What is your practice when you face different responses in your evangelism?

Continuing Contacts

Paul had been away from Corinth for four or five years when he wrote 1 Corinthians. However, the epistle is not devoted to recounting history, but it deals with current problems. Paul kept the church in his heart, in his prayers, and he kept up contact with them during his absence.

Assignment

- Read 1 Corinthians 1:11; 5:9; 7:1; 16:17.
- Read "Continuing Contacts."

Continuing Contacts

The generally accepted view is that Paul wrote 1 Corinthians around AD 56 from Ephesus (1 Cor 16:8) during his third missionary journey. Paul spent three years in Ephesus.

Assuming that Paul departed from Corinth in AD 51, it was four to five years later that 1 Corinthians was written. Thus the church was around six years old.

Clearly, Paul kept up an active relationship with the church at Corinth during the years of his absence from them prior to writing 1 Corinthians. "1 Corinthians" as a title to the letter is somewhat misleading, since it was not the first letter Paul wrote to them.

QUESTION 7

What contacts did Paul have with the church at Corinth between leaving the city in AD 51 and writing 1 Corinthians? Match the contact with the reference.

Contact	Reference
Visit from members of Chloe's household	1 Corinthians 7:1
A letter from Paul to them (now lost)	1 Corinthians 5:9
A letter to Paul from the Corinthians	1 Corinthians 1:11
Visit from Stephanus, Fortunatus, and Achaicus	1 Corinthians 16:17

QUESTION 8

What is your relationship to people you formerly ministered to? What role can you still have in their lives? What roles should you not have? Not being an apostle, in what ways could you continue to encourage their spiritual growth and at the same time affirm their relationship with their current leaders? Record your response in your Life Notebook.

Nature of the Church at Corinth

Assignment

- Read "Nature of the Church at Corinth."

Nature of the Church at Corinth

What did the church at Corinth look like when Paul wrote 1 Corinthians? What was its make-up? Since there were no church buildings in the first century, and because Acts 18:7 records that Paul left the synagogue, undoubtedly the believers met in homes, probably hosted by the wealthier believers. Thus the first century church that Paul wrote to would be one or more house churches.

Converts from both Jewish and Gentile backgrounds are mentioned in Acts 18. It appears that the Jews as a whole rejected the gospel message in Corinth, but that the Gentiles responded, so by the time of the writing of 1 Corinthians we may assume that Gentile believers predominated in the church (see 1 Cor 8:7 and 1 Cor 12:2). Paul also states (1 Cor 1:26) that "not many [of the believers] were wise by human standards, not many were powerful, not many were born to a privileged position." This implies that only a few of the Corinthian believers were well educated or politically or financially powerful. Paul also alludes to slaves in the congregation (1 Cor 7:21).

It appears that primarily the lower classes responded to the gospel under Paul's preaching in Corinth—although not exclusively (1 Cor 1:26). Some of the issues Paul addresses in the letter (which we will study later) may relate to class distinctions among the members.

QUESTION 9

The church at Corinth was homogeneous. *True or False?*

QUESTION 10

How are the people that you minister to different from or similar to the congregation in Corinth? What type of challenges do you face due to socio-economic issues? In what ways could the study of Paul's letter help you with these challenges? Record your responses in your Life Notebook.

Topic 3: Purposes for Writing 1 Corinthians

By today's standards 1 Corinthians is a long letter. It has thousands of words and would take over an hour to read out loud to a congregation. Paul put a lot of effort into its writing. This topic will examine his goals for writing this letter.

Most people really treasure love notes from their family members. Some may file them away for safekeeping all their lives. Would you characterize 1 Corinthians as a love note? Probably not. How then do you perceive the purpose of the letter?

Assignment

- Read "Purposes for Writing 1 Corinthians."

Purposes for Writing 1 Corinthians

As is evident from the content of 1 Corinthians, Paul's purpose for writing was mainly pastoral. The word "pastor," according to the International Standard Bible Encyclopedia, means "literally, a helper, or feeder of the sheep." It is used in Ephesians 4:11 in close connection with "teacher." Usually we think of the pastor as the shepherd of the congregation. A literal shepherd of a flock of sheep does many things for them: he protects, leads, guides, feeds, treats for injury or disease, disciplines, and searches for those who have gone astray.

Paul had heard reports of many problems in the church, plus the church had written him a letter asking certain questions. His responses to problems that had been reported orally and problems raised in their letter form the basis for the overall structure of the letter. Paul's topic by topic responses and answers are reflected in the titles of the remaining lessons of this course.

Most of the problems Paul addressed do not deal with the fundamentals of the gospel (with the exception of the doctrine of the resurrection in chapter 15). Unlike Romans or Galatians, he does not emphasize justification by faith, substitutionary atonement, election, or original sin. Instead, he addresses practical aspects of church life.

Paul is writing to a congregation that he knows, loves deeply, has a deep investment in, but that is failing in many ways to display true spirituality. Instead of love, maturity, and Christlikeness, Paul hears about factions, arrogance, immorality, insensitivity, and disorder. Like a pastor, he writes corrective advice, hoping that they will repent of their errors and get back on the path of spiritual growth.

His secondary purposes for writing this letter are to urge them to continue to collect funds for the poor in Jerusalem (1 Cor 16:1-4), to notify them of Timothy's possible visit (1 Cor 16:10) and his own plans to visit (1 Cor 16:5-7).

Like a parent who really loves his children, or like a pastor serving his flock, Paul wrote 1 Corinthians with deep feeling and concern. Consider how much space Paul devoted to various topics as indicators of his major purpose in writing.

QUESTION 11

What is the primary purpose for writing 1 Corinthians?

    A. To ensure that the fund raising project for the poor is carried out successfully

    B. To alert them to prepare for Timothy's visit

    C. To make sure they are clear about the fundamentals of the gospel

    D. To help them to deal with local church problems

QUESTION 12

Considering the many and serious problems at Corinth and using the principle "judge a tree by its fruit" (Mt 7:17), perhaps some would conclude that Paul was a poor church planter. Their reasoning: If Paul had laid a better foundation at Corinth, then the church would not have had so many serious problems after he left. Record in your Life Notebook how you would respond to this allegation. On what basis do you evaluate your own ministry or the ministry of others?

Topic 4: What Paul Was Thankful for at Corinth (1 Cor 1:1-9)

In view of his pastoral purpose in writing, Paul begins his letter by identifying himself, the recipients, and their relationship to Jesus Christ. Because of the abundant grace of God, there is much to be thankful for despite the many problems. Paul starts off in a positive, uplifting tone.

There is usually some good to praise the Lord for in every bad situation. Paul found many things, despite the negative situation, to give thanks for at Corinth. The effect of this thanksgiving would be to ensure the Corinthians that Paul thought highly of them.

Greetings (1:1-3)

Assignment

- Read 1 Corinthians 1:1-3.
- Read Constable, "Salutation 1:1-3" (refer to the Articles section at the end of this lesson).

- Read "Greetings."

Greetings

Although the content of 1 Corinthians is heavily focused on resolving problems within the congregation, Paul did not write this letter only to the leaders of the church. We may assume that the letter was meant to be read out loud (see Col 4:16) during an assembly of the congregation as a whole. The issues that Paul addresses were not private, but affected the whole church.

Writers usually open a letter with a positive greeting. In his greeting, Paul called the recipients' attention to their privileges in Christ and why they would want to pay close attention to what Paul wrote.

QUESTION 13

Compare 1 Corinthians 1:1-3 with 1 Corinthians 16:21. How was this letter written?

QUESTION 14

Paul writes this letter with the authority of a(n) _____ of Jesus Christ.

QUESTION 15

Paul addresses the church in Corinth as "those who are sanctified in Christ Jesus, and called to be saints." "Sanctified" and "saints" refer to:

A. Their godly behavior

B. Their deep devotion to Christ

C. Their divine calling

D. Their ability to speak in tongues

Thanksgiving (1:4-9)

Assignment

- Read 1 Corinthians 1:4-9.
- Read "Thanksgiving."

Thanksgiving

Paul follows his frequent pattern of offering a thanksgiving for the recipients of the letter, sometimes mentioning prayer (1 Cor 1:4-9).

Paul here refers repeatedly to the second coming, implying that even though they are spiritually "rich" now, much greater blessings are coming in the future. As we will discover, the issues of spirituality and the resurrection of the dead were major issues at Corinth.

When someone says to you, "I thank God for you," you tend to feel encouraged and blessed. Paul started this letter with positive words, showing the Corinthians that he valued them highly, and especially the gifts God had given them.

QUESTION 16

For what things is Paul thankful regarding the church at Corinth? *(Select all that apply.)*

   A. Their financial support
   B. Their godly behavior
   C. God's grace to them
   D. Their spiritual gifts
   E. Their speech
   F. Their knowledge

QUESTION 17

Most of the content of this letter focuses on church problems, including issues of speech (tongues and prophecy), knowledge (the doctrine of the resurrection), and spiritual gifts. How is Paul sincere in this thanksgiving?

QUESTION 18

For a worship interaction, think of someone you have a hard time getting along with. In your Life Notebook, try to make a list of three to five things about them you can thank God for. Pray through that list. What things can you thank the Lord for that you see exhibited in the lives of those who attend or minister in your church?

Topic 5: Closing Remarks (1 Cor 16:1-24)

In 1 Corinthians 16, Paul concludes the letter with a brief mention of a collection for the poor saints in Jerusalem, the plans of Paul, Timothy and Apollos to visit them, an appeal to accept Stephanus' leadership, and final encouragements and blessings.

In promoting a financial collection for the poor in Jerusalem, Paul provided the opportunity for the believers in Corinth to demonstrate love. This show of love would cross cultural and geographic boundaries and unite people in Christ. Traveling with large sums of money in the ancient world was dangerous, and money brings many temptations. Paul briefly wrote his instructions for handling the collection and then finished the letter by explaining his travel plans and giving exhortations.

Principles for Handling the Collection (16:1-4)

Paul wanted to raise a significant amount of money from the predominately Gentile churches to send to Jerusalem. The fundraising was carried out in many churches for perhaps a year before the money was delivered.

Assignment

   * Read 1 Corinthians 16:1-4.
   * Read Romans 15:25-28.

- Read Constable, "Arrangements for the Collection" (refer to the Articles section at the end of this lesson).
- Read "Principles for Handling the Collection."

Principles for Handling the Collection

The collection for the poor in Jerusalem (1 Cor 16:1-4) is explained in greater detail in 2 Corinthians 8-9. When Paul wrote 2 Corinthians, perhaps six months or more after writing 1 Corinthians, the collection project was still unfinished at Corinth. From his wording "with regard to...," it seems that here Paul is responding to some question about the collection in their letter to him.

Paul instructs the church how to participate in this project. That church members were to set aside money on the first day of each week (Sunday) encourages a regular habit of giving on the day of worship. Paul does not specify that they give any particular percentage of their income, but rather that they give according to how much God had prospered them. This instruction fits well with Paul's later teaching in 2 Corinthians 9:7, "Each one of you should give just as he has decided in his heart, not reluctantly or under compulsion, because God loves a cheerful giver."

QUESTION 19

What was an important motivation for Paul to write the verses you read from Romans?

QUESTION 20

What measures did Paul take to ensure that the handling of this collection was above suspicion? *(Select all that apply.)*

    A. More than one person was responsible for the delivery of the collection.

    B. People whom the Corinthians deemed trustworthy would deliver the money.

    C. Paul himself did not have to be part of the delivery.

    D. Letters of explanation would be sent with the deliverers.

    E. Paul was to be in complete control of every detail of handling the money.

QUESTION 21

Are there modifications that you should make in your handling of ministry funds in light of Paul's example? Record your thoughts in your Life Notebook.

Reasons for Paul's Delay (16:5-24)

Paul talked about his and Timothy's plans to visit soon, and about Apollos' plans not to visit soon. In view of the many serious problems in the congregation, we may question why Paul did not make every effort to return to Corinth as soon as possible.

Assignment

- Read 1 Corinthians 16:5-24.

- Read Constable, "The Travel Plans of Paul and His Fellow Apostles," "Final Exhortations," and "Final Greetings and Benedictions" (refer to the Articles section at the end of this lesson).
- Read "Reasons for Paul's Delay."

Reasons for Paul's Delay

Perhaps Paul thought that an immediate personal visit to Corinth would not be the wisest way to handle the problems in the church. After all, there were divisions in the congregation, and some believers attached themselves especially to Paul, but others to other leaders (1 Cor 1:10-17). It was better for him to stay away for a time, to give clear teaching on these matters through this letter, and to pray that the Corinthians themselves would resolve the divisions.

Paul relayed an appeal to Apollos from the Corinthians, apparently from their letter, asking that Apollos visit them. This connection between Paul and Apollos is especially significant since there existed a "Paul party" and an "Apollos party" at Corinth (1 Cor 1:12). Paul demonstrated his unity with Apollos by also urging him to visit them. Apollos refused to go at that time, perhaps for reasons similar to Paul's.

In the final section of the letter, Paul praises the household of Stephanus. He was then visiting Paul, along with two others, Fortunatus and Achaicus. Perhaps these last two were Stephanus' slaves and considered members of his household. Paul urges the Corinthians to recognize and submit to Stephanus' leadership, and to the leadership of similar believers. Many scholars view Stephanus as the one who carried 1 Corinthians back to Corinth.

In Paul's closing to the letter, he sends greetings from the churches of the province of Asia, from Priscilla and Aquila, who had earlier lived in Corinth (Acts 18:1, 2), and from Paul himself.

He urges the believers to greet one another with a holy kiss (1 Cor 16:20). The kiss was holy because it was done among God's holy people (1 Cor 1:2). As a greeting, the holy kiss would indicate love and unity.

The statement, "Let anyone who has no love for the Lord be accursed" (1 Cor 16:22), may seem out of place and harsh at first glance. This is a strong statement of condemnation, similar to Paul's condemnation of Judaizers in Galatia (Gal 1:9). The important thing is a person's relationship to the Lord. Apart from a relationship with Christ, everyone is under God's wrath.

QUESTION 22

Why do you think Paul wanted to wait until after Pentecost to visit Corinth? *(Select all that apply.)*

  A. To give time for his counsel in this letter to take effect
  B. To give time for the Corinthians to complete the collection
  C. To allow more time in his schedule to stay with them, so he could better help them with their problems
  D. To take full advantage of his ministry opportunity in Ephesus
  E. To give time to hear Timothy's report of the situation in Corinth
  F. To be more efficient in his use of travel time—arriving in Corinth after a trip through Macedonia

QUESTION 23

Timothy was unquestionably Paul's co-worker and representative. Why would Paul urge that they see that Timothy had nothing to fear when he visited them, and that they should "let no one treat him with contempt" (1 Cor 16:10, 11)?

QUESTION 24

Why does Paul commend Stephanus as worthy of their submission?

    A. Because of his devotion to the ministry

    B. Because of his obvious spiritual gifts

    C. Because of his high education

    D. Because of his close connection to Paul

QUESTION 25

In letters to various churches, Paul and Peter often close by instructing believers to "greet one another with a holy kiss" (1 Cor 16:20; see also Rom 16:16; 2 Cor 13:12; 1 Thess 5:26; 1 Pet 5:14). What is the principle behind the holy kiss? How is that principle expressed in local churches in your area?

QUESTION 26

How do you speak of your coworkers in ministry? Do you say positive things that highlight their value or do you portray them in a negative light? How could you better follow Paul's example in this area? Record your response in your Life Notebook.

Topic 6: Question of Application

Before embarking on a detailed study of 1 Corinthians, we should consider its relevance for today. The church at Corinth may seem quite different from your own church. How should we approach applying what Paul wrote then to us now?

Have you ever been to a church where the women wear head coverings, or the believers wash each other's feet, or greet one another with a holy kiss? Understanding Paul's advice to a first century Greek church and applying it in a different culture in the twenty-first century is difficult.

Assignment

- Read "Chapter 71" in Ryrie's "Basic Theology" (refer to the Articles section at the end of this lesson).
- Read "Question of Application."

Question of Application

More than any other letter in the New Testament, 1 Corinthians gives detailed insight into the practices and problems of one early church. Of course, those problems were specific to the church at Corinth at that time. Our study of the details of those issues begs the question: How much of what Paul said in 1 Corinthians is applicable today? Perhaps the situation in our churches is quite different. Must we obey today what Paul said almost two thousand years ago in a different context and culture?

The position taken in this course is that the inspired Scriptures teach principles that are relevant and applicable to the local church today. Careful study of the Scriptures includes not just grammatical analysis, but also effort to discover the cultural and historical context in which they were written. The better the student can grasp the nature of the specific problems that Paul was addressing, the better he can understand those timeless principles that apply to the church in all ages, and the better he can apply those principles.

One of the great difficulties in studying 1 Corinthians may be illustrated by the example of a telephone conversation. If you should suddenly walk into a room and overhear someone talking on the phone, you could perhaps understand a great deal of the issues being discussed. However, you probably would not be able to understand everything with clarity because you do not have the ability to overhear the "other half" of the conversation. It is not the same as listening in to the complete conversation on an extension telephone. Similarly, when we study 1 Corinthians, we do not have direct access to the letter the Corinthians wrote to Paul, nor can we overhear the reports from Chloe's people or from Stephanus, Fortunatus, and Achaicus. A lot of information is missing that we would like to have. Thus, for some issues raised in 1 Corinthians, sincere believers have different views as to Paul's meaning and the application of that meaning. We will note these issues as we study through this book.

The study of 1 Corinthians touches on many hotly debated issues in the church today: speaking in tongues, the role of women, marriage and divorce, a Christian's freedom, and the nature of true spirituality. We hope that this study of 1 Corinthians will help guide you to think through these issues.

QUESTION 27

Church practices today should all be exactly the same as in churches of the New Testament. *True or False?*

QUESTION 28

One of the difficulties in interpreting 1 Corinthians is that the letter the Corinthians wrote to Paul, which he mentions in 1 Corinthians 7:1, is now _____.

Lesson 1 Articles

Notes on 1 Corinthians

Dr. Thomas L. Constable; 2003 Edition

Introduction
HISTORICAL BACKGROUND

Corinth had a long history stretching back into the Bronze Age (before 1200 B.C.). (1) In

Paul's day it was a Roman colony and the capital of the province of Achaia. The population consisted of Roman citizens who had migrated from Italy, native Greeks, Jews (Acts 18:4), and other people from various places who chose to settle there.

The ancient city of Corinth enjoyed an ideal situation as a commercial center. It stood just southwest of the Isthmus of Corinth, the land bridge that connected Northern Greece and Southern Greece, the Peloponnesus. This site made Corinth a crossroads for trade by land, north and south, as well as by sea, east and west. In Paul's day large ships would transfer their cargoes to land vehicles that would cart them from the Corinthian Gulf to the Saronic Gulf, or vice

versa. There stevedores would reload them onto other ships. If a ship was small enough, they would drag the whole vessel across the four and a half mile isthmus from one gulf to the other. This did away with the long voyage around the Peloponnesus. Later the Greeks cut a canal linking these two gulfs. (2)

Corinth's strategic location brought commerce and all that goes with it to its populace: wealth, a steady stream of travelers and merchants, and vice. In Paul's day many of the pagan religions included prostitution as part of the worship of their god or goddess. Consequently fornication flourished in Corinth.

> "Old Corinth had gained such a reputation for sexual vice that Aristophanes (*ca.* 450-385 B.C.) coined the verb *korinthiazo* (=to act like a Corinthian, i.e., to commit fornication)." (3)

> "The old city had been the most licentious city in Greece, and perhaps the most licentious city in the Empire." (4)

The most notorious shrine was the temple of Aphrodite that stood on top of an approximately 1,900 foot high mountain just south of the city, the Acrocorinthus. Hundreds of female slaves served the men who "worshipped" there. (5) Other major deities honored in Corinth included Melicertes, the patron of seafarers, and Poseidon, the sea god.

> "All of this evidence together suggests that Paul's Corinth was at once the New York, Los Angeles, and Las Vegas of the ancient world." (6)

There were several other local sites of importance to the student of 1 Corinthians. These included the *bema* (judgment seat or platform), the place where judges tried important cases including Paul's (Acts 18:12). (7) Cenchrea, the port of Corinth on the Saronic Gulf of the Aegean Sea, was the town from which Paul set sail for Ephesus during his second missionary journey (Acts 18:18). Isthmia was another little town east of Corinth, just north of Cenchrea, that hosted the Isthmian Games every two or three years. These athletic contests were important in the life of the Greeks, and Paul referred to them in this epistle (1 Corinthians 9:24-27).

Paul had arrived in Corinth first from Athens, which lay to the east. There he preached the gospel and planted a church. There, too, he met Priscilla and Aquila, Jews who had recently left Rome. After local Jewish officials expelled the church from the synagogue, it met in a large house next door that Titius Justus owned. Paul ministered in Corinth for 18 months, probably in A.D. 51 and 52. He left taking Priscilla and Aquila with him to Ephesus. Paul then proceeded on to Syrian Antioch by way of Caesarea.

Returning to Ephesus on his third journey Paul made that city his base of operations for almost three years (A.D. 53-56). There he heard disquieting news about immorality in the Corinthian church. Therefore he wrote a letter urging the believers not to tolerate such conduct in their midst. Paul referred to this letter as his "former letter" (1 Cor 5:9). It is not extant today.

Then he heard from "Chloe's people" that factions had developed in the church. He also received a letter from the church in Corinth requesting his guidance in certain matters. These matters were marriage, divorce, food offered to idols, the exercise of spiritual gifts in the church, and the collection for the poor saints in Jerusalem. Those who carried this letter also reported other disturbing conditions in the church. These conditions were the condoning rather than disciplining of immorality, Christians suing one another in the pagan courts, and disorders in their church meetings. These factors led Paul to compose another letter, "1 Corinthians." In it he dealt with the problem of factions, promised to visit them soon, and said he was sending Timothy to Corinth (1 Cor 1-4). Paul added his responses to the Corinthians' questions to what he had already written. He dealt next with the oral reports (1 Cor 5-6) and then with the questions that the Corinthian believers had written to him (1 Cor 7-16). He evidently sent this epistle from Ephesus by trusted messengers in the late winter or early spring of A.D. 56 (cf. 1 Cor 16:8).

It seems that a conflict had developed between the Corinthian church and its founder. There was internal strife in the church, as the epistle makes clear. However the larger problem seems to have been that some in the community were leading the church into a view of things that was contrary to that of Paul. This resulted in a questioning of Paul's authority and his gospel. The key issue between Paul and the Corinthians was what it means to be "spiritual." (8)

> "It [1 Corinthians] is not the fullest and clearest statement of Paul's Gospel; for this we must turn to Romans. Nor is it the letter that shows Paul's own heart most clearly, for in this respect it is surpassed by 2 Corinthians, and perhaps by other epistles too. But it has the great value of showing theology at work, theology being used as it was intended to be used, in the criticism and establishing of persons, institutions, practices, and ideas." (9)

Paul's Corinthian Contacts							
Paul's founding visit	His "former letter"	The Corinthians' letter to him	First Corinthians	Paul's "painful visit"	His "severe letter"	Second Corinthians	Paul's anticipated visit

OUTLINE

I. Introduction (1 Cor 1:1-9)

    A. Salutation (1 Cor 1:1-3)

B.Thanksgiving (1 Cor 1:4-9)

II. Conditions reported to Paul (1 Cor 1:10–6:20)

    A. Divisions in the church (1 Cor 1:10–4:21)

        1. The manifestation of the problem (1 Cor 1:10-17)

        2. The gospel as a contradiction to human wisdom (1 Cor 1:18–2:5)

        3. The Spirit's ministry of revealing God's wisdom (1 Cor 2:6-16)

        4. The spiritual yet carnal condition (1 Cor 3:1-4)

        5. The role of God's servants (1 Cor 3:5-17)

        6. Human wisdom and limited blessing (1 Cor 3:18-23)

        7. The Corinthians' relationship with Paul (1 Cor 4:1-21)

    B. Lack of discipline in the church (1 Cor 5-6)

        1. Incest in the church (1 Cor 5)

        2. Litigation in the church (1 Cor 6:1-11)

        3. Prostitution in the church (1 Cor 6:12-20)

III. Questions asked of Paul (1 Cor 7:1-16:12)

    A. Marriage and related matters (1 Cor 7)

        1. Advice to the married or formerly married (1 Cor 7:1-16)

        2. Basic principles (1 Cor 7:17-24)

        3. Advice concerning virgins (1 Cor 7:25-40)

    B. Food offered to idols (1 Cor 8:1-11:1)

        1. The priority of love over knowledge in Christian conduct (1 Cor 8)

        2. Paul's apostolic defense (1 Cor 9)

        3. The sinfulness of idolatry (1 Cor 10:1-22)

        4. The issue of marketplace food (1 Cor 10:23-11:1)

    C. Propriety in worship (1 Cor 11:2-16)

        1. The argument from culture (1 Cor 11:2-6)

        2. The argument from creation (1 Cor 11:7-12)

        3. The argument from propriety (1 Cor 11:13-16)

    D. The Lord's Supper (1 Cor 11:17-34)

        1. The abuses (1 Cor 11:17-26)

        2. The correctives (1 Cor 11:27-34)

    E. Spiritual gifts and spiritual people (1 Cor 12-14)

        1. The test of Spirit control (1 Cor 12:1-3)

        2. The need for varieties of spiritual gifts (1 Cor 12:4-31)

        3. The supremacy of love (1 Cor 13)

4. The need for intelligibility (1 Cor 14:1-25)

    5. The need for order (1 Cor 14:26-40)

F. The resurrection of believers (1 Cor 15)

    1. The resurrection of Jesus Christ (1 Cor 15:1-11)

    2. The certainty of resurrection (1 Cor 15:12-34)

    3. The resurrection body (1 Cor 15:35-49)

    4. The assurance of victory over death (1 Cor 15:50-58)

G. The collection for the Jerusalem believers (1 Cor 16:1-12)

    1. Arrangements for the collection (1 Cor 16:1-4)

    2. The travel plans of Paul and his fellow apostles (1 Cor 16:5-12)

IV. Conclusion (1 Cor 16:13-24)

A. Final exhortations (1 Cor 16:13-18)

B. Final greetings and benediction (1 Cor 16:19-24)

Exposition
I. INTRODUCTION 1:1-9

A. SALUTATION 1:1-3

The apostle Paul began this epistle as he did his others by identifying himself and a fellow worker known to the readers. Then he identified and described the recipients of the letter and greeted them with a benediction. This is the most extensive elaboration of an address that we have in Paul's letters.

1:1 - Paul's description of himself as one whom God had called to be an apostle of Jesus Christ reminded his original readers of his privilege and authority (cf. Rom 1:1). The idea of authority received added strength from the reference to the will of God (cf. 2 Cor 1:1; Eph 1:1; Col 1:1; 2 Tim 1:1).

Sosthenes was probably the same Sosthenes who was the ruler of the synagogue in Corinth (Acts 18:17). He was with Paul in Ephesus when Paul penned this epistle. Though Luke did not record his conversion in the Book of Acts, Sosthenes quite clearly became a believer, assuming this was the same man. Probably he was the same man, and Paul referred to him because the Corinthians knew him well.

1:2 - Paul frequently referred to all the Christians in a particular locality as the church of God in that place (cf. 1 Cor 11:16). However to the Corinthian church, where party spirit was a problem, this reminder focused on the church's true Lord. There may or may not have been more than one house-church in Corinth at this time. God had set the Corinthians apart to be His holy people by uniting them with Him through faith in His Son. "Sanctified" may be a metaphor for conversion (cf. 1 Cor 1:30; 6:11). They were saints by divine calling. The Corinthians were not saintly in their conduct, as this letter makes clear. Perhaps Paul mentioned their saintly calling to inspire them to be more saintly in their conduct. (11)

> "Paul understands Christian ethics in terms of 'becoming what you are,' a perspective that emerges in 1 Corinthians in a number of ways. . . ."

> "Perhaps the single greatest theological contribution of our letter to the Christian faith is Paul's understanding of the nature of the church, especially in its local expression. If the gospel itself is at stake in the Corinthians' theology and behavior, so also is its visible expression in the local community of redeemed people. The net result is more teaching on the church here than in any of Paul's letters." (13)

The saints in other places are probably those in churches in other places some of whom had come to the Savior through the witness of Christians other than Paul. This seems more likely than that they were just Paul's converts near Corinth (cf. 2 Cor 1:1; Rom 16:1). This seems probable in view of "every place" (NASB) or "everywhere" (NIV) and in view of how this verse ends. Paul evidently wanted his readers to remember that they were part of a large body of believers (cf. 1 Cor 12:12); they were not the only church. They needed to fit into the family of God harmoniously rather than being a rebel congregation.

Calling on the name of Christ means to confess faith in Him, to worship and pray to Him (cf. Rom 10:13-14).

1:3 - This greeting is characteristically Christian (cf. Rom 1:7; 2 Cor 1:2; Gal 1:3). It sums up Paul's whole theological outlook.

B. THANKSGIVING 1:4-9

Paul followed his salutation with an expression of gratitude for his original readers, as he usually did in his epistles. In this case the focus of his thanksgiving was on God's grace in giving the Corinthians such great spiritual gifts (cf. Eph 1:3-14).

> "What is remarkable here is the apostle's ability to thank God for the very things in the church that, because of the abuses, are also causing him grief." (14)

1:4 - Paul was grateful that God had poured out His unmerited favor and divine enablement on the Corinthian believers through Christ Jesus. He usually referred to the Lord as Christ Jesus rather than as Jesus Christ. This put the emphasis on His divine character as Messiah rather than on His human nature and encouraged his readers to submit to Him as their Lord.

1:5 - By "speech" (NASB) or "speaking" (NIV; Gr. *logos*) the apostle meant eloquence, the ability to express their "knowledge" (Gr. *gnosis*) fluently and effectively. As we shall see, knowledge and eloquence were two things the Corinthians valued very highly. (15) Paul had to put them in their proper place among the other gifts. Nevertheless they were great gifts, and Paul was thankful that God had given them to the Corinthians.

1:6 - The Corinthians' reception of these gifts had corroborated the truthfulness of the gospel. Giving these gifts was one of the ways God validated the gospel message in the early history of the church (cf. Gal 3:2-5; Heb 2:3-4).

1:7 - God had blessed the Corinthians greatly with spiritual gifts. The revealing of the Lord Jesus Christ to His saints at the Rapture would be God's greatest gift to them. The early Christians awaited His return eagerly. (16)

1:8 - By God's sustaining power Christians will stand free of guilt before Him on that day. The day of the Lord Jesus Christ is the Rapture (cf. Phil 1:6; Col 2:7; 1 Thess 3:13; 5:23; et al.). It is not the day of the Lord, which is a term both Old and New Testament writers used to refer to the period beginning with the Tribulation and extending through the Millennium.

> "The expression 'the day of our Lord Jesus Christ,' identified with 'the coming of our Lord Jesus Christ' (1 Cor 1:7), is the period of blessing for the Church beginning with the rapture. This coming day is referred to as 'the day of the Lord Jesus' (1 Cor 5:5; 2 Cor 1:14), 'the day of Jesus Christ' (Phil 1:6), and 'the day of Christ' (Phil 1:10; 2:16). ('The day of Christ' in 2 Thess 2:2 should be rendered 'the day of the Lord.') 'The day of Christ' in all six references in the N.T. is described as relating to the reward and blessing of the Church at the rapture and in contrast with the expression 'the day of the Lord' (cf. Isaiah 2:12, marg.; Joel 1:15, *note*; Rev 19:19, *note*), which is related to judgment upon unbelieving Jews and Gentiles, and blessing on millennial saints (Zeph 3:8-20)." (18)

The Greek word translated "blameless" (*anegkletos*) means unreprovable or without accusation (cf. Col 1:22; 1 Tim 3:10; Titus 1:6-7). It does not imply that at the judgment seat of Christ there will be complete equality among believers (cf. 1 Cor 3:10-15; 2 Cor. 5:10). Moreover it does not mean that once God regenerates a person that one never sins again (cf. 1 John 1:6-10). It means every Christian will stand before the Lord guiltless, unimpeachable, because God has imputed the guilt of our sins to the Savior and He has borne them (cf. Rom 5:1; 8:1).

1:9 - Paul's confidence that his readers would one day stand without guilt before the Lord did not rest on the Corinthians' ability to persevere faithfully to the end. It rested on God's ability and promises to preserve them. God had begun the good work of calling them into fellowship with His Son, and He would complete that work (cf. Phil 1:6; 1 John 1:1-4).

> ." . . God is the subject of all the actions of the thanksgiving. And in every case that work is mediated by or focused on 'his Son Jesus Christ our Lord.' Thus the christological emphasis that began in the salutation is carried through in an even more emphatic way in this introductory thanksgiving. Everything God has done, and will do, for the Corinthians is done expressly in 'Jesus Christ our Lord.'

> "His concern here is to redirect their focus—from themselves to God and Christ and from an over-realized eschatology to a healthy awareness of the glory that is still future." (19)

The apostle's confidence in God as he expressed this in these verses (1 Cor 1:4-9) enabled him to deal with the problems in the Corinthian church optimistically and realistically. God was for the Corinthians. Now they needed to orient themselves properly toward Him.

G. THE COLLECTION FOR THE JERUSALEM BELIEVERS 16:1-12

I have chosen to include this section with the others that deal with questions the Corinthians had asked Paul rather than with Paul's concluding comments because it begins "*peri de*" (1 Cor 7:1, 25; 8:1; 12:1; 16:12; cf. 1 Cor 8:4). Probably they had asked about the collection Paul was assembling in a letter or through messengers. This is the least confrontational section in this epistle, though we can detect tension here too. (474)

> "This chapter may seem unrelated to our needs today, but actually it deals in a very helpful way with three areas of stewardship: money (1 Cor 16:14), opportunities (1 Cor 16:5-9), and people (1 Cor 16:10-24). These are probably the greatest resources the church has today, and they must not be wasted." (475)

1. Arrangements for the collection 16:1-4

16:1 - It seems that the Corinthian Christians had heard about the collection (Gr. *logeias*, extra collection) Paul was getting together for the poor saints in Jerusalem (1 Cor 16:3) and wanted to make a contribution. James, Peter, and John had encouraged Paul and Barnabas to remember the poor when they were in Jerusalem (Gal 2:10; cf. Acts 11:27-30). There is no record of the directions Paul gave the Galatian churches, to which he referred here, in any of his other surviving epistles. The churches of Galatia evidently were those in southern Galatia including Pisidian Antioch, Iconium, Lystra, and Derbe. Paul had passed through this region as he moved toward Ephesus from which he wrote this epistle (Acts 18:23).

16:2 - From the earliest day of the church's existence Christians assembled on Sundays to worship in commemoration of the Lord's resurrection. The Lord had not commanded this, but it quickly became customary. The Jews met on Saturdays.

> "This is our earliest evidence respecting the early consecration of the first day of the week by the Apostolic Church. Apparently, the name 'Lord's Day' was not yet in use, and the first day of the week is never called 'the sabbath' in Scripture." (476)

Sunday would have been a natural occasion to put money aside for fellow believers since it was particularly on this day that Christians reviewed their responsibilities. Paul did not specify whether the individual Christian should keep the money in his possession or whether a church official should. The former alternative seems more probable in view of the apostle's language (477). Note also that he did not say how much to set aside except that it was to be as the Lord had blessed them. The amount was totally up to the givers. Paul mentioned nothing here about giving proportionately to one's income. We saw earlier that both rich and poor made up this church (1 Cor 11:21). Paul's counsel amounted to, Save a little regularly now so you will not have to make a major withdrawal from your bank account later.

16:3 - Paul planned to send a representative from each of the contributing churches, or possibly groups of churches, to Jerusalem with the gift. The letters he spoke of may have been letters of introduction from himself since it appears that at this time he did not plan to make this trip himself. Such a procedure would guarantee that the money would arrive safely and that people would perceive the whole project as honest (cf. 2 Cor 8:21).

16:4 - The apostle was open to the possibility of going to Jerusalem as part of the group if this seemed best. After he wrote this letter he decided to go (Rom 15:25-26) and indeed went (Acts 20:16, 22; 21:17; 24:17).

These few verses along with 2 Corinthians 8-9 provide guidelines for individual Christians and churches in giving. The principles Paul advocated were that saving up for giving should be regular and in response to the Lord's provision materially. The believers should manage their gifts with integrity. Everything they did should not only be above reproach, but other people should perceive it as such.

Notice that Paul made no mention of tithing. Tithing is a method of giving that God prescribed for the Israelites under the Mosaic Law. People practiced tithing as an act of worship commonly in the ancient Near East (cf. Gen 28:22, NIV) (479). It was also a common tax (480). The Mosaic Law really required that the Israelites give back to God about one-third of their incomes. However, Christians are not under the Mosaic Law (Rom 10:4; et al.). It is therefore understandable that neither Jesus Christ nor the apostles commanded tithing. Some Christians believe that since Abraham paid tithes to Melchizedek (Gen 14:20) tithing antedates the Mosaic Law and is therefore binding on Christians. Nevertheless the absence of any reference to tithing in the New Testament plus the teaching of other guidelines strongly suggest that God wants us to follow a different method. The principles that should govern Christians in our giving appear throughout the New Testament but mainly in 1 Corinthians 16 and 2 Corinthians 8-9.

> "No pressure, no gimmicks, no emotion. A need had to be met, and the Corinthians were capable of playing a role in it. In a day of highly visible campaigns for money on every side, there is something to be said for the more consistent, purposeful approach outlined here." (481)

2. The travel plans of Paul and his fellow apostles 16:5-12

As the preceding verse revealed, Paul's plans were tentative to some extent. He wanted the Corinthians to know that he anticipated a return to Corinth and hopefully a stay of several months. Timothy and Apollos might return too.

16:5 - At the time he wrote, Paul planned to head north from Ephesus and then spend some time in Macedonia. Macedonia was the Roman province north of Corinth where Philippi, Thessalonica, and Berea stood. He then planned to travel south to Corinth. Paul later changed this plan and travelled directly from Ephesus to Corinth (2 Cor 2:1; 12:14; 13:1-2) and returned to Ephesus (cf. 2 Cor 2:5-8; 7:12). Later he visited Macedonia and then Corinth (2 Cor 2:12-13; 7:6-16) (482)

16:6-7 - Paul did spend the winter in Corinth, but it was the winter after the one when he expected to be there, the winter of 57-58 rather than 56-57 (cf. Acts 20:2-3; Rom 16:1, 23). He sensed the need to spend a good long visit in Corinth, and in view of the problems in the church that he mentioned in this letter we can understand why.

16:8 - The Jews celebrated Pentecost in late May or early June so Paul probably wrote 1 Corinthians in the spring of the year (cf. 1 Cor 5:7; 15:20). It is not unusual that since he was a Jewish believer with the evangelization of the Jews on his heart he would refer to important events in the Jewish calendar such as Pentecost (Lev 23:15-21). Perhaps the early Christians paid more attention to the significant events in the life of the church than many independent churches do today. (483) The feast of Pentecost, of course, also marked the coming of the Holy Spirit (Acts 2).

16:9 - Paul occasionally used the door as a metaphor for opportunity (cf. 2 Cor 2:12; Col 4:3). He stayed in Ephesus three years to take advantage of his opportunities there. He did not regard adversaries there as an indication of a closed door or as a sign that God wanted him to move on to more comfortable ministry. He followed his own advice and remained immovable abounding in the work of the Lord in Ephesus (1 Cor 15:58).

16:10-11 - Timothy's visit to Corinth from Ephesus was not very tentative. Paul had already sent him (and Erastus; Acts 19:22) or was about to send him when he penned this epistle (1 Cor 4:17). Evidently Timothy's relative youth tended to make some people despise him, and he tended to be fearful (cf. 1 Tim 4:12). Paul advised the Corinthians, who judged by external appearances, to give him the respect he deserved for doing the Lord's work as Paul did, not just for Timothy's own sake. We do not know the names of Timothy's travelling companions.

It may have been Timothy's report of conditions in Corinth when he returned to Ephesus that moved Paul to go directly to Corinth himself rather than waiting until he had visited Macedonia. Paul referred to this visit as painful because while in Corinth he encountered strong opposition (cf. 2 Cor 2:1-8; 7:12; 12:14; 13:1-2).

16:12 - This verse may contain Paul's final response to the questions the Corinthians had asked him. It is the sixth instance of that key phrase *"peri de"* ("Now concerning"). Paul's relations with this eloquent brother were perfectly friendly, as this verse reveals (cf. 1 Cor 1:12). We do not know why he did not want to revisit Corinth with Timothy or whether he ever did visit that city again.

IV. CONCLUSION 16:13-24

The Apostle Paul concluded this epistle with a series of imperatives, exhortations, and news items.

A. FINAL EXHORTATIONS 16:13-18

As I have pointed out, each section in this epistle concludes with some practical admonition. These verses constitute a summary exhortation for the whole letter.

16:13-14 - Paul urged his somewhat unstable readers to be watchful regarding danger from inside as well as outside the church (cf. Acts 20:29-30). Most of the problems in this church evidently arose from within the congregation. This expression sometimes occurs with anticipation of the Lord's coming, so that may have been in Paul's thinking as well (e.g., Matt 24:42). His readers should also stand firm in their trust in God and their commitment to His Word and will (cf. 1 Cor 15:58). Rather than acting like immature children they should behave as mature men (cf. 1 Cor 1:12). They should be strong in the Lord rather than weak in the faith (cf. Joshua 1:7-8). Above all, love should motivate and mark them (1 Cor 13). This was the great need of this church.

16:15-16 - The Corinthians had a special problem with submission to authority, as we have seen. Many in the church wanted to do their own thing. 1 Cor 16:16-18 would have encouraged them to appreciate some less flashy servants of the Lord.

Stephanus and his family were Paul's first converts in Achaia (1 Cor 1:16). They had given themselves unselfishly to serving the Corinthians. They were probably loyal to Paul and may have been the source from which the apostle received some of his information about conditions in this church. Paul urged that his readers appreciate Stephanus and his family for their ministry and not ride over them but submit humbly to them. They should treat others such as them with similar honor. Service, not status, should be the basis for honor in the church.

16:17-18 - Stephanus had recently visited Paul in Ephesus with the two other Corinthian brothers the apostle named. They may have carried the questions Paul answered in this letter as well as information about conditions in the church. They had all ministered refreshingly to Paul as they typically did in Corinth. Paul wanted the Corinthians to be sure to recognize them too.

B. FINAL GREETINGS AND BENEDICTION 16:19-24

"The letter now concludes with a series of standard (for Paul) greetings (1 Cor 16:19-22) and the grace-benediction (1 Cor 16:23). But Paul cannot quite give up the urgency of the letter, so he interrupts these two rather constant elements of his conclusions with one final word of warning to those who have been causing him grief, this time in the form of an extraordinary curse formula (1 Cor 16:22). The apparent harshness of this warning is matched by the equally unusual addition of a final word of affirmation of his love for them (1 Cor 16:24), found only here in his extant letters. Thus even to the end the unique concerns that have forged this letter find their expression." (484)

16:19 - Several churches in the Roman province of Asia had come into existence while Paul used its capital city, Ephesus, as his base of operations (Acts 19:10). (485)

The names of Aquila and Prisca (Priscilla) usually occur in reverse order in the New Testament. Evidently their friends, of which Paul was one, felt free to use both orders. This suggests that they served the Lord as a harmonious team with individual strengths and talents. They had lived in Corinth after leaving Rome (Acts 18:2), and it was there that Paul first met them. They had left Corinth for Ephesus with Paul and settled in that city (Acts 18:18-21). Their house became a meeting place for the church (cf. Rom 16:5). Church buildings were unknown until the third century. (486)

16:20 - The holy kiss, holy because saints (1 Cor 1:2) exchanged it, was a common practice among believers, and it still is today in some parts of the world. It consisted of women kissing women and men kissing men on the cheek.

16:21 - Paul customarily dictated his letters, and a secretary wrote them down (cf. Rom 16:22). However, he usually added a word of greeting at the end in his own hand that authenticated his epistles as coming from him (cf. Gal 6:11; Col 4:18; 2 Thess 3:17). All of what follows is probably what he added.

16:22 - Normally Paul used the Greek word *agape* for love (except in Titus 3:15). Here he used *phileo*. Consequently this may have been a saying believers used in the congregational worship of the churches. "Maranatha" (NASB) is an Aramaic expression meaning "Our Lord, come." Probably Paul did not translate it into Greek because believers commonly spoke it in Aramaic in the services of the early church (cf. Rev 22:20). Since it was Aramaic it probably originated in Palestine where people spoke that language. They exported it to the Greek-speaking congregations that retained its form.

> "It is strange to meet with an Aramaic phrase in a Greek letter to a Greek Church. The explanation is that that phrase had become a watchword and a password. It summed up the vital hope of the early Church, and Christians whispered it to each other, identified each other by it, in a language which the heathen could not understand." (488)

> "It would appear, then, that the fixed usage of the term 'Maranatha' by the early Christians was a witness to their strong belief in the imminent return of Christ. If they knew that Christ could not return at any moment because of other events or a time period that had to transpire first [i.e., the Tribulation], why did they petition Him in a way that implied that He could come at any moment?" (489)

16:23-24 - Paul concluded this strong but loving epistle with a prayerful benediction of God's grace. Note that this letter also began, "Grace to you" (1 Cor 16:1:3).

> "Grace is the beginning and the end of the Chrstian [*sic*] gospel; it is the single word that most fully expresses what God has done and will do for his people in Christ Jesus." (490)

Paul also added assurance of his own love for all the believers in Corinth, not just those who supported him.

Bibliography

1. See W. Harold Mare, "1 Corinthians," in *Romans-Galatians*, vol 10 of *The Expositor's Bible Commentary*, pp. 175-76, for information helpful to most expositors.

2. Nero began this canal, but it was finally completed in 1893. C. K. Barrett, *A Commentary on the First Epistle to the Corinthians*, p. 1

3. Gordon D. Fee, *The First Epistle to the Corinthians*, p. 2. See also David K. Lowery, "1 Corinthians," in *The Bible Knowledge Commentary: New Testament*, p. 505, for other quotations about Corinth from ancient writers.

4. Archibald Robertson and Alfred Plummer, *A Critical and Exegetical Commentary on the First Epistle of St Paul to the Corinthians*, p. xii.

5. The Greek geographer Strabo wrote of 1,000 prostitutes, but this probably referred to the early history of the old city, and it may have been an exaggeration. See Fee, pp. 2-3.

6. Ibid., p. 3.

7. See the diagram of central Corinth in Mare, p. 186.

8. See Fee, pp. 4-15.

9. Barrett, p. 26.

10. S. L. Johnson Jr., "The First Epistle to the Corinthians," in *The Wycliffe Bible Commentary*, p. 1229.

11. See Robert L. Saucy, "'Sinners' Who Are Forgiven or 'Saints' Who Sin?" *Bibliotheca Sacra* 152:608 (October-December 1995):400-12, for discussion of the Christian's essential identity. He concluded correctly, I believe, that we are primarily saints who sin.

12. Johnson, p. 1230.

13. Fee, pp. 17-18.

14. Ibid., p. 36.

15. These appear by their usage in this letter and in 2 Corinthians to have been common buzzwords in Corinth. *Logos* occurs 26 times in 1 and 2 Corinthians compared to 58 times in Paul's other epistles, and *gnosis* appears 16 times in these two epistles but only seven times in all of Paul's other writings.

16. This is another indication that the apostles taught the imminent (i.e., any moment) return of the Lord for His own (cf. 4:5; 15:51-52; 16:22; Phil. 3:20; 4:5; 1 Thess. 1:10; 2 Thess. 1:10-12; Titus 2:13; James 5:7-9; 1 John 2:28; Rev. 3:11; 22:7, 12, 17, 20). See Wayne A. Brindle, "Biblical Evidence for the Imminence of the Rapture," *Bibliotheca Sacra* 158:630 (April-June 2001):146-48.

17. *The New Scofield Reference Bible*, p. 1233.

18. Ibid.

19. Fee, p. 46. An over-realized eschatology is an understanding of the future that stresses present realities to the exclusion of related future realities. For example, an over-realized view of the resurrection

emphasizes the believer's present spiritually resurrected condition to the exclusion of his or her future physical resurrection

474. Problems over this collection emerge clearly in 2 Corinthians.

475. Wiersbe, 1:621.

476. Robertson and Plummer, p. 384.

477. Fee, *The First . . .*, p. 813.

478. *The New Scofield . . .*, p. 1250.

479. See C. F. Keil and Franz Delitzsch, *Biblical Commentary on the Old Testament: Pentateuch,* 1:207.

480. W. Robertson Smith, *Lectures on the Religion of the Semites*, pp. 245-51. This is still true in some modern countries. For example, in England part of every person's taxes goes to maintain the Church of England. Some residents regard this part of their tax as their contribution to the church or their tithe.

481. Fee, *The First . . .*, p. 817.

482. See Richard Batey, "Paul's Interaction with the Corinthians," *Journal of Biblical Literature* 84 (1985):139-43.

483. Churches that observe "the Christian year" tend to make more of these observances.

484. Fee, *The First . . .,* p. 834.

485. References to "Asia" in the New Testament consistently refer to the Roman province of Asia, which lay in the west and southwest of the geographical region of Asia Minor.

486. Barclay, *The Letter . . .*, p. 187

487. Lowery, "1 Corinthians," p. 548.

488. Barclay, *The Letter . . .,* p. 188.

489. Showers, p. 131. Cf. Rev. 3:11; 22:7, 12, 17, 20.

490. Fee, *The First . . .,* p. 839.

Basic Theology

Charles C. Ryrie

Chapter 71: Principles and/or Pattern?

Before considering the biblical teaching concerning organization, order, and ordinances for local churches, a basic question should be raised. Does the New Testament give principles for these areas to be followed generally, but to be adapted to various cultures and times; or does it expect the pattern practiced in New Testament times to be followed today in all cultures? For example, does the New Testament teach principles of church government that can be adapted in a variety of ways, or does it also prescribe the particular pattern which must be followed? Many would say that flexibility in this area is permitted. The church must have leaders, but it makes little difference whether they are called elders or deacons or whether a group has both. One might even call them stewards and still follow the New Testament principle of leadership.

Or take another example. The New Testament teaches the principle of believers gathering together. But in New Testament times they gathered in homes. Are we today allowed the flexibility of building church buildings, or should we follow the pattern of meeting in homes? Most would allow for flexibility in this case.

Or another example: The principle in water baptism (whatever mode is used) is to show leaving the old life and entering into the new. Is there any way that principle can be followed without using the pattern of actual baptism? Almost all would say no. But why not erect a little closet on the church platform, have the candidate enter it in old clothes, change his clothes inside the closet, and then emerge in new clothes? Would that not illustrate the same truth as baptism does? And is it not a scriptural illustration? (Col. 3:9–12). In church government we allow some flexibility between principle and pattern. In using church buildings we permit complete flexibility between principle and pattern. In water baptism we insist on no flexibility between principle and pattern. Whatever be a person's or group's theoretical views on this question, I doubt that anyone is totally consistent in practice.

Arguments for flexibility are mostly historical and analogical. Historically, it is pointed out that since the early church was influenced by its culture and adopted its forms from that culture, we can do the same today. To be sure, elders came from the synagogue organization (though Gentile communities also had them). Whether the idea of deacons was taken over from the synagogue is much less clear. Baptism was practiced as one of the requirements for proselytes to Judaism and in the mystery religions. The Lord's Supper was new to the church, though it grew out of the Passover feast. Instruction in the Jewish synagogue and instruction in the Christian church were similar. Excommunication was practiced by both groups. Unquestionably many practices that the church used had their antecedents in Judaism. This is to be expected. But the question still remains: When the church took over these practices, did they become divinely sanctioned (to be followed today) or simply divinely exemplified (not necessarily to be followed today in every detail)? The historical argument really does not settle the matter.

Analogies are often drawn to support flexibility between principles and patterns. For example, the Gospel is an inviolable principle, but there are many patterns to follow in presenting it. Salvation is an absolute; but conversion experiences vary. Therefore, it is argued, though the church is an absolute, its forms and functions are variable. But because it is not exegetical the argument is weak.

Those who feel that church practices should conform closely to the principles and patterns of the New Testament point out that the Scriptures claim to be sufficient for every good work, including the work of the local church (2 Tim. 3:16–17). Specifically, Paul wrote 1 Timothy with all its details about church life and government so that Timothy might know how to conduct himself in the house of God and how to instruct others in those same specifics (2 Tim. 3:15). And in the same epistle, cultural conditioning of truth is specifically ruled out (2 Tim. 2:11–14). Furthermore, Paul expected the churches to follow the "traditions," which included both principles and practices (1 Cor. 11).

Can this matter be settled? Probably not conclusively (and no one is entirely consistent). But to conclude, much flexibility seems to ignore the detailed patterns that are revealed in the New Testament. It is one thing to acknowledge a difference of interpretation about some detail, but it is quite another to say it is unimportant. My own feeling is that we should attempt to follow as many details as possible of the patterns for church life as they are revealed in the New Testament. Otherwise, there is no satisfactory answer to the question of why the patterns are there. And since they are there, I want to use them today.

Lesson 1 Notes

Gallio: *Gallio* was proconsul of Achaia from AD 51-52. This date is one of the firmly established dates in Acts. Lucius Junius Gallio was the son of the rhetorician Seneca and the brother of Seneca the philosopher. The date of Gallio's rule is established from an inscription. Thus, the event mentioned here is probably to be dated July-October AD 51.

Lesson 1 Self Check

QUESTION 1

Corinth was an important city for international trade in the first century. *True or False?*

QUESTION 2

Paul's secretary for this letter was Sosthenes. *True or False?*

QUESTION 3

What was Paul's main purpose in writing 1 Corinthians?

    A. To combat heretical doctrine

    B. To urge the congregation to more effective evangelism

    C. To help correct practical problems in the congregation

    D. To bolster his apostolic authority

QUESTION 4

A major topic of 1 Corinthians is justification by faith. *True or False?*

QUESTION 5

A major geographic feature of Corinth was its nearness to two bodies of water near an isthmus. *True or False?*

QUESTION 6

The believers in the church at Corinth when Paul wrote this letter were mostly of Jewish background. *True or False?*

QUESTION 7

Why did Paul give thanks for the Corinthians?

    A. They financially supported him

    B. They were richly blessed with spiritual gifts

    C. They were an example of love

    D. They prayed earnestly for Paul

QUESTION 8

Paul was concerned that Timothy might not be warmly welcomed when he visited Corinth. *True or False?*

QUESTION 9

What was the purpose of the collection project?

    A. Building a church building

    B. Helping poor believers in Jerusalem

    C. Supporting missionaries

    D. Storing up food to prepare for a famine

QUESTION 10

We may ignore whatever teaching we do not like in 1 Corinthians, since the situation in our churches is so different from theirs. *True or False?*

Lesson 1 Answers to Questions

QUESTION 1
    A. Major city
    B. Good transportation
    C. Jewish synagogue
    D. Unevangelized

QUESTION 2: *Your answer*

QUESTION 3: *Your answer should be similar to the following:*
Probably Paul's statement about "weakness, fear and trembling" refers to his condition physically, emotionally and spiritually. Because of all the stress he had been through, he undoubtedly needed strengthening and encouragement. When he arrived in Corinth to proclaim the gospel, he could rely only on the grace and power of the Lord—not on his human connections, wisdom, abilities or resources.

QUESTION 4: False

QUESTION 5

Encouragement	Scripture
In the temporary absence of his team members, Paul found fellow Jews, Priscilla and Aquila (though they may have not been believers yet), to work and live with.	Acts 18:2-3
Paul's team members, Silas and Timothy, arrived in Corinth.	Acts 18:5
Silas and Timothy apparently brought a financial gift from the church in Philippi to enable Paul to devote himself completely to preaching.	Acts 18:5 (see Phil 4:15-16)
In a vision, the Lord told Paul to continue his ministry at Corinth, for God would protect him from harm.	Acts 18:9
The Roman official Gallio refused to hear charges against Paul brought by the Jews.	Acts 18:14-15

QUESTION 6: *Your answer*

QUESTION 7

Contact	Reference
Visit from members of Chloe's household	1 Corinthians 1:11
A letter from Paul to them (now lost)	1 Corinthians 5:9
A letter to Paul from the Corinthians	1 Corinthians 7:1
Visit from Stephanus, Fortunatus, and Achaicus	1 Corinthians 16:17

QUESTION 8: *Your answer*

QUESTION 9: False

QUESTION 10: *Your answer*

QUESTION 11
    D. To help them to deal with local church problems

QUESTION 12: *Your answer*

QUESTION 13: *Your answer should be similar to the following:*
Apparently Paul dictated the letter to a secretary but personally signed it. Perhaps Sosthenes was the secretary.

QUESTION 14: Apostle

QUESTION 15
    C. Their divine calling

QUESTION 16
    C. God's grace to them
    D. Their spiritual gifts
    E. Their speech
    F. Their knowledge

QUESTION 17: *Your answer should be similar to the following:*
The problem is not with the good gifts of God, but with the Corinthians' misuse of those gifts.
QUESTION 18: *Your answer*
QUESTION 19: *Your answer should be similar to the following:*
It was a response of gratitude from Gentile Christians who had benefited from God's grace to the Jews.
QUESTION 20
    A. More than one person was responsible for the delivery of the collection.
    B. People whom the Corinthians deemed trustworthy would deliver the money.
    C. Paul himself did not have to be part of the delivery.
    D. Letters of explanation would be sent with the deliverers.
QUESTION 21: *Your answer*
QUESTION 22
    A. To give time for his counsel in this letter to take effect
    B. To give time for the Corinthians to complete the collection
    C. To allow more time in his schedule to stay with them, so he could better help them with their problems
    D. To take full advantage of his ministry opportunity in Ephesus
    E. To give time to hear Timothy's report of the situation in Corinth
    F. To be more efficient in his use of travel time—arriving in Corinth after a trip through Macedonia
QUESTION 23: *Your answer should be similar to the following:*
This indicates the tension in their relationship with Paul, probably relating to the divisions in the congregation. It may also relate to Timothy's youth and fearfulness.
QUESTION 24
    A. Because of his devotion to the ministry
QUESTION 25: *Your answer should be similar to the following:*
From the contexts of the various references, the principle of the holy kiss is to convey warm greetings, love, and the blessings of being a part of God's family. Today the appropriate expressions in local churches vary widely according to culture. Some examples of this expression may be a handshake, hug, kiss on the cheek, or squeeze of the hand.
QUESTION 26: *Your answer*
QUESTION 27: False
QUESTION 28: *Your answer should be one of the following:*
    Missing, Lost

Lesson 1 Self Check Answers

QUESTION 1: True
QUESTION 2: True
QUESTION 3
    C. To help correct practical problems in the congregation
QUESTION 4: False
QUESTION 5: True
QUESTION 6: False
QUESTION 7
    B. They were richly blessed with spiritual gifts
QUESTION 8: True
QUESTION 9
    B. Helping poor believers in Jerusalem
QUESTION 10: False

Lesson 2: Disunity Problem
(1 Cor 1:10-17)

Disunity is a problem that has plagued local churches since the first century. The effects of disunity are evident: diversion of focus away from Christ, weakness in ministry due to lack of cooperation, bad feelings and attitudes, and diminished witness in the community. Unfortunately, many churches are unsuccessful in healing divisions, with the result of simmering discontentment that stifles growth or perhaps even prompts a church split.

Some feel that 1 Corinthians 1:10 is the thesis statement for the whole letter: "I urge you, brothers and sisters, by the name of our Lord Jesus Christ, to agree together, to end your divisions, and to be united by the same mind and purpose." Indeed, much of the content of this letter deals with unity and disunity, as seen in the issues of a believer's freedom, the observance of the Lord's Supper, and the use of spiritual gifts.

The disunity at Corinth was the first of many problems that Paul addressed. Perhaps he addressed it first not because he considered it the most serious problem, but because it was symptomatic of deeper issues.

In Topic 1, we will investigate the core problem behind the disunity at Corinth.

Topic 2 will reflect on the practical problem of unity that we all face today.

Finally, in Topic 3, we will consider Paul's basic approach to resolving a problem like disunity in a local church.

Lesson Outline

    Topic 1: Divisions at Corinth (1 Cor 1:10-17)

        Parties at Corinth (1:10-12)

        Reasons for the Parties (1:13-17)

    Topic 2: Meaning of Unity

        Definition of Unity

        Basis for Unity

        Paul's Mission and Unity

    Topic 3: Pastoral Approach to Problem Solving

Lesson Objectives

What happened? Lotus wonders. Brothers and sisters in her church are forming cliques and looking down on each other. Thinking back, the divisions seem to have begun when Sister Marie came through last year. She spoke several times and some of the believers were really moved and blessed by her messages. Several of the believers, especially Esther and Sara, started ordering booklets and DVDs from Sister Marie to pass around to others in the church, and they started to hold their own special prayer meeting on Tuesdays. The problem is that Sara and Esther stopped attending Sunday worship regularly, and they are no longer coming to the church's bi-monthly prayer meeting. Lotus tries attending Esther and Sara's meeting, but they just watch a DVD from Sister Marie and then they talk about how much they appreciate her messages. When she asks them why they have the separate prayer meeting, they say that Sister Marie's way is more spiritual.

There are so many people in the village who don't know the Lord, and news of this division among the believers is getting around. It almost seems like another church is developing, splitting up the believers.

Lotus knows of Paul's condemnation of the divisions in the church at Corinth. Why were they divided? Did Paul have a solution for them? Can Paul's teaching be applied to her church?

By the end of this lesson, you will be able to:

- Discern the difference between proper respect for a leader and unhealthy loyalty
- Comprehend the meaning of unity and its barriers—united in Christ, putting Him at the head aligns the rest of the body
- Explain Paul's approach to helping the Corinthians promote unity

Topic 1: Divisions at Corinth (1 Cor 1:10-17)

In 1 Corinthians 1:10-12, Paul makes it clear that there is disunity at Corinth, and of a type that should not exist. Paul learned of this problem through an oral report from Chloe's people—undoubtedly members of a household from Corinth who had visited Paul in Ephesus.

Just about every church has some divisions. It is common for groups and classes to develop within a church based on age (youth group), station in life (couples class), gender (women's missionary society), or even special interests (a drama group). Usually, the local church promotes such divisions, and they are viewed as healthy. What made the divisions at Corinth unhealthy?

Assignment
- Read 1 Corinthians 1:10-17 and read the outline below.

A. Divisions in the church: 1:10-12

    1) Exhortation to unity: 1:10

    2) Source of information on divisions – Chloe's people: 1:11

    3) Example of divisions: 1:12

B. Divisions not God's (or Paul's) will: 1:13-17a

    1) Rebuke for divisions – Christ is one: 1:13

    2) Aside: Paul baptized only a few of them: 1:14-16

    3) Paul's mission: to preach the gospel: 1:17a

Parties at Corinth (1:10-12)
Assignment
- Read 1 Corinthians 1:10-12.
- Read Constable, "Divisions in the Church" and "The Manifestation of the Problem" (refer to the Articles section at the end of this lesson), through the notes on 1 Corinthians 1:12.

When identifying the divisions at Corinth, Paul mentions four names—Paul, Cephas (Peter), Apollos, and Christ. Aside from Christ, the others were all Jews and well-known Christian leaders. We have already examined Paul's relationship to Corinth in Lesson 1. How were Cephas and Apollos related to Corinth?

QUESTION 1

In the Corinthian correspondence (1 and 2 Corinthians), Cephas (Peter) is mentioned in four verses: 1 Corinthians 1:12; 3:22; 9:5; 15:5. Study each verse and state his relationship to Corinth.

QUESTION 2

Apollos is mentioned eleven times in the New Testament. Look up the following verses and write a brief description of Apollos and his relationship to Corinth: Acts 18:24, 27; Acts 19:1; 1 Corinthians 1:12; 3:4, 5, 6; 3:22; 4:6; 16:12; Titus 3:13.

QUESTION 3

What was the relationship of each of these to the church at Corinth?

Relationship to church at Corinth	Person
Founder of the church	Paul
One of the Twelve and possibly a visiting teacher	Cephas
A learned and eloquent teacher who had taught in Corinth	Christ
The Lord and Savior	Apollos

Reasons for the Parties (1:13-17)

Assignment

- Read 1 Corinthians 1:13-17.
- Read Constable, "Notes on 1 Corinthians 1:13-17" (refer to the Articles section at the end of this lesson).
- Read "Reasons for the Parties."

Reasons for the Parties

The last party mentioned by Paul is the "Christ" party. No further explanation is given as to the nature of this group at Corinth. Perhaps they were a group who considered themselves "more spiritual" because they aligned themselves only with Christ and not with any human leader. Paul does not commend this "Christ" party.

If the parties at Corinth was not doctrinally based and was not promoted by the named leaders, on what was it based? The only other option seems to be differences of style, or personality, or gifts among these men.

Peter was one of the Twelve, the main preacher at Pentecost, and a special missionary to the Jews. He was viewed as one of the "pillars" of the early Jerusalem church (Gal 2:9).

Apollos was learned and eloquent. His rhetorical skills enabled him to refute the Jews at Corinth vigorously in public debate.

By contrast, although Paul was the spiritual father to many in the congregation, there is evidence that his rhetorical skills were poor. In 2 Corinthians 10:10, Paul writes that some say, "His letters are weighty and forceful, but his physical presence is weak and his speech is of no account." In 1 Corinthians 2:1, Paul wrote that "I did not come with superior eloquence or wisdom as I proclaimed the testimony of God."

Do you know people who leave one church and go to another just because they like the preacher? Preaching is important, but preachers come and go, and Christian unity goes far deeper than appreciation for any preacher.

QUESTION 4

Groups at Corinth were aligning themselves with Paul, Cephas, or Apollos. Was it because of doctrinal divisions among these three leaders? Would these three men have supported or promoted this disunity? Look up these verses and write out your answer: Acts 15:22-26; 1 Corinthians 16:12; Galatians 1:18; 2:7-9.

QUESTION 5

What is the most likely explanation of the parties at Corinth?

   A. They had doctrinal differences.

   B. Different leaders attempted to secure allegiance to themselves.

   C. People aligned themselves with the leader who had baptized them.

   D. Believers aligned themselves with the teacher they liked the best.

Topic 2: Meaning of Unity

The exhortation to unity is repeated many times in the New Testament. 1 Corinthians helps us discover what true unity is, how it can be achieved, and the best approach to resolving disunity problems in the church.

The church of Jesus Christ exists today in most ethnic and language groups and at every economic level. Yet many people view the church as splintered and, in some cases, as characterized by rivalry and conflict. Jesus prayed for His church, "that they will all be one" (Jn 17:21). In this topic, Paul gives his description of unity in a local church.

Definition of Unity

The early church at Corinth was diverse in many ways. Despite all their differences, Paul urged them to unity in the midst of diversity.

Assignment

- Read 1 Corinthians 1:10-17.
- Read "Definition of Unity."

Definition of Unity

Unity does not mean uniformity. The gospel does not eradicate differences among believers, who are individuals according to gender, race, language, culture, age, education, spiritual gifts, and ethnicity. Later in the letter, Paul will make the point that differences in spiritual gifts are part of God's plan for the building up the church (1 Cor 12).

Unity does not prevent believers from having their own personal convictions on disputable matters, as, for example, regarding one day as holier than another, or the choice to eat meat or be a vegetarian (see Romans 14).

Additionally, Paul does not mean that unity is more important than truth, both in proclamation and in practice. Certainly, Paul had no unity with anyone who came preaching a different gospel (Gal 1:6-8). This is disunity because of heretical doctrine. He also instructed the Corinthians to separate from someone in their church who was flagrantly immoral (1 Cor 5:1-5). This is disunity with another believer because of sinful behavior. Sometimes it is appropriate to have disunity.

Unity is a multi-sided phenomenon. One person cannot have unity with another if the other person wants to be divided! Unity happens when people come together with mutual respect, mutual love and a single purpose that they agree on.

Most of us think of unity according to degrees. For example, we may feel extremely unified with our spouse or with some believers with whom we work closely. With other believers with whom we agree doctrinally and in practice, we may feel a strong sense of unity. Towards other believers with whom we differ on major points of theology or practice, our sense of unity is diminished, although we accept them as members of the body of Christ. We may feel that we can have fellowship with those believers, but that it is very difficult to labor alongside them in the ministry because our ways of doing things are so different from theirs.

QUESTION 6

Is it a sin for believers today to identify with a particular denomination? Record your response in your Life Notebook.

QUESTION 7

How did Paul define unity in 1 Corinthians 1:10-17? *(Select all that apply.)*

- A. To agree together
- B. To end divisions
- C. To have the same mind and purpose
- D. To have the same opinions
- E. To do everything together

QUESTION 8

What specific action did Paul want the believers at Corinth to stop doing?

    A. Stop aligning themselves with particular spiritual leaders

    B. Stop complaining about different parties

    C. Stop allowing different people to baptize converts

    D. Stop encouraging new converts to be baptized

QUESTION 9

Did Paul have unity with the Corinthians when he wrote this letter?

QUESTION 10

Examine two incidents where Paul had a difference with another believer. Then, reflect on the meaning of "unity" and record your response in your Life Notebook.

    (a) Read Acts 15:36-41, where Paul and Barnabas separated. Did Paul have unity with Barnabas in this incident? Was this situation justified?

    (b) Read Galatians 2:11-14. Did Paul have unity with Peter in this incident? Was this situation justified?

    (c) Does Christian unity mean that we accept everybody? Where do we draw the line? Can we have unity with believers we disagree with? What does unity look like?

Basis for Unity

For believers, unity with each other is secondary to unity with one Father, one Lord, and one Spirit. This unity with God means that we are members of one family.

Assignment

- Read 1 Corinthians 1:11-16.
- Read "Basis for Unity."

Basis for Unity

There is an aspect of unity that all believers have with each other—we all have one Father and one Spirit. This is a spiritual unity that God brings about when we believe the gospel and become members of His family. See Ephesians 4:4-6.

The root of the divisions referred to here at Corinth was a spiritual immaturity that overvalued particular leaders in the church. Paul continues to develop his argument to help them come to a proper and balanced view of spiritual leaders in 1 Corinthians 1:17–4:21, which we study in Lessons 2-4. Paul devotes a lot of space in this letter towards educating the Corinthians regarding true wisdom. If they do not understand God's wisdom, then they will have a hard time becoming truly unified. Just telling them to "have unity among yourselves" would not work.

Paul asks three succinct questions focusing on their relationship with Christ:

1. Is Christ divided?

2. Was Paul crucified for you?

3. Were you in fact baptized in the name of Paul?

These rhetorical questions expect "no" as an answer. Of course, Christ is not divided, Paul was not crucified for them, and they were not baptized into the name of Paul. The same argument would apply to Peter and Apollos as well. Christ alone is their Lord and Savior, and allegiance to Him should bring unity. If a relationship to any particular spiritual leader results in divisions in the body of Christ, then that relationship is destructive and needs correction.

Paul wanted them to grow up, to stop overvaluing men, and to focus on Christ. However, the solution is not as simple as just urging them to be unified. They need to understand the roots of their disunity problem, which he goes on to explain involves battling against human wisdom and developing a mature view of spirituality.

QUESTION 11

According to your reading in 1 Corinthians, what kind of practical unity is Paul urging?

   A. That they become Christians.

   B. That they only listen to Paul.

   C. That they give up personal preferences and convictions.

   D. That they focus on Christ rather than men.

QUESTION 12

Suppose Brother Enoch thinks that it is a sin for Christians to drink alcohol. You think that Christians may drink alcohol sparingly, but that it is a sin to get drunk. Can you have unity with Brother Enoch? How should you treat him? How should he treat you?

QUESTION 13

What is the foundation for unity that Paul asserts in this passage?

   A. They are all related to Christ.

   B. They all live in the same location.

   C. They all speak the same language.

   D. They all have spiritual gifts.

QUESTION 14

What are the main barriers to unity in your church? What can you do about them? Record your response in your Life Notebook.

Paul's Mission and Unity

Activities intended to promote unity—such as worship services, communion, and baptism—can become reasons for bickering and dissension. Believers need to keep "first things first" in these matters and realize that each local church has its own practices.

Assignment

- Read 1 Corinthians 1:17.
- Read "Paul's Mission and Unity."

Paul's Mission and Unity

Paul can scarcely believe that the Corinthian believers would divide up into parties following different leaders. He is grasping to understand the reason why they would fail to grasp their fundamental unity in Christ.

Perhaps one of the most divisive issues in the history of the church has been baptism. Churches differ over the age at which baptism may be administered, the method of baptizing (immersion, sprinkling, or pouring), and perhaps even over what words should be said during the ceremony. More importantly, churches differ theologically over the meaning of baptism, especially the relationship of baptism to salvation.

Paul states that "Christ did not send me to baptize, but to preach the gospel" (1 Cor 1:17). Of course, Paul did baptize some people, as he states here, and was himself baptized (Acts 9:18). He was familiar with the Great Commission of Jesus (Matt 28:19-20) which specifically includes baptism. However, he did not consider it necessary to personally baptize everyone he led to the Lord.

The identity of the person who baptizes is not the basis for either unity or disunity among believers. Paul emphasized the unifying aspect of the gospel in his ministry. He did not want what should be a beautiful expression of unity—"one Lord, one faith, one baptism" (Eph 4:5)—to become twisted into a source of division.

QUESTION 15

What is Paul's concern with baptism and divisions at Corinth?

- A. Believers would only view baptism by Paul as valid.
- B. Believers would identify with the one who baptized them.
- C. Believers would think that baptism saves them.
- D. Some would view baptism as unimportant.

QUESTION 16

Baptism is _____ because all believers are baptized into the name of Christ.

QUESTION 17

Paul's regular practice was to personally baptize his converts. *True or False?*

QUESTION 18

Record your response to the following in your Life Notebook. Are there points of disunity in your church or ministry? What seems to be the root cause? How could Paul's message of unity be applied to your situation?

Topic 3: Pastoral Approach to Problem Solving

Many times, when seeking to resolve a problem, a father will simply "lay down the law" and order his small child what to do. Generals often use this method when dealing with problems in their armies, as do business owners with their employees. This method is straightforward, simple and effective. Why didn't Paul use this method with the churches he had planted?

Paul was able to exercise strong apostolic discipline, for instance, when he handed Hymenaeus and Alexander over to Satan so that they would learn not to blaspheme (1 Tim 1:20). He hoped to avoid the exercise of harsh discipline at Corinth by addressing problems by a letter, as 2 Corinthians 13:10 indicates.

Assignment

- Read "Pastoral Approach to Problem Solving."

Pastoral Approach to Problem Solving

Paul began this letter with an assertion of his authority as an apostle of Christ Jesus (1 Cor 1:1). Unlike 2 Corinthians, where Paul's authority as an apostle was being challenged, the content of this letter assumes that the readers accept that he is an apostle. In theory, Paul could have approached problem solving at Corinth by simply commanding that they do things differently— he could have used his apostolic authority directly. Instead, he chose to write thousands of words, addressing their issues topic by topic and giving detailed arguments to answer their questions. Many times Paul quotes or refers to Old Testament Scriptures to support his positions. He uses carefully constructed logical arguments. He uses illustrations from agriculture, building construction, sports, family life, and his own life. He quotes back to them their own slogans, partially agreeing and partially disagreeing. Sometimes he counsels or advises or gives his opinion. He offers himself as an example for them to imitate. Overall his approach is to understand, love, reason with, exhort, and instruct.

Paul seems to exercise his authority with gentleness, preferring to convince his readers to voluntarily change their ways rather than to order them to change. He uses the approach of a wise teacher with his students more than that of a boss with his subordinates. He is acting like a pastor. Clearly, he wants them to learn, to grow spiritually, and to mature. A mark of a mature person is the ability to make wise decisions. If they can grasp the truths that Paul is conveying and grow in wisdom, then even when he is not there with them or not offering advice, they can wisely resolve the problems that come their way. After all, Paul knew he would not always be around. Paul's goal was to guide them to maturity and not to just order them around like young children.

Many would consider that the disunity problem at Corinth was a ploy of Satan. Undoubtedly, Satan was pleased with these divisions. Still, when approaching this problem, Paul did not attribute the problem to Satan, nor did he cast out the "demon of divisiveness" or urge them to pray against the influences of the evil one. Instead, he approached the problem as fundamentally one of immaturity among the Corinthian believers. His problem solving approach was educational and pastoral.

QUESTION 19

Generally, what is Paul's problem-solving approach in this letter? *(Select all that apply.)*

    A. To show them his example

    B. To persuade them to adopt the right course

    C. To order them to change

    D. To threaten to punish them

QUESTION 20

In what ways can Paul's approach to problem solving be modeled in your ministry? What changes should be made to your current approach in light of Paul's example? Record your response in your Life Notebook.

Lesson 2 Articles

Notes on 1 Corinthians

Dr. Thomas L. Constable; 2003 Edition

II. CONDITIONS REPORTED TO PAUL 1:10–6:20

The warm introduction to the epistle (1 Cor 1:1-9) led Paul to give a strong exhortation to unity. In it he expressed his reaction to reports of serious problems in this church that had reached his ears.

"Because Paul primarily, and in seriatim fashion, addresses *behavioral* issues, it is easy to miss the intensely *theological* nature of 1 Corinthians. Here Paul's understanding of the gospel and its ethical demands—his theology, if you will—is getting its full workout.

." . . the central issue in 1 Corinthians is 'salvation in Christ as that manifests itself in the behavior of those "who are being saved."' This is what the Corinthians' misguided spirituality is effectively destroying.

"Thus three phenomena must be reckoned with in attempting a theology of this Letter: (1) Behavioral issues (=ethical concerns) predominate. . . . (2) Even though Paul is clearly after behavioral *change*, his greater concern is with the theological distortions that have allowed, or perhaps even promoted, their behavior. This alone accounts for the unusual nature of so much of the argumentation. . . . (3) In every case but two (11:2-16; chaps. 12—14), Paul's basic theological appeal for right behavior is the work of Christ in their behalf." (20)

A. DIVISIONS IN THE CHURCH 1:10–4:21

The first major problem was the divisions that were fragmenting the assembly.

." . . this opening issue is the most crucial in the letter, not because their 'quarrels' were the most significant error in the church, but because the nature of this particular strife had as its root cause their false theology, which had exchanged the theology of the cross for a false triumphalism that went beyond, or excluded, the cross." (21)

1. The manifestation of the problem 1:10-17

The surface manifestation of this serious problem was the party spirit that had developed. Members of the church were appreciating their favorite leaders too much and not appreciating the others enough. This was really a manifestation of self-exaltation. They boasted about their teachers of wisdom to boast about themselves.

1:10 - By exhorting his readers in the name of their Lord Jesus Christ, Paul was putting what he was about to say on the highest level of authority. (22) The Corinthians were to regard what he was about to say as coming from the Lord Himself.

"That the true source of the Corinthians' illicit behavior is bad theology—ultimately a misunderstanding of God and his ways—is evident from the beginning, especially with Paul's use of crucifixion language in 1:10–2:16." (23)

There was already disagreement among members of the congregation, but there was not yet division in the sense of a church split. Paul urged his original readers to unite in their thinking. The Greek word *katartizo*, translated "made complete," describes the mending of nets in Mark 1:19. He wanted them to take the same view of things, to have the same mind (cf. Phil 2:2), and to experience unanimity in their judgment of what they needed to do.

"The gospel that effects eschatological salvation also brings about a radical change in the way people live. This is the burden of this letter and the theological presupposition behind every imperative. Therefore, although apocalypticcosmological language is also found, salvation is expressed primarily in ethical-moral language. (24)

1:11 - Today no one knows exactly who Chloe was. She evidently had a household or business that included servants some of whom had traveled to Corinth and had returned to Ephesus carrying reports of conditions in the Corinthian church. They had eventually shared this news with Paul. Quarrels and dissension should never mark the church (Gal 5:20).

1:12 - The Corinthians had overdone the natural tendency to appreciate some of God's servants more than others because of their own personal qualities or because of blessings they had imparted.

It was normal that some would appreciate Paul since he had founded the church and had ministered in Corinth with God's blessing for 18 months. Apollos had followed Paul there and was especially effective in refuting Jewish unbelievers and in showing that Jesus was the Messiah. He was a gifted apologist and orator (Acts 18:24-28).

There is no scriptural record that Peter ever visited Corinth, though he may have. Cephas is the Hellenized form of the Aramaic *kepa*, meaning "rock" (cf. Jn 1:42). Since Peter was the leading apostle to the Jews, it is understandable that many of the early Christians, especially the Jewish believers, would have venerated him. A fourth group apparently professed loyalty to no human leader but boasted of their allegiance to Christ alone. They appear to have regarded themselves as the most spiritual element in the church. They had devised their own brand of spiritual elitism that made them no better than the others.

1:13 - This last group was using Christ as the name of a party within the church. This cut Him off from the other members of the church. Such an idea was unthinkable, and by stating it Paul showed its absurdity.

Next Paul addressed his own supporters. How foolish it was to elevate him over Christ since Christ did what was most important. Note the central importance of the Cross in Paul's thinking. His followers had not submitted to baptism in water to identify with Paul but with the Savior. This reference shows how highly Paul regarded water baptism. It is God's specified way for the believer to identify publicly with his or her Lord (Matt 28:19; cf. Acts 8:16; 19:5; Rom 6:3; Gal 3:27). It implies turning over allegiance to the one named in the rite.

1:14 - Crispus was the ruler of the synagogue in which Paul preached when he first came to Corinth (Acts 18:8). Gaius may be the same person as Titius Justus. This man was a Gentile convert who lived next door to the synagogue and opened his home to the church after the Christians could no longer meet in the synagogue (Acts 18:7; Rom 16:23).

"Gaius Titius Justus would be a complete Roman name (*praenomen, nomen gentile, cognomen*)." (25)

Some Christians contend that water baptism is essential for salvation. If it is, it would seem natural that Paul would have emphasized its importance by personally baptizing more than just two new believers in Corinth (cf. Jn 4:2).

1:15 - Paul deliberately did not baptize his converts so there would be no question as to whose disciples they were. This was one way he kept Christ central in his ministry. Paul believed baptism was important, but it was valid whether he or any other believer administered it. He was not superior to other believers in this respect.

1:16 - The members of Stephanus' family were the first converts in the Roman province of Achaia (1 Cor 16:15). It was unimportant to Paul whom he personally baptized. This is clear because he temporarily forgot that he had baptized these people. As he continued to write, the Lord brought them to mind.

1:17 - Obviously baptizing is part of the Great Commission that all Christians are responsible to carry out (Matt 28:19). Paul's point was that preaching the gospel is more important than baptizing. He used a figure of speech, litotes, for emphasis. He would hardly have said this if baptism was necessary for salvation.

> "Cleverness of speech" (NASB) and "words of human wisdom" (NIV) greatly impressed the Greeks.

> "The Greeks were intoxicated with fine words; and to them the Christian preacher with his blunt message seemed a crude and uncultured figure, to be laughed at and ridiculed rather than to be listened to and respected." (28)

One of the features of Paul, Apollos, Peter, and Christ that made them attractive to various segments of the Corinthian church was evidently their individual oratorical styles. Later Paul pointed out that the Corinthian Christians were viewing things through carnal eyes, namely, seeing things as unsaved people do (1 Cor 3:1-4). Paul did not emphasize or place confidence in the method of his preaching but the message of the Cross. He did not want to draw attention away from the gospel message to his style of delivering that message.

> "Paul represents himself as a preacher, not as an orator. Preaching is the proclamation of the cross; it is the cross that is the source of its power." (29)

This verse provides a transition into the next section of the epistle in which Paul contrasted God's wisdom and human wisdom.

> "With this observation Paul is fully launched on his epistle. As in Romans (cf. i. 16 ff.), mention of the Gospel sets his thought and language in motion." (31)

The crux of the Corinthians' party spirit lay in their viewing things as unbelievers did, specifically Christian preachers and teachers. They failed to see the important issues at stake in ministry and instead paid too much attention to external superficial matters. This was a serious condition, so Paul invested many words in the following section to deal with it (1 Cor 1:18–4:21).

Bibliography

20. Gordon D. Fee, "Toward a Theology of 1 Corinthians," in *Pauline Theology. Vol. II: 1 & 2 Corinthians*, pp. 38-39.

21. Idem, *The First . . .*, p. 50. Triumphalism is the belief that Christians are triumphing now over sin and its consequences to the exclusion of persecution, suffering, and some human limitations. It is sometimes, and it was in Corinth, an evidence of an over-realized eschatology, which is that we have already entered into certain blessings of salvation that really lie ahead of us in the eschaton. Prosperity theology is one popular form of triumphalism.

22. This is the tenth reference to Jesus Christ in the first ten verses of the epistle. Clearly Paul was focusing the attention of his audience on Christ, who alone deserves the preeminence.

23. Fee, "Toward a . . .," p. 41.

24. Ibid., p. 47.

25. F. F. Bruce, ed., *1 and 2 Corinthians,* p. 34.

26. A. T. Robertson, *Word Pictures in the New Testament*, 4:76.

27. In litotes a writer makes a negative statement to emphasize the positive alternative. For example, "No small storm" (Acts 27:20), means a very large storm.

28. William Barclay, *The Letters to the Corinthians,* p. 22.

29. Barrett, p. 49.

30. Johnson, p. 1231.

31. Barrett, p. 49.

Lesson 2 Self Check

QUESTION 1

Paul prided himself in his rhetorical skills. *True or False?*

QUESTION 2

To what were the divisions at Corinth Paul identifies in this passage probably related?

- A. Economic differences among believers
- B. Theological differences among believers
- C. Preferences for particular teachers
- D. Ethnic differences among believers

QUESTION 3

What does unity mean in 1 Corinthians 1:10-17?

- A. Doing everything together
- B. Always having the same opinions
- C. Being of the same purpose
- D. Tolerating everybody

QUESTION 4

Unity among believers is more important than preserving the truth of the gospel. *True or False?*

QUESTION 5

The Christian leaders named in this passage are Paul, Apollos, and Cephas. *True or False?*

QUESTION 6

The primary basis for Christian unity is relationship to Christ. *True or False?*

QUESTION 7

Paul learned of the divisions at Corinth through a report from Chloe's people. *True or False?*

QUESTION 8

Paul made sure that he personally baptized everyone he led to the Lord. *True or False?*

QUESTION 9

Paul considered that his primary calling was to preach the gospel. *True or False?*

QUESTION 10

Paul's approach to solving the problems at Corinth may be described as pastoral. *True or False?*

Lesson 2 Answers to Questions

QUESTION 1: *Your answer should be similar to the following:*
In 1 Corinthians 9:5, Paul uses Cephas as an example of an apostle who carried along a believing wife and accepted financial support from those he ministered to. Paul writes as if the Corinthians were quite familiar with Cephas as an apostle of the Lord who traveled to spread the gospel. Possibly Cephas had spent time at Corinth teaching, but the evidence does not allow for a firm conclusion on this point.

QUESTION 2: *Your answer should be similar to the following:*
Apollos was a Christian Jew from Alexandria. He accepted the baptism of John the Baptist and spoke boldly, effectively, and accurately about Jesus in the synagogue at Ephesus, where Priscilla and Aquila heard him. They educated him further about Jesus, and then he went on to Corinth after Paul had left there on his second missionary journey. Apollos ministered in Achaia and at Corinth, edifying the believers and refuting Jewish unbelievers in public. Later, Paul urged him to revisit Corinth.

QUESTION 3

Relationship to church at Corinth	Person
Founder of the church	Paul
One of the Twelve and possibly a visiting teacher	Cephas
A learned and eloquent teacher who had taught in Corinth	Apollos
The Lord and Savior	Christ

QUESTION 4: *Your answer should be similar to the following:*
These three men were unified and mutually supportive. There were no major doctrinal divisions among them. They would have each upheld the unity of the church.

QUESTION 5
    D. Believers aligned themselves with the teacher they liked the best.

QUESTION 6: *Your answer*

QUESTION 7
    A. To agree together
    B. To end divisions
    C. To have the same mind and purpose

QUESTION 8
    A. Stop aligning themselves with particular spiritual leaders

QUESTION 9: *Your answer should be similar to the following:*
He had many points of unity with them: He regarded them as fellow-believers and as his spiritual children. He loved them and wanted to help them. On the other hand, he could not be completely united with them because of their sinful and immature attitudes and behaviors.

QUESTION 10: *Your answer*

QUESTION 11
    D. That they focus on Christ rather than men.

QUESTION 12: *Your answer*

QUESTION 13
    A. They are all related to Christ.

QUESTION 14: *Your answer*

QUESTION 15
    B. Believers would identify with the one who baptized them.

QUESTION 16: Unifying

QUESTION 17: False

QUESTION 18: *Your answer*

QUESTION 19
    A. To show them his example
    B. To persuade them to adopt the right course

QUESTION 20: *Your answer*

Lesson 2 Self Check Answers

QUESTION 1: False

QUESTION 2

    C. Preferences for particular teachers

QUESTION 3

    C. Being of the same purpose

QUESTION 4: False

QUESTION 5: True

QUESTION 6: True

QUESTION 7: True

QUESTION 8: False

QUESTION 9: True

QUESTION 10: True

Lesson 3: True Wisdom
(1 Cor 1:17–2:16)

In the section from 1 Corinthians 1:17 through the end of chapter 2, Paul addresses the subject of wisdom. Why does he devote so much space to discussing wisdom? His discussion of wisdom here is the second part of his longer discussion on the problem of *disunity*, from 1 Corinthians 1:10–4:21. In the first part of his discussion, from 1 Corinthians 1:10-17, Paul stated the problem and urged the Corinthians to come together rather than divide. Now, in the second part of his argument, he discusses wisdom, both God's and man's. In the third part, he will apply God's wisdom to the problem of their view of Christian leaders. True wisdom does not lead to behavior that is divisive and quarrelsome, but rather leads to righteousness, peace, and unity. Paul knows that the Corinthians' divisiveness is a reflection of their immaturity. In order to grow spiritually, they need to grasp the nature of true wisdom.

In Topic 1 we will examine what Paul means by the difference between God's wisdom and man's wisdom and the basic approaches to life that each involves. It is possible for believers to mistakenly evaluate things using human wisdom and thus miss out on the power of God's wisdom.

Topic 2 makes clear the basic distinction within humans—the spiritual man and the natural man. A person's basic values and perspective on life should flow out of his status as a spiritual or natural man.

Lesson Outline

Topic 1: The Wisdom of God and the Wisdom of the World (1 Cor 1:17–2:5)

Two Types of Wisdom (1:17-21)

Gospel as a Stumbling Block (1:22-25)

Corinthian Church Is Foolish (1:26-31)

Paul's "Foolish" Preaching (2:1-5)

Human Wisdom Robs the Cross of Its Power

Topic 2: Spiritual and Natural Man (1 Cor 2:6-16)

God's Mystery Not Understood (2:6-9)

Revealed by the Spirit (2:10-13)

Discerned by the Spiritual Man (2:14-16)

Lesson Objectives

Lotus' husband, Shan, laughs at her spending so much time going to church and associating with Christians, whom he says are not the power brokers in the town. His thinking is, "Why waste so much time with people who cannot help you get what you want?" Shan spends much time trying to build relationships to get more work in his handyman business. He keeps income flowing by doing welding, carpentry, and masonry work around the town. Of course, he's not the only one who can do this work, so he has made relationships with the owners of the lumber yard, the gravel pit, and the local metal supplier. Whenever people come around looking for cost quotations for materials to do building projects, those owners will recommend Shan to do the work. If Shan gets the job, then he pays the owners a referral fee. In addition, several times a year Shan takes these people out for expensive restaurant meals, and he always gives them gifts at the New Year. For Shan there is a lot of payback in these relationships with people of influence.

Relationships with church people mean a tremendous amount to Lotus, not because they are people of high status in the town, but because they are her brothers and sisters in the Lord. In the early days of the church, when people had needs, they would rally around each other, pray, and help each other. Now, though, people seem to care less about those who are not in their "group." Those that follow Sister Marie's teaching are cliquish with each other, and they are always talking about "Sister Marie this," and "Sister Marie that." Although they get such a blessing out of Sister Marie, they seem to be withholding the blessing of their presence and participation from the church. To a certain extent, they seem to be more interested in what they can get than in what they can give.

As Lotus reads through 1 Corinthians 1 and 2, Paul's teaching about this world's wisdom and God's wisdom speaks to her heart. This world's wisdom is so attractive, but it comes from self-interest and ends in ungodliness. The thinking of Shan, her unsaved husband, seems to be permeating the church. Lotus wants to understand God's wisdom and work to apply it in her church.

By the end of this lesson, you will be able to:

- Explain the difference between God's wisdom and man's wisdom
- Learn how to evaluate situations using God's wisdom instead of man's wisdom
- Understand how the gospel is "foolish" and take steps to make your evangelism more effective
- Distinguish between the spiritual and the natural man, and apply this truth in your ministry

Topic 1: The Wisdom of God and the Wisdom of the World (1 Cor 1:17–2:5)

The 2004 Presidential inauguration in the United States cost approximately $40,000,000. It was a huge pageant attracting media attention from around the world. Tickets to attend one of the inaugural balls were much sought after and coveted.

In 1931 the forty meters tall "Christ the Redeemer" statue was completed in Rio de Janeiro at a cost of $250,000. Then in 2007, Brazilian corporate sponsors spent large amounts of money to have it declared one of the New Seven Wonders of the World.

Some people may think that Christians should do similar big things to attract the world's attention. This topic will explore the contrast between the wisdom of the world and the wisdom of God.

Christians must walk a balanced line between being **in** the world and being **of** the world (Jn 17:15-16). We face the constant temptation to be conformed to the thinking, values and behaviors of this world. We do not want to withdraw from this world and lose our ability to influence it. We need God's wisdom, so that unhealthy worldly practices will not corrupt our lives and our churches.

Two Types of Wisdom (1:22-25)

Assignment

- Read 1 Corinthians 1:17-21.

- Read Constable, "The Folly of a Crucified Messiah" (refer to the Articles section at the end of this lesson), through the note on 1:21.

- Read "Two Types of Wisdom."

Two Types of Wisdom

Wisdom was a high value in ancient Greek culture, just as it was highly valued in Old Testament Jewish culture (Prov 8). Paul distinguishes two types of wisdom in 1 Corinthians 1:17–2:5.

Paul uses the word "foolish" or "foolishness" seven times in this passage. "Foolish" is a negative word, meaning "absurd; ridiculous; despicable; contemptible." Thus, "foolish" would be the opposite of "wise" in normal usage. Sometimes Paul says the gospel is "foolish," (note the quotation marks) by which he means that *unsaved humanity views the gospel as foolish*, simply because they cannot understand it (1 Cor 2:14). On the other hand, Paul says that *the wisdom of the world is foolish in God's sight*. This is because all human knowledge, worldly power, status, and philosophy cannot remedy the sin problem so as to bring salvation. When studying this passage, be careful to note whether Paul is referring to something as foolish from God's point of view or from unsaved man's point of view.

There is a similar need to be careful when studying the meaning of "wisdom" or "wise" in this passage. "Wisdom" and its related forms are used twenty-one times in this passage! Normally, we think of wisdom as a positive thing. The dictionary defines "wise" as "discerning and judging soundly concerning what is true or false, proper or improper." Yet, Paul identifies two types of wisdom and evaluates them from the point of view of salvation. Paul is not saying that all human knowledge is bad or useless in and of itself. There is much value in poetry, philosophy, math, science and art. However, none of this knowledge and wisdom can save a sinner.

Human wisdom in this passage is more than just knowledge. It denotes mankind's philosophies, values and ways of achieving success apart from God. Human wisdom focuses on man and what he can do. Sometimes we call this self-effort. For the Greeks, this would have meant putting oneself forward, climbing the social ladder, and reaching for fame and influence. Skill in rhetoric was viewed as critical to achieving these goals. For the Jews, the road to social status often meant mastering the intricacies of the Law and the rabbinic traditions, like a scribe or Pharisee (1 Cor 1:20). Paul states that all these efforts are really foolishness to God, because they cannot bring about salvation. Paul's point is that no one comes to know God through such human wisdom. The result of following the path of human wisdom is pride in one's own efforts.

Conversely, God's wisdom is centered on the message of the cross and manifests itself in humble service based on truth and love. Jesus and Paul are examples of lives showing forth God's wisdom—not man's. God saves people through the simple, sometimes inelegant, preaching of the gospel. Most of the people who responded to the gospel message at Corinth were not from the top of the social pyramid. God's wisdom is humbling for those who understand it. Because salvation is entirely the gift of God's grace, no believer can boast that he has done anything to merit it. Any reliance on human achievement is actually a hindrance to salvation. God's wisdom means a way of thinking and doing that is the opposite of the world's way. Indeed, the world views God's wisdom as foolish or stupid.

The message of the gospel is for everyone—not just the privileged, rich, powerful, and intelligent. Many who hear the gospel and accept its truth do so when they are children—a time when social status is perhaps less important to them.

QUESTION 1

Match the characteristics of true wisdom with the corresponding verses in 1 Corinthians.

Characteristics of True Wisdom	Verses
Source is God	1 Corinthians 2:5
Viewed by the world as weak, low, despised	1 Corinthians 1:21
Centered on the crucified Christ	1 Corinthians 1:27-28
Is God's power	1 Corinthians 1:23-24
Viewed by the world as foolishness	1 Corinthians 1:18

QUESTION 2

Match the characteristics of human wisdom with the corresponding verses in 1 Corinthians.

Characteristics of Human Wisdom	Verses
Does not bring salvation	1 Corinthians 1:17; 2:1
Clever speech and eloquence	1 Corinthians 1:21
Linked with power and privilege in this world's system	1 Corinthians 1:20
Is called the wisdom of the world	1 Corinthians 2:6
Is called the wisdom of this age	1 Corinthians 1:19
Is called the wisdom of the wise	1 Corinthians 1:26

Gospel as a Stumbling Block (1:22-25)

Assignment

- Read 1 Corinthians 1:22-25.
- Read Constable, "The Folly of a Crucified Messiah" (refer to the Articles section at the end of this lesson), through the note on 1:25.
- Read "Gospel as a Stumbling Block."

Gospel as a Stumbling Block

In Galatians, Paul talks about the offense of the cross (Gal 5:11). A stumbling block is something in your path, an obstacle that you trip over. Metaphorically, the stumbling block prevents you from journeying forward. Instead, you fall down and perhaps are injured.

In 1 Corinthians 1:23, the message of the cross is a *stumbling block* to Jews and *foolishness* to Greeks. "Stumbling block" and "foolishness" have the same function—an obstacle hindering people from receiving salvation through the gospel.

The particular Jewish stumbling block was a demand for miraculous signs. Jesus frequently encountered this request in his earthly ministry .(See Mt 12:38-39; Mt 16:1-4; Jn 6:30). Jesus was not willing to perform signs on demand, but he did perform many miracles publicly. Still, the Jewish leaders and most of the Jewish people did not believe, even when Jesus was raised from the dead.

For the Greeks, steeped in rational philosophies, the simple message of a crucified Savior seemed ridiculous. In Athens, Luke reported that "all the Athenians and the foreigners who lived there used to spend their time in nothing else than telling or listening to something new." (Acts 17:21) Traveling philosophers would seek an audience to impress others with their speeches, and the hearers would judge the speaker according to their standards of cogency, oratorical skill, logic, and sophistication of argument.

Generally when we think about evangelism, we want to clear away as many obstacles as possible to make it "easy" for the unbeliever to understand. Consequently, we will take pains to select the Scripture passage that we want to use, and we will carefully craft our message to appeal to the needs of the hearers. We will often emphasize points in common with the audience. Perhaps we will use illustrations that the listeners are familiar with. Above all, we will speak to them in their own language, so that we have hope of their grasping our points. This approach is skillful and strategic and does eliminate many hindrances to the gospel. Still, Paul emphasizes in this passage that *the major obstacle to successful evangelism is the gospel message itself*. The simple message of Christ dying for the sins of the world on the cross cannot be understood by the unsaved man.

QUESTION 3

Think about how and why the cross could be a stumbling block. Record your thoughts in your Life Notebook.

Paul says that neither miraculous signs nor human wisdom are the focus of his message. Yet, today, much evangelism is centered on "miracle" services, "charismatic" speakers, or special techniques.

QUESTION 4

In 1 Corinthians 1:22-25, how is the message of the cross a stumbling block to Jews?

QUESTION 5

The gospel message was foolishness to the Greeks because Jesus' death on the cross did not fit their philosophies. *True or False?*

QUESTION 6

Since the gospel is a stumbling block and foolishness, how then do we have any hope of success in evangelism?

QUESTION 7

Answer the following questions in your Life Notebook. How will you apply the truth that the message of the cross is "a stumbling block to Jews and foolishness to Gentiles" in your personal evangelism? What might Paul call "wisdom of this age" in your cultural setting? How have you seen people react to the gospel negatively? Did they view it as foolishness or as unbelievable? In what ways does Paul's message encourage you to persevere in your witness?

Corinthian Church Is Foolish (1:25-31)

After receiving God's blessings, we are tempted to congratulate ourselves as deserving of those blessings. Paul makes clear that God saves people by grace irrespective of status or accomplishments.

Assignment

- Read 1 Corinthians 1:26-31.
- Read Constable, "The Folly of the Corinthian Believers" (refer to the Articles section at the end of this lesson).
- Read "Corinthian Church Is Foolish."

Corinthian Church Is Foolish

In an effort to shake the Corinthian believers out of their pattern of behavior based on human wisdom, Paul asks them to consider the circumstances of their coming to faith in Christ (1 Cor 1:26-31). He says that not many of them were wise by human standards. With few exceptions, they did not come from the ranks of the powerful of society—the nobility, the wealthy, the famous, or from those holding high political office. Instead, they came mostly from the opposite end of the social scale.

For Paul, Jesus was everything. There was nothing else to boast about except the Lord and what flowed out of his relationship to the Lord. As he said, "I have been crucified with Christ, and it is no longer I who live, but Christ lives in me" (Gal 2:20).

Here he calls Jesus "our wisdom, righteousness, sanctification and redemption." By this he means that our whole spiritual life and hope is in Jesus. We have nothing to boast about apart from our relationship to him.

QUESTION 8

Read Matthew 11:25 and 1 Corinthians 1:26-31. God chooses the lowly, the weak, and what the world considers foolish to shame human wisdom so that no one can boast before God. *True or False?*

Boasting in one's own achievements is the natural outcome of human wisdom, for its premise is self-effort. All such boasting comes out of human pride. However, not all boasting is bad. There is a type of boasting that Christians can legitimately do.

QUESTION 9

According to Philippians 3:3-6, what things did Paul boast about before his conversion? *(Select all that apply.)*

    A. Circumcision

    B. Ancestry

    C. Legalistic righteousness

    D. Persecution of the church

Before you answer Question 10, read Romans 15:17-19; 1 Corinthians 1:31; 2 Corinthians 11:30-33; and 2 Corinthians 12:5.

QUESTION 10

What things did Paul boast about after his conversion? *(Select all that apply.)*

    A. Things that show his weakness

    B. The Lord

    C. What the Lord has done through him

    D. The heavenly visions the Lord gave him

    E. How cunning he was in escaping from his captors

QUESTION 11

Do you think that it is possible to be rightly proud of our spiritual achievements? (For example, how many people we have led to Christ, how much we have grown in faith, how effectively we have utilized our spiritual gifts?) Is it ever allowable for us to speak of such things? If yes, what is the right way to do it? Record your responses in your Life Notebook.

QUESTION 12

How is Paul's focus on "Christ, as one who had been crucified" like or unlike the messages you proclaim? Are there times when you neglect or even hide the message of the cross? If so, why? How does Paul's example encourage you to do things differently? In what ways could you better communicate and even highlight "Christ, crucified"? Record your responses in your Life Notebook.

Paul's "Foolish" Preaching (2:1-5)

Have you ever listened to an "evangelistic" message where the cross of Christ was barely mentioned? Such was not Paul's practice.

Assignment

- Read 1 Corinthians 2:1-5.

- Read Constable, "The Folly of Paul's Preaching" (refer to the Articles section at the end of this lesson).

- Read "Paul's 'Foolish' Preaching."

Paul's "Foolish" Preaching

Paul did not come preaching with polished rhetorical style (1 Cor 2:1-5). He would certainly not have been classed as a Sophist (from which the Greek word for "wisdom" comes), defined as a teacher of eloquence, philosophy, and politics in ancient Greece. Whether he was capable of such speech techniques or not is not the issue here. Rather, his purpose was to avoid such displays and to concentrate on the message of the cross. From a critical Greek perspective, his preaching was unappealing—he appeared weak and fearful. Compared to Apollos, Paul must have come across second rate. Still, Paul's preaching brought results, as he points out to the Corinthians (See 1 Cor 4:15). Paul had a different power that he relied on—the power of the Holy Spirit. Paul did not want to attract people to himself, but only to the Lord, who had died for their sins.

Paul did not want inconsistency between his message and his manner. He is making a case here for orthodoxy of practice to go along with orthodoxy of doctrine, or for using God's ways to preach the gospel. Paul knew that using human ways to spread the gospel would be counter-productive. The ultimate result would be to empty the cross of its power.

QUESTION 13

The best evangelist makes no preparation for his messages. *True or False?*

QUESTION 14

What is the most important factor in evangelism?

    A. The appearance of the speaker

    B. The confidence with which the message is presented

    C. High quality audio-visuals

    D. Presentation of the message of the cross

Human Wisdom Robs the Cross of Its Power

Assignment

- Read "Human Wisdom Robs the Cross of Its Power."

Human Wisdom Robs the Cross of Its Power

Paul understood that his commission from the Lord to preach the gospel meant that he should not use the ways of the world to evangelize. He did not do the Lord's work in the world's way. For Paul, that meant that he refused to preach with "clever speech" (1 Cor 1:17). This phrase in the Greek is literally "in wisdom of word." The wisdom he is talking about is human wisdom, implying using flowery language, rhetorical technique and philosophy to impress the hearers. This was common practice in the Greek world. Good speakers built quite a reputation and following according to their use of these tools. Apparently some people looked down on Paul at Corinth for his poor oral performance.

Paul says that an evangelist using "wisdom of word" would cause the cross of Christ to "be emptied." (1 Cor 1:17) This Greek word for "emptied" is also used by Paul to describe Christ in Philippians 2:7, where it describes Jesus' humiliation. He laid aside the glory of heaven to become a man, took the form of a servant, and died on the cross. According to Strong's Concordance, the word means "to make empty, i.e. (figuratively) to abase, neutralize, falsify." The NET Bible translates this phrase as "so that the cross of Christ would not become useless." Some translations add the phrase "emptied *of its power*" (the italicized words are not in the Greek) to try to clarify the meaning.

The message of the cross is humbling, for eternal life cannot be merited. Any presentation of the gospel that fails to focus on Christ is misguided, if not false.

QUESTION 15

Evangelizing with human wisdom could cause the cross of Christ to become useless in which of the following ways? *(Select all that apply.)*

    A. People could focus on the speaker rather than on the message of the cross.

    B. People could assume that believing the gospel brings worldly success.

    C. Such methods could lead to boasting in man rather than to humble trust in God.

    D. Using such methods could neglect the important work of the Holy Spirit in evangelism.

QUESTION 16

Is it better for the church to have poor speakers, so that by their preaching they will not cause the cross to be emptied? Give a short reason in your response.

QUESTION 17

Are there any ways in which you utilize this world's wisdom through your ministry? Are your methods sometimes influenced by a desire to become popular, or to earn a lot of money, or to impress people with your skills? How can we deal with the problem of impure motives and human wisdom in our ministries? Record your responses in your Life Notebook.

Topic 2: Spiritual and Natural Man (1 Cor 2:6-16)

Since God's "foolishness" is conveyed in the message of the cross, only "foolish" people will appreciate those "foolish" preachers. Those who think themselves wise miss out. There is a crucial distinction here among humans, a distinction that has eternal consequences.

Especially in Western cultures, it has become fashionable to disavow the importance of distinctions between people, for we do not want to be accused of prejudice based on age, gender, race, disability, or cultural differences. Paul himself affirmed that in Christ "there is neither Jew nor Greek, there is neither slave nor free, there is neither male nor female" (Gal 3:28). Yet, there is a major difference between people that is not outwardly observable, but is instead inward and spiritual.

God's Mystery Not Understood (2:6-9)

Assignment

- Read 1 Corinthians 2:6-9.

- Read Constable, "The Spirit's Ministry of Revealing God's Wisdom" (refer to the Articles section at the end of this lesson), through the note on 2:9.

- Read "God's Mystery Not Understood."

God's Mystery Not Understood

In 1 Corinthians 2:6-9, Paul shows that God's wisdom was not understood by the rulers of this age. Thus, instead of being truly wise, they crucified Jesus rather than worshipping Him.

In Paul's writing, "mystery" often means revealed truth, something formerly hidden but now made known. God had predetermined the plan of salvation from the creation of the world (Rev 13:8), but unbelievers knew nothing of it.

Who are the rulers of this age (1 Cor 2:6)? Are they human rulers? Could Paul be referring to supernatural demonic powers? It is possible that Paul refers to both here, but his emphasis seems to be on human rulers, for they are the ones who sent Jesus to His death (although Satan certainly had a hand in it—see John 13:27).

Paul quotes from Isaiah 64:4 to prove that even the wisest man according to human wisdom cannot know God apart from God's revelation.

Paul says that "we do speak wisdom among the mature" (1 Cor 2:6). The wisdom he refers to is, of course, God's wisdom, and the aspect of God's wisdom he has been emphasizing is the message of the cross. But who are the "mature"? This word "mature" is sometimes translated in English versions as "perfect" or "full grown." Scholars are divided on what Paul means here. Some think that by "mature" he means the spiritually mature believer. Evidence supporting this view is that in Chapter 3 Paul makes a big issue of their immaturity. Others think that by "mature" Paul means *any* believer. The NET Bible gives the following note supporting this interpretation:

> "In extrabiblical literature this word was applied to an initiate of a mystery religion. It could here refer to those who believed Paul's message, the mystery of God (v. 1), and so be translated as 'those who believe God's message.'"

Since the emphasis in 1 Corinthians 2:6-16 is on the clear difference between the natural and the spiritual man, and since Paul closes his argument with the surprising statement, "We have the mind of Christ," the second interpretation seems best. Probably "mature" here refers to all believers.

QUESTION 18

In your opinion, what did Paul mean by "mystery"? Record your response in your Life Notebook.

Believers are absolutely dependent on revelation and enlightenment to understand the things of God. Jesus understood this when He prayed on the cross, "Father, forgive them, for they don't know what they are doing" (Lk 23:34).

QUESTION 19

Why did the human leaders crucify Christ?

QUESTION 20

What are two possible meanings for "mature" in 1 Corinthians 2:6? *(Select all that apply.)*

    A. All believers

    B. Mature believers

    C. Adult believers

    D. People who have believed for years

Revealed by the Spirit (2:10-13)

QUESTION 21

What do you think Paul means by "the one who is spiritual discerns all things, yet he himself is understood by no one"? Or "we have the mind of Christ"? Record your response in your Life Notebook.

Assignment

- Read 1 Corinthians 2:10-13.

- Read Constable, "The Spirit's Ministry of Revealing God's Wisdom" (refer to the Articles section at the end of this lesson), through the note on 2:13.

- Read "Revealed by the Spirit."

Revealed by the Spirit

The role of the Holy Spirit in revealing things to people and giving them understanding is indispensable. Jesus said that people did not believe Him because they were not His sheep (Jn 10:26). Paul gives a similar principle here in 1 Corinthians 2:10-13.

It is sometimes pointed out that unsaved people can be very familiar with the Bible. Paul himself, as an unsaved Pharisee, had undoubtedly memorized large sections of the Old Testament. Yet, when Jesus spoke to the Pharisee Nicodemus, He chastised him: "Are you the teacher of Israel and yet you don't understand these things?" (Jn 3:10) Clearly, study of the Bible without the enlightenment of the Holy Spirit does not bring spiritual life.

People can study religions—even Christianity—as a scholarly exercise, and thus on one level gain knowledge. Paul is talking about a different level of knowledge in this passage—a knowledge of God's grace.

QUESTION 22

What seems to be Paul's main point in 1 Corinthians 2:10-13?

QUESTION 23

The unsaved man can grasp the truth of the gospel without the ministry of the Holy Spirit. *True or False?*

QUESTION 24

What is the best choice for Paul's meaning "the things that are freely given to us by God" (1 Cor 2:12)?

    A. Salvation

    B. Orthodox doctrines

    C. Secret knowledge

    D. Baptism

Discerned by the Spiritual Man (2:14-16)

Assignment

- Read 1 Corinthians 2:14-16.

- Read Constable, "The Spirit's Ministry of Revealing God's Wisdom" (refer to the Articles section at the end of this lesson), through the note on 2:16.

- Read "Discerned by the Spiritual Man."

Discerned by the Spiritual Man

There is a radical distinction among human beings. In the Old Testament, people were primarily divided between Jews and Gentiles. According to everyday human wisdom today, the main distinctions between people are racial, sexual, national, cultural, or economic. Paul uses God's wisdom to divide humankind into only two groups—the natural and the spiritual. We first see this distinction in 1 Corinthians 1:18, where Paul refers to "those who are perishing" and "us who are being saved."

In 1 Corinthians 2:14–2:15, the two types of people are most clearly differentiated. One section of humanity is called "natural." The Greek word is *psychikos*. (The NET Bible uses the term "unbeliever" instead of "natural," but the Greek literally reads "natural person.") The other part of humanity is called "spiritual." The Greek word here is *pneumatikos*.

Although Paul teaches that all believers are spiritual people because of the indwelling Holy Spirit, apparently the Corinthians were confused over the definition of a spiritual person. As we shall discover in later lessons, some in Corinth probably viewed themselves as "super-spiritual," which led to overemphasis on the gifts of the Spirit, feelings of pride and/or living a life of indulgence. They may have seen themselves as already resurrected in a spiritual sort of way that did not involve their physical bodies. This error is called "over-realized eschatology." It is true that believers already have "every spiritual blessing in the heavenly realms in Christ" (Eph 1:3). But it is also true that some of those blessings are not actualized until after Christ comes again, when we receive our glorified bodies. This is part of the "already-not yet" tension for believers.

Note that there is a major difference between the natural man and the spiritual man in his response to the things of the Spirit of God.

Paul makes very broad and difficult-to-understand statements in 1 Corinthians 2:15-16. These are not typical statements that most Christians make today. Would you feel comfortable saying, "The one who is spiritual discerns all things, yet he himself is understood by no one"? Or, "we have the mind of Christ"? From the context, Paul's subject is every believer—not some group of super-spiritual elite. What does he mean by such statements?

To analyze Paul's meaning, we should first look at the meanings of several words: "discern," "understood," and "mind."

The word translated both as "discern" (1 Cor 2:14) and as "understood" (1 Cor 2:15) by the NET Bible is *anakrino* in the Greek. Paul used this verb ten times in 1 Corinthians, but never in any other letter. Clearly it is an important word for understanding this letter, and perhaps it was a popular word among the Corinthians. According to Strong's Concordance, the word means "to scrutinize, i.e. (by implication) investigate, interrogate, determine." It is often translated in other English versions as "judge." The NET Bible gives the alternate translation "evaluate" for this word in 1 Corinthians 2:15.

Paul's point is that the indwelling Holy Spirit gives discernment to believers that unbelievers do not have. This understanding is so radical as to touch on every aspect of life and give believers God's perspective. Believers simply view things differently from non-believers, because believers have a new value system, a new life, and a new Lord. Paul does not mean that believers become omniscient like God.

The word translated "mind" in the NET Bible is used twice in 1 Corinthians 2:16. The first time it occurs is in Paul's quote of Isaiah 40:13. In Isaiah the context is the wonder of God's creation, and "mind" refers to God's knowledge of all things. Paul quotes this Old Testament verse to show that God's "mind" is unfathomable, except by God's Spirit (1 Cor 2:10). Since believers have the Spirit indwelling them, we have the "mind" of God (or Christ) in us. The Holy Spirit empowers us to evaluate things with God's wisdom.

Having the mind of Christ does not mean that we have no need to ask God for wisdom or to learn. Indeed, just by writing this letter, Paul was teaching the believers at Corinth in hopes that they would learn. Furthermore, one of the gifts of the Spirit is teaching (Eph 4:11). "Having the mind of Christ" is a powerful way of expressing that we are indwelt by the Holy Spirit. Therefore, Christians are spiritual people, essentially different from unbelievers. God's wisdom comes to us through the Holy Spirit.

The following quote from the Studying the Bible course will clarify Paul's meaning (from Lesson 1, Topic 4: The Holy Spirit Gives Understanding to Believers):

> "Believers can understand the Bible only because the Holy Spirit enables them to understand it. The Holy Spirit clarifies the written Word in the minds of believers. They are able to recognize the spiritual truths that the Lord wants them to know. Having the Holy Spirit makes all the difference in how people read, study, and understand the Scriptures. People are forever changed once the Spirit of God is within them. The Lord equips believers to spiritually judge the words in the Bible.
>
> Having the mind of Christ does not mean that believers understand absolutely everything. It does mean, however, that they see the Bible from the perspective of Jesus Christ and not from the perspective of the world. As believers study the Bible, humbly depending on the Holy Spirit to teach them, they will gradually comprehend more and more of God's Word."

All believers, indwelt by the Holy Spirit, are spiritual people and have the mind of Christ. Those displaying the mind of Christ are people who promote unity based on humble service.

QUESTION 25

From 1 Corinthians 2:12-15, what is the critical difference between the natural man and the spiritual man?

    A. The Holy Spirit indwells the spiritual man but does not indwell the natural man.

    B. The spiritual man is God's elect, but the natural man is not.

    C. The spiritual man can speak in tongues, but the natural man cannot.

    D. The spiritual man is spiritually mature, but the natural man is carnal.

QUESTION 26

What is the response of the natural man to the things of the Spirit? *(Select all that apply.)*

    A. He does not receive them.

    B. He regards them as foolish.

    C. He cannot understand them.

    D. He has no interest in studying them.

QUESTION 27

If unbelievers cannot understand the gospel message, then why do we evangelize? How does this truth affect your personal evangelism? How does this affect your prayer life? Record your responses in your Life Notebook.

QUESTION 28

As believers we need teachers, even though we have the mind of Christ. *True or False?*

Lesson 3 Articles

Notes on 1 Corinthians

Dr. Thomas L. Constable; 2003 Edition

2. The gospel as a contradiction to human wisdom (1:18–2:5)

Paul set up a contrast between cleverness of speech and the Cross in verse 17. Next he developed this contrast with a series of arguments. Boasting in men impacts the nature of the gospel. He pointed out that the gospel is not a form of *sophia* (human wisdom). Its message of a crucified Messiah does not appeal to human wisdom (1 Cor 1:18-25). Second, its recipients are not specially wise in the eyes of humanity (1 Cor 1:26-31). Third, Paul's preaching was not impressive in its human wisdom, but it bore powerful results (1 Cor 2:1-5).

> "There are . . . three particularly important expository passages in 1 Corinthians. They may be regarded as the letter's principal theological discourses and as such deserve special attention.

> "These three key discourses deal, respectively, with the wisdom of the cross (1 Cor 1:18–2:16), the nature of Christian community (1 Cor 12:4-13:13), and the resurrection of the dead (1 Cor 15). In each instance Paul's reflections on the topic are deliberate and focused, and lead him to develop a more or less extended and coherent argument. Moreover, each of these passages occurs at an important point within the overall structure of the letter. The discourse on wisdom, situated prominently at the beginning of the letter, supports the apostle's urgent appeals for unity (1 Cor 1:10–4:21). It can be argued that the discourse on Christian community undergirds, directly or indirectly, all of the counsels and instructions in chaps. 8 through 14. And the discourse on resurrection, a response to those who claim that 'there is no resurrection of the dead' (1 Cor 15:12), is located prominently at the end of the letter." (32)

> "In this part of the [first] discourse [i.e., 1 Cor 1:18–2:5] the argument proceeds in three steps: Paul makes his main point in 1 Cor 1:18-25, confirms it in 1 Cor 1:26-31 with an appeal to the Corinthians' own situation, and then further confirms it in 1 Cor 2:1-5 with reference to what and how he had preached in Corinth.

> "The apostle's thesis is registered first in 1 Cor 1:18 and then twice restated (in 1 Cor 1:21 and 1 Cor 1:23-24). (33)

Superficial displays of oratory that to them appeared to be demonstrations of wisdom impressed the Corinthian Christians excessively. Paul pointed out that the wisdom of God, the gospel of Christ, had power that mere worldly wisdom lacked.

The folly of a crucified Messiah (1:18-25)

> "This paragraph is crucial not only to the present argument (1 Cor 1:10–4:21) but to the entire letter as well. Indeed, it is one of the truly great moments in the apostle Paul. Here he argues, with OT support, that what God had always intended and had foretold in the prophets, he has now accomplished through the crucifixion: He has brought an end to human self-sufficiency as it is evidenced through human wisdom and devices." (34)

1:18 - The message (*logos*) of the Cross, in contrast to the speech (*logos*) of human wisdom (1 Cor 1:17), has the Cross as its central theme. When people hear it, it produces opposite effects in those who are on the way to perdition and in those on the way to glory. Paul contrasted foolishness and weakness with wisdom and power (cf. Rom 1:16).

> "What would you think if a woman came to work wearing earrings stamped with an image of the mushroom cloud of the atomic bomb dropped over Hiroshima?
>
> "What would you think of a church building adorned with a fresco of the massed graves at Auschwitz? . . .
>
> "The same sort of shocking horror was associated with *cross* and *crucifixion* in the first century." (35)

1:19 - Paul's quotation of Isaiah 29:14 shows that it has always been God's method to show the folly of merely human wisdom.

1:20 - The first three questions in this verse recall similar questions that Isaiah voiced when the Assyrians' plans to destroy Jerusalem fell through (Isa 33:18; cf. Job 12:17; Isa 19:12). Paul's references to the age (Gr. *aion*) and the world (*kosmos*) clarify that he was speaking of purely natural wisdom in contrast to the wisdom that God has revealed. God's wisdom centers on the Cross.

> "In first-century Corinth, 'wisdom' was not understood to be practical skill in living under the fear of the Lord (as it frequently is in Proverbs), nor was it perceived to be some combination of intuition, insight, and people smarts (as it frequently is today in the West). Rather, wisdom was a public philosophy, a well-articulated world-view that made sense of life and ordered the choices, values, and priorities of those who adopted it. The 'wise man,' then, was someone who adopted and defended one of the many competing public world-views. Those who were 'wise' in this sense might have been Epicureans or Stoics or Sophists or Platonists, but they had this in common: they claimed to be able to 'make sense' out of life and death and the universe." (36)

1:21 - Human reasoning does not enable people to get to know God nor does it deliver them from their sins. These benefits come only through the "foolishness" (in the eyes of the natural man) of the message preached (Gr. *kerygma*), namely, the gospel. The true estimation of things, therefore, is that human reasoning is folly.

Paul was not saying that all the wisdom that unbelievers have produced is worthless. However in comparison with what the wisdom that God has revealed about Himself can accomplish human wisdom is of little value.

> "Not every human knowledge about any given topic—physics or medicine, for instance—is under debate in our text (at least not primarily). Paul has something more specific in mind . . . Paul aims specifically at the human wisdom *about God* as 'wisdom of the world,' at 'theology' as 'wisdom of the world.'" (37)

1:22 - The Jews characteristically asked for signs as demonstrations of God's power (cf. Matt 16:1-4; Mk 8:11-12; Jn 2:18). In contrast, the message of the Cross seemed to be a demonstration of weakness, namely, Jesus' inability to save Himself from death.

Likewise the Greeks typically respected wisdom, an explanation of things that was reasonable and made sense. However the message of the Cross did not appear to make sense. How could anyone believe in and submit to One who was apparently not smart enough to save Himself from suffering execution as a criminal when He was not one? Furthermore how could anyone look to such a One as a teacher of wisdom?

> ." . . the 'Jews' and 'Greeks' here illustrate the basic idolatries of humanity. God must function as the all-powerful or the all-wise, but always in terms of our best interests—power in our behalf, wisdom like ours! For both the ultimate idolatry is that of insisting that God conform to our own prior views as to how 'the God who makes sense' ought to do things." (38)

1:23 - A crucified Messiah was a stumbling block to the Jews because they regarded Messiah as the Person on whom God's blessing rested to the greatest degree (Isa 11:2). However, Jesus' executioners hung Him on a tree, the sure proof that God had cursed Him (Deut 21:23; Gal 3:13).

Paul used the terms "Greeks" (1 Cor 1:22) and "Gentiles" (1 Cor 1:23) interchangeably.

> "It is hard for those in the christianized West, where the cross for almost nineteen centuries has been the primary symbol of the faith, to appreciate how utterly mad the message of a God who got himself crucified by his enemies must have seemed to the first-century Greek or Roman. But it is precisely the depth of this scandal and folly that we *must* appreciate if we are to understand both why the Corinthians were moving away from it toward wisdom and why it was well over a century before the cross appears among Christians as a symbol of their faith." (39)

1:24 - The "called" contrast with the unsaved among both Jews and Gentiles (1 Cor 1:2; Rom 8:28, 30). Christ is the instrument of God's power in conquering the forces of evil and delivering people from their control. Moreover He is the instrument of God's wisdom in solving the problem human reasoning could not unravel, namely, how people can know God and come to God. The wisdom literature of the Old Testament personified wisdom as God's agent in revelation, creation, and redemption. Jesus Christ personally is that wisdom because He is the power of God for the salvation of everyone who believes (Rom 1:16; cf. v. 1 Cor 1:30).

> "This is Paul's most brilliant epigrammatic description of the world in which the Gospel is preached, and of the Gospel itself." (40)

1:25 - The "foolishness" of God, the gospel of the Cross, is wiser than human wisdom, and the "weakness" of God, in the eyes of unbelievers, is stronger than human strength.

> "At the moment, books are pouring off the presses telling us how to plan for success, how 'vision' consists in clearly articulated 'ministry goals,' how the knowledge of detailed profiles of our communities constitutes the key to successful outreach. I am not for a moment suggesting that there is nothing to be learned from such studies. But after a while one may perhaps be excused for marveling how many churches were planted by Paul and Whitefield and Wesley and Stanway and Judson without enjoying these advantages. Of course all of us need to understand the people to whom we minister, and all of us can benefit from small doses of such literature. But massive doses sooner or later dilute the gospel. Ever so subtly, we start to think that success more critically depends on thoughtful sociological analysis than on the gospel.... We depend on plans, programs, vision statements—but somewhere along the way we have succumbed to the temptation to displace the foolishness of the cross with the wisdom of strategic planning. Again, I insist, my position is not a thinly veiled plea for obscurantism, for seat-of-the-pants ministry that plans nothing. Rather, I fear that the cross, without ever being disowned, is constantly in danger of being dismissed from the central place it must enjoy, by relatively peripheral insights that take on far too much weight. Whenever the periphery is in danger of displacing the center, we are not far removed from idolatry." (41)

In these verses (1 Cor 1:18-25) Paul sought to raise the Corinthians' regard for the gospel message by showing its superiority over anything humans can devise through reasoning and philosophizing. His purpose in doing so was to encourage them to value the content of the message more highly than the "wisdom" evident in the styles of those who delivered it.

> "One can scarcely conceive a more important—and more difficult—passage for the church today than this one. It is difficult, for the very reason it was in Corinth. We simply cannot abide the scandal of God's doing things his way, without our help. And to do it by

means of such weakness and folly! But we have often succeeded in blunting the scandal by symbol, or creed, or propositions. God will not be so easily tamed, and, freed from its shackles, the preaching of the cross alone has the power to set people free." (42)

The folly of the Corinthian believers (1:26-31)

Paul turned from the content of the gospel to the Corinthian believers to strengthen his argument that the gospel he preached contradicted human expectations. God had chosen "nobodies" rather than the "beautiful people" of Corinth. They themselves were evidence that God's "foolishness" confounds the wise. Jeremiah 9:23-24, with its emphasis on boasting in one proper thing or another improper thing, lies behind this pericope.

1:26 - This verse reflects that there were few in the Corinthian assembly who came from the higher intellectual and influential levels of their society. This characteristic has marked most local churches throughout history.

1:27-28 - The Old Testament is full of illustrations of God choosing less than promising material for His instruments. His method did not change with the coming of Christ nor has it changed since then.

> "Things that are not" are things that are nothing. They are non-entities in the eyes of the world. The "things that are" are those things and individuals that the world values highly. Paul did not mean that God cannot or will not save the affluent, but the glory of the gospel is that God's mercy extends to those whom the affluent tend to write off.

1:29 - God has chosen this method so the glory might be His and His alone. How wrong then to glorify His messengers! Glorying here has the idea of putting one's full confidence in some inappropriate object to secure ourselves.

1:30 - God is the source of the believer's life in Christ (cf. 1 Cor 1:2). Righteousness, sanctification, and redemption are metaphors of salvation, the result of the wisdom we find in Christ (cf. 1 Cor 6:11). Righteousness focuses on our right standing in the sight of God, sanctification on His making us more holy, and redemption on our liberation from sin.

1:31 - This loose quotation from Jeremiah 9:24 summarizes Paul's point. Instead of emphasizing the Lord's servants and what they have done we should focus on what the Lord Himself has done in providing wisdom and power in Christ.

God's purpose was not to make a superficial splash but to transform lives, something the Corinthians could see in their own experience.

> "The issue of election is particularly strong in 1 Corinthians. Paul opens the letter by affirming not only his call ('called to be an apostle of Christ Jesus by the will of God') but also that of the Corinthians ('called to be saints,' 1 Cor 1:2). This conviction reappears in the final verse of the thanksgiving, functioning there as part of the ultimate ground for Paul's confidence (1 Cor 1:9): 'God is faithful; by him you were called into the fellowship of his Son, Jesus Christ our Lord.' When the issue surfaces again a few verses later with renewed rhetorical emphasis (1 Cor 1:24, 26-30), it becomes clear that the concept of election or call no longer merely undergirds Paul's argument; it has instead become the focus of this argument. The Corinthians, it seems, have not grasped what election means." (43)

The folly of Paul's preaching (2:1-5)

Paul offered the example of his preaching among the Corinthians as a further illustration of what the wisdom of God can do in contrast to what the words that humans regard as wisdom can do.

> "The matters of *literary context* and *the continuity of the argument* are all important in understanding I Corinthians 2. Otherwise, much of the chapter reads like pure gnosticism,

and Paul is made the advocate of a private religion reserved for the spiritual elite (1 Cor 2:6-16)." (44)

2:1 - The apostle's preaching in Corinth was "not in excellence of rhetorical display or of philosophical subtlety." (45)

Some early texts have "mystery" (Gr. *mysterion*) instead of "testimony" (*martyrion*). The difference is not significant. The gospel was both the message God had previously not revealed that the apostles made known and the message to which they bore witness.

2:2 - As far as his preaching went, Paul only spoke about Christ crucified. This was his regular practice (Gal 3:1). He left all other knowledge aside.

> "According to Acts xviii. 1 Paul moved on to Corinth from Athens, and it is often supposed that after an attempt to marry the Gospel to Greek philosophy in his Areopagus speech (Acts xvii. 22-31), which was attended with indifferent success (Acts xvii. 32 ff.), he determined to change his tactics and preach nothing but the cross. (46) For this imaginative picture there is no evidence whatever."(47)

> ." . . 1 Corinthians is more than a practical letter aimed at telling the readers what to do and what not to do. The letter in fact primarily seeks to influence the minds, dispositions, intuitions of the audience in line with the message Paul had initially preached in the community (1 Cor 2:2), to confront readers with the critical nature of God's saving action in the crucified Christ in such a fashion that it becomes the glasses to refocus their vision of God, their own community, and the future. The advancing of such an epistemology gives the letter a theological purpose that unifies its otherwise unconnected structure." (48)

Centering his preaching on Christ crucified was not a new tack Paul took in Corinth because of previous lack of response (cf. Acts 17:22-31).

> "What Paul avoided was artificial communication that won plaudits for the speaker but distracted from the message. Lazy preachers have no right to appeal to 1 Corinthians 2:1-5 to justify indolence in the study and careless delivery in the pulpit. These verses do not prohibit diligent preparation, passion, clear articulation, and persuasive presentation. Rather, they warn against any method that leads people to say, 'What a marvelous preacher!' rather than, 'What a marvelous Savior!'" (49)

2:3 - The reason Paul felt weak, fearful, and trembling was probably his sense of personal inadequacy in the face of the spiritual needs he faced when he entered Corinth (cf. Acts 18:9-10).

> "If this was epilepsy, or malarial fever (Ramsay), it might well be the recurrent trouble which he calls a 'thorn for the flesh' (2 Cor. xii. 7)." (50)

2:4 - Paul did not design his content ("message," *logos*) and or his delivery ("preaching," *kerygma*) to impress his hearers with his eloquence or wisdom. Rather he emphasized the simple message he announced. His preaching was a demonstration, not a performance. Conviction came as a result of the Holy Spirit's power, not the "wisdom" of the preacher. We should not interpret this verse as deprecating persuasion but as a warning that conviction does not come as a result of persuasive arguments. It comes as the Holy Spirit opens blind eyes when we herald the gospel. The warning is against self-reliance in the preacher.

> "Those who minister the Word must prepare and use every gift God has given them—but they must not put their confidence in themselves." (51)

"Mere human *sophia* may dazzle and overwhelm and seem to be unanswerable, but . . . it does not penetrate to those depths of the soul which are the seat of the decisions of a lifetime." (52)

"It is possible for arguments to be logically irrefutable, yet totally unconvincing." (53)

2:5 - Paul's reason for this approach was so his converts would recognize that their faith rested on a supernatural rather than a natural foundation, namely, the enlightenment of the Holy Spirit (cf. Matt 16:15-17).

The apostle's conviction concerning the importance of the superior power of the gospel message was clear in his own preaching.

3. The Spirit's ministry of revealing God's wisdom (2:6-16)

Paul's reference to the Holy Spirit's power (vv. 1 Cor 2:4-5) led him to elaborate on the Spirit's ministry in enlightening the minds of believers and unbelievers alike. The Corinthians needed to view ministry differently. The key to this change would be the Holy Spirit's illumination of their thinking. People who are pursuing wisdom (*sophia*) cannot perceive it except as the Holy Spirit enlightens them.

Paul constructed his argument in this section with three contrasts that overlap slightly. The first contrast is between those who receive God's wisdom and those who do not (vv. 1 Cor 2:6-10a), and the second one is the Spirit of God and the spirit of the world (vv. 1 Cor 2:10b-13). The third contrast is the "natural" person and the "spiritual" person (vv. 1 Cor 2:14-16). (54)

> "Paul is not here rebuilding what he has just torn down. He is retooling their understanding of the Spirit and spirituality, in order that they might perceive the truth of what he has been arguing to this point.

> "While it is true that much of the *language* of this paragraph is not common to Paul, the explanation of this phenomenon is, as before, to be found in his using *their* language but filling it with his own content and thus refuting them. The theology, however, is his own, and it differs radically from theirs. . . . Paul's concern throughout is to get the Corinthians to understand who they are—in terms of the cross—and to stop acting as non-Spirit people." (55)

2:6 - Even though Paul's preaching of the gospel was simple and clear, there was a depth to his message that he did not want the Corinthians to overlook. Immature Christians cannot understand the real depths of the gospel fully. Later Paul would say the Corinthians were not mature (1 Cor 3:1-3).

Paul could have been using the word "mature" as synonymous with "Christian." He may have selected the word "mature" because the Corinthians apparently loved to apply it to themselves.

> "All Christians are 'mature' in the sense that they have come to terms with the message of the cross, while all others, by definition, have not." (56)

However, Paul later distinguished the natural person, the spiritual person, and the carnal person (1 Cor 2:14–3:4). Consequently by spiritual he may have meant one who has followed God's Spirit for some time, not just one who has His Spirit (cf. Heb 6:1).

The deep things of God require a type of wisdom that is different from secular wisdom. Presently those who control the climate of public opinion dominate secular wisdom. These rulers are those individuals who set the standard of what people who disregard God's revelation consider as true (cf. 1 Cor 1:20, 26), particularly those who were responsible for Jesus' crucifixion (1 Cor 2:8). However these people are on the way out because the popular perception of what is true changes and because Christ will end their rule eventually (1 Cor 15:24-25; Col 2:15).

2:7 - The wisdom Paul proclaimed was wisdom that God had not revealed previously. It was not a revelation in addition to the gospel. The message about Christ crucified embodies the wisdom of God. This message was unknown before Christ came. The message of the Cross is a further unfolding of God's plan and purpose beyond what He had revealed and what people had known previously.

Paul expounded on the fact that God had decreed this mystery from before creation in Ephesians 3:2-12. The Ephesian church was more mature and better able to understand this revelation than was the Corinthian congregation.

The end purpose of this new revelation was the saints' ultimate glorification by conformity to the image of God's Son.

2:8 - The rulers of this age are probably the intellectual trend-setters Paul mentioned above (1 Cor 2:7). Those responsible for the death of Christ were members of this group (cf. Acts 3:17-18; 4:25-28). If they had understood the central place that Jesus Christ occupied in God's plan, they would not have crucified Him thus assuring their own doom (cf. Lk 23:34).

> "The key [to this section of Paul's argument] is verse 8. The rulers of this age (whether understood as political and religious figures or as apocalyptic powers) demonstrated their ignorance of divine wisdom when they crucified the Lord of glory. The very mention of the crucifixion shows the argument very much in continuity with the preceding section and reminds us that the wisdom of God, which is incomprehensible to the world, is nothing other than the word of the cross (1 Cor 1:23-24)." (57)

The phrase "Lord of glory" implies the divine fullness. It also ties in with the saints' glory (1 Cor 2:7). It is through union with Him that we will experience glory.

2:9 - The source of this quotation is evidently Isaiah 64:4; 65:17. It summarizes Paul's point well. There are many things we can know only by revelation. The more God reveals the more clearly we see that He has designed His plans for humanity for our blessing.

> "Paul's thought is that there is no method of apprehension open to man (eyes, ears, or understanding) which can give him any idea of the wonderful things that God has made ready for *them that love him* (cf. Rom. viii. 28)." (58)

2:10 - The wonderful mysteries God has prepared for those who love Him are not knowable only by a select group of Christians. Any and every believer can understand and appreciated them because the indwelling Holy Spirit can enlighten us. The mystery religions of Greece promised deeper insights and new knowledge to their devotees. However any Christian can apprehend the very best that God has revealed because we all possess the spiritual organ of perception, namely, the Holy Spirit. "Searches" (Gr. *ereuna*) means continually examines.

> "Apparently they have thought of spirituality mostly in terms of ecstasy and experience, which has led some of them to deny the physical body, on the one hand, and to a sense of 'having arrived' (cf. 1 Cor 4:8), on the other. . . .

> "They considered Paul's preaching to be 'milk'; on the contrary, he implies, redemption through the cross comes from the profound depths of God's own wisdom, which his Spirit, given to those who love him, has searched out and revealed to us." (59)

2:11 - It is necessary for someone to be a human being to understand things having to do with human life. Likewise it is necessary for someone to have the indwelling Spirit of God to understand the things of God.

2:12 - "We" is emphatic in the Greek text. All believers have received the Holy Spirit (1 Cor 12:13; Rom 8:9). He helps us understand the mind of God and the things God has given us. This Spirit is vastly different from the spirit (viewpoint) of the world. Unbelievers cannot understand the things of God as believers can because they have no one who can help them perceive these supernatural things.

> ." . . as a man's own spirit best understands his inner thoughts, so the Spirit of God alone can grasp divine truths (verse 11), and alone can interpret to those within whom he dwells 'the things that are freely given to us by God' (RV)." (60)

2:13 - Paul and the other apostles spoke the truths that the Holy Spirit had helped them understand (cf. 1 Cor 2:6-7). They did not choose their words because of what people generally regarded as the best ones to persuade. They did not rely on the rhetorical forms that the orators used either. The Holy Spirit guided them in their communication of divine truth as well as in their perception of it. Spiritual thoughts or truths are concepts the Holy Spirit enables us to understand. Spiritual words are those He guides us to use in expressing these thoughts. The Spirit enables us to speak in language appropriate to the message rather than with human wisdom. In short, the Holy Spirit plays an indispensable role both in our understanding and in our communicating God's revelation.

2:14 - The natural man is any person who does not possess the Holy Spirit, namely, unbelievers. (62) Every human being is a natural man until he or she trusts Christ and receives the Spirit. Paul called this person a natural (Gr. *psychikos*) man because he or she is only natural. He has no supernatural Person indwelling him, and his viewpoints and ideas are only natural. He cannot accept all that God has revealed because he does not possess the indwelling Spirit of God.

The natural person can, of course, understand the gospel and experience salvation but only because the Holy Spirit illuminates his or her understanding. Paul did not mean that an unbeliever is incapable of understanding Scripture. However an unbeliever rejects and does not *accept* all that God wants him or her to have. One of these things is eternal life through faith in His Son. It is as though God is speaking in a language that the unbeliever does not understand. He or she needs an interpreter. That is a ministry that only the Holy Spirit can perform (63).

> "It will help us to think clearly about this issue if we recognize that 1 Corinthians 2 is not concerned with the mechanics of how people understand their Bibles generally, or with the quality of a particular scholar's exegesis of some specific Hebrew text. . . . His focus is the fundamental message of the crucified Messiah. And this, he insists, is fundamentally incomprehensible to the mind without the Spirit." (64)

2:15 - In contrast to the natural man stands the spiritual (Gr. *pneumatikos*) man. He or she is a natural man who now has the Holy Spirit dwelling within. Consequently he or she is a different person and has a different outlook.

One of the things the spiritual person is able to do is appraise or make judgments (Gr. *anakrino*) regarding all things. In other words, the spiritual man looks at everything somewhat differently than the natural man because he has spiritual perception. This affects his values and decisions. For this very reason he is a puzzle to the natural man. The profane person cannot understand holiness, but the holy person can understand the depths of evil. Even carnal fellow believers cannot fully understand the spiritual person. That is all right because the spiritual person's judge is ultimately God, not other people. (66)

This verse is not saying believers are responsible only to God but that the Christian is answerable to God alone ultimately (cf. 1 Cor 4:3-4). Paul recognized the value of church discipline (1 Cor 5:3-8), constructive criticism (1 Cor 11:17-18), and self-judgment (1 Cor 11:31) as having immediate value.

2:16 - To summarize his thought Paul again cited Isaiah (Isaiah 40:13; cf. Rom 11:34). That prophet marveled at the mind of God. Who can fully understand what God understands? Certainly no one can. On the other hand, believers can understand to a much greater degree than unbelievers can because we have the Spirit of God in us. Since we have Him, we have the mind of Christ. That is, we view life to some extent as Jesus did because we understand things from God's perspective at least partially.

In his epistle to the Philippians, Paul urged his readers to adopt the mind of Christ (Phil 2:5). Even though we have the mind of Christ we need to adopt it and use it to view life as He did. One evidence of Christian maturity is the believer's consistent employment of Christ's attitude and viewpoint in all of life.

In this section (1 Cor 2:6-16) Paul elaborated on the subject of the Holy Spirit's ministry of illuminating the believer about what God has revealed. He had previously reminded his readers that he had conducted himself in their midst with this supernatural viewpoint (1 Cor 2:1-5).

The basic theological point of tension between Paul and the Corinthians in this epistle was over what it means to be *pneumatikos*, a Spirit person. Because of their experience of glossolalia (speaking in tongues) they considered themselves to be "as the angels" and in need only of shedding their bodies. The sources of this distorted view were popular philosophy tainted with Hellenistic dualism. (67) The result was a "spirituality" and "higher wisdom" that had little connection with ethical behavior. (68)

The concern from here on will be to force them to acknowledge the folly of their 'wisdom,' which is expressing itself in quarrels and thereby destroying the very church for which Christ died.

> "Paul's concern needs to be resurrected throughout the church. The gift of the Spirit does not lead to special status among believers; rather, it leads to special status vis-à-vis the world. But it should do so always in terms of the centrality of the message of our crucified/risen Savior. The Spirit should identify God's people in such a way that their values and worldview are radically different from the wisdom of this age." (69)

Bibliography

32. Victor Paul Furnish, "Theology in 1 Corinthians," in *Pauline Theology. Vol. II: 1 & 2 Corinthians*, p. 63.

33. Ibid., p. 65.

34. Fee, *The First . . .*, p. 68.

35. D. A. Carson, *The Cross & Christian Ministry*, p. 12.

36. Ibid., pp. 15-16.

37. Peter Lampe, "Theological Wisdom and the 'Word About the Cross' The Rhetorical Scheme in I Corinthians 1-4," *Interpretation* 44:2 (April 1990):120.

38. Fee, *The First . . .*, p. 74.

39. Ibid., p. 76.

40. Barrett, p. 54.

41. Carson, p. 26.

42. Fee, *The First . . .*, pp. 77-78.

43. Jouette M. Bassler, "Paul's Theology: Whence and Whither?" in *Pauline Theology. Vol. II: 1 & 2 Corinthians*, p. 15.

44. Charles B. Cousar, "Expository Articles: I Corinthians 2:1-13," *Interpretation* 44:2 (April 1990):169.

45. J. B. Lightfoot, *Notes on the Epistles of St Paul*, p. 170.

46. E.g., Barclay, p. 26.

47. Barrett, p. 63.

48. Charles B. Cousar, "The Theological Task of 1 Corinthians," in *Pauline Theology. Vol. II: 1 & 2 Corinthians*, p. 102.

49. Carson, p. 35.

50. Robertson and Plummer, p. 31.

51. Warren W. Wiersbe, *The Bible Exposition Commentary*, 1:573.

52. Robertson and Plummer, p. 33.

53. Leon Morris, *The First Epistle of Paul to the Corinthians*, p. 52.

54. Carson, pp. 46, 52, 56.

55. Fee, *The First . . .*, p. 100.

56. Carson, p. 47.

57. Cousar, "Expository Articles . . ", p. 171.

58. Morris, p. 57.

59. Fee, *The First . . .*, pp. 110, 111.

60. Bruce, p. 40.

61. Robertson, 4:87.

62. See Barrett, p. 77.

63. See Robert A. Pyne, "The Role of the Holy Spirit in Conversion," *Bibliotheca Sacra* 150:598 (April-June

1993):204-5.

64. Carson, p. 64.

65. Johnson, p. 1233.

66. See Charles C. Ryrie, "What Is Spirituality?" *Bibliotheca Sacra* 126:503 (July-September 1969):204-13, or idem, *Balancing the Christian Life*, pp. 12-23.

67. Hellenistic dualism viewed anything material as evil and anything non-material or "spiritual" as good.

68. Fee, "Toward a . . .," pp. 37-38.

69. Idem, *The First . . .,* p. 120.

Lesson 3 Self Check

QUESTION 1

Paul's teaching about God's wisdom and man's wisdom was intended to help solve the Corinthians' disunity problem. *True or False?*

QUESTION 2

The message of the gospel is a stumbling block to Jews and foolishness to Gentiles. *True or False?*

QUESTION 3

Why did Paul concentrate only on Jesus Christ and Him crucified?

    A. Paul was not knowledgeable about Greek philosophy.

    B. They already knew the teachings of the Old Testament.

    C. Paul felt that teaching about the Holy Spirit was unimportant.

    D. Paul did not want people to be attracted to Christ through human wisdom.

QUESTION 4

The ability to quote large sections of the Bible is an indication of spirituality. *True or False?*

QUESTION 5

In 1 Corinthians 2:12-16, who does the spiritual man refer to?

    A. People who have been baptized

    B. People who have devoted themselves wholly to God

    C. People indwelt by the Holy Spirit

    D. People with miraculous spiritual gifts

QUESTION 6

The unbeliever understands the things of the Spirit of God. *True or False?*

QUESTION 7

"We have the mind of Christ" refers to which one of the following?

    A. We know all things.

    B. We always do God's will.

    C. We are indwelt by the Holy Spirit.

    D. We understand God's will.

QUESTION 8

The unbeliever can understand the gospel only with the illumination of the Holy Spirit. *True or False?*

QUESTION 9

In Paul's writings, "mystery" often means revealed truth, something formerly hidden but now made known. *True or False?*

QUESTION 10

According to Paul, the most important distinction between people is spiritual—not physical, racial, educational, etc. *True or False?*

Unit One Exam

QUESTION 1

Paul probably went to Corinth to evangelize for what reason?

A. It already had a church before he arrived

B. Priscilla and Aquila invited him to come

C. Jesus told him to go there in a vision

D. It was an important city

QUESTION 2

Paul's main purpose in writing 1 Corinthians was to address problems in the church. *True or False?*

QUESTION 3

When the Jews brought charges against Paul at Corinth, the consul Gallio threw out the case. *True or False?*

QUESTION 4

The believers at Corinth when Paul wrote 1 Corinthians were _____.

A. Mostly Jewish

B. Mostly Gentiles

C. Mostly from the upper classes

D. Mostly women

QUESTION 5

The church at Corinth financially supported Paul. *True or False?*

QUESTION 6

Which one of the following it **not** a reason that understanding and applying the teaching of 1 Corinthians is difficult?

A. Prior correspondence between Paul and the church is lost.

B. Corinthian culture of two thousand years ago is quite different from ours today.

C. The principles Paul teaches in the letter are irrelevant to us today.

D. Specific issues in the church at Corinth may not be issues in our church today.

QUESTION 7

The collection project was for helping the poor in Jerusalem. *True or False?*

QUESTION 8

When Paul wrote 1 Corinthians, Apollos had already visited the church. *True or False?*

QUESTION 9

Unity among believers is secondary to unity with Christ. *True or False?*

QUESTION 10

How is the unity Paul advocated at Corinth shown?

    A. Keeping silent about problems in the church

    B. Hiding potentially divisive spiritual gifts

    C. Focusing on Christ and the message of the cross

    D. Refusing to talk about spiritual leaders

    E. Allowing only one person to baptize

QUESTION 11

The different parties at Corinth were based mainly on differences in social class. *True or False?*

QUESTION 12

One step Paul took to solve their disunity problem was to cast out the demon of divisiveness. *True or False?*

QUESTION 13

The church at Corinth had so many problems because they lacked certain spiritual gifts. *True or False?*

QUESTION 14

What was Paul's main approach to resolving problems at Corinth?

    A. Don't judge anyone

    B. Promote allegiance to himself

    C. Ridicule the enemies

    D. Ignore the problems

    E. Teach as a pastor

QUESTION 15

Unless the Corinthians could grasp and apply God's wisdom, they would continue in disunity. *True or False?*

QUESTION 16

Paul consciously chose to avoid flashy rhetorical displays in evangelism. *True or False?*

QUESTION 17

Paul uses all the following in 1 Corinthians **except** which one?

    A. Quoting the Old Testament

    B. Illustrations from agriculture and sports

    C. Personal example

    D. Quoting slogans from the Corinthians

    E. Appealing to Peter's authority

QUESTION 18

Paul viewed baptizing converts as his primary calling. *True or False?*

QUESTION 19

Believers still need teachers even though they have the mind of Christ. *True or False?*

QUESTION 20

Paul's instruction about human wisdom and God's wisdom was intended to help solve the Corinthians' disunity problem. *True or False?*

QUESTION 21

What things display human wisdom?

    A. The message of a crucified Messiah

    B. The membership of the church at Corinth

    C. Polished rhetoric

    D. Paul's preaching style

QUESTION 22

Paul concentrated on the message of the cross because he knew little about Greek philosophy. *True or False?*

QUESTION 23

In Paul's writings, the word "mystery" often means revealed truth. *True or False?*

QUESTION 24

According to Paul, what is the reason that the unbeliever cannot understand the things of God?

    A. He does not study them.

    B. He lacks the Holy Spirit.

    C. He has not been baptized.

    D. He is God's enemy.

QUESTION 25

The most important distinction between people is between believers and unbelievers. *True or False?*

Lesson 3 Answers to Questions

QUESTION 1

Characteristics of True Wisdom	*Verses*
Source is God	1 Corinthians 1:21
Viewed by the world as weak, low, despised	1 Corinthians 1:27-28
Centered on the crucified Christ	1 Corinthians 1:23-24
Is God's power	1 Corinthians 2:5
Viewed by the world as foolishness	1 Corinthians 1:18

QUESTION 2

Characteristics of Human Wisdom	*Verses*
Does not bring salvation	1 Corinthians 1:21
Clever speech and eloquence	1 Corinthians 1:17; 2:1
Linked with power and privilege in this world's system	1 Corinthians 1:26
Is called the wisdom of the world	1 Corinthians 1:20
Is called the wisdom of this age	1 Corinthians 2:6
Is called the wisdom of the wise	1 Corinthians 1:19

QUESTION 3: *Your answer*

QUESTION 4: *Your answer should be similar to the following:*
The Jews could not conceive of a Messiah who died shamefully on the cross like a criminal.

QUESTION 5: True

QUESTION 6: *Your answer should be similar to the following:*
Our only hope for success in evangelism is God's Spirit working in the hearts of the hearers.

QUESTION 7: *Your answer*

QUESTION 8: True

QUESTION 9
- A. Circumcision
- B. Ancestry
- C. Legalistic righteousness
- D. Persecution of the church

QUESTION 10
- A. Things that show his weakness
- B. The Lord
- C. What the Lord has done through him

QUESTION 11: *Your answer*

QUESTION 12: *Your answer*

QUESTION 13: False

QUESTION 14
- D. Presentation of the message of the cross

QUESTION 15
- A. People could focus on the speaker rather than on the message of the cross.
- B. People could assume that believing the gospel brings worldly success.
- C. Such methods could lead to boasting in man rather than to humble trust in God.
- D. Using such methods could neglect the important work of the Holy Spirit in evangelism.

QUESTION 16: *Your answer should be similar to the following:*
No. Evangelism and prophecy are spiritual gifts. The real issue is one of basic values. What are we emphasizing—human ways or God's grace?

QUESTION 17: *Your answer*

QUESTION 18: *Your answer*

QUESTION 19: *Your answer should be similar to the following:*
They did not understand God's wisdom.
QUESTION 20
    A. All believers
    B. Mature believers
QUESTION 21: *Your answer*
QUESTION 22: *Your answer should be similar to the following:*
The necessity of the Spirit to understand the things of God.
QUESTION 23: False
QUESTION 24
    A. Salvation
QUESTION 25
    A. The Holy Spirit indwells the spiritual man but does not indwell the natural man.
QUESTION 26
    A. He does not receive them.
    B. He regards them as foolish.
    C. He cannot understand them.
QUESTION 27: *Your answer*
QUESTION 28: True

Lesson 3 Self Check Answers

QUESTION 1: True

QUESTION 2: True

QUESTION 3

    D. Paul did not want people to be attracted to Christ through human wisdom.

QUESTION 4: False

QUESTION 5

    C. People indwelt by the Holy Spirit

QUESTION 6: False

QUESTION 7

    C. We are indwelt by the Holy Spirit.

QUESTION 8: True

QUESTION 9: True

QUESTION 10: True

Unit 1 Exam Answers

QUESTION 1
  D. It was an important city
QUESTION 2: True
QUESTION 3: True
QUESTION 4
  B. Mostly Gentiles
QUESTION 5: False
QUESTION 6
  C. The principles Paul teaches in the letter are irrelevant to us today.
QUESTION 7: True
QUESTION 8: True
QUESTION 9: True
QUESTION 10
  C. Focusing on Christ and the message of the cross
QUESTION 11: True
QUESTION 12: False
QUESTION 13: False
QUESTION 14
  E. Teach as a pastor
QUESTION 15: True
QUESTION 16: True
QUESTION 17
  E. Appealing to Peter's authority
QUESTION 18: False
QUESTION 19: True
QUESTION 20: True
QUESTION 21
  C. Polished rhetoric
QUESTION 22: False
QUESTION 23: True
QUESTION 24
  B. He lacks the Holy Spirit.
QUESTION 25: True

Unit 2: Applying Wisdom to Solve Problems

Unit Introduction

True spirituality for a church is not just a matter of lively, stirring worship services. Churches can have exciting music and displays of the Spirit's gifts but still be racked by disunity, immorality, and ungodliness. True spirituality is reflected in righteousness, peace, and the joy of the Holy Spirit (Rom 14:17). Training a diverse group of believers to use God's wisdom to resolve their problems is a tough task.

In Lesson 4, we examine how Paul applies God's wisdom to resolve the Corinthians' disunity problem. He knows that as people indwelt by the Holy Spirit, they have the power to come together. By rejecting human wisdom and looking at leaders from the perspective of the cross of Christ, they can overcome their factions.

Once they are unified, they can deal with further destructive challenges facing the church—immorality and lawsuits between believers. Lesson 5 delves into these two issues. A divided congregation cannot handle such cases of church discipline. Only by using God's wisdom and by being united under apostolic leadership can they overcome these challenges.

Unit Outline

Lesson 4: Right Attitude Toward Leaders (1 Cor 3:1–4:21)

Lesson 5: Immorality and Lawsuits (1 Cor 5:1–6:20)

Unit Objectives

Lotus is so troubled about what is going on in her church that she calls Brother Thomas. Not only are cliques forming in the church, but a recent case of adultery where Daniel, a baptized church member, has left his wife for another woman, has really grieved her. She asks him to come back for an extended visit to take care of these problems. Brother Thomas is glad for her call, but he says that God has given him church planting work eight hundred kilometers away, and he has no plans to be back in her area any time soon.

Lotus pleads with him to reconsider, since the problems in the church are so deep, and she is sure he is the only one who can help. Brother Thomas says that he certainly will pray, but that he knows that they have the Bible and the Holy Spirit, and the church should seek God's wisdom to handle their issues. He says that even though they are facing many trials, God has not abandoned them, and He will give them strength and the grace they need. Resolving problems like this will be painful, he says, and every church member needs to examine his own heart before trying to correct others. He suggests that they study 1 Corinthians in depth, and look to Jesus for the solution, instead of to any former leader.

Lesson 4: Right Attitude Toward Leaders (1 Cor 3:1–4:21)

It is certainly true that strong and gifted Christian leaders make a name for themselves. This was the case in the early church. Paul himself admits that Peter, James, and John were among the pillars of the Jerusalem church (Gal 2:9). Understandably, such well-known leaders also attract a following, similar to Jesus when He traveled, preached and healed. Wherever such people go to minister, others gather to have a chance to see them and benefit from their ministries.

Some mega-churches have become so large because they have a gifted pastor whose ministry attracts people. A survey of the congregation might reveal that many say they attend the church primarily because the messages excite and stimulate them. At their previous church, they did not have the same feeling. When a gifted leader sees his church grow, a good question to ask is, whether this is genuine conversion growth, or just a rearrangement of believers from other churches to his.

Respect for gifted leaders is certainly proper, but undue allegiance is unhealthy and a sign of spiritual immaturity on the part of the follower. Addressing the problem of factions at Corinth, Paul urges the believers to apply God's wisdom to resolve their divisions, which were rooted in allegiances to particular leaders.

In Topic 1, we will examine Paul's assessment that he is dealing with a carnal congregation whose real need is spiritual maturity. This is the core problem underlying their improper view of Christian leaders.

Topic 2 directly addresses the problem of divisions by defining the true role of leaders in the church, and by assigning the glory to God.

Any leader who does not minister for the Lord with integrity will fall under God's judgment and lose his reward, as Topic 3 explains. This is a warning to all who engage in Christian ministry.

Topic 4 lays out the proper view of leaders in the church, according to the standards of God's wisdom— the cross of Christ.

Finally, Topic 5 challenges us to consider imitating Paul's balanced use of warning and exhortation in ministry, a skill vital for effective leaders.

Lesson Outline

Topic 1: Carnal Christians (1 Cor 3:1-4)

    Carnal Characteristics

    Categorizing Christians

Topic 2: Paul and Apollos Compared (1 Cor 3:5-9)

    Difference Between Paul and Apollos

    Glory Belongs to God

Topic 3: Building Solidly—God's Temple (1 Cor 3:9-17)

    Laying a Solid Foundation (3:9-11)

Lesson Objectives

Lotus knows that God wants unity in their church. She knows that the church people can come together. From studying 1 Corinthians 2, she is convinced that all the believers had the Holy Spirit, but some people were focusing too much on their own interests.

Maybe she could talk to Esther and Sara, who have started their own meeting centered around Sister Marie's teachings, about this issue of unity and discuss and pray with them about Paul's teaching in 1 Corinthians. Instead of forming a special group, for the sake of unity couldn't they rejoin the church as a whole? Lotus really misses their smiles, prayers, service, and presence. After all, there are many traveling speakers who come through from time to time, and they bless everybody. Why not have everybody enjoy them all?

From her study of 1 Corinthians 3 and 4, Lotus can see that no individual's teaching style justifies splitting up the church. However, she hesitates to bring up that passage with them, because she knows they view themselves as more spiritual than she. She wonders whether she should warn Esther and Sara of the danger of what they are doing. How can she approach them when they think Sister Marie is so spiritual?

By the end of this lesson, you will be able to:

- Understand the importance of spiritual maturity in members in the church

- Appreciate God's orchestration of the work or building His church

- Identify the roles God has given leaders in the Church and that it is for His glory alone

- Apply Paul's use of warning and exhortation in your own area of ministry

Topic 1: Carnal Christians (1 Cor 3:1-4)

From Paul's statements at the end of 1 Corinthians 2, the believers at Corinth were assured that he viewed them as spiritual people. Observably, they had many characteristics of a healthy Christian congregation: they met together for worship, they possessed and used every spiritual gift, they were in communication with the apostle Paul, and they were raising money for the poor in Jerusalem. Clearly the Holy Spirit was working among them.

Despite these positive behaviors, Paul chastised them for being "worldly" or "carnal." This assessment must have stung, since they viewed themselves as the opposite—as rich, wise, strong and spiritual. What did Paul mean by "worldly"? How could they have failed to perceive it? After all, didn't they have many prophets among them to help them understand spiritual truth (1 Cor 14:31)?

Carnal Characteristics (3:1-4)

Assignment

- Read 1 Corinthians 3:1-4.
- Read Constable, "The Immature and Carnal Condition—3:1-4" (refer to the Articles section at the end of this lesson).
- Read "Carnal Characteristics."

Carnal Characteristics

Paul's comments must be seen against the background of the incorrect view of spirituality at Corinth. Some viewed themselves as having "arrived" spiritually, or having become perfect. They had become proud and arrogant, ignoring biblical evidence of true spirituality (the fruit of the Spirit) and substituting such things as speaking in tongues and prophecy as signs of true spirituality. The whole congregation was caught up in this, or at least greatly affected by it.

The interpretative questions are:

1. What does Paul mean by "of the flesh" (i.e., carnal)?

2. Is Paul dividing believers into categories—such as spiritual, mature, carnal, and infants?

3. What did Paul mean by "milk" and "solid food"?

4. In saying this, how did Paul hope the Corinthians would respond?

1. What does Paul mean by "of the flesh" (i.e., carnal)?

As we saw at the end of 1 Corinthians 2, Paul made a clear distinction between the spiritual man and the natural man. That distinction was based on the indwelling of the Spirit. The believer is indwelt by the Holy Spirit and has entered into spiritual life. The unbeliever is spiritually dead and thus a natural man.

The Greek *sarkikos* can be translated as "pertaining to the flesh," "worldly," or "carnal." Even though Paul describes the Corinthians in this way, it is clear from 1 Corinthians 3:1 that he considered them to be genuine believers in Christ, for the calls them "brothers and sisters." He also considers them to be spiritual people, but in verse 3, he says they were "behaving *like* unregenerate people." Therefore, he is careful to say "I could not speak to you *as* spiritual people, but instead *as* people of the flesh, *as* infants in Christ."

In other words, they really were true believers and therefore really were spiritual people. However, they suffered from immaturity, as evidenced by their jealousy, dissension, and divisions. Paul uses "of the flesh" to describe the poor behavior of Christians who behave the same way that unsaved people do.

2. Is Paul dividing believers into categories—such as spiritual, mature, carnal, and infants?

Is being "of the flesh" the same as being an "infant in Christ"? Based on the grammar and the reference to "milk," it seems that Paul is making this identification. In this case, "infant" would have a negative meaning—immaturity. They should have grown up and should be behaving better.

There is debate over categorizing believers. Some believe that "spiritual" means both indwelling by the Holy Spirit **and** maturity, and they distinguish between believers as in the following chart:

1 Corinthians 2:14 Natural Man	1 Corinthians 2:15, 3:1 Spiritual Man	1 Corinthians 3:1 Babe in Christ	1 Corinthians 3:3 Carnal Christian
Dominated by the flesh—no spiritual capacity	Dominated by the Holy Spirit—spiritually mature	Characterized by fleshly conduct, but is willing to serve God	Has a spiritual capacity, but continually yields to the flesh
Does not welcome spiritual things	Spiritual discernment in life	Limited capacity for understanding God's world	Willful rebellion
Cannot know them experientially	Comprehends the "solid food" of God's word	Not reprimanded for his immaturity	Reprimanded—a moral issue
Jude 19 James 3:15	Cannot be "examined" spiritually by non-Christians	Needs milk	Evidence is he is out of touch with everyone; he is selfish and proud

In this passage, Paul reprimands the church for their jealousy, quarrels and divisions, but he considers all true believers to be spiritual. Even though they are spiritual, they are not living as spiritual people should live. It's like a father reprimanding his teenager: "Act your age!"

Was their carnality an issue of the Lordship of Jesus Christ in their lives? At Corinth, apparently everyone believed that Jesus was the Lord and had the right to rule (see 1 Cor 8:6; 12:3). The question was how to apply the Lordship of Christ in particular situations. They needed to identify and turn away from their human wisdom ways of doing things.

3. What did Paul mean by "milk" and "solid food"?

Paul implies that the believers at Corinth need to grow up, for he says that they were fed on milk when he first came to plant the church, and they are still not ready for solid food. "Milk" is used here to imply elementary instruction, and "solid food" refers to deeper teaching.

We know that when Paul first came to Corinth, he was "concerned about nothing among you except Jesus Christ, and him crucified" (1 Cor 2:2). This statement would seem to imply that by "milk" Paul meant the basic doctrines of Jesus' person and work.

Since Paul states that they "are *still not ready*" for solid food, it would seem logical that the whole content of 1 Corinthians would also have to be classified as "milk"! After all, why would he go on to give solid food to a congregation that is not ready for it? However, Paul wrote a lot of solid food content in this letter—like the teaching about human wisdom and God's wisdom, church discipline, food offered to idols, spiritual gifts, and the resurrection body. (Interpreters have the same problem with Hebrews. See Heb 5:11–6:3.) How do we resolve this puzzle?

In trying to answer this question, it is helpful to try to discern Paul's tone in writing 1 Corinthians 3:1-4. Undoubtedly Paul is writing to rebuke them for their immature behavior. Although they viewed themselves as having reached a high spiritual state, their behavior and attitudes betrayed just the opposite. The fundamental problem was not with Paul's teaching (whether it was milk or solid food), but rather with their living *as* people of the flesh.

"Milk" may have been a derogatory term some "super-spiritual" Corinthians were using to criticize Paul's teaching, implying that what Apollos and Peter taught was "meat." Ironically, Paul admits that his teaching was "milk"—the message of the cross—but that they still have not grasped and applied that basic message in their lives. Thus, they still need "milk," but they also need to go on to maturity.

4. By saying this, how did Paul hope the Corinthians would respond?

Paul hoped that they would examine themselves and repent. They should be capable of digesting (understanding and applying) everything that Paul wrote in this letter, but instead they have shown themselves to be incapable of digesting even the most elementary Christian teaching. They must have heard basic gospel teachings repeatedly (after all, some of them had been believers for five to six years, and Paul had personally taught them for a year and a half), but it had failed to take root in their lives so as to bring maturity.

QUESTION 1

Consider and answer the following questions in your Life Notebook:

a. What does Paul mean by "of the flesh" (i.e. carnal)?

b. Is Paul dividing believers into categories—such as spiritual, mature, carnal, and infants?

c. What did Paul mean by milk and solid food?

d. By saying this, how did Paul hope the Corinthians would respond?

e. At this stage in its life does my church need "milk" or "solid food"? Perhaps it needs both. With this need in mind what should I be addressing in my teaching during the next few months?

The Corinthians' basic problem with disunity was immaturity—not a lack of saving faith, heresy, or the failure to make a Lordship decision. They needed to grasp God's wisdom and resist the pull of the culture towards partisanship.

QUESTION 2

Some Bible teachers divide Christians into four types. Please match the characteristic with the type.

Characteristic	Type
Natural man	Has limited capacity for understanding God's Word
Spiritual man	Willful rebellion against God
Babe in Christ	Has spiritual discernment
Carnal Christian	Does not welcome spiritual things

QUESTION 3

All the teaching of 1 Corinthians is milk. *True or False?*

Categorizing Christians

Assignment

- Read "Categorizing Christians."

Categorizing Christians

Is it appropriate to categorize believers as spiritual, carnal, or spiritual infants?

Few people would have any problem with referring to a new believer as a spiritual baby, since nothing derogatory is meant. A new believer has just begun his walk of faith and is spiritually healthy, although not mature. Given the right conditions and the passing of time, he should grow beyond the infant stage. He should become more convinced of his faith and be able to explain it to others, and he should grow more in the image of Christ.

The problem arises when we try to label as carnal believers who are not new Christians. One problem is that the people who make such an evaluation usually view themselves as spiritual. There is a temptation to fall into spiritual pride. This pride can lead church members to become judgmental of other believers. Another consideration is that no matter how long someone has been walking with Christ, there is always room to mature. Having considered these cautions, it must be recognized that Paul did refer to the Corinthians "as people of the flesh, as infants in Christ" (1 Cor 3:1).

An important observation to make here is that Paul *is addressing the church as a whole.* He is not singling out some individuals within the congregation as infants or influenced by the flesh, whereas others are mature and spiritual. His point is that everyone in the whole church is behaving as people of the flesh.

As a Christian, we sometimes look at ourselves and all that we do—study the Bible, memorize Scripture, witness to others—and consider ourselves "better" Christians than others. Sadly, this is a very immature and proud mindset. How does the issue of pride play into the issue of categorizing Christians in 1 Corinthians?

QUESTION 4

Paul's calling the Corinthians carnal was a sign of his own spiritual pride. *True or False?*

QUESTION 5

How do you view the issue of categorizing believers according to spiritual, carnal, and infants in Christ? How would you view yourself? Is it possible to be more mature in some areas and less mature in others? Open your Life Notebook and write your reflections.

Topic 2: Paul and Apollos Compared (1 Cor 3:5-9)

The Corinthians' disunity problem, which bore the bad fruit of jealousy and dissension, focused on various Christian leaders, giving undue allegiance to one over and against another. They had failed to grasp basic teaching in this matter and displayed human wisdom rather than God's wisdom.

To instruct them, Paul chose Apollos and himself to illustrate the essential unity of God's servants in the work of the ministry. As important as these servants may be in the eyes of the people whose lives they touch, still, their work is fruitless unless God is working through them. This properly gives the glory to God.

Difference Between Paul and Apollos (3:5-9)

God has given a rich variety of evangelists, preachers, scholars, musicians, counselors, and servants to His church. Each makes his contribution, and we can praise God for them all.

Assignment

- Read 1 Corinthians 3:5-9 and note how the ministries of Paul and Apollos differed.

- Read Constable, "The Role of God's Servants" (refer to the Articles section at the end of this lesson), through the note on 3:5-9.

- Read "Difference Between Paul and Apollos."

Difference Between Paul and Apollos

Paul and Apollos had different ministries at Corinth. Paul "planted" and Apollos "watered." Based on the history of the church, Paul's planting refers to the starting of the church, when he was engaged in much evangelism, discipleship, and church organizing. Apollos came later, after Paul had left, and "he assisted greatly those who had believed by grace, for he refuted the Jews vigorously in public debate, demonstrating from the Scriptures that the Christ was Jesus" (Acts 18:27).

Under God's sovereign orchestration, Paul and Apollos were actually working together in unity. Even though there is no evidence that Paul and Apollos were ever physically present at the same time or consciously working together as a team in Corinth, Paul nevertheless paints a picture of their working toward the same goal. Anticipating extensive teaching about the body of Christ in 1 Corinthians 12, Paul insists that the two of them are servants and coworkers, working under God's direction. They are not in competition with each other for influence, honor or reputation at Corinth. Instead, they supported each other by performing complementary ministries.

QUESTION 6

From Paul's use of the metaphor in 1 Corinthians 3:6-8, what activities would be included in "watering"? *(Select all that apply.)*

- A. Publicly defending the faith
- B. Building up believers
- C. Modeling effective use of the Scriptures
- D. Pioneer evangelism

QUESTION 7

Paul considered his planting work more important than Apollos' watering work. *True or False?*

Glory Belongs to God

Recognizing the value of another's ministry is a sign of maturity, provided we don't overvalue that person. Assigning the proper value of God's coworkers is an application of Paul's teaching in 1 Corinthians 2:12-14 about the indispensable work of the Holy Spirit. No coworker can produce spiritual fruit without the work of the Holy Spirit.

Assignment

- Read 1 Corinthians 3:5-9.
- Read "Glory Belongs to God."

Glory Belongs to God

Paul uses an agricultural metaphor—that of plant growth. As any gardener knows, nothing he does really causes the growth of a plant. He can have the best soil, work and plow it, add fertilizer, and supply the best quality seeds. However, he cannot make the plants grow. All he can do is try to provide suitable conditions for growth. Similarly, Paul recognizes that neither he nor Apollos can cause spiritual growth in the Corinthians. No man can change a natural man into a spiritual man. This miracle is purely the work of God. All God's servants can do is to try to provide conditions for spiritual growth, such as a godly example, the proclamation of the truth, loving care and discipline. Given this truth, no glory properly belongs to any of the servants, even though each servant will receive a reward for faithful service. The Corinthians may appreciate their spiritual leaders, but first and foremost their thanks should go to God.

QUESTION 8

What truth is a major antidote to spiritual pride in this passage?

QUESTION 9

What is an appropriate response to someone who honors, thanks, or praises you for your gospel work?

Topic 3: Building Solidly—God's Temple (1 Cor 3:9-17)

God's coworkers are laboring in a mighty, eternal construction project that must be able to withstand the ultimate test. Each worker will be held accountable for his contribution.

During the Middle Ages in Europe, constructing great cathedrals took hundreds of years and huge sums of money. Famous artists were often engaged to provide artwork for these great worship halls, such as Michelangelo, who painted the ceiling of the Sistine Chapel in Rome. As wonderful and magnificent as these construction projects were, they are only the handiwork of men, and they will not last for eternity.

The church, however, God's true temple and dwelling place, will last forever. Using the metaphor of a building project, Paul depicts two roles: those who lay the foundation and those who build the superstructure for the church. Just as the construction of a medieval cathedral required careful design, use of the right materials, and great effort, so does the building of God's true temple.

The quality of a Christian leader's work will be judged. Much false or poor quality construction will be tested in the fires of God's judgment. How then can we ensure that our labors in building the church will withstand the test?

Laying a Solid Foundation (3:9-11)

Within the realms of "foundation laying," Paul would probably include all of his church planting work at Corinth—not just the evangelistic messages. Laying a proper foundation is fundamental to the rest of the building project, and it takes time to do it properly.

Assignment

- Read 1 Corinthians 3:9-11.
- Read Constable, "Builders of God's Temple" (refer to the Articles section at the end of this lesson), through the note on 3:11.
- Read "Laying a Solid Foundation."

Laying a Solid Foundation

Paul shifts the metaphor from agriculture to building construction. Similar to his illustration about gardening, Paul identifies different roles associated with building—laying a foundation and constructing the building. Foundation-laying is fundamental, and Paul assigns that role to himself. This is another way of illustrating his church planting activities at Corinth. "Someone else builds on it" could easily refer to the follow-up work that Apollos did in strengthening the believers, but it also refers to the ministry of any of God's servants who labored to build the church subsequent to Paul. Again, the point is the essential unity of the workers, working toward one goal, but with different functions.

Paul clearly identifies the foundation of the building—Jesus Christ. By this he means the message of the gospel of Jesus Christ (based on the Person and work of Christ), by which sinners are saved. Spreading the gospel was Paul's passion and calling, especially "where Christ has not been named, so as not to build on another person's foundation" (Rom 15:20). For the church of Jesus Christ, no other foundation can be laid.

QUESTION 10

In Paul's metaphor of building in 1 Corinthians 3:10, to what do the builders refer?

- A. Apostles
- B. Any Christian
- C. False teachers
- D. Christian leaders

QUESTION 11

What teachings do you consider foundational? What do you consider non-foundational? Categorize the following list and add three or four more topics. Record your answer in your Life Notebook and give reasons for your choices.

- The Trinity
- Sin
- Grace
- Faith
- Eternal life
- Church discipline

- Predestination
- Communion
- Church structure
- Spiritual gifts
- Baptism
- Prayer
- Scripture
- Evangelism
- Fellowship
- The second coming
- Judgment day
- The millennium
- Stewardship
- New birth

Testing a Man's Work (3:12-15)

Christian leaders are not exempt from God's judgment. Even though lasting fruit only comes by God's grace, God's servants will still be held responsible for the quality of their labor.

Assignment

- Read 1 Corinthians 3:12-15.
- Read Constable, "The Role of God's Servants" (refer to the Articles section at the end of this lesson), through the note on 3:15.
- Read "Testing a Builder's Work."

Testing a Builder's Work

The caution Paul mentions here concerns the quality of each builder's work. By listing various building materials, Paul warns against using materials of inferior quality. The materials listed here are symbolic of the quality of a Christian leader's ministry.

On the day, the quality of each builder's work will be clearly seen, for it will be tested by fire. The day refers to a day of judgment, and the fire is a metaphor for God's judgment. Other passages in Scripture also teach that there will be a judgment for believers. (See Rom 14:10-12; 1 Cor 4:5; 2 Cor 5:10.)

The fire destroys anything built of inferior quality materials and reveals the permanent quality of construction using gold, silver and precious stones. What is meant here is the fruit of a ministry that lasts for eternity. If a servant of the Lord passes the test of fire, then "he will receive a reward," but we are not told what that reward will be. From the immediate context, the reward could simply be the work that has stood the test of judgment (1 Thess 2:19-20). In 1 Corinthians 4:5, Paul's phrase "recognition from God" could refer to this reward.

Conversely, if all his work is burned up, he suffers loss, but not the loss of his salvation. (Some would challenge this view and translate the verse this way: "If anyone's work is consumed, he will suffer loss, and he himself will be saved but in the same manner, as through fire."

If the Jews took care to construct the tabernacle on earth according to God's design, how much more should the Lord's servants soberly and carefully labor to build His church?

Paul warns against destroying God's temple. Probably he is referring to those at Corinth who are promoting divisions in the church. Although they may think they are building on the foundation with gold, silver and precious stones, Paul affirms that they are not building, but rather are tearing down. They are using human wisdom in a vain attempt to build God's house. Their work will not last.

QUESTION 12

In the metaphor of building in 1 Corinthians 3:12-15, "wood, hay, or straw" describes what kinds of materials?

QUESTION 13

What characteristics relate to materials of high quality? *(Select all that apply.)*

    A. Expensive

    B. Unburnable

    C. Beautiful

    D. Eternal

QUESTION 14

In this metaphor, what are the effects of the fire on the builders?

    A. Purification or cleansing of the builders

    B. Testing the quality of their works

    C. Punishment for their sins

    D. Separating the saved from the unsaved

Building God's Temple (3:16-17)

Far more important and long lasting than any medieval cathedral building project is the work of building God's church. Such work must not be taken lightly or done shoddily.

Assignment

- Read 1 Corinthians 3:16-17.
- Read Constable, "A Warning Against Destroying the Church" (refer to the Articles section at the end of this lesson).

QUESTION 15

Another translation for the word "destroys" in 1 Corinthians 3:17 is _____.

QUESTION 16

Please open your Life Notebook and write your reflections on the following questions.

(a) What factors do you think make for a ministry of gold, silver and precious stones in your ministry?

(b) What factors do you think will result in your ministry not standing the test of fire on the Day of Judgment?

Topic 4: Proper View of Leaders (1 Cor 3:18–4:13)

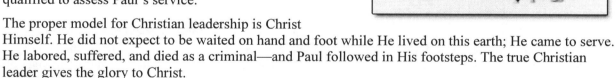

Have you ever wondered what would happen to the church you attend if the main leader left? Have you ever longed to be in that top position yourself? Leadership often means increased visibility and recognition, greater privilege and influence. In many groups, top leaders are almost worshipped by the group members. Followers sense that the way to climb the organizational ladder is to obtain the favor of the top leader.

We have no indication in the New Testament that Paul, Apollos, or Cephas ever abused their leadership roles. Nevertheless, human wisdom at Corinth resulted in many believers rallying around a particular leader, and in pride judging the others. Their judgment of Paul was groundless and unauthorized, for Paul was serving Jesus, who alone is qualified to assess Paul's service.

The proper model for Christian leadership is Christ Himself. He did not expect to be waited on hand and foot while He lived on this earth; He came to serve. He labored, suffered, and died as a criminal—and Paul followed in His footsteps. The true Christian leader gives the glory to Christ.

False vs. True Wisdom (3:18-23)

Factionalism is restrictive and limiting. When God has provided such a breadth of leaders in the church, it is foolishness not to benefit from them all.

Assignment

- Read 1 Corinthians 3:18-23.
- Read Constable, "Human Wisdom and Limited Blessing" (refer to the Articles section at the end of this lesson).
- Read "False vs. True Wisdom."

False vs. True Wisdom

Paul returns to his theme of two types of wisdom (see 1 Cor 1:18–2:5). The wisdom of this age is not true wisdom, even though the world regards it as the path to success.

The Corinthians had been going around saying, "I am with Paul," or "I am with Apollos," or "I am with Cephas." This mindset is the exact opposite of God's wisdom. Twice Paul says, "everything belongs to you" (1 Cor 3:21-22), and he alludes specifically to their divisions—"whether Paul or Apollos or Cephas." For Christians to say that they belong to some particular Christian leader is ridiculous, no matter how exalted or capable he may be. On the contrary, those leaders are merely "servants" of the Lord and "coworkers belonging to God." God gave them to His church—not the reverse! It would be much more accurate for the Corinthians to say, "Paul belongs to us," or "Apollos belongs to us," or "Cephas belongs to us"—and the "us" is the whole church. Such statements would put these pillars of the church in their proper role. We are all one body, just with different roles and functions. No one part is complete without the rest of the body, and we all need each other. God's wisdom enables us to view Christian leaders properly.

QUESTION 17

How does Paul refer to the wisdom of this age in 1 Corinthians 3:18-20? *(Select all that apply.)*

   A. Self-deception

   B. Foolishness

   C. Futile

   D. Boasting

QUESTION 18

Why should believers not over-value human leaders?

Judgment of Paul (4:1-5)

Everything the Lord's servants do is foolishness according to human wisdom. Believers' viewpoints need to be transformed from this world's standards and renewed according to Christ. Even then, believers do not have exhaustive knowledge. Even the best judgments must be viewed as tentative, awaiting the day of judgment.

Assignment

- Read 1 Corinthians 4:1-5.
- Read Constable, "The Corinthians' Relationship With Paul." (refer to the Articles section at the end of this lesson), through the note on 4:5.
- Read "Judgment of Paul."

Judgment of Paul

Paul continues with the subject of how he (and any Christian leader) should be viewed by other believers—as a servant and steward. These terms, rich in meaning, imply that Paul worked under the direction and coordination of Jesus, the Lord of the church.

Paul makes this argument toward those at Corinth who are judging him: the task of the servant/steward is to please his master. It is his master alone who has the right and responsibility to judge his performance. Therefore, Paul is out of their jurisdiction—they have no right to judge him. In fact, as a matter of principle, believers should not judge anything before the Lord comes. Paul does not even judge himself. We shouldn't judge other believers because only Jesus can reveal what is in people's hearts and make a true judgment.

Do Paul's words seem odd to you? Would you say that "it is a minor matter that I am judged by you or by any human court" when you sense believers having a critical attitude toward you? After all, is not Paul judging them when he says they are "as people of the flesh" (1 Cor 3:1)? How is Paul exempt from their judgment of him, yet he may judge them?

Paul is not being hypocritical. It's important to recognize the context of Paul's remarks. Undeniably, the Corinthians were making judgments about various Christian leaders and dividing themselves into factions. Perhaps even the majority at Corinth had decided against Paul, indicating this by aligning themselves with Apollos or Cephas. The context is not about accusing Paul of some obvious sinful behavior, like sexual immorality, theft of money, drunkenness, or heresy. Paul would certainly have affirmed the Corinthians' right and responsibility to exercise church discipline against him if he were guilty of serious sin. No one is above the law of Christ (1 Cor 9:21). Paul, however, can judge them for their carnal behavior, because the evidence is obvious and Paul has spiritual authority over them both as an apostle and as their spiritual father. Conversely, what is Paul's sin against them? They can name none. Instead, they judged Paul superficially, without a firm basis. If they felt they could accuse him of the sin of improper motives, Paul points out that only Jesus can judge the secrets of the heart.

QUESTION 19

To be acquitted on the day of judgment, you should keep a clean conscience. *True or False?*

QUESTION 20

What is the major criterion for receiving praise from the Lord on the day of judgment?

- A. Having led many to Christ
- B. Faithfulness
- C. A good report from your church
- D. Self-sacrifice
- E. A good conscience

Their Pride vs. Paul's Humiliation (4:6-13)

Assignment

- Read 1 Corinthians 4:6-13.
- Read Constable, "Taking Pride in the Wrong Things" (refer to the Articles section at the end of this lesson).
- Read "Their Pride vs. Paul's Humiliation."

Their Pride vs. Paul's Humiliation

Once again Paul discusses their attitudes toward Apollos and him—how they improperly value one leader over the other. Their judgment, flowing out of human wisdom, is wrong and promotes human pride. In a passage full of sarcasm, Paul reflects their attitude of having "arrived" spiritually, viewing themselves as reigning kings, the privileged wealthy, the wise and distinguished. Not only are they carnal, but they are also self-deceived (1 Cor 3:18) and spiritually blind.

This text, along with others in 1 Corinthians, leads many Bible students to the conclusion that one of the root problems at Corinth was a type of false teaching called over-realized eschatology (or triumphalism). The definition of over-realized eschatology: "an understanding of the future that stresses present realities to the exclusion of related future realities" (Constable, *Notes on 1 Corinthians*, 2003 edition, footnote 16), in effect denying that the experience of certain blessings assured to believers is still in the future. Triumphalism over-emphasizes the believer's present victory over sin, suffering and weakness, a view that often leads to pride and/or the denial of reality (ibid., footnote 18.) Such a view would explain how the Corinthians could dismiss Paul, who obviously did not fit their picture of the triumphant, successful apostle. Repeatedly in the Corinthian correspondence, Paul talks about his weakness as an apostle of Christ. Since Paul is a true apostle, obviously the Corinthians' views have been influenced by human wisdom rather than God's wisdom.

QUESTION 21

What do you think Paul meant by the statement "We are fools for Christ, but you are wise in Christ?" Record your response in your Life Notebook.

When Paul gives his apostolic job description, he emphasizes sufferings. His lifestyle is far removed from the definition of success according to human wisdom: comfort, honor, servants, fine clothes, ownership of large estates, etc. The present age is the time of humble service for God, awaiting the rewards of the age to come.

QUESTION 22

The antidote to spiritual pride is a proper understanding of grace. *True or False?*

QUESTION 23

Which things were characteristics of true apostles? *(Select all that apply.)*

    A. Free from suffering

    B. Financially poor

    C. Hardworking

    D. Victims of abuse

    E. Respected by all

    F. Without enemies

Topic 5: Exhortation and Warning (1 Cor 4:14-21)

Paul hopes for change in the church at Corinth. As a father dealing with his own children, he both encourages and warns the congregation.

Some (perhaps the "Paul" group in particular) would be struck to the heart over the realization that they were disappointing their spiritual father by their carnal behavior. This letter, the word of exhortation to imitate Paul, and the reminder of Timothy would be sufficient motivation to bring about genuine change.

Others, those arrogant people who are also those guilty of judging Paul, need stronger words—a warning that if they do not heed, Paul will come and exercise church discipline. The opportunity to repent is now, before Paul comes personally to set things straight.

Exhortation (4:14-17)

Paul calls on the believers at Corinth to imitate him. He repeats this call later in 1 Corinthians 11:1, where he makes clear that he is imitating Christ. Christ and Paul lived by God's wisdom.

Assignment

- Read 1 Corinthians 4:14-17.
- Read Constable, "A Final Appeal and Exhortation" (refer to the Articles section at the end of this lesson), through the note on 4:17.
- Read "Exhortation."

Exhortation

Paul must have known that the Corinthians would sense his sarcastic tone in the previous paragraph and may have felt he was trying to shame them. Here Paul insists that shame is not his purpose (although, see 1 Cor 6:5; 15:34), rather his purpose is correction. He appeals for them to imitate him based on his special relationship with them as their spiritual father. As such he is sending another spiritual son and his right-hand man, Timothy, to personally remind them of his ways. Paul offers himself as the example for them to follow, and he is confident that Timothy would display the same attitudes.

QUESTION 24

In what ways does Paul use his authority to correct the problems at Corinth? *(Select all that apply.)*

- A. He usually orders them to obey him.
- B. He instructs the "Paul" party to separate from the others.
- C. He tells them to choose between him and the other leaders.
- D. He says that Apollos is not really an apostle and thus has less authority than he.
- E. He appeals to them as their spiritual father.
- F. He reasons with them, laying out clear arguments and using Scripture.

Warning (4:18-21)

Evidently those in the arrogant opposition at Corinth had eloquent speech but lacked the fruit of the Holy Spirit. As a father with his children, Paul was not afraid to take disciplinary measures.

Assignment

- Read 1 Corinthians 4:18-21.
- Continue reading Constable, "A Final Appeal and Exhortation" (refer to the Articles section at the end of this lesson), through the note on 4:21.
- Read "Warning."

Warning

Although Paul hopes that the Corinthians will respond favorably to his appeal as their spiritual father, he does not neglect to warn them that he can be forceful in the exercise of discipline. Just as fathers sometimes resort to the rod in correcting their children, Paul threatens the same. Practically, this would mean a face-to-face confrontation with the "arrogant" people who reject Paul's authority. If they don't repent before he arrives, they will face certain rebuke, humiliation, and possible expulsion from the church. Paul says that "the kingdom of God is demonstrated not in idle talk but with power."

Is Paul's remedy to the problem of divisions at Corinth likely to work? His approach has been primarily instructional. He treats the Corinthians as misguided and immature, but recognizes that the Spirit is still working among them. They need to learn, to mature, and to grasp God's wisdom. He treats this as a problem in the congregation as a whole rather than just singling out the leaders, for he wrote to the whole church.

QUESTION 25

What does Paul mean by the "kingdom of God" in 1 Corinthians 4:20?

    A. The future millennial kingdom

    B. The visible church

    C. God's present rule in the lives of His people

    D. Heaven

QUESTION 26

Paul uses both exhortation and warning here. Open your Life Notebook and write down your thoughts on how to balance exhortation and warning in your ministry. What are the dangers in over-emphasizing one to the neglect of the other?

Lesson 4 Articles

Notes on 1 Corinthians

Dr. Thomas L. Constable; 2003 Edition

4. The immature and carnal condition 3:1-4

The apostle proceeded to tell the Corinthians that they had not been viewing things from the spiritual point of view. He was referring specifically to their exaltation of one or another of God's servants above the others (1 Cor 1:10-17). Paul urgently appealed to them to change.

3:1 - Here Paul introduced a third category of humanity, namely, the "fleshly" (Gr. *sarkinos*) or "worldly" (NIV) man. The Corinthians were spiritual rather than natural because they possessed the Holy Spirit. Notwithstanding Paul said he could not speak to them as spiritual men. He explained the reason in verse 3. Instead he had to address them as fleshly people, even as babes in Christ. The fleshly believer then is an immature Christian. Immaturity is not blameworthy if one is very young. However if a person has been a Christian for some time and is still immature, his or her condition is blameworthy (cf. 1 Cor 2:6). Such was the condition of the Corinthians.

3:2 - When Paul had been with them they were new converts, so he gave them the milk of the Word, the ABCs of the faith (cf. 1 Pet 2:2). Now when they should have been able to take in more advanced teaching they were not able to do so (cf. Heb 5:11-14). Their party spirit was one evidence of spiritual immaturity, lack of growth. Their fundamental need was not a change of diet but a change of perspective.

Paul's use of the vocative ("brothers [and sisters]") and second person plural pronouns in verses 1 and 2 indicates that he was addressing the whole church, not just a faction within it (cf. 1 Cor 1:10). The actions of many in the congregation had defiled the whole body. (70)

3:3 - The reason Paul did not feel he should give them more advanced instruction was that their flesh (Gr. *sarkikos*) still dominated them. As believers they were making provision for the flesh to fulfill its desires rather than following the leading of the Holy Spirit. They were not only immature believers but also carnal Christians. The carnal believer is the fourth type of person Paul mentioned in 1 Cor 2:14–3:4 (71).

Paul let the Corinthians diagnose themselves. Are not jealousy and strife the works of the flesh (Gal 5:20)? Did these qualities not indicate that they were conducting themselves as unbelievers, as people who do not even possess the Holy Spirit? (72)

> "Being human is not a bad thing in itself, any more than being *sarkinoi* is (v. 1). What is intolerable is to have received the Spirit, which makes one more than merely human, and to continue to live as though one were nothing more." (73)

3:4 - Partisanship is a manifestation of human wisdom. All the philosophical schools in Greece had their chief teachers. There was keen competition among these teachers, and there were strong preferences among the students as to who was the best. However this attitude is totally inappropriate when it comes to evaluating the servants of Christ. It is completely contrary to the mind of Christ who Himself stooped to raise others.

> "It is sinful for church members to compare pastors, or for believers to follow human leaders as disciples of men and not disciples of Jesus Christ. The 'personality cults' in the church today are in direct disobedience to the Word of God. Only Jesus Christ should have the place of preeminence (Col 1:18)." (74)

This section of verses makes it very clear that it is possible for genuine Christians to behave as and to appear to be unbelievers. The Corinthians' conduct indicated carnality, not lack of eternal life. Prolonged immaturity as a result of carnality is a condition all too prevalent in modern Christianity. Often we mistake carnal Christians for natural men, unbelievers.

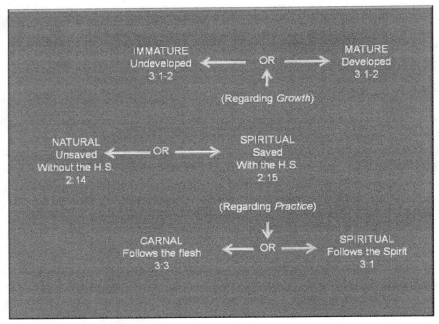

5. The role of God's servants 3:5-17

Paul turned next to a positive explanation of how his readers should view himself and his fellow workers.

> "At issue is their radically misguided perception of the nature of the church and its leadership, in this case especially the role of the teachers." (75)

Fellow workers under God 3:5-9

> "Besides evidencing a misapprehension of the gospel itself, the Corinthians' slogans bespeak a totally inadequate perception of the church and its ministry."

3:5 - Paul, Apollos, and, of course, Cephas were only servants of Christ each serving in his own way and sphere of opportunity under the Master's direction.

3:6-8 - Obviously God deserved more credit for the church in Corinth than either its planter or its nurturer. Next to Him the others were nothing. Human laborers are all equal in that they are human laborers with human limitations. Nevertheless the Lord will reward each one at the judgment seat of Christ because of his or her work. Note that it is our labor that will be the basis of our reward, not the fruit of our labor.

3:9 - Paul and Apollos were fellow workers *for* God. Elsewhere Paul spoke of believers as fellow workers *with* God (2 Cor 6:1), but that was not his point here. The Corinthians were the field in view in the preceding illustration (2 Cor 6:6-8). Paul now compared them to a building. He proceeded to develop this illustration in the following verses (2 Cor 6:10-17). This verse is transitional.

To help the Corinthians abandon the party spirit that marked their church, Paul stressed the equality of their teachers as fellow workers *under* God's sovereign authority (2 Cor 6:5-9).

> "Everything is God's-the church, its ministry, Paul, Apollos—everything. Therefore, it is absolutely not permissible to say 'I belong to Paul,' since the only legitimate 'slogan' is 'we all belong to God.'" (78)

"A sermon on our text [3:1-9] would focus on the attitudes of preachers and congregations about one another as they relate to the gospel of the cross. Peruse this brief sermon sketch:

"'I belong to Paul.' 'I belong to Apollos.' Familiar cries in a world of hi-tech religion. See huge Sunday crowds squint under the glare of spotlights as 'their' preachers dazzle millions of electronic viewers with wisdom and rhetorical charm. Overhear the Christian public admire TV evangelists and big-time clergy: 'Oh, I like to listen to_____.' 'Well, he's O.K. but I like better.' You fill in the blanks. Yes, everyone has their favorite preacher nowadays. In spite of all the notorious hucksters, 'preacher religion' is in. The result? An increasingly fragmented church. 'I belong to Paul and you don't.' It is enough to make Corinth look tame by comparison. " (79)

Builders of God's temple 3:10-15

"The usual explanation of this passage is that it describes the building of the Christian life. We all build on Christ, but some people use good materials while others use poor materials. The kind of material you use determines the kind of reward you will get.

"While this may be a valid *application* of this passage, it is not the basic *interpretation*. Paul is discussing the building of the local church, the temple of God." (80)

3:10 - In the new illustration Paul laid the foundation of the church in Corinth by founding the church, and others added the walls and continued building on that foundation. Paul's special mission from God was to found churches (Rom 15:20). He readily acknowledged that it was only by God's grace that he could do so as a skillful master-builder. He added a word of warning that the quality of the materials and workmanship that went into building the church are very important.

"By laying the foundation he did—Jesus Christ and him crucified—he was the truly 'wise' master-builder in contrast to the 'wise' in Corinth, who are building the church of totally incongenial materials and are therefore in danger of attempting to lay another foundation as well." (81)

3:11 - Christ Himself is the foundation of the church (Matt 16:18; cf. Isa 28:16; Rom 9:33; 1 Pet 2:6). Basing a church on the work of any other person, even Peter, is improper. Paul laid the foundation for the church in Corinth when he preached Christ and Him crucified there. The apostles and prophets are the foundation of the church in a secondary sense only (Eph 2:20). (82)

3:12-13 - Even though the quality of the foundation was the best, the condition of the building also depended on what others built on top of the foundation. In Paul's day contractors built buildings of durable and or combustible materials, as they do today. In the building of the Corinthian church durable materials were those activities that sprang from reliance on Christ and Him crucified, the foundation. These works contributed to the permanent spiritual strengthening of the believers. The combustible materials were activities that arose out of human "wisdom" in all its forms. These made no lasting contribution though they may have served some temporary need. Examples of the former include instruction in the Word of God, training in evangelism, and the refutation of error. Illustrations of the latter would be the teaching of popular ideas not rooted in Scripture, social work that excluded the gospel message, and the use of time and money for simply temporal purposes. However, Paul's main concern in this metaphor was those doing the building rather than the building itself.

"The six materials in 1 Cor 3:12 are arranged to denote a descending scale by moving from a unit of three good qualities to a unit of three bad ones. The verse uses pictures to represent what Paul calls 'work' in vv 13 and 14. Paul's main point is to encourage building with quality materials that will meet with God's approval and receive eternal reward. Interpreters sometimes restrict the meaning of the symbols either to doctrine, to people, to activity, or to character. The [proper] conclusion is that Paul in the symbols combines several things that lead to Christ's good pleasure and a believer's reward. These are sound doctrine, activity, motives and character in Christian service." (83)

God will expose the work of each of God's servants on "the day." This is a reference to the day when the believer will stand before God and give an account of the stewardship of his or her life at Christ's judgment seat (cf. Lk 19:11-27; 1 Cor. 1:8; 2 Cor 5:10; Phil 1:6, 10; 2 Tim 1:12, 18; 4:8; Rev 22:12; et al.). (84) Then the fire of God's judgment will test the quality of each person's work and his workmanship, but not his person. The durability or transience of those works will then become apparent.

3:14-15 - If the servant of the Lord has made a lasting contribution to the building of the church by emphasizing the gospel, he or she will receive a reward. If someone has not because he or she has pursued human "wisdom," that person will not, though he or she will retain his or her salvation. Paul likened the unfaithful servant to a man pulled to safety through the flames of his burning house (cf. Matt 25:14-30; Lk 19:11-27). The context identifies those who suffer loss as being Christians who seek to build the church with materials that fail to withstand God's assessment. They do not refer to all carnal Christians (1 Cor 3:1-4), though carnal Christians may fail to make lasting contributions to the church. (85)

The rewards in view seem to be opportunities to glorify God by serving Him (cf. Matt 25:14-30; Lk 19:11-27). The Christian will have greater or lesser opportunities to do so during the Millennium and forever in proportion to his or her faithfulness on earth now. (86) The New Testament writers spoke of these rewards symbolically as crowns elsewhere (cf. 1 Cor 9:25; Phil 4:1; 1 Thess 2:19; 2 Tim 4:8; James 1:12; 1 Pet 5:4; Rev 2:10; 3:11). It is perfectly proper to serve Christ to gain a crown. We will one day lay it at the feet of our Savior. It is a symbol of a life of faithful service that we performed out of gratitude for His grace to us (cf. Rev 4:4, 10). (87)

The testing in view here provides no support for the unbiblical doctrine of purgatory. It is the believer's works that God subjects to the fires of testing, not the believer personally. God applies the fire to determine the quality of the works, not to purify the believer.

> "[The] whole subject of rewards for the believer is one, I am afraid, rarely thought of by the ordinary Christian, or even the average student of the Scriptures. But it is both a joyous and solemn theme and should serve as a potent incentive for holiness of life." (88)

> "The Bible describes the judgment seat of Christ for one main purpose: to affect the way we think and live—to motivate us to anticipate with joy His return and to live our lives to please Him, not worrying about the way others treat us or what they may think about us. . . ."Though not the only motivating factor, I am convinced that the doctrine of the judgment seat (*bema*) is meant to be one of the major scriptural motivations for godly living." (89)

> "It is unfortunately possible for people to attempt to build the church out of every imaginable human system predicated on merely worldly wisdom, be it philosophy, 'pop' psychology, managerial techniques, relational 'good feelings,' or what have you. But at the final judgment, all such building (and perhaps countless other forms, where systems have become more important than the gospel itself) will be shown for what it is: something merely human, with no character of Christ or his gospel in it." (90)

A warning against destroying the church 3:16-17

This is perhaps the strongest warning in the New Testament against taking the church lightly and destroying it with the world's wisdom and division.

3:16 - The Corinthian church was a temple that God's Spirit indwelt. Paul was not speaking here of individual believers being temples of God, though we are (1 Cor 6:19), nor of the church universal as the temple of God, though it is (Eph 2:19-22; 1 Pet 2:5). He meant the collective body of believers that made up the local church as is clear from his use of the plural "you" in the Greek text and the singular "temple." The local congregation was not just any building (v. 9) but a sanctuary (Gr. *naos*) that God inhabited. The presence of the Spirit alone marked them off as God's sanctuary in Corinth. (91)

The New Testament writers spoke often of the church (a group of believers) as God's temple. They did not make the distinction between the holy place and the holy of holies that existed in the Israelites' physical temples. They viewed the temple as a whole. However here Paul did distinguish the place of God's dwelling, the temple building itself (*naos*), from the temple precincts that surrounded and included the sanctuary (Gr. *hieron*).

3:17 - If any servant of the Lord tears down the church instead of building it up, God will tear him or her down (Acts 9:1-4). He usually does this by sending temporal discipline in one form or another (cf. 1 Cor 5:5). The Greek word translated "destroys" (*phtheiro*) also means "defiles." It is a very serious thing to destroy or defile a holy temple, and that is what the local church is. (92) In the ancient world destroying a temple was a capital offense. The church is holy in that God has set it aside to glorify Himself even though it is not always as holy in its conduct as it is in its calling. (93)

Paul ended his discussion of the local church (1 Cor 3:5-17) as he did to stress the importance of the work that all God's servants were doing at Corinth. He also did so to stress the need for unity of viewpoint in the congregation.

> ." . . this is one of the few texts in the NT where we are exposed both to an understanding of the nature of the local church (God's temple indwelt by his Spirit) and where the warning of v. 17 makes it clear how important the local church is to God himself." (95)

6. Human wisdom and limited blessing 3:18-23

The apostle now combined the threads of his argument, which began at 1 Cor 1:18, and drew a preliminary conclusion. If his readers insisted on taking the natural view of their teachers and continued to form coteries of followers, they would limit God's blessing on themselves needlessly. Rather than their belonging to Paul or Apollos, both Paul and Apollos, and much more, belonged to them because they were Christ's and Christ is God's.

3:18 - Paul continued the subject of spiritual rather than natural wisdom. He urged his readers to turn away from attitudes the world regards as wise and to adopt God's viewpoint so they would be truly wise.

3:19-20 - Again Paul used Old Testament quotations to give added authority to his thought (cf. 1 Cor 1:19, 31; 2:9, 16). Here he referred to Job 5:13 and Psalm 94:11. The best wisdom the natural man can produce is foolishness compared with the wisdom God has revealed in His Word. Unbelieving humanity cannot avoid God's judgment through its own rationalizing. The reasoning of the wise of this world is useless regarding the most important issues of life. In 1 Cor 1:18-25 Paul had said that the wisdom of God, namely, Christ crucified, is foolishness to the world. Here he made the same point in reverse: the wisdom of the world is foolishness in God's sight.

3:21 - "So then" marks the apostle's conclusion. It is wrong to line up in cliques behind one or another of God's servants. In doing so, the Corinthians were only limiting God's blessing on them. They were rejecting God's good gifts by not appreciating all the people God had sent to help them.

> "Perhaps we cannot help but have our personal preferences when it comes to the way different men minister the Word. But we must not permit our personal preferences to become divisive prejudices. In fact, the preacher I may enjoy the least may be the one I need the most!" (96)

3:22 - All of God's servants were God's gifts to them. The world (Gr. kosmos, universe) belongs to the Christian in the sense that we will inherit it and reign over it with Christ one day. Life and all it holds contains much blessing for us. Even death is a good gift because it will usher us into the presence of our

Savior. This list is similar to the one in Romans 8:38-39 and, as there, is a way of saying "everything." The figure of speech is a merism. (97)

> "The five things . . . represent the fundamental tyrannies of human life, the things that enslave us, the things that hold us in bondage." (98)

3:23 - All the Corinthians belonged to Christ, not just those of the "Christ party" (1 Cor 1:12). They belonged to Him, not to one of His servants. Even Christ belongs to God in the sense of being under the authority and protection of the Father (cf. 1 Cor 8:6; 11:3; 15:28). This is functional rather than ontological subordination. All things belong to the Christian because the Christian belongs to Christ, and all things are His. Thus in Him we possess all things, but it is only in Him that we do.

Paul made several references to the administrative order of God when correcting disorders of various kinds in the Corinthian church. This order is the Father over the Son, the Son over the man, and the man over the woman (e.g., 1 Cor 8:6; 11:3; et al.). The apostle stressed divine order because the Corinthians were disorderly having failed to submit to the Holy Spirit's control.

> "On this high note Paul's response to the Corinthian pride in man and wisdom has come to a fitting conclusion. But the problem is larger still; so he turns next to deal with their attitudes toward him in particular." (99)

7. The Corinthians' relationship with Paul 4:1-21

The apostle now returned to the subject of himself and the other teachers of the Corinthians as servants of God. He did so to say more about what it means to be a servant of God. In this section he clarified the essential features of an acceptable servant of God. He did this so his readers would appreciate them all more and so they would follow Paul's example as a servant themselves. However, Paul stressed his authority too since the factions in the church that favored Apollos, Peter, or Christ really opposed Paul.

> "Throughout 1 Corinthians 1—4 Paul is primarily concerned to address the factionalism that was tearing the church apart with squabbles, jealousy, and one-upmanship. But because not a little of this quarreling arose from the habit of different groups in the church associating themselves with various well-known Christian leaders ('I follow Paul,' . . .), Paul found it necessary to address several Corinthian misconceptions regarding the nature of genuine Christian leadership. These believers were adopting too many models from their surrounding world." (100)

> "What Paul is trying to do above all else is to get the Corinthians to enter his orbit, to see things from his eschatological perspective. Therefore, it is not simply a matter of his being right and their being wrong on certain specific issues. It has to do with one's whole existence, one's whole way of looking at life, since 'you are Christ's, and Christ is God's.'" (101)

Judging God's servants 4:1-5

> "The first paragraph (vv. 1-5) leads the way by making an application of the servant model and showing how that relates to their treatment of him [Paul]. He changes images from farm to household and insists that he is *God's* servant, not theirs; and they are not allowed to judge another's servant. While on the theme of judgment, he gently broadens the perspective to remind them again of the future judgment that all must experience." (102)

4:1 - Learners should view teachers as stewards of God's mysteries rather than as party leaders. Paul used a different word for servants here (*hyperetai*) than he did in 1 Cor 3:5 (*diakonoi*). This word means an under-rower, a figure taken from the galley ships of the time. Slaves who rowed under the authority of the man who coordinated their individual efforts propelled the ship. The ship sailed straight ahead rather than in circles as the slaves followed the instructions of their leader. The other word (*diakonoi*) is the normal word for a servant.

A steward ("those entrusted with," NIV) was a servant whom his master entrusted with the administration of his business or property. His job was to devote his time, talents, and energy to executing his master's interests, not his own. The figure stresses both the apostles' humble position as belonging to Christ and their trusted yet accountable position under God. The mysteries of God refer to the truths of the Christian faith.

4:2 - The most important quality in a steward is that he manage his master's affairs so the desires of his lord materialize (cf. Matt 25:14-30; Luke 16:1-13; 19:11-27; 1 Pet 4:10). He must be faithful to his master's trust. For Paul this meant remaining faithful to the gospel as he had received it and preached it (cf. 1 Cor 15:1-11). God's requirement is not eloquence, wisdom, initiative, or success.

4:3 - It mattered little to Paul how well the Corinthians or anyone else thought he was carrying out his stewardship, how popular or unpopular he was. His personal evaluations of his own performance were irrelevant too. What did matter to him was God's estimation of his service. Paul did not give much time and attention to introspection, though he sought to live with a good conscience before God. Rather he concentrated on doing the job God had put before him to the best of his ability since he was accountable (cf. 1 Cor 3:13).

4:4 - As far as Paul knew he was serving God faithfully. However, he realized that his conscience might not be as sensitive as it should be. (103) Only his Master had the insight as well as the authority to judge him.

4:5 - Since only one Person has enough insight and is authoritative enough to pass final judgment, it is unwise for us to try to do so. Of course, we must make judgments from time to time, but we should always do so with the knowledge that our understanding is imperfect. The place God will judge our lives is the judgment seat of Christ. If Paul's references to his judgment by God in his epistles are any measure of how he regarded that event, he took it very seriously and thought about it often (cf. 2 Cor 1:14; 5:10; Phil 2:16; 1 Thess 2:19-20; 2 Tim 1:12, 18; 4:8; et al.).

> "Paul lives in expectation of the imminent coming again of Christ." (105)

The things hidden in the darkness probably include the unconscious motives of God's servants. Evidently God will find something in every faithful Christian's life for which to praise him or her on that day. Paul did not just say each servant would receive what he or she deserves but that each would receive some praise. Of course, the more faithful among us will receive more praise than the less faithful.

> "He [Paul] says nothing here about those who will receive not praise but blame; he is still thinking in terms of the Corinthian situation, in which some have praise for Paul, some for Apollos, some for Cephas." (106)

Verses 1-5 help us to view those who minister to us as God's servants, not our servants. They also help us as servants of God to remember to serve for the future approval of our Lord rather than for the present praise of people. The Corinthian church was not the only one that ever became disillusioned with its minister because he lacked "charismatic" qualities.

Taking pride in the wrong things 4:6-13

> "With rhetoric full of sarcasm and irony he [Paul] goes for the jugular. His own apostleship, which he portrays in bold relief, contrasting his own 'shame' with their perceived 'high station,' is alone consonant with a theology of the cross." (107)

4:6 - Paul had used various illustrations to describe himself and Apollos: farmers, builders, servants, and stewards. To exceed what God has written would be to go beyond the teaching of the Scriptures (cf. 1 Cor 15:3-4). If his readers avoided this pitfall, they would not take pride in one of their teachers over another.

In this letter Paul often used the verb translated "arrogant" or "puffed up" (Gr. *physioomai*) to describe attitudes and activities that smacked of human pride rather than godly wisdom and love (cf. 1 Cor 4:18-19; 5:2; 8:1; 13:4). The frequent use of this word identifies one of the Corinthians' main problems. Their attitude was wrong because their outlook was wrong. Paul proceeded to deal with it, and the rejection of him that it produced, in the remainder of this pericope.

4:7 - The apostle reminded the Corinthians that they were not intrinsically superior to anyone else, an attitude that judging others presupposes. God had given them everything they had. Consequently they should be grateful, not boastful.

4:8 - His readers were behaving as though they had already received their commendation at the judgment seat of Christ. This is an indication of their over-realized eschatology. They should have been conducting themselves as under-rowing stewards and paying attention to serving God faithfully (v. 1). Ironically Paul wished the time for rewards had arrived so he could enjoy reigning with his readers. Unfortunately suffering must precede glory.

> "The irony is devastating: How they perceive themselves, masterfully overstated in vv. 8 and 10, is undoubtedly the way they think *he* ought to be. But the way he actually is, set forth in the rhetoric of vv. 11-13, is the way *they* all ought to be." (108)

4:9 - Paul may have had the Roman games in mind here, specifically the battles between condemned criminals and wild beasts in the amphitheaters. (110) Another view is that Paul was thinking of the Roman triumph, a figure that he developed more fully elsewhere (2 Cor. 2:14). At the end of that procession came the captives of war who would die in the arena. (Fee) In either case, Paul seems to have been thinking of the apostles as the ultimately humiliated group. They were the leaders, and their sufferings for the cause of Christ were common knowledge. How inappropriate it was then for the Corinthians to be living as kings rather than joining in suffering with their teachers.

> "The Corinthians in their blatant pride were like the conquering general displaying the trophies of his prowess; the apostles were like the little group of captives, men doomed to die. To the Corinthians the Christian life meant flaunting their pride and their privileges and reckoning up their achievement; to Paul it meant a humble service, ready to die for Christ." (111)

Paul evidently meant good angels since he used "principalities and powers" to refer to what we call bad angels.

4:10 - These contrasts between the apostles and the Corinthians clarify the differences in their conditions. Natural men thought the apostles were fools, but they were willing to suffer this judgment for Christ's sake. The Corinthians and others, on the other hand, regarded themselves as prudent in their behavior as Christians. To the naturally wise the apostles looked weak, but the Corinthians appeared strong. They looked distinguished while the apostles seemed to be dishonorable.

4:11-13 - Paul proceeded to detail the dishonor that befalls those who bear the message of the cross. The Greeks despised people who did manual labor, as Paul had done in Corinth (cf. 1 Cor 9:4-18; Acts 18:3, 5; 2 Cor. 11:9; 12:13-17); they regarded it as the work of slaves. (112) To the world it is foolish to bless those who curse us, but that is what Paul did following the teaching and example of Jesus (cf. Lk 6:28; 23:34). All of these descriptions of the apostles emphasize the depths to which they were willing to stoop to proclaim the gospel (cf. Phil 2). They did so even though people who viewed things naturally called them fools.

In this section (1 Cor 4:6-13) Paul contrasted the viewpoint of the Corinthians with that of the apostles. The viewpoint of the Corinthians was virtually identical to that of natural unsaved people. The viewpoint of the apostles whom his readers professed to venerate and follow was quite different. Not only were the Corinthians unwise, but they were also proud.

A final appeal and exhortation 4:14-21

Paul concluded this first major section of the epistle (1 Cor 1:10–4:21) by reasserting his apostolic authority, which had led to his correcting the Corinthians' shameful conduct and carnal theology. He changed the metaphor again and now appealed to them as a father to his children. He ended by warning them that if they did not respond to his gentle approach he would have to be more severe.

4:14-15 - It was not Paul's purpose in writing the immediately preceding verses to humiliate the Corinthians. Other congregations would read this epistle. However, he did want to admonish them strongly as their father in the faith. They had many "tutors" or "guardians" (Gr. *paidagogoi*) who sought to bring them along in their growth in grace, but he was their only spiritual father.

> "The *paidagogos* was the personal attendant who accompanied the boy, took him to school and home again, heard him recite his 'lines', taught him good manners and generally looked after him; he was entitled to respect and normally received it, but there was no comparison between his relation to the boy and that of the boy's father." (113)

4:16 - The Corinthians were to learn from Paul as a son learns by observing the example of his father.

> ." . . Paul's actual ethical instruction as it appears in his Epistles rarely uses the language of Jesus as it is recorded in the Gospels; but on every page it reflects his example and his teaching . . ." (114)

4:17 - Timothy would serve as Paul's personal representative in Corinth soon (along with Erastus; Acts 19:22). Several factors point to the probability that Timothy had already departed from Ephesus but had not yet arrived in Corinth when Paul wrote this epistle (cf. Acts 19:22). One of these is Paul's lack of reference to Timothy in this epistle's salutation. A second is the tense of the verb translated "have sent" (NASB) or "am sending" (NIV; *epempsa*, aorist tense). A third is Paul's later reference to Timothy (1 Cor 16:10-11). Timothy was, of course, one of Paul's closest and most trusted fellow workers.

Paul's way of life here refers to the ethical principles that he taught and practiced.

> ." . . the Christian leader today not only must teach the gospel, but also must teach how the gospel works out in daily life and conduct. And that union must be modeled as well as explained.

> "The need is evident even at a confessional seminary like the one at which I teach. Increasingly, we have students who come from thoroughly pagan or secular backgrounds, who have been converted in their late teens or twenties, and who come to us in their thirties. Not uncommonly, they spring from dysfunctional families, and they carry a fair bit of baggage. More dramatically yet, a surprising number of them cannot easily make connections between the truths of the gospel and how to live.

> "A couple of years ago a student who was about to graduate was called in by one of our faculty members who had learned the student was planning to return to computer science and abandon plans to enter vocational ministry. The student was pleasant, with a solid B+ to his credit. But as the faculty member probed, it became obvious that this student had not put it all together. He could define propitiation but did not know what it was like to feel forgiven. He could defend the priority of grace in salvation but still felt as if he could never be good enough to be a minister. He could define holiness but found himself practicing firm self-discipline rather than pursuing holiness. His life and his theological grasp had not come together.

> "Mercifully, this particular faculty member was spiritually insightful. He took the student back to the cross and worked outward from that point. The student began to weep and weep as he glimpsed the love of God for him. Today he is in the ministry." (115)

Paul gave another gentle reminder that it was the Corinthians and not he who had departed from the Christian way. What he reminded them of here was standard teaching in all the churches (cf. 1 Cor 1:2; 7:17; 11:16; 14:33, 36).

4:18 – Some of the Corinthians who did not value Paul as highly as they should have had become puffed up in their own estimation of themselves and their ideas (cf. 1 Cor 4:6). They had done so as though they would not face him again. Evidently they felt he would not return to Corinth, and even if he did, they could overcome his influence.

4:19 - However, Paul did plan to return if God allowed him to do so. Evidently he was not able to return for some time. In 2 Corinthians he responded to criticism from within the church to the effect that he had promised to come but did not (2 Cor 1:15-18).

Paul knew that all the pretension to superior wisdom in the church was a result to viewing things from a worldly perspective; there was no reality behind it.

4:20 - The apostle returned to his earlier contrast between words and real power (1 Cor 2:1-5). Real power is the power of the Holy Spirit working through humble messengers. The kingdom of God here does not refer to the future millennial kingdom but to God's present rule over His people in the church, as the context clarifies.

4:21 - The Corinthians' response to this epistle would determine whether the apostle would return to them as a disciplining or as a delighted father. A spirit of gentleness also marked the Lord Jesus (Matt 11:29), though it stood in stark contrast to the spirit of arrogance in Corinth.

Paul concluded this part of 1 Corinthians with a strong confronting challenge.

> "Christian leadership means being entrusted with the 'mysteries' of God (1 Cor 4:1-7).

> "Christian leadership means living life in the light of the cross (1 Cor 4:8-13). "Christian leadership means encouraging—and if necessary, enforcing—the way of the cross among the people of God (4:14-21)." (116)

The depreciation of some of their teachers resulted in the Corinthians' not deriving benefit from them. It also manifested a serious error in the Corinthians' outlook. They were evaluating God's servants as natural unbelieving people do. This carnal perspective is the main subject of chapters 1-4. The Corinthians had not allowed the Holy Spirit to transform their attitudes.

> "Paul's view of the Christian ministry as revealed in this section (1 Cor 3-4) may now be summed up. The ministry is a divine provision which is responsible to Christ. It is a part of the Church given to the rest of the Church to be employed in its service. It comprises a multiplicity of gifts and functions, but is united by the unity of God and the unity of the Church. It serves the Church by itself first living out the life of suffering and sacrifice exhibited by the Lord on earth, thereby setting an example for the Church as a whole to follow." (117)

> "Even though at times Paul seems to be weaving in and out of several topics, the concern throughout is singular: to stop a current fascination with 'wisdom' on the part of the Corinthians that has allowed them not only to 'boast,' but to stand over against Paul and his gospel. With a variety of turns to the argument he sets forth his gospel over against their 'wisdom' and tries to reshape their understanding of ministry and church. . . .

> "The changes of tone in this passage reveal some of the real tensions that continue to exist in Christian ministry. How to be prophetic without being harsh or implying that one is above the sins of others. How to get people to change their behavior to conform to the gospel when they think too highly of themselves. There is no easy answer, as this passage

reveals. But one called to minister in the church must ever strive to do it; calling people to repentance is part of the task." (118)

Perhaps Paul originally intended to end this epistle here. (119) This opinion rests on the fact that the first four chapters could stand alone. This view points out the unity of this section of the letter. However it is impossible to prove or to disprove this hypothesis.

> "It becomes evident in chaps. 5 through 14 as specific problems in the Corinthian community are considered and as pastoral directions are given that at the same time something else is going on. With statements here and there, the epistemology presented in 1:18–2:16 is kept before the readers. They are nudged into viewing themselves and their congregational life in new and different ways, consistent with the message of the crucified Messiah." (120)

Bibliography

70. Ibid., p. 123.

71. See Stanley D. Toussaint, "The Spiritual Man," *Bibliotheca Sacra* 125:498 (April-June 1968):139-46, for fuller exposition of the four-man view. Lewis S. Chafer, *He That Is Spiritual*, pp. 3-14, saw only three kinds of people here: the natural man, the carnal man, and the spiritual man. John F. MacArthur Jr., *Faith Works*, p. 126, saw only two, "the unsaved person and the Christian."

72. For an excellent discussion of carnal believers, see Joseph C. Dillow, *The Reign of the Servant Kings*, pp. 311-31.

73. Fee, *The First . . .*, p. 127.

74. Wiersbe, 1:569.

75. Fee, *The First . . .*, p. 128.

76. Johnson, p. 1231.

77. Fee, *The First . . .*, p. 129.

78. Ibid., p. 134.

79. C. Thomas Rhyne, "Expository Articles: I Corinthians 3:1-9," *Interpretation* 44:2 (April 1990):177.

80. Wiersbe, 1: 579.

81. Fee, *The First . . .*, p. 138.

82. See Barrett, pp. 87-88.

83. James E. Rosscup, "A New Look at 1 Corinthians 3:12—'Gold, Silver, Precious Stones,'" *Master's Seminary Journal* 1:1 (Spring 1990):33.

84. See Joe L. Wall, *Going for the Gold,* pp. 31-37; Arlen L. Chitwood, *Judgment Seat of Christ*, p. 10.

85. Cf. Carson, pp. 79-80. John Proctor, "Fire in God's House: Influence of Malachi 3 in the NT," *Journal of the Evangelical Theological Society* 36:1 (March 1993):9-14, suggested that Malachi 3:2-3 may have been in Paul's mind when he wrote verse 15. However, Malachi predicted a future cleansing of Israel whereas Paul spoke of a future testing of Christians.

86. See Wall, pp. 112-21, for an explanation of the negative judgment at the *bema*.

87. If the idea of serving God for a reward makes you uncomfortable, may I suggest that you read again the Sermon on the Mount (Matt. 5—7)? There Jesus repeatedly appealed to His hearers to follow His teaching with the prospect of receiving an eternal reward for doing so. For a helpful introduction to the study of the Christian's rewards, see Wall, or Zane C. Hodges, *Grace in Eclipse.*

88. Wilbur Smith, "Inheritance and Reward in Heaven," *Eternity*, March 1977, p. 79.

89. Wall, pp. 19, 21.

90. Fee, *The First . . .*, p. 145.

91. Ten times in this epistle Paul asked, "Do you no know?" (cf. 5:6; 6:2, 3, 9, 15, 16, 19; 9:13, 24), and each time the question introduces an indisputable statement.

92. See James Sweeney, "Jesus, Paul, and the Temple: An Exploration of Some Patterns of Continuity," *Journal of the Evangelical Theological Society* 46:4 (December 2003):605-31.

93. Brian S. Rosner, "Temple and Holiness in 1 Corinthians 5," *Tyndale Bulletin* 42 (1991):137-45, argued convincingly that verses 16 and 17 anticipate the discussion of church discipline in 5:1-13.

94. Johnson, pp. 1234-35. Cf. Lowery, p. 511.

95. Fee, *The First . . .,* p. 149.

96. Wiersbe, 1:581.

97. In a merism two objects that are poles apart stand for everything between them.

98. Carson, p. 86.

99. Fee, *The First . . .*, p. 155.

100. Carson, p. 93.

101. Fee, *The First . . .,* p. 157.

102. Ibid., p. 156.

103. See Roy B. Zuck, "The Doctrine of Conscience," *Bibliotheca Sacra* 126:504 (October-December 1969):329-40.

104. Johnson, p. 1235.

105. *Theological Dictionary of the New Testament*, s.v. *"erchomai,"* by Johannes Schneider, 2:674.

106. Barrett, p. 104.

107. Fee, *The First . . .,* p. 156.

108. Ibid., p. 165.

109. Bruce, p. 50.

110. Fee, *The First . . .*, pp. 174-75.

111. Barclay, p. 45.

112. Morris, p. 81.

113. Bruce, p. 51.

114. Fee, *The First . . .,* p. 187. For example, Paul never used the word "disciple" in his epistles. Instead he appealed to his readers as his children or his brethren. The metaphor of father and children to refer to a teacher and his disciples was also common in Judaism.

115. Carson, p. 111.

116. Ibid., pp. 94, 103, 108.

117. Ronald Y. K. Fung, "The Nature of the Ministry according to Paul," *Evangelical Quarterly* 54 (1982):132.

118. Fee, *The First . . .,* pp. 193-94.

119. Bruce, pp. 52-53.

120. Cousar, "The Theological . . .," p. 101.

Lesson 4 Self Check

QUESTION 1

Sometimes the poor behavior of believers is indistinguishable from that of unbelievers. *True or False?*

QUESTION 2

When God builds His Church, He does not use human instruments. *True or False?*

QUESTION 3

Paul uses agricultural and construction metaphors in this section to describe the work of Christian leaders. *True or False?*

QUESTION 4

In God's wisdom, Christian leaders belong to the whole church. *True or False?*

QUESTION 5

Which response best explains Paul's statement that he does not judge himself (1 Cor 4:3)?

    A. He does not examine his own heart.

    B. He recognizes that final and true judgment belongs to the Lord.

    C. He considers himself perfect and without sin.

    D. He knows that the Lord has already justified him.

QUESTION 6

Which response best describes the relationship between Paul and Apollos?

    A. Rivals in ministry

    B. Coworkers in ministry

    C. Apostles of Christ

    D. Spiritual father and son

QUESTION 7

Paul was unwilling to use discipline to correct the problems at Corinth. *True or False?*

QUESTION 8

Some scholars think the underlying problem at Corinth was a theological error known as triumphalism. *True or False?*

QUESTION 9

On the day of judgment, God will test the quality of each Christian's work. *True or False?*

QUESTION 10

Which response best describes carnal Christians?

    A. Can never change

    B. Need to repent

    C. Are really unsaved people

    D. Neglect attending worship services

    E. Have never made a Lordship decision

Lesson 4 Answers to Questions

QUESTION 1: *Your answer*

QUESTION 2

Characteristic	Type
Natural man	Does not welcome spiritual things
Spiritual man	Has spiritual discernment
Babe in Christ	Has limited capacity for understanding God's Word
Carnal Christian	Willful rebellion against God

QUESTION 3: False

QUESTION 4: False

QUESTION 5: *Your answer*

QUESTION 6

   A. Publicly defending the faith

   B. Building up believers

   C. Modeling effective use of the Scriptures

QUESTION 7: False

QUESTION 8: *Your answer should be similar to the following:*
Only God gives the growth.

QUESTION 9: *Your answer*

QUESTION 10

   D. Christian leaders

QUESTION 11: *Your answer*

QUESTION 12: *Your answer should be similar to the following:*
Should include words like: cheap, burnable, temporary, inferior.

QUESTION 13

   A. Expensive

   B. Unburnable

   C. Beautiful

   D. Eternal

QUESTION 14

   B. Testing the quality of their works

QUESTION 15: Defiles

QUESTION 16: *Your answer*

QUESTION 17

   A. Self-deception

   B. Foolishness

   C. Futile

   D. Boasting

QUESTION 18: *Your answer should be similar to the following:*
Human leaders are just men whom God has specially gifted and given to the church. Fundamentally, they are just servants of God, just like any other godly believer.

QUESTION 19: False

QUESTION 20

   B. Faithfulness

QUESTION 21: *Your answer*

QUESTION 22: True

QUESTION 23
B. Financially poor
C. Hardworking
D. Victims of abuse

QUESTION 24
E. He appeals to them as their spiritual father.
F. He reasons with them, laying out clear arguments and using Scripture.

QUESTION 25
C. God's present rule in the lives of His people

QUESTION 26: *Your answer*

Lesson 4 Self Check Answers

QUESTION 1: True
QUESTION 2: False
QUESTION 3: True
QUESTION 4: True
QUESTION 5
    B. He recognizes that final and true judgment belongs to the Lord.
QUESTION 6
    B. Coworkers in ministry
QUESTION 7: False
QUESTION 8: True
QUESTION 9: True
QUESTION 10
    B. Need to repent

Lesson 5: Immorality and Lawsuits (1 Cor 5:1–6:20)

Lesson Introduction

Have you ever heard anyone say that they long to get back to the situation of the early church? Sometimes Christians romanticize the first-century church, viewing it as pure and ideal. Certain congregations even advertise themselves as being patterned after the apostolic church. Certainly the Spirit moved powerfully at that time, but the Bible does not paint the picture of the early church as perfect or as an earthly paradise. In fact, many things at the church at Corinth displeased Paul, and one issue moved him to take concrete action in church discipline.

Have you ever been associated with a church that practiced church discipline? In some countries, principles of church discipline are now only rarely applied. In Topic 1 we will examine one case of early church discipline. Paul had to chastise the church to take action, because the sin was painful for all involved. We will see important principles for church discipline in this topic.

Paul's condemnation of lawsuits among believers is the subject of Topic 2. This was another grievous issue for Paul, and it should have grieved the congregation.

Topic 3 examines the extent of a Christian's freedom as it relates to sexual behavior. Just as relevant today as it was two thousand years ago, Paul offers counsel and a call to holiness.

Lesson Outline

Topic 1: Church Discipline for Immorality (1 Cor 5:1-13)

Responsibility for Discipline (5:1-4)

Method of Discipline (5:5)

Purposes of Discipline (5:6-8)

Only for Church Members (5:9-13)

Topic 2: Lawsuits Among Believers (1 Cor 6:1-11)

Shame of Lawsuits (6:1-8)

Warning and Encouragement (6:9-11)

Topic 3: Freedom and Immorality (1 Cor 6:12-20)

Freedom's Limits (6:12-17)

Flee Immorality (6:18-20)

Lesson Objectives

It happened suddenly four weeks ago. Nobody guessed anything was going on between Daniel and Lily until it happened. Daniel left his wife Ai and moved in with Lily. What is so shocking is that Daniel and Ai had both been baptized and had been coming to church for six or seven years! Lily, of course, makes no pretense that she believes in Jesus. She is Daniel's fellow worker at the post office and has been married twice before. Currently she is divorced.

Now poor Ai is very upset and depressed even more. Their son is at university, and Lotus heard that he is very upset about this, too.

Through town gossip, Lotus heard that Daniel was tired of Ai's nagging and complaining, fell in love with Lily, and that he plans to divorce Ai and marry Lily.

Both Daniel and Ai stopped attending church when this happened. Some of the brothers and sisters in the church have been trying to comfort and support Ai in the wake of this mess, but nobody seems to be ministering to Daniel.

Many of the brothers and sisters disapprove of what Daniel has done. Some are threatening to stop coming to church unless there is some discipline. Others at church say that we should not judge and that this type of thing happens all the time. Another complicating factor in the church taking action is that Lily is a cousin of Ruth (the church pianist and hostess for their meetings), and they are very close.

Lotus turns to 1 Corinthians 5 and 6 for guidance. She feels that the church needs wisdom and courage to act. If things like this keep on happening and nobody does anything, she fears even more for the unity and witness of their church.

By the end of this lesson, you will be able to:

- Understand there is no "ideal" or "perfect" church, even the early church had problems
- List four purposes of church discipline
- Explain the reasons for believers to handle problems within the church differently than they handle problems outside the church
- Apply the lesson to your life that all believers are called to holiness even amidst our "freedom in Christ"

Topic 1: Church Discipline for Immorality (1 Cor 5:1-13)

Paul wrote in 1 Corinthians 4:21: "What do you want? Shall I come to you with a rod of discipline or with love and a spirit of gentleness?" With the next verse, he criticizes the proud Corinthians for their toleration of an obvious case of terrible immorality in their midst.

Although this case was well known in their church, they apparently neglected to mention it in their letter to Paul, for he begins to answer their letter in 1 Corinthians 7:1. Instead, Paul had heard about it from others, probably "members of Chloe's household" (1 Cor 1:11).

Paul reacts with sorrow and indignation—not just at the perpetrators of this immorality, but also at the entire church for failing to take action.

Responsibility for Discipline (5:1-4)

Assignment

- Read 1 Corinthians 5:1-4.
- Read Constable, "Incest in the Church" (refer to the Articles section at the end of this lesson), through the note on 5:4.
- Read "Responsibility for Discipline."

Responsibility for Discipline

What was this horrible sin? "Someone is cohabiting with his father's wife." This was a case of incest. A man in the church was persisting in an immoral sexual relationship with his stepmother.

Both Jews and Gentiles uniformly considered such immorality heinous and evil. Apparently, this was being done openly and shamelessly.

It is possible that Paul means that the Corinthians were proud of this sin, reflecting some twisted view of Christian freedom. Perhaps, though, he means that they were spiritually proud in general (1 Cor 4:6, 8, 18), when they should have been humbling themselves before the Lord because of this sin of incest.

Paul instructed the congregation to take action to discipline this member. The reason is that church discipline is the responsibility of the entire congregation.

Why did Paul only command discipline for the man in this instance? A possible answer to this question is that only the man was a member of the church; otherwise, Paul would have commanded discipline for both the man and the woman. This interpretation of Paul's actions is in line with the principle of 1 Corinthians 5:12: "For what do I have to do with judging those outside (the church)? Are you not to judge those inside?"

Paul was aghast at the church's failure to take action against this rank evil in their midst. The church as a whole was guilty of negligence. Yet, in order to take disciplinary action, the church needed to be first unified.

QUESTION 1

What is a possible reason that Paul was only concerned to discipline the male offender in this case?

- A. Males carry the greater responsibility in cases of sexual immorality.
- B. The man was a member of the church, whereas the woman was not.
- C. Paul looked down on women.
- D. Paul did not want to embarrass the woman.
- E. Paul knew the woman would not repent.

Method of Discipline (5:5)

Assignment

- Read 1 Corinthians 5:5.
- Read "Method of Discipline."

Method of Discipline

Analyzing the steps of church discipline from Matthew 18:15-17, in this case Paul seems to be advising the last step: "If he refuses to listen to the church, treat him like a Gentile or a tax collector." Paul assumes that this sinner will not listen to the church. There are other cases of discipline in the New Testament where the steps in Matthew 18 were not rigidly carried out—for example, when Paul rebuked Peter in Galatians 2:11-14, or with Ananias and Sapphira in Acts 5:1-11.

What precisely did Paul mean in 1 Corinthians 5:5 by "turn this man over to Satan for the destruction of the flesh"? The interpretative questions are many:

(A) What did Paul mean by "the flesh"?

(B) What does it mean to turn someone over to Satan?

(C) In what way is the "destruction of the flesh" helpful to the sinner?

(A) "The flesh" could mean either his physical body or his sin nature. In a discipline situation, it would seem that "physical body" would be the intended meaning, and thus turning someone over to Satan would result in physical pain or death. It is difficult to see how the alternative makes sense: Would not Satan be fighting against himself if he destroyed someone's sin nature? Also, nowhere does Scripture teach that Satan has the power (or the desire) to destroy someone's sin nature.

(B) The meaning of "turn this man over to Satan" seems to be the same as "remove the evil person from among you" (1 Cor 5:13; see also 1 Cor 5:2). Probably the meaning is that the offender is cast outside of the protection of the church into Satan's domain, the world (1 Jn 5:19). He is cut off from Christian fellowship, from the teaching and ordinances of the church, from participating in the ministries of the church and from using his own gifts in the church. His unrepentant spirit places him in the evil one's hands.

(C) As to "the destruction of the flesh": We know that Satan can inflict physical pain (the case of Job) and even cause death (the case of Job's children). Physical suffering, however, can be instructive to believers. Many times in the Old Testament, God brought suffering to His errant people so that they would turn back to Him (Judg 3:7-11). If the meaning is "premature death," then the benefit to the sinner would be that he could no longer continue in his sin.

QUESTION 2

Please answer the following questions in your Life Notebook.

> A. What did Paul mean by "the flesh"?
>
> B. What does it mean to turn someone over to Satan?
>
> C. In what way is the "destruction of the flesh" helpful to the sinner?

Church discipline of this type would be a distasteful affair for the whole congregation. Not only was the need for discipline a grievous matter, but also the discipline itself would be painful to the church. Paul's pronouncement should have helped to galvanize the church to act.

QUESTION 3

What did Paul instruct the church to do about this immorality?

> A. Pray about it.
>
> B. Leave it to the pastor to handle.
>
> C. Forgive and forget, since we have all already committed adultery in our hearts.
>
> D. Remove the sinner from their fellowship.

QUESTION 4

Paul advised the church to discipline the man guilty of incest in a gathering of the whole church. *True or False?*

In this particular case in Corinth, the sin was longstanding, open, and detestable. Look up Numbers 15:30-31 and read the note on "defiant sin" (refer to the Notes section at the end of this lesson).

QUESTION 5

Do you think this sin at Corinth qualifies as a sin "with a high hand"? Why or why not?

Purposes of Discipline (5:6-8)

No reputable hospital would tolerate infection in the operating room. No quality restaurant would allow tainted food to be served to its customers. In the same manner, the local church must not allow gross sin to defile it.

Assignment

- Read 1 Corinthians 5:6-8.
- Read Constable, "The Analogy of the Passover" (refer to the Articles section at the end of this lesson).
- Read "Purposes of Discipline."

Purposes of Discipline

Church discipline in the New Testament is never done for vengeance, hate, or only to punish. The overall motive must be love for God, for the offender, and for the church. Our reaction when we learn of serious sin in the body of Christ should be deep sorrow. As the Holy Spirit is grieved, so we should be grieved—for the harm done to Christ's body, for the plight of the sinner, and for the offense to God.

Is church discipline punishment? Church discipline is actually called punishment in 2 Corinthians 2:6. One purpose of the punishment is to communicate formally and forcefully that the offender's actions are unacceptable among believers. In criminal law, society views punishment for crimes as paying for the crime. Church discipline is fundamentally different in this respect. The only solution for sin is the sacrificial death of Jesus Christ appropriated by faith and repentance. Undergoing church discipline does not cleanse the offender of his sin. On the other hand, neither does church discipline—even being cast out of fellowship—cancel a believer's salvation (1 Cor 5:5).

For the sinner in this case, Paul undoubtedly hoped that this man would repent in the face of the discipline and turn back to God. Whether or not the man referred to in 2 Corinthians 2:5-11 is the same man as in 1 Corinthians 5:1 may be debated; nevertheless, it is clear that Paul rejoices over that man's restoration to Christian fellowship after repenting. Thus, a second major purpose of church discipline is to help restore the sinner to fellowship with God and the body of Christ.

A third major purpose of church discipline is for the purity of the body of Christ. In 1 Corinthians 5:6-8, Paul expresses this purpose with the analogy of cleaning out the yeast. As one lump of yeast affects the whole loaf of bread, so sin spreads and negatively affects the whole group of believers. Letting serious sin go undisciplined sets a poor example and tempts others to do the same. Furthermore, it gives the church a bad reputation among unbelievers, thus damaging the church's witness.

Implied in this passage is another purpose of church discipline—to stir up fear of sinning among the believers. This may sound sub-Christian to some, but it seems to be supported by Acts 5:11

and 1 Timothy 5:20. After the deaths of Ananias and Sapphira, "great fear gripped the whole church, and all who heard about these things." Being publicly cast out of fellowship, such as this man in Corinth was to be, should be humiliating. The prospect of being delivered to Satan for the destruction of the flesh is fearful. Believers who hear about such discipline would react naturally with grief and horror.

QUESTION 6

Match the purposes of church discipline with appropriate Scripture.

Scripture	Purposes
Deuteronomy 19:19-20	To restore the sinner to fellowship.
1 Corinthians 5:6-7	To punish the offender.
Galatians 6:1	To purify the Body of Christ
2 Corinthians 2:6	To warn believers and to give them fear of sinning.

Only for Church Members (5:9-13)

Assignment

- Read 1 Corinthians 5:9-13.
- Read Constable, "The Christian's Relationship to Fornicators" (refer to the Articles section at the end of this lesson).
- Read "Only for Church Members."

Only for Church Members

In a previous letter (now lost, see 1 Cor 5:9) Paul had instructed the Corinthian believers not to associate with immoral people; however, they misunderstood him. Paul did not mean for believers to insulate themselves from interaction with unbelievers, whose lives are characterized by sin. Instead, believers are to imitate Jesus, who was criticized for eating with tax collectors and sinners (Lk 15:1-2). The local church has no authority to discipline non-believers. God will judge them on judgment day.

How was the church at Corinth to carry out Paul's instruction not to associate with immoral believers? The context here is a case of formal church discipline. In 1 Corinthians 5:13, Paul alludes to verses in the law of Moses (Deut 17:7; 19:19; 22:21, 24; 24:7) where people who sin were removed from the community. Capital punishment is not a part of New Testament church discipline (but premature death remains one of God's direct disciplinary methods—see 1 Cor 11:30), so expulsion from the church is Paul's meaning here. Church members were to cut off fellowship with the offender, even to the point of refusing to eat with him.

Most Christians do not think that when they join a local church, they are agreeing to come under the discipline of that church. The function of discipline has two sides—being corrected for unrepentant sin, and supporting the congregation in applying discipline to others. Church discipline is one of the marks that distinguishes a local church from a Bible study group or fellowship group.

QUESTION 7

To what immoral people in 1 Corinthians 5:9 was Paul referring?

    A. Any immoral people

    B. Weak believers who are struggling with sin

    C. Hypocrites, who say they are believers but refuse to repent

    D. True believers who have fallen into sin and refused to repent of it

QUESTION 8

Match the sins with the correct references that discuss how the church was to address them.

Verse References	Sins
1 Corinthians 5:1-5	Disobedience to apostolic teaching
1 Timothy 1:20	Divisiveness
Titus 3:10	Serious sexual immorality
2 Thessalonians 3:14, 15	Blasphemy
2 Thessalonians 3:6	Idleness

QUESTION 9

It is the responsibility of the local church to discipline its members. *True or False?*

QUESTION 10

Part A:

Suppose Sister Mary, who used to be the church treasurer, has been disciplined by the church but refuses to repent of her repeated thefts of church funds. She has had her church membership revoked, and church members have been instructed not to associate with her. How would you answer the following questions: (a) If Mary is your close family member, are you to cut off contact with her? (b) If you work for Mary in her store, how are you to act? (c) Should church members no longer shop at her store?

Part B:

Suppose James discovers that his colleague at work, David, is committing adultery. David claims to be a Christian, but he's not a member of any local church and seldom attends worship anywhere. Should James cut off contact with him and refuse to eat lunch at work with him?

Topic 2: Lawsuits Among Believers (1 Cor 6:1-11)

How many times have you lent money or property to a fellow believer and it was never returned to you? Perhaps you made an arrangement to help a brother who said he had a need, and he promised to pay you back the money at a certain time, or to return the item in the same condition as when you lent it. After the deadline had passed, you sought out the brother, but he made excuse after excuse. What should you do? It seems that one solution to such problems in the church at Corinth was to sue the brother in the local courts. Paul says this is a defeat for the church.

Shame of Lawsuits (6:1-8)

If the church is competent to handle the discipline of a member living in unrepentant sexual immorality, they are also able to decide other disputes. In this case, Paul does not counsel church discipline of the parties involved, but rather church intervention. This matter can be settled within the church family if both parties will agree to it.

Assignment

- Read 1 Corinthians 6:1-8.

- Read Constable, "The Shame on the Church" and "Paul's Judgment on the Matter" (refer to the Articles section at the end of this lesson).

- Read "Lawsuits Among Believers."

Lawsuits Among Believers

Another negative report that came to Paul about the church at Corinth concerned lawsuits among believers. Paul is not as concerned about the dispute as he is concerned with what such a situation says about the church as a whole. It is another indication of their being "influenced by the flesh and behaving like unregenerate people" (1 Cor 3:3).

Although it is impossible to say with certainty, the dispute probably involved property or money. Paul calls it an "ordinary lawsuit" (1 Cor 6:3). It seems to be a dispute between individuals, both of whom are members of the church. There is no indication that church property is involved.

Paul argues that believers are more than competent to handle such cases, because, eventually, believers will judge angels. Many at Corinth placed a high value on human philosophy and wisdom. Paul now chastises them by asking ironically, "Is there no one among you wise enough to settle disputes between fellow Christians?" Apparently, the disputing individuals did not think so, or perhaps the possibility of settling their dispute within the church had never crossed their minds.

By taking such a dispute before the secular courts to resolve, word gets out in the community that believers cannot get along with each other and cannot resolve their own differences. Such behavior gives non-believers a low view of the faith. Believers look like hypocrites. Although they proclaim the gospel of love and forgiveness, instead, they wrong and cheat each other. The reputation and attractiveness of the church are damaged.

Does Paul mean that believers should avoid the secular courts in all cases? This does not seem to be his teaching. For example, certain cases, such as murder, necessarily involve the secular courts. Rather, Paul's emphasis is that believers should consider higher values when they have disputes with fellow believers. Consider what effect suing your brother in the local courts would have on your witness for the Lord or on the unity of your congregation. Try to handle your dispute within the church so as to minimize the bad effects. Sometimes, it is better just to suffer loss and drop a case. After all, the progress of the gospel is a much higher value than material gain.

QUESTION 11

What type of lawsuit between believers is referred to in 1 Corinthians 6:1? Record your response in your Life Notebook.

QUESTION 12

If no church property is involved, why is Paul even interested in this case? *(Select all that apply.)*

A. It reflects the low spiritual life of the entire church.

B. It results in a bad witness to the unbelieving community.

C. It affects the fellowship and harmony in the church.

D. It is unnecessary for believers to take such cases to the courts.

QUESTION 13

To settle the matter referred to in 1 Corinthians 6:1-8, Paul counsels mediation by the church. *True or False?*

QUESTION 14

The modern church has often neglected this ministry of helping resolve believers' disputes with each other. Open your Life Notebook and record your thoughts on what your church can do to apply this teaching.

Warning and Encouragement (6:9-11)

Assignment

- Read 1 Corinthians 6:9-11.
- Read Constable, "Notes on 1 Corinthians 6:9-11" (refer to the Articles section at the end of this lesson).
- Read "Warning and Encouragement."

Warning and Encouragement

Paul states that the unrighteous will not inherit the kingdom of God. The kingdom of God refers to the future kingdom program, involving both the one-thousand-year reign of Christ on earth and the phase of the kingdom called the new heavens and the new earth. Paul insists that Christians should not continue to live in such sins, because if they do they will forfeit their inheritance in the kingdom of God.

The Greek word for "unrighteous" in 1 Corinthians 6:1; 6:9 could refer either to the unsaved (as it does in 1 Cor. 6:1) or to unrighteous Christians. Because the verbal form of the noun "unrighteous" is used in the immediately preceding verse, it may be better to understand this word as referring to carnal Christians. Paul says that the Corinthian believers were once unrighteous, but now they have been saved. He lists a series of ten sinful behaviors that some of them have been redeemed from. However, in 1 Corinthians 6:7 Paul uses the verb form of this word "unrighteous" (NET Bible translation: "[do] wrong") to describe the actions of the Corinthian believers toward their brothers and sisters in the Lord! The intended effect is to shame the church and move them to live in step with their current position in the Lord. "Unrighteous" behavior is unsuited for righteous people. It is because of this wicked behavior that unrighteous Christians will not inherit the kingdom of God. It is likely that Paul has true Christians in view because in Galatians 5:21 he applies the warning of not inheriting the kingdom of God directly to true believers who "belong to Christ" (Gal. 5:24).

To "inherit the kingdom" means to have special honor there, co-rulership with Christ. An inheritance is a reward paid to faithful Christians (Col. 3:24). All Christians will enter the kingdom, but not all will have an inheritance there. This distinction between entering and inheriting is common to most cultures. It is one thing to enter a friend's house, but it is entirely another to inherit or "possess" it.

The Bible frequently warns Christians of the danger of loss of reward at the judgment seat of Christ (see 1 Cor 3:15; 2 Cor 5:10-11; 1 Jn 2:28; 2 Jn 8; Col 2:18-19).

Of particular concern in some parts of the church today is the issue of homosexuality. With the recent rampant increase in open homosexuality in some societies, questions have been raised as to the Biblical view of such acts. A key passage in understanding the Bible's teaching on this issue is 1 Corinthians 6:9-11.

The argument is sometimes made that homosexual orientation is natural, or a predisposition from birth. Note that the list of sins in 1 Corinthians 6:9-10 includes other sins for which similar arguments are sometimes made. However, Paul would not accept the argument that predisposition toward heterosexual promiscuity justifies adultery. Having a sin nature that tends toward covetousness does not justify greed, theft or swindling, either. Certainly Paul would not agree that a predisposition toward homosexuality justifies homosexual acts. People who continue to live in such wickedness after claiming to know Christ should examine themselves. Perhaps they do not really know Him (Mt 7:21-23).

Jesus came to save His people from their sin, starting at the point of conversion. Believers are not only given power over sin through the Holy Spirit, but also are called to live lives worthy of God's kingdom.

QUESTION 15

What is the function of 1 Corinthians 6:9-11 in Paul's argument?

  A. To warn and encourage self-examination

  B. To list sins that require church discipline

  C. To teach that excessive sinners are not true Christians

  D. To build a case that true believers can lose their salvation

QUESTION 16

Look up these key passages relating to the Bible's view of homosexuality. Match the passage with its main content:

Passages	Content
Leviticus 18:22	Prohibition of male homosexuality
Leviticus 20:13	Lesbianism and homosexuality as evidence of God's wrath
Genesis 19:1-13	Death penalty for male homosexual acts
Romans 1:26-27	Destruction of Sodom for the sin of homosexuality

QUESTION 17

According to 1 Corinthians 6:11, believers were washed, _____, and justified at conversion.

Topic 3: Freedom and Immorality (1 Cor 6:12-20)

The internet, billboards, television, movies, magazines and books continually bombard us with temptations to immorality. Temptations to sexual sin in Corinth two thousand years ago must have also been rampant, since at one time, the Greek for acting immorally was "to corinthianize." Shockingly, it appears that some church members approved of visiting prostitutes, asserting that believers were free to do so! How could they have been so confused? What does Paul advise in the face of such temptation?

Freedom's Limits (6:12-17)

Assignment

- Read 1 Corinthians 6:12-17.

- Read Constable, "Prostitution in the Church" (refer to the Articles section at the end of this lesson) through the note on 6:17.

- Read "Freedom's Limits."

Freedom's Limits

With this section, Paul begins to address directly the topic of Christian freedom—a topic that undergirds much of his argument and teaching in the rest of 1 Corinthians. In subsequent chapters, Paul instructs the Corinthians regarding the nature and limits of Christian freedom in a number of areas: marriage, food, and worship. In this passage, he concentrates on freedom versus immorality.

There are two extreme positions that Christians sometimes mistakenly fall into regarding the physical body. Both positions separate the spiritual from the physical in an unbalanced and unhealthy way. One position (antinomianism) completely denies the importance of the physical body, saying that only the spiritual is of value. This view can lead to extremely sinful self-indulgent behavior, since the activities of the body do not matter at all. The second position (asceticism) views the physical as evil. The only way to deal with it is by denial of bodily desires. Such people may punish their own bodies or refuse to express natural functions, even to the point of abstaining from sexual activity within marriage.

The first part of 1 Corinthians 6:13, "all things are lawful for me," is put in quotes in many modern Bible translations. Additionally, "food is for the stomach and the stomach is for food, but God will do away with both," is listed in quotes in the NET Bible. These translators' views that the words in quotes are most likely slogans from the Corinthians that Paul is quoting back to them, perhaps from their letter to him. Possibly Paul had actually made statements like these previously, but he now acts to correct their misuse of them.

The Corinthians had gone too far in asserting their freedom in Christ. They had taken fundamental Christian truth—Christ has set us free—and tried to apply it in ungodly ways. They asserted "all things are lawful," by which they meant that they could do anything they wanted. "All things are lawful" is true in one sense—Christians are no longer under the law of Moses. We no longer have to be concerned about fulfilling Old Testament regulations regarding clean and unclean foods, observing holy days, or offering sacrifices. We can eat whatever we want; hence, "food is for the stomach and the stomach is for food" is true, if the meaning is that we can freely eat and enjoy anything.

However, Christian freedom is not a license to sin. Paul made this argument later in Romans 6. We have been set free from sin to live a new life that is holy, dedicated to God, and pleasing to

Him. We have been set free from sin to become slaves of righteousness. In 1 Corinthians 6, Paul puts limits on our freedom in Christ with the expressions "but not everything is beneficial" and "but I will not be controlled by anything." True, Christians are free to eat any food without concern for ceremonial regulations, but that does not mean we are free to become gluttons, or to get drunk, or to become addicted to substances.

The Corinthians had misapplied the slogan "all things are lawful" to the area of sexual relations. We can almost imagine them also saying, "the body for sex and sex for the body"! Paul argues that such thinking is mistaken.

QUESTION 18

What does Paul mean by "all things are lawful for me"? Record your response in your Life Notebook.

Believers are set free from many rules and regulations of the Old Testament law, but we remain morally constrained by the law of Christ (1 Cor 9:21). We are freed in Christ to do what pleases Him.

QUESTION 19

What principle of Christian freedom is implied in 1 Corinthians 6:12-13?

    A. Christian freedom means freedom from sinning.

    B. Christian freedom means different things to different people.

    C. Christian freedom means freedom from the penalty of sin.

    D. Christian freedom means freedom from moral standards.

QUESTION 20

What is the proper application of the teaching, "the body is not for sexual immorality, but for the Lord, and the Lord for the body" (1 Cor 6:13)?

    A. Avoid all sexual expression.

    B. Make sure you are not tempted sexually.

    C. Get married and have regular sexual activity with your spouse.

    D. Flee immorality.

Flee Immorality (6:18-20)

Assignment

- Read 1 Corinthians 6:18-20.
- Read Constable, "The Reason Participating in Prostitution is Wrong" (refer to the Articles section at the end of this lesson).
- Read "Flee Immorality."

Flee Immorality

The NET Bible views "every sin a person commits is outside of the body" (1 Cor 6:18) as another Corinthian slogan:

> It is debated whether this is a Corinthian slogan. If it is not, then Paul is essentially arguing that there are two types of sin, nonsexual sins which take place outside the body and sexual sins which are against a person's very own

body. If it is a Corinthian slogan, then it is a slogan used by the Corinthians to justify their immoral behavior. With it they are claiming that anything done in the body or through the body had no moral relevance. A decision here is very difficult, but the latter is to be preferred for two main reasons. (1) This is the most natural understanding of the statement as it is written. To construe it as a statement by Paul requires a substantial clarification in the sense (e.g., "All *other* sins…" [NIV]). (2) Theologically the former is more difficult: Why would Paul single out sexual sins as more intrinsically related to the body than other sins, such as gluttony or drunkenness? For these reasons, it is more likely that the phrase in quotation marks is indeed a Corinthian slogan which Paul turns against them in the course of his argument, although the decision must be regarded as tentative. (NET Bible, note on 1 Cor 6:18. 2006, Biblical Studies Press; reprinted with permission from http://bible.org.)

That this is another Corinthian slogan would make sense coming from an antinomian position which denies the importance of the physical body. Again, Paul argues to correct this error. He says they are wrong for "the immoral person sins against his own body" (1 Cor 6:18).

The proper application to Paul's teaching here is to "flee sexual immorality." What precisely does that mean?

Sexual immorality has been the downfall of many Christian leaders, and it seems to be a sin to which Christian leaders are particularly susceptible. There are perhaps many reasons for this:

   a. Pastors often deal with situations that require counseling with members of the opposite sex.

   b. Day-to-day ministry frequently places leaders in close contact with co-workers of the opposite sex.

   c. In some situations, missionaries and evangelists are separated from their spouses for extended periods of time to do the work of the ministry.

   d. Like everyone else, Christian leaders do not have perfect marriages.

The command to flee immorality means that believers are to keep separating themselves far enough from immorality so they do not fall into it. The word "flee" in the Greek is in the present tense, implying continued action. Exactly the same grammatical construction is used later in 1 Corinthians 10:14 where the object is idolatry.

Applying this command personally means taking specific actions which differ from person to person and situation to situation. The Bible's teaching is clear that sin begins in the heart (James 1:14). Our sinful nature, the temptations of Satan, and the lure of the world leave us all susceptible to sexual sin. Falling into sexual sin does not usually happen suddenly and without warning. First, there are temptations, compromising situations, improper touching, unhealthy reading or movies, marriage problems, etc. The believer should start to flee immorality as soon as any of these things begin to happen.

As believers, we are not our own. Christ bought us with His own blood so that we would be His—a pure, holy, and living sacrifice.

QUESTION 21

Match the reference with the corresponding argument Paul uses in 1 Corinthians 6:14-19 to support sexual purity for believers.

Verse	Argument
1 Corinthians 6:14	Sexual sin is sin against our own body.
1 Corinthians 6:15	We will receive glorified bodies.
1 Corinthians 6:17	The Holy Spirit lives in our bodies.
1 Corinthians 6:18	We are one spirit with the Lord.
1 Corinthians 6:19	Our bodies are members of Christ.

QUESTION 22

Open your Life Notebook and record your reflections.

Part A:

Take an inventory of your life with respect to sexual temptation and warning signs. Consider whether the following statements are true of you:

- I sometimes read or view pornographic material.
- I counsel members of the opposite sex one-on-one.
- Although I am married, I sometimes do not see my spouse for long periods of time.
- I can most easily share my heart with a person of the opposite sex who is not my spouse.
- I have serious marriage problems.
- I have physical contact with members of the opposite sex other than my spouse.

Part B:

What should you do if you identify warning signs of sexual immorality in your life?

Lesson 5 Articles

Notes on 1 Corinthians

Dr. Thomas L. Constable; 2003 Edition

B. LACK OF DISCIPLINE IN THE CHURCH CHS. 5-6

The second characteristic in the Corinthian church reported to Paul that he addressed concerned a lack of discipline (cf. Gal 5:22-23). This section of the epistle has strong connections with the first major section. The lack of disciple in the church (1 Cor 5-6) reflected a crisis of authority in the church (1 Cor 1:10–4:21). The Corinthians were arrogant and valued a worldly concept of power. This carnal attitude had produced the three problems that Paul proceeded to deal with next: incest, litigation, and prostitution in the church.

1. Incest in the church ch. 5

First, the church had manifested a very permissive attitude toward a man in the congregation who was committing incest. Paul explained his own reaction to this situation and demanded that his readers take a different view of immorality than the one they held (1 Cor 5:1-8). Then he spoke to the larger issue of the Christian's relationship to the immoral both within and outside the church (1 Cor 5:9-13).

> "What is at stake is not simply a low view of sin; rather, it is the church itself: Will it follow Paul's gospel with its ethical implications? or will it continue in its present 'spirituality,' one that tolerates such sin and thereby destroys God's temple in Corinth (1 Cor 3:16-17)? Thus Paul uses this concrete example both to assert his authority and to speak to the larger issue of sexual immorality." (122)

> "The unusual feature of 5:1-13 is the manner in which the community is addressed first and more extensively than the man involved in an incestuous relationship. The congregation is distinguished by its arrogance and boasting and its failure to mourn. At the heart of Paul's rebuke is an urgent plea for a new, communal self-understanding (5:6-8). Mixing the cultic images of unleavened bread and the Passover lamb, the text pushes the Corinthians to think of themselves differently—as an unleavened community that demonstrates honesty and dependability, as a community for whom the paschal lamb has been sacrificed. The crucified Messiah lies at the heart of the new perspective, critically needed by the readers." (123)

Paul's judgment of this case 5:1-5

5:1 - "Immorality" is a general translation of the Greek word *porneia*, which means fornication, specifically sexual relations with a forbidden mate. The precise offense in this case was sexual union with the woman who had married the man's father (cf. Matt 5:27-28, 32; 15:19; 19:9; Mk 7:21). Had she been his physical mother other terms would have been more appropriate to use. Evidently the woman was his step-mother, and she may have been close to his own age.

> "The woman was clearly not the mother of the offender, and probably (although the use of *porneia* rather than *moicheia* does not prove this) she was not, at the time, the wife of the offender's father. She may have been divorced, for divorce was very common, or her husband may have been dead." (124)

The verb translated "to have," when used in sexual or marital contexts, is a euphemism for a continuing relationship in contrast to a "one night stand" (cf. 1 Cor 7:2). This man and this woman were "living together." Since the man is the object of Paul's censure, it seems that the woman was not in the church.

"The word *porneia* ('sexual immorality') in the Greek world simply meant 'prostitution,' in the sense of going to the prostitutes and paying for sexual pleasure. The Greeks were ambivalent on that matter, depending on whether one went openly to the brothels or was more discreet and went with a paramour. But the word had been picked up in Hellenistic Judaism, always pejoratively, to cover all extramarital sexual sins and aberrations, including homosexuality. It could also refer to any of these sins specifically, as it does here. In the NT the word is thus used to refer to that particular blight on Greco-Roman culture, which was almost universally countenanced, except among the Stoics. That is why *porneia* appears so often as the first item in the NT vice lists, not because Christians were sexually 'hung up,' nor because they considered this the primary sin, the 'scarlet letter,' as it were. It is the result of its prevalence in the culture, and the difficulty the early church experienced with its Gentile converts breaking with their former ways, which they did not consider immoral." (125)

The leaders of Israel and the early churches regarded fornication of all kinds as sin to avoid (Lev 18:8; Deut 22:30; 27:20; Acts 15:20, 29; 21:25). (126) As depraved as Greek culture was, even the pagans looked down on incest. (127)

5:2 - The Corinthians' attitude about this situation was even worse than the sin itself. Rather than mourning over it and disciplining the offender they took pride in it. They may have viewed it as within the bounds of Christian liberty thinking that their position in Christ made sexual morality unimportant. Another possibility is that their worldly "wisdom" encouraged them to cast off sexual restraints.

."... Paul is not here dealing with 'church discipline' as such; rather, out of his Jewish heritage he is expressing what should be the *normal* consequences of being the people of God, who are called to be his holy people (1:2). It is this lack of a sense of sin, and therefore of any ethical consequences to their life in the Spirit, that marks the Corinthian brand of spirituality as radically different from that which flows out of the gospel of Christ crucified. And it is precisely this failure to recognize the depth of their corporate sinfulness due to their arrogance that causes Paul to take such strong action as is described in the next sentence (vv. 3-5)." (128)

5:3 - Paul had spoken earlier about not judging others (1 Cor 4:5). That kind of judging had to do with one's degree of faithfulness to the Lord. Here the issue was blatant immorality. This needed dealing with, and Paul had already determined what the Corinthian Christians should do in this case even though he was not present. The case was so clear that he did not need to be present to know the man was guilty of a serious offense that required strong treatment.

5:4 - The apostle wanted the believers to view his ruling as the will of the Lord. He assured them that God would back it up with His power as they enforced the discipline. The phrase "in the name of the Lord Jesus" probably modifies "I have decided to deliver such a one to Satan for the destruction of the flesh" (v. 5) (129). In passing the following judgment Paul was acting in Jesus' name, with His authority.

5:5 - Paul had determined to deliver the man to Satan for the destruction of his flesh. Probably Paul meant that he had delivered the man to Satan, with God's permission of course, for his premature death. (130) This was the result of Peter's dealings with Ananias and Sapphira, though the text does not say he delivered them to Satan for the destruction of their flesh. God was bringing premature death on other Corinthians for their improper conduct during the Lord's Supper (1 Cor 11:30; cf. 1 Jn 5:16). We have no record that this man died prematurely, though he may have. Premature death might be his judgment (the "worst case scenario") if he did not repent.

Paul passed similar judgment on Hymenaeus and Alexander (1 Tim 1:20). In that case he said he just delivered them to Satan. He wrote nothing about the destruction of the flesh. Deliverance to Satan must mean deliverance to the authority and control of Satan in a way that is different from the way all believers are under Satan's control. Everyone is subject to temptation and demonic influence under the sovereign authority of God (cf. Job 1-2).

A variation of this view is that the delivery to Satan would eventuate in a wasting physical illness but not death (131). However the term "the destruction of the flesh" seems to imply death rather than simply disease.

A third interpretation understands the term "flesh" metaphorically as referring to the destruction of the man's sinful nature (132). The destruction of the flesh in this case refers to the mortification of the lusts of the flesh. However it seems unusual that Paul would deliver the man to Satan for this purpose. Satan would not normally put the lusts of the flesh to death but stir them up in the man. It is hard to see how handing a person over to Satan would purify him.

Still another view takes the flesh and spirit as referring to the sinful and godly character of the church rather than the individual (133). Paul may have been identifying the sinful element within the Corinthian church that needed destroying. This would result in the preservation of the spirit of the church. The main problem with this view is that Paul seems to be referring to an individual rather than to the church as a whole. Certainly the man's actions would affect the church, so it is probably proper to see some involvement of the church here even though the judgment seems to be primarily against the man.

Another interpretation is that Paul was speaking of the man's excommunication from the church (134). Probably Paul meant that he was turning the man over to live in the sphere of Satan's authority, the world, from the sphere of the Spirit's authority, the church.

I think Paul meant both excommunication and premature death. (136) His analogy concerning the Passover (1 Cor 5:6-8) stresses separating what is sinful from what it pollutes.

Is this a form of church discipline that we can and should practice today? There are no other Scripture passages in which the Lord instructed church leaders to turn sinners over to Satan. Consequently some interpreters believe this was one way in which the apostles in particular exercised their authority in the early church for the establishment of the church (cf. Acts 5). I think modern church leaders can turn people over to Satan by removing them from the fellowship of other Christians and the church. People may commit sins that may ultimately lead to their premature deaths today, and there are, of course, other biblical examples of excommunication as church discipline.

The last part of the verse gives the purpose of Paul's discipline. "Spirit" contrasts with "flesh." "Flesh" evidently refers to the body so "spirit" probably refers to the immaterial part of the man. The "day of the Lord Jesus" refers to the return of Christ at the Rapture and the judgment of believers connected with it (cf. 1 Cor 1:8). From what did his punishment save the incestuous man? It did not save him eternally since faith in Christ does that, nor did it save him from physical death since that appears to have been his punishment. Probably it saved him from a worse verdict when Christ would evaluate his stewardship of his life at the judgment seat. Evidently Paul regarded it better for this sinning Christian, as well as best for the church, that he die prematurely, assuming that he would not repent, than that he go on living. Perhaps Paul had reason to believe he would not turn from his sin but only worsen.

Some have interpreted Paul's allusion to "such a one" in 2 Corinthians 2:6-7 as referring to this incestuous man. The text does not warrant that definite a connection. "Such a one" is simply a way of referring to someone, anyone, without using his or her name (137).

The analogy of the Passover 5:6-8

Paul argued for the man's removal from the church with this analogy. It was primarily for the sake of the church that they should remove him, not for the man's sake.

5:6 - It was not good for the Corinthians to feel proud of their permissiveness (cf. v. 2). Sin spreads in the church as yeast does in dough (cf. Gal 5:9; Mk 8:15). Eventually the whole moral fabric of the congregation would suffer if the believers did not expunge this sin.

5:7 - In Jewish life it was customary to throw away all the leaven (yeast) in the house when the family prepared for the Passover celebration (Ex 12:15; 13:6-7). They did this so the bread they made for Passover and the feast of Unleavened Bread that followed would be completely free of leaven. This may have been for hygienic reasons as well as because of the symbolism of the act. This is what the Corinthians needed to do as a church so they could worship God acceptably. In one sense they were already free of leaven; their trust in Christ had removed their sins. However in another sense they possessed leaven since they had tolerated sin in their midst. Paul described the same situation earlier in this epistle when he said the Corinthians were saints (1 Cor 1:2) even though they were not behaving as saints. God had sanctified them in their position, but they were in need of progressive sanctification. They needed to become what they were. This is Paul's basic exhortation.

> "1 Corinthians emphasizes that the gospel issues in transformed lives, that salvation in Christ is not complete without God/Christlike attitudes and behavior.

> "The classic expression of Paul's understanding of the relationship between gospel and ethics (indicative and imperative) is to be found in 5:7.

> "Ethics for Paul is ultimately a *theological* issue pure and simple. Everything has to do with God and with what God is about in Christ and the Spirit. Thus (1) the *purpose* (or basis) of Christian ethics is the glory of God (10:31); (2) the *pattern* for such ethics is Christ (11:1); (3) the *principle* is love, precisely because it alone reflects God's character (8:2-3; 13:1-8); and (4) the *power* is the Spirit (6:11, 19)" (138).

The mention of the removal of leaven before the Passover led Paul to develop his analogy further. Christ, the final Passover Lamb, had already died. (139) Therefore it was all the more important that the believers clean out the remaining leaven immediately.

5:8 - The feast of Unleavened Bread began the day after Passover. The Jews regarded both Passover and the feast of Unleavened Bread as one festival (cf. Ex 23:15; 34:18; Deut 16:6). As believers whose Pascal Lamb had died, it was necessary that the Corinthians keep celebrating the feast and worshipping God free of leaven that symbolically represented sin. The old leaven probably refers to the sins that marked the Corinthians before their conversion. Malice and wickedness probably stand for all sins of motive and action. Sincerity and truth are the proper motive and action with which we should worship God. This verse constitutes a summary exhortation.

The Christian's relationship to fornicators 5:9-13

Paul proceeded to deal with the larger issue of the believer's relationship to fornicators inside and outside the church. He did this so his readers would understand their responsibility in this area of their lives in their immoral city and abandon their arrogant self-righteousness.

5:9 - Paul had written this congregation a previous letter that is no longer extant. (140) In it he urged the Corinthians to avoid associating with fornicators. The same Greek word, *pornois*, occurs here as in verse 1. In view of this instruction the Corinthians' toleration of the incestuous brother in the church was especially serious.

5:10 - However, Paul hastened to clarify that in writing what he had he did not mean a believer should never associate with fornicators outside the church. He did not mean either that they should avoid contact with unbelievers who were sinful in their attitudes and actions toward people and God. Even our holy Lord Jesus Christ ate with publicans and sinners. Such isolationism would require that they stop living in the real world and exist in a Christian ghetto insulated from all contact with unbelievers. This approach to life is both unrealistic and unfaithful to God who has called us to be salt and light in the world (Matt 5:13-16; 28:19-20). Many Christians today struggle with an unbiblical view of separation that tends more toward isolationism than sanctification.

In 2 Thessalonians 3:14 Paul used the same phrase (Gr. *sunanamignusthai*, lit. mix up together), translated "to associate with" (v. 9), with regard to busybodies in the church. There not associating was to be the last resort of faithful believers in their social dealings with their disobedient brethren (cf. 1 Thess 4:11-12; 5:14). They were not to treat them as enemies, however, but as brothers. Probably Paul had the same type of disciplinary behavior in view here. Some interpreters view this as excluding the offender from the community of believers gathered for worship. (141) I tend to think it means not socializing with such a person.

5:11 - Paul now clarified that he had meant that the Corinthian Christians should not associate with such a person if he or she professed to be a believer. The Greek phrase *tis adelphos onomazomenos* literally means one who bears the name brother. The translation "so-called brother" (NASB) implies that the sinner was only a professing Christian. Only God and that person knew for sure whether he or she was a genuine Christian or not. (142) In particular they were to exclude such a person from table fellowship with the other Christians in the church.

In the early history of the church eating together was a large part of the fellowship that the Christians enjoyed with one another (cf. Acts 2:46-47; 6:1; et al.). To exclude a Christian from this circle of fellowship would have made a much stronger statement to him than it normally does today in American church life.

> "The Apostle is not thinking of Holy Communion, in which case the *mede* ["not even"] would be quite out of place: he is thinking of social meals; 'Do not invite him to your house or accept his invitations.'" (143)

This exclusion was a strong form of discipline that Paul designed to confront the offender with his or her behavior and encourage him or her to repent. Some modern congregations have adopted the policy of excluding such offenders from participation in the Lord's Supper. However this form of discipline does not carry much impact when a congregation observes the Lord's Supper only monthly or quarterly. Modern church leaders need to give careful thought to what form of discipline would have the same impact and effect on such a person in their particular society.

> "Church discipline is not a group of 'pious policemen' out to catch a criminal. Rather, it is a group of brokenhearted brothers and sisters seeking to restore an erring member of the family." (144)

Paul's list of sins here seems to be suggestive rather than comprehensive (cf. 1 Cor 6:9-10). It includes fornicators, the greedy, idolaters, people who abuse others verbally, drunkards and perhaps others addicted to enslaving substances, and swindlers. The failure of many church leaders to discipline professing Christians who practice these things today is a sad commentary on the carnality of the modern church.

5:12 - Paul's authority as an apostle did not extend to judging and prescribing discipline on unbelievers for their sins. He did, of course, assess the condition of unbelievers (e.g., Rom 1; et al.), but that is not what is in view here. His ministry and the ministry of other Christians in judging and disciplining sin took place only within church life. Judging means more than criticizing. It involves disciplining, too, as the context shows.

5:13 - Judging and disciplining unbelievers is the Lord's work. Obviously this does not mean that Christians should remain aloof when justice needs maintaining in the world. God has delegated human government to people as His vice-regents (e.g., Gen 9:5-6). As human beings Christians should bear their fair share of the weight of responsibility in these matters. The point here is that the Corinthians and all Christians should exercise discipline in church life to an extent beyond what is our responsibility in civil life.

Paul did not explain the objective in view in church discipline in this passage. Elsewhere we learn that it is always the restoration of the offender to fellowship with God and His people (2 Cor 2:5-11). It is also the purity of the church. (145)

Chapter 5 deals with the subject of immoral conduct by professing Christians. (146) The first part (1 Cor 5:1-8) contains directions for dealing with a particular case of fornication that existed in the church. The Corinthian Christians were taking a much too permissive attitude toward sin. The second part (1 Cor 5:9-13) clarifies our duty in all instances of immoral conduct inside and outside the church.

2. Litigation in the church 6:1-11

The apostle continued to deal with the general subject of discipline in the church that he began in 1 Cor 5:1. He proceeded to point out some other glaring instances of inconsistency that had their roots in the Corinthians' lax view of sin. Rather than looking to unsaved judges to solve their internal conflicts, they should have exercised discipline among themselves in these cases. (147)

> "In this section Paul is dealing with a problem which specially affected the Greeks. The Jews did not ordinarily go to law in the public law-courts at all; they settled things before the elders of the village or the elders of the Synagogue; to them justice was far more a thing to be settled in a family spirit than in a legal spirit. . . . The Greeks were in fact famous, or notorious, for their love of going to law." (148)

> ." . . the congregation's root problem lies in its lack of theological depth. It shames itself by not understanding itself as an eschatological community ('Do you not know that we are to judge angels?') and as a community redeemed by Christ." (149)

> "Paul has not finished with the theme of church discipline in regard to sexual life; see vi. 12 and chapter vii; but in v. 12 f. he had spoken of judgement [sic], and this brings to his mind another feature of Corinthian life of which he had heard . . ." (150)

The shame on the church 6:1-6

The failure of the two men who were suing each other was another evidence that the Corinthian church was not functioning properly. It indicated how lacking in true wisdom these Christians were. Paul argued with a series of rhetorical questions in this pericope.

6:1 - Again Paul used a rhetorical question to make a point (cf. 1 Cor 3:16; 4:21). The answer was self-evident to him.

In view of the context the "neighbor" (NASB) must be a fellow Christian. The "unrighteous" or "ungodly" (NIV) contrasts with the "saints" and refers to an unbeliever (v. 6). When people had disputes with each other in Corinth and wanted official arbitration, they went to the *bema* (judgment seat) in the center of town.

> "The phrase translated 'has a dispute' is a technical term for a lawsuit, or legal action; and the verb *krino* ('judge') in the middle voice can carry the sense of 'going to law,' or 'bringing something for judgment,' as it does here." (151)

> "He does not mean that Christian courts ought to be instituted, but that Christian disputants should submit to Christian arbitration." (152)

6:2 - The earlier revelation that the saints will have a part in judging unbelievers in the future may be Daniel 7:18, 22, 27. This judgment will evidently take place just after the Lord returns to earth at His second coming to set up His millennial kingdom. We will be with Him then (1 Thess 4:17).

Since the Lord will delegate the authority to judge unbelievers to Christians in the future, Paul concluded that we are competent to settle disputes among ourselves now. In the light of future eschatological judgment, any decisions that believers must make in church courts now are relatively trifling. (153)

Obviously some cases involving Christians arguing with one another are more difficult to sort out than some of those involving unbelievers. Paul's point was that Christians are generally competent to settle disputes between people. After all, we have the help and wisdom of the indwelling Holy Spirit available to us.

Earlier Paul wrote that the Corinthians were judging him (cf. 1 Cor 4:3-5, 7), which was inappropriate in view of God's final judgment. Now they were judging in the courts, which was inappropriate since the saints will participate in eschatological judging.

6:3 - Evidently God had not revealed the fact that believers will play a role in judging angels earlier in Scripture. He apparently revealed that for the first time here through Paul (cf. Jude 6).

6:4 - The first part of this verse seems to refer to the disputes and judicial procedures the Christians should have used with one another rather than to the heathen law courts. The context seems to argue for this interpretation. Paul was speaking here of Christians resolving their differences in the church rather than in the civil law courts.

The second part of the verse is capable of two interpretations. Paul may have been speaking ironically, as the next verse may imply (cf. 1 Cor 4:8). If so, he may have meant that the Corinthians should select the least qualified people in the church to settle these disputes. His meaning in this case was that any Christian was capable of settling disputes among his brethren. He did not mean that the Corinthians should really choose as judges the most feebleminded Christians in the church. The statement is ironical. This is the interpretation of the NIV. (154)

On the other hand he may have been asking a question rather than making an ironical statement. This is how the NASB translators have taken Paul's words. In this case he was asking if the Corinthians chose as judges in their church disputes the members who had the fewest qualifications to arbitrate. The obvious answer would be no. They would choose the best qualified brethren. This interpretation understands Paul as advocating the choice of the best qualified in the church forthrightly rather than ironically. This seems to me to be a better interpretation (155).

A third possibility is that Paul really advocated the selection of the least qualified in the church for these judicial functions. He was not speaking ironically. The main argument against this view is its improbability. Why choose less qualified people for any job when better qualified people are available?

6:5-6 - What was to the Corinthians' shame? It was that by going into secular courts to settle their church problems they seemed to be saying that there was no one in their church wise enough to settle these matters. Certainly they could count on the Holy Spirit to give them the wisdom they needed to do this (cf. John 14:26; 16:13).

> "A church has come to a pretty pass when its members believe that they are more likely to get justice from *unbelievers* than from their own brothers." (156)

Clearly this church did not understand its identity as an eschatological community nor did it demonstrate much concern about its witness to the world.

> "Every Jewish community throughout the Roman Empire and beyond its frontiers had its own *bet-din*, its own competent machinery for the administration of civil justice within its own membership; the least that could be expected of a Christian church was that it should make similar arrangements if necessary, and not wash its dirty linen in public." (157)

This passage does not deal with how Christians should respond when pagans defraud or sue us. We should participate in public litigation only as a last resort.

Paul's judgment in the matter 6:7-11

The apostle now addressed the two men involved in the lawsuit but wrote with the whole church in view.

6:7 - By hauling one another into court the Corinthians were intent on winning damages for themselves. Evidently a business or property dispute was the root of this case (cf. v. 10). Paul reminded them that they had already lost before the judge gave his verdict. The shame of people who professed to love one another and put the welfare of others before their own suing each other was a defeat in itself. This defeat was far more serious than any damages they may have had to pay. It would be better to suffer the wrong or the cheating than to fight back in such an unchristian way (Matt 5:39-40; 1 Pet 2:19-24).

> "It is possible that this use of *meth heauton* ["with your own selves"] for *met allelon* ["with one another"] is deliberate, in order to show that in bringing a suit against a fellow-Christian they were bringing a suit against themselves, so close was the relationship." (158)

Christians should be willing to give to one another rather than trying to get from one another. In other words, there should be no going to court with one another at all. Nevertheless if the Corinthians insisted on going to court, it should be a court of believers in the church, not unbelievers outside the church.

6:8 - An even more shocking condition was that some of the Christians in Corinth were more than the victims of wrong and fraud. They were the perpetrators of these things (cf. Matt 5:39-41).

6:9-10 - Who are the "unrighteous" (NASB) or "wicked" (NIV) in view? Paul previously used this word (Gr. *adikos*) of the unsaved in verse 1 (cf. v. 6 where he called them unbelievers). However he also used it of the Corinthian Christians in verse 8: "you yourselves wrong [*adikeo*]."

Christians as well as unbelievers have been guilty of unrighteous conduct, even all the offenses listed in these verses. Therefore what Paul said about the unrighteous in this verse seems to apply to anyone who is unrighteous in his or her behavior whether saved or unsaved. It does not apply just to the unrighteous in their standing before God, namely, unbelievers. (159)

What will be true of the unrighteous? They will "not inherit the kingdom of God." Elsewhere Paul used this expression to describe the consequences of the behavior of unbelievers when he compared it to the behavior of believers (cf. Gal 5:21; Eph 5:5).. (160) That appears to be its meaning here too. Paul was contrasting what the Corinthians did before their conversion with their conduct after conversion (v. 11). He did not mean that Christians are incapable of practicing these sins, but they typically characterize unbelievers.

Paul warned his readers about being deceived on this subject (v. 9). (161) Probably many of them failed to see that how Christians choose to live here and now will affect our eternal reward. Many Christians today fail to see this too. The fact that we are eternally secure should not lead us to conclude that it does not matter how we live now even though we will all end up in heaven. (162)

The meanings of most of these sins are clear, but a few require some comment. "Effeminate" (NASB) or "male prostitutes" (NIV; Gr. *malakoi*) refers to the passive role in a homosexual union whereas "homosexuals" refers to the active role. (163)

> "We can scarcely realize how riddled the ancient world was with it [homosexuality]. Even so great a man as Socrates practised [*sic*] it; Plato's dialogue *The Symposium* is always said to be one of the greatest works on love in the world, but its subject is not natural but unnatural love. Fourteen out of the first fifteen Roman Emperors practised unnatural vice." (164)

Note the seriousness of the sin of covetousness or greed (cf. 1 Cor 5:10-11; 6:8). Greed may manifest itself in a desire for what one should not have (Ex 20:17; Rom 7:7) or in an excessive desire for what one may legitimately have (Eph 5:5; Col 3:5).

> "The universality of wine drinking was of course due to the inadequate water-supplies. But normally the Greeks were sober people, for their drink was three parts of wine mixed with two of water." (165)

"The order of the ten kinds of offenders is unstudied. He enumerates sins which were prevalent at Corinth just as they occur to him." (166)

6:11 - Some of the Corinthian Christians had been fornicators and had practiced the other sins Paul cited before they trusted in Christ. However the blood of Christ had cleansed them, and God had set them apart to a life of holiness. The Lord had declared them righteous through union with Christ by faith (cf. 1 Cor 1:30) and through the sanctifying work of the Holy Spirit who indwelt them. He had made them saints. Consequently they needed to live like saints.

> "The quite unconscious Trinitarianism of the concluding words should be noted: *the Lord Jesus Christ, the Spirit, our God*. Trinitarian theology, at least in its New Testament form, did not arise out of speculation, but out of the fact that when Christians spoke of what God had done for them and in them they often found themselves obliged to use threefold language of this kind." (167)

This verse does not support the idea that once a person has experienced eternal salvation he will live a life free of gross sin. Normally this is the consequence of conversion thanks to the sanctifying work of the Holy Spirit. However believers can grieve and quench the Holy Spirit's ministry in their lives. In this letter we have seen that not only were some of the Corinthian saints fornicators before their conversion, but one of them had continued in or returned to that sin (1 Cor 5:1).

Paul's point in this whole section (vv. 1-11) was that genuine Christians should not continue in or return to the sinful practices that mark unbelievers. We should become what we are because of what Jesus Christ has done for us. This appeal runs throughout the New Testament and is latent in every exhortation to pursue godliness. It is especially strong in this epistle. Rather than assuming that believers will not continually practice sin, the inspired writers constantly warned us of that possibility.

3. Prostitution in the church 6:12-20

The apostle proceeded to point out the sanctity of the believer's body as the temple of the Holy Spirit. He wanted to help his readers realize the seriousness of the sins that marked them to some extent as a church.

> "The Greeks always looked down on the body. There was a proverbial saying, 'The body is a tomb.' Epictetus said, 'I am a poor soul shackled to a corpse.'" (168)

> "Apparently some men within the Christian community are going to prostitutes and are arguing for the right to do so. Being people of the Spirit, they imply, has moved them to a higher plane, the realm of the spirit, where they are unaffected by behavior that has merely to do with the body. So Paul proceeds from the affirmation of v. 11 to an attack on this theological justification.

> "As before, the gospel itself is at stake, not simply the resolution of an ethical question. The Corinthian pneumatics' understanding of spirituality has allowed them both a false view of freedom ('everything is permissible') and of the body ('God will destroy it'), from which basis they have argued that going to prostitutes is permissible because the body doesn't matter." (170)

This is one of the more important passages in the New Testament on the human body.

Refutation of the Corinthians' false premises 6:12-14

Paul began by arguing against his recipients' distortion of Christian freedom and their misunderstanding of the nature of the body. (171)

6:12 - Paul was and is famous as the apostle of Christian liberty. (172) He saw early in his Christian life and clearly that the Christian is not under the Mosaic Law. His Epistle to the Galatians is an exposition of this theme. He preached this freedom wherever he went. Unfortunately he was always subject to misinterpretation. Some of his hearers concluded that he advocated no restraints whatsoever in Christian living. Perhaps those in Corinth who were practicing sexual immorality and suing their brethren in pagan courts appealed to Paul to support their actions, though they took liberty farther than Paul did. (173)

> "'Everything is permissible for me' is almost certainly a Corinthian theological slogan." (174)

> "It could have been argued in Corinth . . . that the right course was for a husband to keep his wife 'pure', and, if necessary, find occasional sexual satisfaction in a harlot." (175)

In this verse the apostle restated his general maxim but qualified it (cf. 1 Cor 10:23). Legality is not the only test the Christian should apply to his or her behavior. Is the practice also profitable (helpful, admirable, beneficial, expedient, good)? Furthermore even though I have authority over some practice, might it gain control over me? The Christian should always be able to submit to the Lord's control. We should give the Lord, not anyone or anything else, control of our bodies.

> "Freedom is not to be for self but for others. The real question is not whether an action is 'lawful' or 'right' or even 'all right,' but whether it is good, whether it benefits. . . . Truly Christian conduct is not predicated on whether I have the right to do something, but whether my conduct is helpful to those about me." (176)

> "We have no longer any right to do what in itself is innocent, when our doing it will have a bad effect on others. . . . We have no longer any right to do what in itself is innocent, when experience has proved that our doing it has a bad effect on ourselves" (177)

6:13-14 - The first part of this verse is similar to the two parts of the previous verse. It contains a statement that is true, but a qualifier follows. Food is not a matter of spiritual significance for the Christian, except that gluttony is a sin. As far as what we eat goes, we may eat anything in the will of God (Mark 7:19). He has not forbidden any foods for spiritual reasons, though there may be physical reasons we may choose not to eat certain things. Both food and the stomach are temporal. Paul referred to food here not because it was an issue but to set up the issue of the body and sexual immorality. As food is for the stomach, so the body is for the Lord.

> "Not only are meats made for the belly, but the belly, which is essential to physical existence, is made for meats, and cannot exist without them." (178)

Paul constructed his argument like this:

Proposition 1:

Part 1: Food is for the stomach [A, B], and the stomach is for food [B, A].

Part 2: God will destroy the stomach [B] and the food [A].

Proposition 2:

Part 1: The body is for the Lord [A, B] (not for sexual immorality), and the Lord is for the body [B, A].

Part 2: God has raised the Lord [B], and He will raise us [A] (by His power).

One might conclude, and some in Corinth were evidently doing so, that since sex was also physical and temporal it was also irrelevant spiritually. (179) However this is a false deduction. The body is part of what the Lord saved and sanctified. Therefore it is for Him, and we should use it for His glory, not for fornication. Furthermore the Lord has a noble purpose and destiny for our bodies. He is for them in that sense.

The Lord will resurrect the bodies of most Christians in the future, all but those that He catches away at the Rapture (1 Thess. 4:17). The resurrection of our bodies shows that God has plans for them. Some in

Corinth did not believe in the resurrection, but Paul dealt with that later (ch. 15). Here he simply stated the facts without defending them.

> "The body of the believer is *for* the Lord because through Christ's resurrection God has set in motion the reality of our own resurrection. This means that the believer's physical body is to be understood as 'joined' to Christ's own 'body' that was raised from the dead." (180)

Arguments against participating in prostitution 6:15-17

Building on the preceding theological base, Paul argued against participating in fornication with prostitutes. The Corinthians had not understood the nature of sexual intercourse or the nature of Christian conversion.

6:15 - Another rhetorical question affirmed the truth. As we are members of Christ's body, so our bodies are members of Him. This is not just clever word play. Our physical bodies are just as much a part of Christ—united with Him in a genuine spiritual union—as we are part of the mystical body of Christ, the church. Paul was not speaking here of the believer's union with Christ by becoming members of His mystical body, the church (1 Cor 12:12-26). He was metaphorically speaking of our individual union with Christ's physical body.

When a Christian has sexual relations with a prostitute, he or she takes what belongs to God and gives it to someone else. This is stealing from God. When a Christian marries, this does not happen because God has ordained and approves of marriage (cf. 1 Cor 7:14). He permits us to share our bodies with our lawful mates. Taking a member of Christ and uniting it to a harlot also involves the Lord in that immoral act. Paul's revulsion at the thought of this comes through graphically in his characteristic *me genoito* (lit. "May it not happen!").

> "Sex outside of marriage is like a man robbing a bank: he gets something, but it is not his and he will one day pay for it. Sex within marriage can be like a person putting money into a bank: there is safety, security, and he will collect dividends. Sex within marriage can build a relationship that brings joys in the future; but sex apart from marriage has a way of weakening future relationships, as every Christian marriage counselor will tell you." (181)

6:16 - Paul urged his readers not to think of sexual intercourse as simply a physical linking of two people for the duration of their act. Intercourse involves the whole person, not just the body. It is the most intimate sharing that human beings experience. A spiritual union takes place. Sexual relations affect the inner unseen conditions of the individuals involved very deeply. This is what is in view in the reference to two people becoming "one flesh" in Genesis 2:24. Consequently it is improper to put sexual relations on the same level of significance as eating food.

6:17 - In contrast to the union that takes place when two people have sex, the person who trusts Christ unites with Him in an even stronger and more pervasive oneness. This is an even stronger spiritual union. Consequently, it is a very serious thing to give to a prostitute what God has so strongly united to Christ.

The argument again contains a chiasm.

A Your bodies are members of Christ's body.

> **B** So they must not be members of a prostitute's body.

> **B'** Joined to a prostitute your members become one body with her.

A' Joined to Christ your members become one spirit with Him.

The reason participating in prostitution is wrong 6:18-20

Sexual immorality is wrong, Paul concluded, because it involves sinning against one's body, which in the case of believers belongs to the Lord through divine purchase.

6:18 - In conclusion, believers should flee from fornication (*porneian*). Joseph is a good example to follow (Gen 39:12). Fornication is more destructive to the sinner than other sins because the people who engage in it cannot undo their act. Gluttony and drunkenness hurt the body as well, but they involve excess in things morally neutral, and abstinence may correct their effects.

Fornication is also a specially serious sin because it involves placing the body, which is the Lord's (vv. 19-20), under the control of another illegitimate partner (cf. 1 Cor 7:4). (182) No other sin has this result. All other sins are outside or apart from the body in this sense.

> "Does God then forbid the restoration of fallen leaders? No. Does He leave open the possibility? Yes. Does that possibility look promising? Yes and no. If both the life and reputation of the fallen elder can be rehabilitated, his prospects for restoration are promising. However, rehabilitating his reputation, not to mention his life, will be particularly difficult, for squandering one's reputation is 'a snare of the devil' (1 Tim 3:7), and he does not yield up his prey easily." (183)

6:19 - Another rhetorical question makes a strong important statement. Previously Paul taught his readers that the Corinthian church was a temple (*naos*; 1 Cor 3:16). The believer's body is also one. The Holy Spirit is really indwelling each of these temples (Rom 8:9). (184) He is a gift to us from God (cf. 1 Thess 4:8). He is the best gift God has given us thus far.

Consequently we have a moral obligation to the Giver. Moreover because He indwells us we belong to Him.

6:20 - Furthermore, God has purchased (Gr. *agorazo*) every Christian with a great price, the blood of Jesus Christ (Rom 3:24-25; Eph 1:7; et al.). We belong to Him for a second reason. In view of this we should glorify God in our bodies rather than degrading Him through fornication (cf. Rom 12:1-2). Usually the New Testament emphasis is on redemption leading to freedom from sin (e.g., Gal 3:13; 4:5; Rev 5:9; 14:3), but here it is on redemption leading to faithfulness to God. Even our physical bodies are to be faithful to the Lord with whom we are joined.

> "The reason to glorify God in the body and not engage in sexual immorality is rooted in a new way of understanding the self." (185)

> "What Paul seems to be doing is taking over their own theological starting point, namely, that they are 'spiritual' because they have the Spirit, and redirecting it to include the sanctity of the body. The reality of the indwelling Spirit is now turned against them. They thought the presence of the Spirit meant a negation of the body; Paul argues the exact opposite: The presence of the Spirit in their present bodily existence is God's affirmation of the body." (186)

Paul's solution to the problem of the lack of discipline (1 Cor 5-6) was the same as his solution to the problem of divisions in the church (1 Cor 1:10-4:21). He led his readers back to the Cross (1 Cor 6:20; cf. 1 Cor 1:23-25).

Incest was one manifestation of carnality in the church (1 Cor 5), suing fellow believers in the public courts was another (1 Cor 6:1-11), and going to prostitutes was a third (1 Cor 6:12-10). Nevertheless the underlying problem was a loose view of sin, a view the unbelievers among whom the Corinthian Christians lived took. In this attitude, as in their attitude toward wisdom (1 Cor 1:10–4:21), their viewpoint was different from that of the Apostle Paul and God. God inspired these sections of the epistle to transform their outlook and ours on these subjects.

Bibliography

122. Fee, *The First . . .,* p. 197.

123. Cousar, "The Theological . . .," p. 98.

124. Robertson and Plummer, p. 96. Cf. Barclay, p. 49.

125. Fee, *The First . . .,* pp. 199-200.

126. If the guilty man's father was still alive and married to the woman, adultery would also have been involved. Most interpreters have concluded that this was a case of incest rather than incest and adultery. If Paul had been living under the Mosaic Law, he should have prescribed the death penalty for both the guilty man and the woman (Lev. 18:8, 29), but he lived under the New Covenant and advocated a different penalty (v. 5).

127. Johnson, p. 1236.

128. Fee, *The First . . .,* p. 203. See also Barrett, p. 122.

129. See Fee, *The First . . .,* pp. 206-8, for supporting arguments.

130. Advocates of this view include H. Conzelmann, *1 Corinthians: A Commentary on the First Epistle to the Corinthians,* p. 97; S. M. Gilmour, "Pastoral Care in the New Testament Church," *New Testament Studies* 10 (1963-64):395; J. C. Hurd Jr., *The Origin of I Corinthians,* p.137, p. 286, n. 5; G. W. H. Lampe, "Church Discipline and the Interpretation of the Epistles to the Corinthians," in *Christian History and Interpretation: Studies Presented to John Knox,* pp. 349, 353; Morris, pp. 88-89; Johnson, p. 1237; and Bruce, pp. 54-55.

131. Advocates include William Barclay, *By What Authority?* p. 118; M. Dods, *The First Epistle to the Corinthians,* p. 118; H. Olshausen, *Biblical Commentary on St. Paul's First and Second Epistles to the Corinthians,* p. 90; H. Ridderbos, *Paul: An Outline of His Theology,* p. 471; W. G. H. Simon, *The First Epistle to the Corinthians: Introduction and Commentary,* p. 78; and M. E. Thrall, *The First and Second Letters of Paul to the Corinthians,* p. 40.

132. See F. W. Grosheide, *Commentary on the First Epistles to the Corinthians,* p. 123; R. C. H. Lenski, *The Interpretation of St. Paul's First and Second Epistles to the Corinthians,* p. 217; J. J. Lias, *The First Epistle to the Corinthians,* p. 67; and G. Campbell Morgan, *The Corinthian Letters of Paul,* p. 83;

133. B. Campbell, "Flesh and Spirit in 1 Cor 5:5: An Exercise in Rhetorical Criticism of the NT," **Journal of the Evangelical Theological Society** 36:3 (September 1993):341. Campbell saw his view as similar to those of K. P. Donfried, "Justification and Last Judgment in Paul," *Interpretation* 30 (April 1976):150-51; H. von Campenhausen, *Ecclesiastical Authority and Spiritual Power in the Church of the First Three Centuries,* pp. 134-135, n. 50; and the early church father Tertullian.

134. Fee, *The First . . .,* pp. 208-15; Barclay, *The Letters . . .,* p. 50; Robertson, 4:113.

135. Fee, *The First . . .,* p. 209. See also Craig L. Blomberg's discussion of this verse in William D. Mounce, *Basics of Biblical Greek Grammar: Second Edition,* p. 54.

136. Cf. Lowery, p. 514.

137. Bruce, p. 54.

138. Fee, "Toward a . . .," pp. 51, 53.

139. A type is a divinely intended illustration of something else, the antitype. A type may be a person (cf. Rom. 5:14), a thing (cf. Heb. 10:19-20), an event (cf. 1 Cor. 10:11), a ceremony, as here, or an institution (cf. Heb 9:11-12).

140. See my comments on this letter in the Introduction section of these notes.

141. E.g., Fee, *The First . . .*, p. 226.

142. F. F. Bruce, *1 and 2 Thessalonians*, p. 210, regarded this person as not a genuine believer. Robert N. Wilkin presented evidence that the man in view was a genuine Christian in "The So-Called So-Called Brother," *Grace Evangelical Society News* 6:10 (October 1991):2-3. The important point is that this person's behavior threw into question whether he was a genuine Christian or not.

143. Robertson and Plummer, p. 107.

144. Wiersbe, 1:586.

145. For general studies of church discipline, see J. Carl Laney, "The Biblical Practice of Church Discipline," *Bibliotheca Sacra* 143:572 (October-December 1986):353-64; and Ted G. Kitchens, "Perimeters of Corrective Church Discipline," *Bibliotheca Sacra* 148:590 (April-June 1991):201-13. On the subject of lawsuits against local churches and church leaders who practice church discipline, see Jay A. Quine, "Court Involvement in Church Discipline," *Bibliotheca Sacra* 149:593 (January-March 1992):60-73, and 594 (April-June 1992):223-36.

146. See Timothy D. Howell, "The Church and the AIDS Crisis," *Bibliotheca Sacra* 149:593 (January-March 1992):74-82.

147. Gallio had refused to get involved in Jewish controversies in Corinth and had told the Jews to deal with these matters themselves (Acts 18:14-16). Paul now counseled a similar approach for the Christians.

148. Barclay, *The Letters . . .*, pp. 55, 56.

149. Cousar, "The Theological . . .," pp. 98-99.

150. Barrett, p. 134.

151. Fee, *The First . . .*, p. 231.

152. Robertson and Plummer, p. 111.

153. The marginal reading in the NASB "try the trivial cases" probably gives the better sense than "constitute the smallest courts." See Fee, *The First . . .*, pp. 233-34.

154. See also Robertson and Plummer, p. 113.

155. See also Barrett, p. 137.

156. Ibid., p. 138.

157. Bruce, *1 and 2 Corinthians,* p. 59.

158. Robertson and Plummer, p. 116.

159. MacArthur took the reference as describing only unbelievers, pp. 127-29. See also J. Dwight Pentecost, *Thy Kingdom Come*, p. 283.

160. Inheriting the kingdom and entering the kingdom are synonyms in the Gospels (cf. Matt. 19:16; Mark 10:17; Luke 18:18).

161. René A. López, "Does the Vice List in 1 Corinthians 6:9-10 Describe Believers or Unbelievers?" *Bibliotheca Sacra* 164:653 (January-March 2007):59-73, concluded that Paul was exhorting Corinthian believers to live like saints.

162. See Wall.

163. See P. Michael Ukleja, "Homosexuality in the New Testament," *Bibliotheca Sacra* 140:560 (October-December 1983):350-58; Sherwood A. Cole, "Biology, Homosexuality, and Moral Culpability,"

Bibliotheca Sacra 154:615 (July-September 1997):355-66. David E. Malick showed that Paul was condemning all homosexual relationships, not just "abuses" in homosexual behavior, in "The Condemnation of Homosexuality in 1 Corinthians 6:9," *Bibliotheca Sacra* 150:600 (October-December 1993):479-92.

164. Barclay, *The Letters . . .*, p. 60.

165. Ibid., p. 59.

166. Robertson and Plummer, p. 119.

167. Barrett, p. 143.

168. Barclay, *The Letters . . .,* p. 62.

169. Johnson, p. 1238.

170. Fee, *The First . . .,* pp. 250-51.

171. The influence of Greek dualism on the Corinthians continues to be obvious.

172. Similarly the Protestant reformers fell under the same criticism by their Roman Catholic opponents. The Catholics said that the reformers were teaching that since Christians are saved by grace they could live sinful lives. Unfortunately John Calvin's successor in Geneva, Theodore Beza (1519-1605), overreacted and argued that a true Christian *cannot* commit gross sin. This assertion led to the conclusion that the basis of assurance of salvation is the presence of fruit in the life rather than the promise of God (e.g., John 6:47; et al.). This view, that a true Christian will not commit gross sin, has become popular in reformed theology, but it goes further than Scripture does. Scripture never makes this claim but constantly warns Christians against abusing their liberty in Christ and turning it into a license to sin. See Dillow, pp. 245-69.

173. See Robert N. Wilkin, "Are All Things Lawful for Believers?" *Grace Evangelical Society Newsletter* 4:7 (July 1989):2.

174. Fee, *The First . . .*, p. 251. Cf. 10:23.

175. Barrett, p. 145.

176. Fee, *The First . . .*, p. 252.

177. Robertson and Plummer, p. 122.

178. Ibid., p. 123.

179. Barrett, p. 147.

180. Fee, *The First . . .*, p. 258.

181. Wiersbe, 1:589.

182. Fee, *The First . . .*, p. 262.

183. Jay E. Smith, "Can Fallen Leaders Be Restored to Leadership? *Bibliotheca Sacra* 151:604 (October-December 1994):480.

184. See Sweeney, p. 629.

185. Cousar, "The Theological . . .," p. 99.

186. Fee, *The First . . .*, p. 264.

Lesson 5 Notes

Defiant sin: The sin is described literally as acting "with a high hand." The expression means that someone would do something with deliberate defiance, with an arrogance in spite of what the Lord said. It is as if the sinner was about to attack God, or at least lifting his hand against God. The implication of the expression is that it was done in full knowledge of the law (especially since this contrasts throughout with the sins of ignorance). Blatant defiance of the Word of the Lord is dealt with differently (from NET Bible, note on Num 15:30-31).

Lesson 5 Self Check

QUESTION 1

Church discipline is the responsibility of the whole church, not just the church leaders. *True or False?*

QUESTION 2

The most likely meaning in 1 Corinthians 5:5 for "the flesh" in "turn this man over to Satan for the destruction of the flesh" is the physical body. *True or False?*

QUESTION 3

Church discipline is not punishment. *True or False?*

QUESTION 4

What does "remove the evil person from among you" mean (1 Cor 5:13)?

- A. Cut off Christian fellowship with the person.
- B. Stop doing business with the person.
- C. Stop talking to the person for any reason.
- D. Avoid the sinner's family.

QUESTION 5

When a believer is removed from the church for serious sin, he loses his salvation. *True or False?*

QUESTION 6

Instead of one believer taking another believer to court, he should appeal to the church for help in resolving the dispute. *True or False?*

QUESTION 7

If a Christian has a homosexual orientation, then the practice of homosexual acts is acceptable. *True or False?*

QUESTION 8

Why are believers competent to judge disputes between church members?

- A. Such cases are easy to decide
- B. In the future, believers will judge angels
- C. Believers have the gift of distinguishing spirits
- D. Believers are unbiased

QUESTION 9

"All things are lawful for me" is most likely a slogan from the church at Corinth. *True or False?*

QUESTION 10

The word "flee" in the command "flee sexual immorality" (1 Cor 6:18) is in the past tense in the Greek. *True or False?*

Unit 2 Exam

QUESTION 1

A sin "with a high hand" is sometimes called a defiant sin. *True or False?*

QUESTION 2

On judgment day, what will Christian workers be judged for?

    A. How long they have been in the ministry

    B. The size of their ministry

    C. How well known their ministry is

    D. The quality of their ministry

QUESTION 3

Christians sometimes behave just like unsaved people. *True or False?*

QUESTION 4

Church discipline may include capital punishment. *True or False?*

QUESTION 5

Triumphalism is a theological error also known as over-realized eschatology. *True or False?*

QUESTION 6

By calling the church at Corinth "carnal" (or influenced by the flesh), Paul hoped they would examine themselves and repent. *True or False?*

QUESTION 7

Paul rejoiced that his labor was indispensible for the salvation of the believers at Corinth. *True or False?*

QUESTION 8

Paul did not judge himself because he had a clear conscience. *True or False?*

QUESTION 9

In the building metaphor of 1 Corinthians 3, Paul and Apollos are coworkers building God's temple. *True or False?*

QUESTION 10

Paul threatened to use the rod of discipline to correct problems at Corinth. *True or False?*

QUESTION 11

"The kingdom of God" in the clause "the unrighteous will not inherit the kingdom of God" (1 Cor 6:9, 10) refers to what?

    A. The church

    B. Heaven

    C. The fruit of the Spirit

    D. Future blessings at the second coming

QUESTION 12

One characteristic of true apostles is suffering for Christ. *True or False?*

QUESTION 13

In 1 Corinthians 3, Paul used the following metaphor to describe the work of Christian leaders

A. Fishing

B. Farming

C. Shepherding

D. Rescuing

QUESTION 14

Church discipline is only the leaders' responsibility. *True or False?*

QUESTION 15

Immorality, theft, greed, idolatry, homosexuality, and drunkenness describe those who will not inherit the kingdom of God. *True or False?*

QUESTION 16

"All things are lawful for me" is most likely a Corinthian church slogan. *True or False?*

QUESTION 17

Why is "all things are lawful" true for believers in one sense?

A. We are set free from all moral restraints

B. We are not subject to government regulations

C. We have already become perfect

D. We are no longer under the Old Testament ceremonial or food laws

QUESTION 18

Cutting off Christian fellowship is an unacceptably harsh church discipline. *True or False?*

QUESTION 19

It is ridiculous for Christians to say they belong to a particular Christian leader. *True or False?*

QUESTION 20

To what does "the flesh" in "turn this man over to Satan for the destruction of the flesh" probably refer?

A. The physical body

B. The sin nature

C. The carnal behavior of the congregation as a whole

D. Spiritual blindness

QUESTION 21

Which one of the following is **not** an acceptable motive for church discipline?

A. Preventing evil from spreading in the church

B. Restoration of the offender

C. Vengeance against the offender

D. Punishing the offender

QUESTION 22

When a believer is removed from the church for serious sin, what happens to him?

    A. He loses his salvation.

    B. He can never repent.

    C. He is cast into Satan's sphere.

    D. He falls further into sin.

QUESTION 23

Fleeing immorality is an important aspect of glorifying God with your body. *True or False?*

QUESTION 24

Antinomianism is a theological error that leads to extremely self-indulgent behavior. *True or False?*

QUESTION 25

The problems of the church at Corinth that Paul identifies in 1 Corinthians 1–4 do **not** include

    A. Pride

    B. Immaturity

    C. Persecution

    D. Immorality

    E. Negligence

Lesson 5 Answers to Questions

QUESTION 1

    B. The man was a member of the church, whereas the woman was not.

QUESTION 2: *Your answer*

QUESTION 3

    D. Remove the sinner from their fellowship.

QUESTION 4: True

QUESTION 5: *Your answer should be similar to the following:*

This sin seems to qualify as a defiant sin, since even the non-believers viewed it as wrong.

QUESTION 6

Scripture	Purposes
Deuteronomy 19:19-20	To warn believers and to give them fear of sinning.
1 Corinthians 5:6-7	To purify the Body of Christ
Galatians 6:1	To restore the sinner to fellowship.
2 Corinthians 2:6	To punish the offender.

QUESTION 7

    D. True believers who have fallen into sin and refused to repent of it

QUESTION 8

Verse References	Sins
1 Corinthians 5:1-5	Serious sexual immorality
1 Timothy 1:20	Blasphemy
Titus 3:10	Divisiveness
2 Thessalonians 3:14, 15	Disobedience to apostolic teaching
2 Thessalonians 3:6	Idleness

QUESTION 9: True

QUESTION 10: *Your answer*

QUESTION 11: *Your answer*

QUESTION 12

    A. It reflects the low spiritual life of the entire church.

    B. It results in a bad witness to the unbelieving community.

    C. It affects the fellowship and harmony in the church.

    D. It is unnecessary for believers to take such cases to the courts.

QUESTION 13: True

QUESTION 14: *Your answer*

QUESTION 15

    A. To warn and encourage self-examination

QUESTION 16

Passages	Content
Leviticus 18:22	Prohibition of male homosexuality
Leviticus 20:13	Death penalty for male homosexual acts
Genesis 19:1-13	Destruction of Sodom for the sin of homosexuality
Romans 1:26-27	Lesbianism and homosexuality as evidence of God's wrath

QUESTION 17: Sanctified

QUESTION 18: *Your answer*

QUESTION 19

    A. Christian freedom means freedom from sinning.

QUESTION 20

    D. Flee immorality.

QUESTION 21

Verse	Argument
1 Corinthians 6:14	We will receive glorified bodies.
1 Corinthians 6:15	Our bodies are members of Christ.
1 Corinthians 6:17	We are one spirit with the Lord.
1 Corinthians 6:18	Sexual sin is sin against our own body.
1 Corinthians 6:19	The Holy Spirit lives in our bodies.

QUESTION 22: *Your answer*

Lesson 5 Self Check Answers

QUESTION 1: True
QUESTION 2: True
QUESTION 3: False
QUESTION 4
    A. Cut off Christian fellowship with the person.
QUESTION 5: False
QUESTION 6: True
QUESTION 7: False
QUESTION 8
    B. In the future, believers will judge angels
QUESTION 9: True
QUESTION 10: False

Unit 2 Exam Answers

QUESTION 1: True

QUESTION 2

    D. The quality of their ministry

QUESTION 3: True

QUESTION 4: False

QUESTION 5: True

QUESTION 6: True

QUESTION 7: False

QUESTION 8: False

QUESTION 9: True

QUESTION 10: True

QUESTION 11

    D. Future blessings at the second coming

QUESTION 12: True

QUESTION 13

    B. Farming

QUESTION 14: False

QUESTION 15: True

QUESTION 16: True

QUESTION 17

    D. We are no longer under the Old Testament ceremonial or food laws

QUESTION 18: False

QUESTION 19: True

QUESTION 20

    A. The physical body

QUESTION 21

    C. Vengeance against the offender

QUESTION 22

    C. He is cast into Satan's sphere.

QUESTION 23: True

QUESTION 24: True

QUESTION 25

    C. Persecution

Unit 3: Freedom Has Limits in Personal Behavior

Unit Introduction

Freedom is an emotive word that people react positively to. Many are familiar with the words of Jesus, "you will know the truth, and the truth will set you free" (Jn 8:32). But for the Christian, what exactly does freedom mean? For many people, the definition that comes to mind is unrestricted behavior. To them, the free person can do whatever he wants. It's easy to imagine, however, how unrestricted behavior could lead to a lot of pain in a fallen world.

Jesus was not mistaken when He declared that the truth will set you free. Paul and the church at Corinth debated what freedom means. Apparently some at Corinth advocated the unrestricted behavior idea, but Paul advocated a freedom that limits its behavior according to God's truth and the principle of love. Jesus set the believer free from bondage to sin for a purpose—to please God and benefit his neighbor.

This freedom does not mean that anything goes, or "all things are lawful" as the Corinthians put it. In Lesson 6, Paul gives extensive teaching on marriage, explaining what a believer is free to do, but also how the responsibilities of marriage must be upheld. Trusting Christ is no reason to change marriage status.

Although it is strange to many of us, freedom and food sacrificed to idols is the subject of Lesson 7. By addressing a very practical, everyday issue in first century Corinth, Paul brings out universal principles showing how a believer's freedom is limited both by exclusive worship of the true God and by consideration for the weaker brother.

In Paul's own life he exemplifies setting aside his own rights and freedoms for the sake of the gospel. In Lesson 8, Paul gives powerful examples of self-sacrifice, financially and culturally. He exercises his freedom by giving up his rights in order to win more people to Christ.

Unit Outline

Lesson 6: Freedom in Marriage (1 Cor 7:1-40)

Lesson 7: Freedom and Food Sacrificed to Idols (1 Cor 8:1-13; 10:1–11:1)

Lesson 8: Freedom and Ministry (1 Cor 9:1-27)

Unit Objectives

Brother Thomas gave up a lot to plant their church. Although he wasn't from their area, he gladly ate their province's trademark sour cuisine, coped with their local dialect, and stayed in his own rented apartment while he worked to evangelize and start worship services. Although from the beginning he insisted that they take up offerings, he never touched the money. He said the Lord provided the money he needed from other sources, and they should use their offerings for needs in their town. Dorcas, his wife, came with him and endeared herself to the ladies by holding women's meetings and starting the children's ministry. Although it was obvious that they were outsiders, they tried every way they could to fit in and make friends. Lotus remembers their sacrifices, hard work, and voluntary separation from their grown-up children and grandchildren who lived eight hundred kilometers away. When the weather got cold that winter, Lotus was sure that Brother Thomas' bad leg hurt him even more, but he didn't head for a warmer climate to ease the pain. He stayed right on in the church planting work until the church was strong enough to stand on its own.

Lotus remembers Brother Thomas and all his sacrifices, and then she remembers her own sacrifices after becoming a Christian. Every year there is the continuing stress of the New Year's activities when Shan's family goes to the shrine to pray to the ancestors for blessings. She doesn't participate, and she feels it deeply from Shan's extended family. Shan doesn't really talk to her about it much anymore. She wonders sometimes if Shan is tempted to leave her because her faith kept her out of this important expression of family solidarity.

Lotus wonders if she is doing the right thing. She wonders if it is necessary for her to stay away from the annual visit to the town shrine at New Year's. After all, there is only one true God, and the dead ancestors can't really answer prayers. She looks to 1 Corinthians for understanding and encouragement.

Lesson 6: Freedom in Marriage
(1 Cor 7:1-40)

The family is an institution established by God as the fundamental unit of human society. New families begin with marriage. Today, the traditional definition of marriage is being challenged, and the importance of marriage in many societies is diminishing. Attacks on marriage and family in recent decades have spurred the growth of evangelical organizations.

Not surprisingly, the Christian faith should be greatly concerned about marriage, and that many questions about marriage should arise in a place like first-century Corinth. The city had a reputation for immorality and was steeped in Greco-Roman views, plus Christianity was a new faith. There were tensions in the congregation, with some favoring casting away all sexual constraints under the rubric of "freedom in Christ," while others advocated strict abstinence. Misunderstandings regarding the importance of the physical body, the meaning of spirituality, and the blessings of the future kingdom of God gave rise to such extreme positions. Perhaps some in Corinth felt that since "in the resurrection they neither marry nor are given in marriage, but are like angels in heaven" (Mt 22:30) that marriage in this life is not so important either.

Paul is answering questions about marriage from a letter the church at Corinth wrote to him. In the first part of the chapter, he answers their questions about those already married or previously married, then he responds to the issue of the unmarried. He repeatedly brings up the principle of "remain as you are." Although marriage is important, it is not the most important value in a believer's life.

In Topic 1, we discuss Paul's answers to questions regarding the married or widowed.

Topic 2 explains his overarching principle for believers: that they stay as they were when they came to faith.

Finally, in Topic 3, Paul addresses the unmarried, or people engaged to be married.

Lesson Outline

Topic 1: Advice to the Married (1 Cor 7:1-16)

    Celibacy and Marriage (7:1-7)

    Unmarried and Widows (7:8-9)

    Christian Marriages (7:10-11)

    Mixed Marriages (7:12-16)

Topic 2: Principle—Remain as You Were Called (1 Cor 7:17-24)

    General Principle (7:17)

    Specific Application (7:18-24)

Topic 3: Advice to the Unmarried (1 Cor 7:25-40)

    Recognize the Crisis (7:25-31)

    Principle—Freedom From Concern (7:32-35)

    Application for Virgins and Widows (7:36-40)

Lesson Objectives

Rebekah is so dedicated to the Lord. She is from Lotus' town, and she trusted the Lord during the first visit of Brother Thomas. That was about ten years ago, when she was eighteen. She so fell in love with Jesus, God's Word and the ministry that she decided to go on to the training school for evangelists in the neighboring province. The church supported her financially to do this, since she had such a good reputation and had served so faithfully with children's ministries. Two years ago she came back to the town and regularly serves with children's outreach in the local area, sometimes traveling to nearby villages for special meetings. The church views her as a resident missionary.

Now that she is twenty-eight years old, her family is pressing her to get married, have children, and raise a family. Already she's passed the age when most women marry, and her mother and grandmother keep bringing up the issue with her and trying to find a husband for her. Several men have come to see her, but either they weren't believers or they didn't impress her very much. In the church, there aren't any single men near her age. They have all gone to the big city to work, and they only come back home to the village at New Year's.

It's become a troublesome issue for Rebekah, because she would like to get married, but only to the "right" man. She's been praying about it for a long time, but what can she do? Whenever she goes to special training sessions for children's ministry workers, there are not many eligible men to meet. She has thought about trying to move to the big city to get a job and meet more Christian men, but then she thinks about the need for children's work in her home town and in the surrounding villages. Plus, the church is supporting her now, and what job could she get in the big city?

When she shares her heart with Lotus, Lotus suggests they read and pray together over 1 Corinthians 7. Lotus thinks that Rebekah has a heart and situation in life a lot like Paul's, but perhaps with some significant differences.

By the end of this lesson, you will be able to:

- Define what Paul means by the statement "remain as you are," whether you are married or unmarried
- Explain the importance of maintaining physical relations within marriage
- Examine why God has you in the circumstances you are in and how that applies to your calling He has placed on you
- Recognize being called to singleness as a gift
- Understand that neither being married nor unmarried is immoral in itself, so such decisions are an area of Christian freedom.

Topic 1: Advice to the Married (1 Cor 7:1-16)

The overall thrust of Paul's instruction to the married is to "remain as you are," which will become more clear in Topic 2. Those who are already married retain that marital status, with all its rights and responsibilities, after conversion to Christ. Becoming a believer should not alter regular sexual expression in marriage, nor should it promote a believer to seek divorce. There were many mixed marriages at Corinth, with one believer and one unbeliever, and they brought both special problems as well as opportunities.

Celibacy and Marriage (7:1-7)

Assignment

- Read 1 Corinthians 7:1-7.

- Read Constable, "The Importance of Sexual Relations in Marriage 7:1-7" (refer to the Articles section at the end of this lesson).

- Read "Celibacy and Marriage."

Celibacy and Marriage

One of the interpretive issues of this section is how to translate 1 Corinthians 7:1. Paul wrote in Greek without punctuation marks. There are two good options for punctuating this verse:

(A) Now with regard to the issues you wrote about: "It is good for a man not to have sexual relations with a woman." (Here Paul is seen as quoting from their letter.)

(B) Now with regard to the issues you wrote about. It is good for a man not to have sexual relations with a woman. (Here Paul is giving his advice and not quoting their letter.)

How does one decide between the two? The main reasons for choosing (A) are:

1. The immediate context shows Paul's disagreement with the statement in quotes.

2. Such a statement could easily have been made by the ascetic elements in the church.

3. Paul's general teaching about marriage does not support such a statement.

Reasons for favoring (B) are:

1. Paul is seen as generally advising against marriage, especially in the face of the "impending crisis" (1 Cor 7:26). This is an argument from the broader context.

2. This translation is simpler and more straightforward. It does not require inserting quotation marks.

However, since the statement is not about marriage per se, but rather about sexual relations, translation (A) seems to be the better choice. This is the choice of the NET Bible.

Abstaining from sex within marriage is not viewed by Paul as "spiritual." Paul considers it a dangerous temptation to stop regular sexual relations with one's spouse. Even someone in such a demanding ministry as an apostle of the Lord has the right to take along a believing wife with him in his travels (1 Cor 9:5). Similarly, Paul does not view celibacy as a more "spiritual" state than marriage, although he prefers singleness for reasons he will make clear later.

QUESTION 1

To what does Paul's "concession" (1 Cor 7:6) refer?

A. Sex within marriage

B. Abstention from sex within marriage

C. Prayer

D. Lack of self-control

QUESTION 2

In Christian marriage, neither husband nor wife has exclusive _____ to his/her own body.

QUESTION 3

Both marriage and singleness are spiritual gifts. *True or False?*

Unmarried and Widows (7:8-9)

The sexual drive is God-given, and the God approved way to express it is in marriage. Although certainly not the only reason for getting married, the fulfillment of sexual needs is a valid reason for getting married.

Assignment

- Read 1 Corinthians 7:8-9.
- Read Constable, "The Legitimate Option of Singleness 7:8-9" (refer to the Articles section at the end of this lesson).
- Read "Unmarried and Widows."

Unmarried and Widows

Paul views sexual relations as an important part of marriage, and sexual needs as an important reason for getting married. Sexual fulfillment within marriage is God's way of escape when faced with the temptation to immorality.

QUESTION 4

It is better for a believer to marry a non-believer than to burn with desire. *True or False?*

Christian Marriages (7:10-11)

God's original intention for marriage was confirmed by Jesus and by Paul: "What God has joined together, let no one separate" (Mt 19:6).

Assignment

- Read 1 Corinthians 7:10-11.
- Read Constable, "No Divorce for Christians Whose Mates are Believers 7:10-11" (refer to the Articles section at the end of this lesson).
- Read "Christian Marriages."

Christian Marriages

"The married" refers to marriages where both spouses are believers (1 Cor 7:10). This is evident from the context that follows, where Paul discusses "mixed" marriages.

Paul's teaching here dovetails with Jesus' teaching about divorce in Matthew 19:9. If divorce occurs for reasons other than immorality, then the divorced people are to either remain unmarried or be reconciled to their previous spouse. If they marry someone else, then they commit adultery. The concept here is that in God's eyes the original marriage has not been dissolved.

QUESTION 5

What does Paul's statement, "—not I, but the Lord—" (1 Cor 7:10), mean?

    A. Jesus said this when He taught on earth.

    B. Paul disagrees with Jesus.

    C. Jesus revealed this directly to Paul.

    D. Jesus' statements have more authority than Paul's.

Mixed Marriages (7:12-16)

Assignment

- Read 1 Corinthians 7:12-16.

- Read Constable, "No Divorce for Christians Whose Mates are Unbelievers 7:12-16" (refer to the Articles section at the end of this lesson).

- Read "Mixed Marriages."

Mixed Marriages

"Mixed" marriages can come about in two ways. Probably what Paul had in mind was the situation where only one spouse becomes a believer in a marriage that was originally between two unbelievers. The other way is when a believer marries a non-believer and violates God's command for believers to only marry other believers (see 1 Cor 7:39). Since many marriages in first-century Roman society were arranged by the families involved, there could well have been pressure for Christian singles to marry unbelievers.

Here Paul makes it clear that conversion to Christ does not alter one's marital state, nor does it provide grounds for the believer to initiate divorce. This instruction is in line with his general principle to remain as you were called (1 Cor 7:20).

However, the conversion of the spouse may be a reason the unbelieving partner uses to terminate the marriage. If the unbeliever does want a divorce, then the believer should accept the marriage dissolution as permitted by God.

Mixed marriages are often difficult, tense, and restrictive, but may have evangelistic and sanctification results. Just as believing parents have much influence on their children, so also a believing spouse has a great effect on the unbelieving partner. Hopefully, through the believer's witness, the unbelieving spouse and the children will come to faith.

The permission to accept divorce under the circumstances of 1 Corinthians 7:15 is sometimes referred to as the "Pauline privilege." Although Paul grants permission, he does not encourage divorce, but rather emphasizes the positive points of remaining in a mixed marriage.

QUESTION 6

What does "—I, not the Lord—" (1 Cor 7:12) mean? *(Select all that apply.)*

    A. Jesus disagrees with Paul.

    B. Jesus never said this when He taught on earth.

    C. The Lord did not inspire Paul to write this.

    D. This is Paul's own apostolic instruction.

QUESTION 7

Please match the Scripture with the reason for those in mixed marriages not to seek a divorce:

Scripture	Reason
1 Corinthians 7:14	"Remain as you are" as a general principle
1 Corinthians 7:16	Witness to the unbeliever
1 Corinthians 7:17	Special blessings to the spouse and children because of the believer

QUESTION 8

How would you advise a believer who reports that her unbelieving husband is physically violent when he drinks too much? Should she seek a divorce? How should she respond to the problem? Record your thoughts in your Life Notebook.

Topic 2: Principle: Remain as You Were Called (1 Cor 7:17-24)

When a person becomes a Christian, he is "in Christ" no matter what his social or ethnic standing. Being "in Christ" should change a believer's values and behaviors, but Paul advises against seeking a radical change of circumstances. Instead, the believer should look for why God has called him in those circumstances.

General Principle (7:17)

God has a plan and a purpose for every believer's life, from the circumstances of his conversion to the end of his earthly life. This principle encourages believers to recognize God's sovereignty in their lives.

Assignment

- Read 1 Corinthians 7:17.
- Read Constable, "The Basic Principle" (refer to the Articles section at the end of this lesson), through the note on 7:17.
- Read "General Principle."

General Principle

The "place in life" refers to one's whole situation, such as: vocation, marital status, freedman vs. slave status, citizenship, language, culture, and physical characteristics, regardless of their religious nature.

Of course, Paul is not referring to sins of your pre-Christian life, such as immorality or idolatry, when he counsels to remain as you were called. Such things must be turned away from immediately.

QUESTION 9

Paul teaches that a believer's station in life is irrelevant to his spirituality. *True or False?*

QUESTION 10

What does Paul regard as of great importance?

    A. Marital status

    B. Jewish identity

    C. Freedman status

    D. Keeping God's commands

Specific Application (7:18-24)

God's calling changes the person radically, but not the person's circumstances. Instead, the believer becomes God's agent in his circumstances.

Assignment

- Read 1 Corinthians 7:18-24.

- Read Constable, "The Basic Principle" (refer to the Articles section at the end of this lesson).

- Read "Specific Application."

Specific Application

Why does Paul tell believers to remain as they were called? Paul's response is the relative unimportance of a person's circumstances when he was called. Your human circumstances when called do not affect your relationship with God. Whether you were Jew or Gentile, slave or free, married or single does not matter in your relationship with God. There is no reason to seek to change your status to try to somehow get "closer to God."

On the other hand, Paul recognizes God's sovereign plan for believers' lives. God had His purpose in calling you to faith just as you were, and He wants to use you in that situation. Your circumstances when called are important for God's purposes. He has previously stated, "For how do you know, wife, whether you will bring your husband to salvation? Or how do you know, husband, whether you will bring your wife to salvation?" (1 Cor 7:16).

It is an established evangelistic principle that generally the most effective witnesses for Christ are new believers. For these people, the changes in their lives are most apparent in the first few years after conversion. Their friends and relatives see these changes, interact with the new believer, and have to deal with the changes. However, after several years, attitudes among the unbelievers may have become hardened, plus the believer will have formed a new set of friendships among other believers. Witnessing opportunities among the old circle of friends and relatives diminish. Unless the believer takes direct steps to continue to develop friendships with non-believers, gradually he loses influence on non-believers.

QUESTION 11

In 1 Corinthians 7 Paul states his principle "remain as you were called" _____ times.

QUESTION 12

"Remain as you were called" is a new law for believers. *True or False?*

QUESTION 13

In what ways would a new believer in your culture be tempted to change his "situation" in order to appear or feel more spiritual? How would you counsel them in light of this passage? Open your Life Notebook and record your thoughts.

Topic 3: Advice to the Unmarried (1 Cor 7:25-40)

Undoubtedly the social pressure to marry was great at Corinth, particularly after someone had become engaged. Paul advised remaining unmarried. He reasoned that the unmarried believer could more easily be single minded in devotion to Christ, and this is so important be since He is coming again soon. Still, Paul recognized that Christian marriage is godly and a great blessing.

Recognize the Crisis (7:25-31)

Paul counsels believers to grasp the reality that they are in the world but not of the world. As much as possible, avoid entanglements with the things of this world.

Assignment

- Read 1 Corinthians 7:25-31.
- Read Constable, "Advice Concerning Virgins" (refer to the Articles section at the end of this lesson), through the note on 7:31.
- Read "Recognize the Crisis."

Recognize the Crisis

Paul's statements advising singleness for those never married come in the category of wise advice—not moral rulings.

How are we to understand Paul's reasoning?

Those who have wives should be as those who have none

Those with tears like those not weeping

Those who rejoice like those not rejoicing

Those who buy like those without possessions

Those who use the world as though they were not using it to the full (1 Cor 7:29-31)

Specifically, he refers to the "impending crisis," the "short time," and "difficult circumstances." These verses poetically counsel an attitude of freedom from the things of this world. Believers are foreigners and exiles (1 Pet 2:11), people just passing through this world. From the perspective of the second coming and eternity, such things as marriage, children, houses, fame, and emotions all fade in importance. Those things will pass away. What is important is the "eternal weight of glory" (2 Cor 4:17).

QUESTION 14

What does "I have no command from the Lord, but I give my opinion" mean? *(Select all that apply.)*

    A. This is Paul's apostolic command.

    B. This is Paul's wise advice.

    C. Jesus has not spoken about this matter.

    D. Paul is speaking as a prophet.

QUESTION 15

Most probably, the "impending crisis" (1 Cor 7:26) refers to what?

    A. The last days before Christ's return

    B. Local persecution

    C. Famine

    D. Future problems in the church

QUESTION 16

How does the truth, "the present shape of this world is passing away" (1 Cor 7:31), affect your day-to-day activity? Open your Life Notebook and record your thoughts.

Principle—Freedom From Concern (7:32-35)

Assignment

- Read 1 Corinthians 7:32-35.

- Read Constable, "Reasons for Remaining Single" (refer to the Articles section at the end of this lesson), through the note on 7:35.

- Read "Principle—Freedom From Concern."

Principle—Freedom From Concern

Marriage is a huge commitment for a whole lifetime. Preserving a good marriage requires work, time, attention, emotional and spiritual energy, and a focus on the spouse's needs. Paul calls these concerns about the things of the world. He does not mean that such things are "worldly" in a negative or moral sense. In fact, working to preserve a good marriage is God's will. Rather, he refers to their transient sense—they are passing away.

Unquestionably, if a person does not have the responsibility of marriage, he is comparatively free from concentrating on "the things of this world" and can instead focus on "the things of the Lord." Here he is referring to things which last for eternity—holiness in body and spirit.

Despite his counsel, Paul recognized that marriage/singleness is an area of freedom for the Christian. A believer can decide either way, in accordance with his spiritual gift. It stands to reason that, for those without the gift of singleness, marriage is the appropriate choice.

The top priority for a Christian is serving the Lord. Such things as marriage, property ownership, a demanding job, or perhaps pursuing an educational degree can be distracting. However, none of these things is immoral in itself, and so such decisions are an area of Christian freedom.

QUESTION 17

What is the limitation that married people face in their service for the Lord?

QUESTION 18

The devoted Christian will avoid marriage. *True or False?*

Application for Virgins and Widows (7:36-40)

Societal expectations or family pressure should not be the major factor for believers deciding to marry or remain single. Assuming that the goal in life is to serve Christ, believers are free to make their own decisions regarding marriage.

Assignment

- Read 1 Corinthians 7:36-40.
- Read Constable, "The Legitimacy of Marriage" (refer to the Articles section at the end of this lesson).
- Read "Application for Virgins and Widows."

Application for Virgins and Widows

Scholars are uncertain as to Paul's meaning in 1 Corinthians 7:36-40, and there are strong arguments for and against possible translations. Regardless of translation, however, Paul gives freedom of choice to marry or remain single. Neither choice is viewed as more "spiritual," but Paul says that remaining single is "better" for keeping undivided focus on eternal things. This is not to say that remaining single is the better choice for everyone—just for those with the gift of singleness.

QUESTION 19

Marriage of a Christian widow to a Christian man is a matter of _____.

QUESTION 20

What would you say to someone who tells you that he got married by mistake—that he thinks he has the gift of singleness even though he is already married? Open your Life Notebook and record your thoughts.

QUESTION 21

How will this chapter help you counsel people who are considering marriage or singlehood? How does this differ from what your family, culture or society desires? Open your Life Notebook and record your thoughts.

Lesson 6 Articles

Notes on 1 Corinthians

Dr. Thomas L. Constable; 2003 Edition

III. QUESTIONS ASKED OF PAUL 7:1—16:12

The remainder of the body of this epistle deals with questions the Corinthians had put to Paul in a letter. Paul introduced each of these with the phrase *peri de* ("now concerning," 1 Cor 7:1, 25; 8:1; 12:1; 16:1, 12).

> "Rather than a friendly exchange, in which the new believers in Corinth are asking spiritual advice of their mentor in the Lord, their letter was probably a response to Paul's Previous Letter mentioned in 5:9, in which they were taking exception to his position on point after point. In light of their own theology of spirit, with heavy emphasis on 'wisdom' and 'knowledge,' they have answered Paul with a kind of 'Why can't we?' attitude, in which they are looking for his response." (187)

A. MARRIAGE AND RELATED MATTERS CH. 7

The first subject with which Paul dealt was marriage. He began with some general comments (vv. 1-7) and then dealt with specific situations.

> "The transition from chapter 6 to chapter 7 illustrates the necessity Paul was under of waging a campaign on two fronts. In chapter 6 he dealt with libertines who argued that everything was permissible, and in particular that sexual licence *[sic]* was a matter of ethical indifference. In chapter 7 he deals with ascetics who, partly perhaps in reaction against the libertines, argued that sexual relations of every kind were to be deprecated, that Christians who were married should henceforth live as though they were unmarried, and those who were unmarried should remain so, even if they were already engaged to be married." (188)

> ."... the controlling motif of Paul's answer is: 'Do not seek a change in status.' This occurs in every subsection (vv. 2, 8, 10. 11. 12-16, 26-27, 37, 40) and is the singular theme of the paragraph that ties the ... sections together (vv. 17-24)—although in each case an exception is allowed." (189)

> "Two other features about the nature of the argument need to be noted: First, along with 11:2-16, this is one of the least combative sections of the letter. Indeed, after the argumentation of 1:10—6:20, this section is altogether placid. Furthermore, also along with 11:2-16, this is one of the least 'authority-conscious' sections in all of his letters. Phrases like 'I say this by way of concession, not of command' (v. 6), 'it is good for them' (vv. 8, 26), 'I have no command, but I give my opinion' (v. 25; cf. 40) are not your standard Paul. Second, in a way quite unlike anything else in all his letters, the argument alternates between men and women (12 times in all). And in every case there is complete mutuality between the two sexes." (190)

1. Advice to the married or formerly married 7:1 16

Paul proceeded to give guidelines to the married or formerly married. The statement "It is good for a man not to touch a woman" (v. 1) may well have been a Corinthian slogan. (191) Paul responded to that view in all that follows in this section.

The importance of sexual relations in marriage 7:1-7

Paul advised married people not to abstain from normal sexual relations.

7:1 - Again Paul began what he had to say by citing a general truth. Then he proceeded to qualify it (cf. 1 Cor 6:12-13). The use of the Greek word *anthropos* (man generically, people) rather than *aner* (man as distinguished from woman) indicates that the statement pertains to human beings generally. To "touch a woman" (NASB) is a euphemism for sexual intercourse. (192) Evidently the Corinthians' question was something like this. Isn't it preferable for a Christian man to abstain from sexual relations with a woman? This would reflect the "spiritual" viewpoint of the Corinthians that held a negative attitude toward the material world and the body (cf. 1 Cor 6:13; 15:12).

> "Some difficulty is alleviated if these words are regarded as a quotation from the Corinthian letter, and this is a hypothesis that may very probably be accepted [cf. 1 Cor 6:12-13] . . ." (193)

Another view is that "touch a woman" is a euphemism for marrying. (194) However this meaning is difficult to prove, and I do not prefer it. If this is what he meant, Paul's advice was to abstain from marrying. Paul wrote later that because of the present distress his readers would do well to remain in their present marital state (v. 26). Nevertheless throughout the passage Paul viewed marriage as God-ordained and perfectly proper for Christians.

7:2 - This verse probably begins Paul's extended qualification of the Corinthians' view of marriage. He proceeded to urge them strongly that the type of abstinence that they were arguing for within marriage was totally wrong. Notice the three sets of balanced pairs in this verse and in the two that follow. In this verse Paul urged married couples to have sexual relations with one another because of the prevalence of temptations to satisfy sexual desire inappropriately.

The view of verse 1 that understands Paul to be saying that it is better to avoid marrying sees Paul making a concession to that statement here. Those who hold this view believe that Paul was saying that it is better to marry since many single people cannot live in the single state without eventually committing "immoralities" (fornication, Gr. *porneias*). This is obviously not the only reason to marry (cf. Gen 2:18-24), but it appears to have been an important consideration in Corinth where temptations to fornicate abounded. As noted above, I do not favor this interpretation.

> "This [i.e., "each . . . each"] forbids polygamy, which was advocated by some Jewish teachers." (195)

7:3 - In view of the temptation to commit fornication, each partner in marriage needs to fulfill his or her sexual duty to the spouse. Part of the responsibility of marriage is to meet the various needs of the partner (Gen 2:18) including sexual needs.

7:4 - Moreover in marriage each partner relinquishes certain personal rights, including the exclusive right to his or her own body, to which he or she gives the mate a claim. Neither person has *complete* authority over his or her own body in marriage. Note that Paul was careful to give both husband and wife equal rights in these verses. He did not regard the man as having sexual rights or needs that the woman does not have or vice versa.

7:5 - Evidently the Corinthians had concluded that since they were "spiritual" they did not need to continue to have sexual relations as husband and wife. Another less probable situation, I think, is that there were some married Christians in the church who were overreacting to the immorality in Corinth by abstaining from sexual relations with their mates. For whatever reason Paul viewed this as depriving one another of their normal sexual needs and urged them to stop doing it. Husbands and wives should commit themselves to honoring the spirit of mutual ownership that these verses describe.

There are legitimate reasons for temporary abstinence, but couples should temporarily abstain only with the agreement of both partners. When there are greater needs, spiritual needs, the couple may want to set aside their normal physical needs. However they should only do so temporarily. (196)

"Three conditions are required for lawful abstention: it must be by mutual consent, for a good object, and temporary." (197)

Normally we think of sexual activity as an indication of lack of self-control, but Paul also viewed the failure to engage in sex as a lack of self-control for a married person.

7:6 - Paul's concession was allowing temporary abstinence from sex. The concession was not having sex. He did not command abstinence. He viewed regular marital relations as the norm. Paul was no ascetic who favored as little sex as possible. Abstinence was the exception to what was normal in his view.

7:7 - Paul evidently was not a married man when he wrote this epistle (v. 8). We do not have enough information about his life to know whether he had never married, had become a widower, or if his wife had left him.

To Paul the single state had certain advantages for a servant of the Lord such as himself. He had to put up with many hardships in his ministry that it would have been difficult for a wife to share. Moreover God had given him grace to live as a single person without feeling consumed by the fires of lust (cf. 1 Cor 7:9).

He wished everyone could live as he did, but he realized that most could not. Each person has his or her own special gift (Gr. *charisma*) from God, some to live single and some to live married (cf. Matt 19:12). These are spiritual gifts just as those gifts listed in chapters 12-14 are. The gift of celibacy is a special ability that God gives only some people to feel free from the desire or need of sexual fulfillment in marriage. (198)

The legitimate option of singleness 7:8-9

Paul moved from advice to the married regarding sexual abstinence to advice to the unmarried. He advised this group, as he had the former one, to remain in the state in which they found themselves, but he allowed them an exception too.

7:8 - Who are the "unmarried" (Gr. *agamois*) that Paul had in view? Most interpreters have taken this word in its broadest possible meaning, namely, all categories of unmarried people. Others, however, take it to refer to widowers since Paul also specified widows in this verse and since he dealt with males and females in balance in this chapter. (199) I prefer the former view.

The unmarried state has some advantages over the married state even though it is better for most people to marry (Gen 2:18). Since it is not a sinful condition, married people should not look down on single people or even pity them because they are unmarried. Sometimes married people tend to do this because singles do not enjoy the pleasures of married life. Notwithstanding they enjoy the pleasures of single life that married individuals do not. Married people should not pressure single people to get married just because they are single.

7:9 - However if a single person cannot or does not control his or her passions, it would be better to marry than to burn with lustful temptation (cf. 1 Cor 7:2). If a single has very strong sexual urges that may very well drive him or her into fornication, he or she would be wise to get married if possible. Of course a believer should marry a suitable Christian mate. This may be easier said than done, especially for a woman. The Lord has promised to provide the basic needs of those who put Him first in their lives (e.g., Matt 6:33). I believe He will do so in answer to prayer either by providing a suitable mate or by relieving the sexual passion. In either case He gives more grace (1 Cor 10:13).

No divorce for Christians whose mates are believers 7:10-11

Again Paul advised remaining as they were, but he also allowed an exception.

"While Paul displays ambivalence toward whether widowers and widows should get married (vv. 8-9), he consistently rejects the notion that the married may dissolve their marriages." (200)

7:10 - The Lord Jesus Christ gave instruction concerning what believers are to do in marriage when He taught during His earthly ministry (Matt 5:27-32; 19:3-12; Mark 10:1-12). Paul cited some of this teaching and added more of his own. (201) Of course God's instructions through Paul are just as inspired and authoritative as His teaching through Jesus Christ during His earthly ministry. This is one of Paul's few commands in this chapter (cf. 1 Cor 7:2-5).

The main point of Paul's advice is that Christians should not break up their marriages (Matt 19:4-6; Mark 10:7-9). "Leaving" and divorcing (1 Cor 7:12-13) were virtually the same in Greco-Roman culture. (202) "Separate" (Gr. chorizo) was vernacular for "divorce." (203) In our day one popular way to solve marriage problems is to split up. Nevertheless the Lord's will is that all people, including believers, work through their marital problems rather than giving up on them by separating permanently.

7:11 - If separation (divorce) occurs, they should either remain unmarried (i.e., stay as they are) or reconcile with their mate. Paul said this was to be the wife's course of action because if she left her husband she would be the mate who had to decide what to do. However the same procedure would be appropriate for the husband.

I believe Paul did not deal with the exception that Jesus Christ allowed on the grounds of fornication (Gr. porneia; Matt 5:32; 19:9) because it is an exception. Paul wanted to reinforce the main teaching of Christ on this subject, namely, that couples should not dissolve their marriages.

The Corinthian Christians appear to have been separating for ascetic reasons, to get away from sexual activity. In modern western culture the reason is usually the opposite; people usually divorce to marry someone else. Regardless of the reason for the temptation, Paul commanded Christian husbands and wives to stay together and to share their bodies as well as their lives with each other. It is impossible for a Christian husband and wife to provide a model of reconciliation to the world if they cannot reconcile with each other.

No divorce for Christians whose mates are unbelievers 7:12-16

In this situation, too, Paul granted an exception, but the exceptional is not the ideal. He also reiterated his principle of staying in the condition in which one finds himself or herself.

> ." . . one of the great heathen complaints against Christianity was exactly the complaint that Christianity did break up families and was a disruptive influence in society. 'Tampering with domestic relationships' was in fact one of the first charges brought against the Christians." (204)

7:12-13 - "The rest" refers to persons not in the general category of verse 10. Paul had been speaking of the typical married persons in the church, namely, those married to another believer. Now he dealt with mixed marriages between a believer and an unbeliever, as the following verses make clear.

For these people he could not repeat a teaching of Jesus because He had not spoken on this subject. At least as far as Paul knew He had not. Nevertheless the risen Lord inspired Paul's instructions on this subject so they were every bit as authoritative as the teaching Jesus gave during His earthly ministry.

The Corinthians may have asked Paul if a believing partner should divorce an unbelieving mate rather than living mismatched with him or her. This is the problem he addressed. He counselled the believer to go on living with the unbeliever if the unbeliever was willing to do so.

> "The point is clear: in a mixed marriage the Christian partner is not to take the initiative . . . in a move towards [permanent] separation." (205)

In Judaism, wives could not divorce their husbands, but under Greek and Roman law they could. (206)

7:14 - Even though an unbeliever might affect his or her mate negatively morally or ethically, it was still better to keep the marriage together. This was so because the believing mate would affect the unbeliever positively. "Sanctified" (Gr. hagiadzo) means to be set apart for a special purpose. God has set aside the unsaved spouse of a believer for special blessing some of which comes through his or her mate (cf. Exodus 29:37; Lev 6:18). God will deal with such a person differently than He deals with those not married to Christians.

I do not believe Paul would have objected to a couple separating temporarily if the believer was in physical danger from the unbeliever (cf. 1 Cor 7:15). What he did not want was for believers to initiate the termination of their marriages for this or any other reason.

Likewise the children in such a marriage would enjoy special treatment from God rather than being in a worse condition than the children in a Christian home. This probably involves their protection in the mixed home and the supply of grace needed for that sometimes difficult situation. "Holy" (Gr. *hagios*) means set apart as different.

I do not believe Paul was saying unsaved spouses and children of mixed marriages are better off than the spouses and children in Christian families. His point was that God would offset the disadvantages of such a situation with special grace.

> "This verse throws no light on the question of infant baptism." (207)

7:15 - On the other hand if the unbeliever in a mixed marriage wants to break up the marriage, the believing partner should allow him or her to do so. The reason for this is that God wants peace to exist in human relationships. It is better to have a peaceful relationship with an unbelieving spouse who has departed than it is to try to hold the marriage together. This is true if holding the marriage together will only result in constant antagonism in the home. However notice that the Christian does not have the option of departing (1 Cor 7:10-11).

When the unbeliever departs, the Christian is no longer under bondage (Gr. *douleuo*, lit. to be a slave). Does this refer to bondage to hold the marriage together or bondage to remain unmarried? Most of the commentators believe it means that the Christian is free to let the unbeliever depart; he or she does not have an obligation to maintain the marriage.. (209) Among these some hold that the believer is not free to remarry (cf. 1 Cor 7:11). (210) Most of these believe that the Christian is free to remarry. (211) The Greek text does not solve this problem. I think Paul was not addressing the idea of remarrying here.

I would counsel a Christian whose unsaved spouse has divorced him or her to remain unmarried as long as there is a possibility that the unsaved person may return. However if the unsaved spouse who has departed remarries, I believe the Christian would be free to remarry since, by remarrying, the unsaved partner has closed the door on reconciliation. (212)

7:16 - It is possible that Paul meant Christians should not separate from their unbelieving spouses because by staying together the unbeliever may eventually become a Christian (cf. 1 Pet 3:1). (213) However he may have meant the believer should not oppose the unbeliever's departing because he may become a Christian through channels other than the witness of the believing spouse. Both possibilities are realistic so even though we cannot tell exactly what the apostle meant here what we should do is clear. The Christian can have hope that God may bring the unsaved spouse to salvation while the believer does the Lord's will.

Verse 16 is a positive note on which to close instructions to Christians who have unsaved spouses.

2. The basic principle 7:17-24

At this point Paul moved back from specific situations to basic principles his readers needed to keep in mind when thinking about marriage (cf. 1 Cor 7:1-7). He drew his illustrations in this section from circumcision and slavery.

> "Under the rubric 'It is good not to have relations with a woman,' they were seeking to change their present status, apparently because as believers they saw this as conforming to the more spiritual existence that they had already attained. Thus they saw one's status

with regard to marriage/celibacy as having *religious* significance and sought change because of it. Under the theme of 'call' Paul seeks to put their 'spirituality' into a radically different perspective. They should remain in whatever social setting they were at the time of their call since God's call to be in Christ (cf. 1 Cor 1:9) transcends such settings so as to make them essentially irrelevant." (214)

7:17 - Whether he or she is unmarried or married, married to a believer or to an unbeliever, the Christian should regard his condition as what God has placed him or her in for the present. The concept of "call" is a way of describing Christian conversion (cf. 1 Cor 1:2, 9). He or she should concentrate on serving the Lord therein rather than spending most of one's time and energy on trying to change that condition. Paul taught the priority of serving Christ, over trying to change one's circumstances, in all the churches.

> "Paul's intent is not to lay down a rule that one may not change; rather, by thus hallowing one's situation in life, he is trying to help the Corinthians see that their social status is ultimately irrelevant as such (i.e., they can live out their Christian life in any of the various options) and therefore their desire to change is equally irrelevant—because it has nothing to do with genuine spirituality as their slogan would infer (v. 1b)." (215)

This is the second of four instances where Paul appealed to what was customary in all the churches (cf. 1 Cor 4:17; 11:16; 14:33). He never did this in any of his other letters. He was reminding this church that its theology was off track, not his.

7:18-19 - This principle applies to being circumcised as well as to being married. Both conditions were secondary to following the Lord obediently. God did not command celibacy or marriage, circumcision or uncircumcision. These are matters of personal choice in the church. One's ministry might be one factor in his or her decision (e.g., Acts 16:3; cf. Gal 5:6; 6:15).

The idea of becoming uncircumcised after one has been circumcised seems strange, but some Jews did this to avoid being known as Jews when they participated in activities at the public gymnasiums. (216)

7:20 - The "condition" (NASB) or "situation" (NIV; Gr. *klesis*) is the calling (1 Cor 7:17) in life in which a person was when God called him or her into His family (cf. 1 Cor 1:2; Eph 4:1). Our calling as Christians, to bear witness to Jesus Christ, is more important than our calling in life, namely, the place we occupy in the social, economic, and geographical scheme of things.

7:21 - Paul did not mean that a Christian should take a fatalistic view of life and regard his or her physical condition as something he or she should definitely remain in forever. If we have the opportunity to improve ourselves for the glory of God, we should do so. If we do not, we should not fret about our state but bloom where God has planted us. We should regard our call to Christ as sanctifying our present situation. In the context, of course, Paul was appealing to those who felt compelled to dissolve their marriages.

Another example of this principle would be if a person became a Christian while uneducated, he can serve Christ effectively as an uneducated person in a variety of ways. Many outstanding servants of the Lord have done so. If he has the opportunity to get an education and so serve God more effectively, he should feel free to take advantage of that opportunity. Unfortunately some Christians put more emphasis on getting an education than they do on serving the Lord. This is putting the cart before the horse and is the very thing Paul warned against here.

7:22 - Paul's emphasis on the wisdom of the world and the wisdom of God comes back into view in this section of verses (cf. 1 Cor 1:10–4:21). Priorities are in view. Does the Corinthian slave view himself primarily as a slave or as a freedman? (217) He was both, a slave of men but the freedman of God. Does the freedman view himself primarily as a freedman or as a slave? He was both, a freedman socially but the Lord's slave spiritually.

"This imagery, of course, must be understood in light of Greco-Roman slavery, not that of recent American history. Slavery was in fact the bottom rung on the social order, but for the most part it provided generally well for up to one-third of the population in a city like Corinth or Rome. The slave had considerable freedom and very often experienced mutual benefit along with the master. The owner received the benefit of the slave's services; and the slave had steady 'employment,' including having all his or her basic needs met—indeed, for many to be a slave was preferable to being a freedman, whose securities were often tenuous at best. But the one thing that marked the slave was that in the final analysis, he did not belong to himself but to another. That is Paul's point with this imagery." (218)

It is unfortunate that many Christians today choose to focus on their limitations rather than on their possibilities as representatives of Jesus Christ. We should use the abilities and opportunities that God gives us rather than feeling sorry for ourselves because we do not have other abilities or opportunities.

7:23 - Paul's thought returned to the Cross again (cf. 1 Cor 6:20). God has set us free from the worst kind of slavery having purchased us with the precious blood of His Son. How foolish then it would be for us to give up any of the liberties we enjoy that enable us to serve Jesus Christ. How ridiculous it would be to place ourselves back into a slave relationship to anyone or anything but Him. This applies to physical and spiritual bondage.

7:24 - For the third time in this pericope (1 Cor 7:17, 20, 24) Paul stated the basic principle that he advocated. Evidently there was much need for this exhortation in the Corinthian church.

In our day upward mobility has become a god to many Christians, and its worship has polluted the church. We need to be content to serve the Lord, to live out our calling, whether in a mixed marriage, singleness, a white collar or blue collar job, or whatever socioeconomic condition we may occupy.

In this section Paul chose his examples from circumcision and uncircumcision, slavery and freedom. However the larger context of the chapter is singleness and marriage. His point was that those who were single when God called them to follow Him should be content to remain single, and those who were married should stay married. Faithfulness to God or effectiveness for God do not require a change.

3. Advice concerning virgins 7:25-40

The second occurrence of the phrase *peri de* ("now concerning") occurs in verse 25 and indicates another subject about which the Corinthians had written Paul (1 Cor 7:1). This was the subject of single women. This section belongs with the rest of chapter 7 because this subject relates closely to what immediately precedes. Paul continued to deal with questions about marriage that the Corinthians' asceticism raised.

The advantage of the single state 7:25-28

In view of the verses in this section it seems that the question the Corinthians had asked Paul was whether an engaged girl should get married or remain single. One might understand verses 17-24 as saying no unmarried person should change her situation and get married (cf. 1 Cor 7:8), but this was not what Paul advocated necessarily.

7:25 - The "virgins" (Gr. *parthenoi*) were a group within the "unmarried" (*agamoi*) of verse 8. Paul used the feminine gender in five out of the six uses of this noun in verses 25-38. Consequently it seems clear that he was speaking of female virgins in particular.

There are three major views about the identity of these virgins. One view is that they were the virgin daughters of men in the Corinthian church and that these fathers had questions about giving their daughters in marriage. A second view is that the virgins were both men and women who were living together in a "spiritual marriage" (i.e., without sexual relations). A third view is that the virgins were females who were engaged, or thinking of becoming engaged, but were experiencing pressure from the "spiritual" in the church to forgo marriage. I believe the text supports the third view best.

The Lord Jesus had not addressed this problem during His earthly ministry as far as Paul knew (cf. 1 Cor 7:12). Paul gave his inspired opinion as a trustworthy (wise) steward of the Lord who had received mercy to be such (1 Cor 4:2). Note that Paul appealed to the Lord's mercy, not His command. As in the first part of this chapter, Paul was offering good advice, but he was not commanding that everyone do the same thing. Thus to choose not to follow Paul's advice did not amount to sinning.

7:26 - What is the present distress or crisis (Gr. *anagke*) to which the apostle referred? It may have been a crisis in the Corinthian church or in Corinth about which we have no more specific information. However in view of Paul's description of this distress (1 Cor 7:29-31) it seems as though he was speaking of the fact that we live in the last days. (219) They are last days because the Lord's return for us could end them at any time.

If this is correct, we live in the same present distress as the Corinthian believers did. It is a time of distress because of the hostility of unbelievers and increasing apostasy (cf. 1 Tim 4; 2 Tim 3). The Apostle Paul consistently viewed the inter-advent age as a time of crisis and distress.

The last part of the verse restates Paul's basic principle of abiding in one's calling (1 Cor 7:17, 20, 24). "Man" (NASB) or "you" (NIV) is *anthropos*, meaning "person."

7:27 - Paul thought it prudent to stay married rather than seeking a life of singleness with a view to serving the Lord more effectively. Obviously it would be wrong to split up a marriage for this purpose. If an unbelieving spouse had abandoned the Christian, or if he or she had lost his or her spouse to death, a single life would provide greater opportunity for Christian ministry.

7:28 - Nevertheless marrying in such a case is not sinful. Furthermore if a young woman decides to marry rather than staying single, she has not sinned. However the decision to marry may complicate her service of the Lord.

For example, suppose a single woman gets into a position where an adversary may torture her for her faith. She could face that possibility more easily than a married woman who has children for whom she has responsibility could. It is that kind of "trouble" that Paul evidently had in mind.

> "One of the unfortunate things that has happened to this text in the church is that the very pastoral concern of Paul that caused him to express himself in this way has been a source of anxiety rather than comfort. Part of the reason for this is that in Western cultures we do not generally live in a time of 'present distress.' Thus we fail to sense the kind of care that this text represents. Beyond that, what is often heard is that Paul prefers singleness to marriage, which he does. But quite in contrast to Paul's own position over against the Corinthians, we often read into that preference that singleness is somehow a superior status. That causes some who do not wish to remain single to become anxious about God's will in their lives. Such people need to hear it again: Marriage or singleness per se lies totally outside the category of 'commandments' to be obeyed or 'sin' if one indulges; and Paul's preference here is not predicated on 'spiritual' grounds but on pastoral concern. It is perfectly all right to marry." (220)

Reasons for remaining single 7:29-35

Paul next called his readers to take a different view of their relationship to the world since they lived in distressing times and the form of the world was passing away. We, too, need this view of the world since we also live in distressing times and the form of the world is still passing away.

7:29a - While it is true that the time a person has to serve Christ grows shorter with every day he or she lives, Paul probably meant that the Lord's return is closer every day. However it is not the amount of time that we have left that concerned Paul but the fact that we know our time is limited. Christians should live with a certain perspective on the future and, therefore, we should live with eternity's values consciously in view. We should be ready to make sacrifices now in view of the possibility of greater reward later (1 Cor 3:14).

7:29b-31a - Married men should live as soldiers of the Cross willing to forgo some of the comforts and pleasures of family life, but not its responsibilities, since we are in a spiritual battle. Those who weep should remember that present sorrow will be comparatively short (cf. Luke 6:21). Likewise those who rejoice should bear in mind that we have a serious purpose to fulfill in life (Luke 6:25). When we make purchases, we need to consider that we are only stewards of God and that everything really belongs to Him. The Christian should use the world and everything in it to serve the Lord, but we must not get completely wrapped up in the things of this world. Therefore, whether a person is single or married he or she should live with an attitude of detachment from the world. We should not let it engross or absorb us.

7:31b - The reason for viewing life this way is that earthly life as we know it is only temporary and is passing away.

7:32a - Paul wanted his readers to be free from concerns about this present life so devotion to the Lord would be consistent (1 Cor 7:35; cf. Matt 6:25-34; Phil 4:11; 1 Pet 5:7). He wanted us to live as eschatological people. Our new existence in Christ should determine our lives, not the world in its present form. Buying and marrying should not determine our existence. A clear view of the future should do that.

7:32b-34 - Comparing two equally committed Christians, an unmarried man can give more concentrated attention to the things of the Lord. A married man also needs to think about his family responsibilities. This is true of women, and particularly virgins, as well as men. (221) Some interpreters put more emphasis on the negative anxiety feeling while others stress the positive legitimate care that each person needs to show. Both aspects of concern are probably in view. Even though the unmarried state is desirable, it is not intrinsically better. (222)

7:35 - Paul did not want his readers to regard his preceding comments as an attempt to build too strong a case for celibacy, as ascetics do. He wanted to help his readers appreciate the realities of the single and married states so they could express unhindered devotion to the Lord. Christians have genuine freedom under the Lord to choose to be single or married. (223) However, we need to view life in view of the "present distress" and the "shortened times" as we consider our options.

Single women have freedom to choose whether they want to get married as do single men. Nevertheless the realities of life in Christ that Paul outlined in this pericope need to inform that decision.

The legitimacy of marriage 7:36-40

This section concludes Paul's entire teaching on marriage in this chapter. However it contains problems related to the meaning of "virgin" as is clear from the three different interpretations in the NASB, the NIV, and the NEB. I tend to think that these verses do not introduce a special case (advice to fathers of virgins [224]) but connect with verse 35. Probably the man in view is the fiancé of the virgin who is considering the possibility of marriage with her. (225) The pericope then summarizes what Paul has already taught.

7:36 - Paul urged any man not to feel that he must remain single or that he and his virgin girlfriend must forgo sexual fulfillment after marriage (1 Cor 7:1-7). He might have been reluctant to marry because of what Paul had written about the single state being preferable (1 Cor 7:8, 28-34). He might also have hesitated because of ascetic influences in the church that were due to a false sense of "spirituality" and possibly an overreaction to the fornication in Corinth.

7:37 - Likewise the man who preferred to take Paul's advice to remain single should feel at peace about his decision. External pressure from the ascetic Corinthians or from what Paul himself had just written need not constrain him. He should follow his own convictions about marrying or not marrying.

7:38 - The decision in view is one involving the good and the better rather than the right and the wrong or not sinning and sinning. This is a good example of an amoral situation. Paul addressed other amoral situations later in this epistle (cf. 1 Cor 8:1-13; 9; 10; 11:1).

> "So at the end Paul has agreed, and disagreed, with the Corinthians in their letter. They prefer celibacy for 'spiritual' reasons; he prefers it for pastoral and eschatological ones. But quite in contrast to them, he also affirms marriage; indeed, he does so strongly: Such a man 'does well.' But there is one final word. These verses are addressed to the man; but in keeping with his response throughout, there is a final word for married women as well." (227)

7:39 - The remaining two verses conclude both major sections of the discussion by repeating that women should not separate from their husbands (cf. 1 Cor 7:1-24). This concluding reminder is especially important for virgins considering the possibility of marrying. Again Paul referred to marriage as a binding relationship (cf. 1 Cor 7:15, 27). The wife is bound (Gr. *deo*) to her husband as long as he lives. Does this mean that even if he leaves her the marriage tie is unbroken? That is what many interpreters have concluded. If that is the case, remarriage after a divorce or separation would constitute adultery (cf. Matt 19:9; Mk 10:11-12). In that case, one should avoid remarriage before the death of the spouse.

Another possibility is that Paul conceded, but did not restate, the fact that desertion by an unbelieving spouse freed the Christian and he or she was no longer under bondage to the mate (1 Cor 7:15). This applied only to mixed marriages, however.

Paul regarded death as the only thing that always breaks the marriage bond. This may imply that present marital relationships will not continue in heaven just as they are now (cf. Luke 20:34-36). Jesus taught that fornication may break the marriage bond if the marriage partners do not reunite (Matt 19:9). God may permit separation or divorce in certain circumstances (cf. Matt 19:9; 1 Cor 7:15), but remarriage usually results in adultery.

When a Christian woman's husband dies, she is at liberty to marry whomever she chooses provided he is a believer (cf. 2 Cor 6:14). The same rule would apply to a Christian man whose wife dies.

> "Long, long ago Plutarch, the wise old Greek, laid it down, that 'marriage cannot be happy unless husband and wife are of the same religion.'" (228)

7:40 - Paul expressed his opinion, that a widow would probably be better off to remain unmarried, with a very light touch, one that he used throughout this chapter. This decision, as well as all decisions about whether to marry or not, pivots on a delicate balance. I suspect that Paul would have acknowledged that given certain conditions a widow might be better off to marry.

For example, faced with the prospect of choosing between a fine Christian husband and a life of destitute poverty it would probably be better for her to remarry. However if all other things are equal, the single state seemed preferable to the apostle. Notice that the issue is the widow's happiness, not her obedience.

Paul undoubtedly knew he represented the mind of the Spirit in what he said. He simply expressed himself as he did to avoid laying too much weight on his preference.

Bibliography

187. Ibid., pp. 266-67.

188. Bruce, *1 and 2 Corinthians*, p. 66.

189. Fee, *The First . . .*, p. 268.

190. Ibid., pp. 269-70.

191. Ibid., p. 270. This hypothesis, which seems valid to me in light of the passage, results in a different interpretation of the text than has been traditional. The traditional view takes the entire section as

explaining Paul's position on marriage in general in response to the Corinthians' question about its advisability (e.g., Godet, Lightfoot, Grosheide, Morris, Mare, Wiersbe).

192. Fee, *The First . . .*, p. 275; Lowery, p. 517.

193. Barrett, p. 154.

194. Morris, p. 105.

195. Robertson and Plummer, p. 133.

196. Laying aside eating (fasting) or sleeping (watching) temporarily to engage in more important spiritual duties (e.g., prayer) is similar.

197. Robertson and Plummer, p. 134.

198. Fee, *The First . . .*, p. 284.

199. There is a Greek word for "widowers," but it does not appear in the koine period. Agamos served in its place. See ibid., pp. 287-88, for additional support for this view.

200. Ibid., p. 291.

201. This is one of the rare instances when Paul appealed directly to Jesus' teachings (cf. 9:14; 11:23; 1 Tim. 5:18). Usually he taught in harmony with Jesus without citing Him.

202. Fee, *The First . . .*, p. 293.

203. William F. Arndt and F. Wilbur Gingrich, *A Greek-English Lexicon of the New Testament*, p. 899.

204. Barclay, *The Letters . . .*, p. 70.

205. Barrett, p. 164.

206. Bruce, *1 and 2 Corinthians*, p. 69.

207. Robertson and Plummer, p. 142.

208. Johnson, p. 1240.

209. E.g., Robertson and Plummer, p. 143; Fee, *The First . . .*, pp. 302-3.

210. E.g., William A. Heth and Gordon J. Wenham, *Jesus and Divorce*.

211. E.g., Barrett, p. 166; Bruce, *1 and 2 Corinthians*, p. 70; Lenski, pp. 294-95; Lowery, p. 518; Morris, p.

111.

212. See Robertson, 4:128.

213. Barrett, p. 167.

214. Fee, *The First . . .*, p. 307.

215. Ibid., p. 311. Cf. Robertson and Plummer, p. 144.

216. Ibid., p. 146.

217. A freedman was a person who had formerly been a slave but had received manumission, been set free.

218. Fee, *The First . . .*, p. 319.

219. Barrett, p. 175; Barclay, *The Letters . . .*, p. 77; et al.

220. Fee, *The First . . .*, p. 334.

221. Queen Elizabeth I said that England was her husband. Robertson and Plummer, p. 158.

222. Barrett, p. 181.

223. Similarly we have freedom to choose how many children to have and when to have them, assuming we can have them. There is no New Covenant legislation in this regard.

224. E.g., Robertson and Plummer, p. 158; Lowery, p. 520.

225. Barrett, p. 184.

226. Robertson, 4:135.

227. Fee, *The First . . .*, p. 355.

228. Barclay, *The Letters . . .*, p. 79.

Lesson 6 Self Check

QUESTION 1

Paul's advice about virgins (1 Cor 7:35) could refer to the situation of engaged people, or to the situation of a father with his marriageable age daughter, or possibly to the situation of men and women in a "spiritual marriage." *True or False?*

QUESTION 2

Paul distinguishes between the authority of Jesus' statements and the authority of his own apostolic instruction. *True or False?*

QUESTION 3

Why should a believer remain in the situation in life in which he was called?

    A. Too many changes at once are not good.

    B. It is sin to make any changes.

    C. One's status does not affect his relationship with God.

    D. God doesn't make mistakes.

QUESTION 4

According to Paul, one good reason for Christians to marry is to avoid _____.

    A. Immorality

    B. Shame

    C. Childlessness

    D. Parental pressure

QUESTION 5

It is not God's will for a Christian to marry a non-believer. *True or False?*

QUESTION 6

Which of the following is **not** a necessary condition for believers to abstain from sexual relations within marriage?

    A. By mutual agreement

    B. For a short time

    C. For the purpose of prayer

    D. For becoming more holy

QUESTION 7

Marriage and singleness are both spiritual gifts. *True or False?*

QUESTION 8

It is abnormal to remain single. *True or False?*

QUESTION 9

Paul permits divorce in mixed marriages under what circumstances?

    A. If the non-believer leaves

    B. If the believer suffers abuse

    C. If the believer has prayed about it

    D. If the local church permits it

QUESTION 10

Children with at least one Christian parent are saved. *True or False?*

Lesson 6 Answers to Questions

QUESTION 1
B. Abstention from sex within marriage

QUESTION 2: Rights

QUESTION 3: True

QUESTION 4: False

QUESTION 5
A. Jesus said this when He taught on earth.

QUESTION 6
B. Jesus never said this when He taught on earth.
D. This is Paul's own apostolic instruction.

QUESTION 7

Scripture	Reason
1 Corinthians 7:14	Special blessings to the spouse and children because of the believer
1 Corinthians 7:16	Witness to the unbeliever
1 Corinthians 7:17	"Remain as you are" as a general principle

QUESTION 8: *Your answer*

QUESTION 9: True

QUESTION 10
D. Keeping God's commands

QUESTION 11: *Your answer should be one of the following:*
Three, 3

QUESTION 12: False

QUESTION 13: *Your answer*

QUESTION 14
B. This is Paul's wise advice.
C. Jesus has not spoken about this matter.

QUESTION 15
A. The last days before Christ's return

QUESTION 16: *Your answer*

QUESTION 17: *Your answer should be similar to the following:*
Divided interests

QUESTION 18: False

QUESTION 19: *Your answer should be one of the following:*
Freedom, Liberty

QUESTION 20: *Your answer*

QUESTION 21: *Your answer*

Lesson 6 Self Check Answers

QUESTION 1: True
QUESTION 2: False
QUESTION 3
    C. One's status does not affect his relationship with God.
QUESTION 4
    A. Immorality
QUESTION 5: True
QUESTION 6
    D. For becoming more holy
QUESTION 7: True
QUESTION 8: False
QUESTION 9
    A. If the non-believer leaves
QUESTION 10: False

Lesson 7: Freedom in Food
(1 Cor 8:1-13; 10:1-11:1)

Lesson Introduction

The topics covered in 1 Corinthians 8:1-11:1 constitute one large section. In it, Paul discusses what at first seems to be two separate topics: food offered to idols in 1 Corinthians 8 and 10, and Paul's rights as an apostle in 1 Corinthians 9. Many students puzzle over why the subject of food offered to idols seems to be interrupted in Paul's discussion. However, careful study reveals that Paul has one overriding theme for this long segment—freedom. As we will see, chapter 9, which discusses Paul's apostolic rights, is an illustration of the principle of foregoing rights or freedom for a higher purpose. Although it is integral to Paul's argument in this long segment, we wait until Lesson 8 to consider that passage.

Many Western believers may consider eating food offered to idols an irrelevant topic, for they can hardly imagine people giving food to idols. However, for many people from Asia this is quite common even today. Any tourist to Hong Kong, for example, will see "god shelves" in just about every restaurant, and temples to false gods all over the city. What the tourist may not see are the "god shelves" in the vast majority of homes, where regular worship of ancestors and false gods takes place.

Topic 1 addresses Corinthian arguments for the freedom to eat food offered to idols. These arguments are cogent and true, but Paul shows that they omit love for the weaker brother.

In Topic 2 the consequences of exercising freedom without love become clear.

Paul reinforces his case with lessons from Israel's history in Topic 3. Moving beyond the weaker brother argument, Paul warns against testing a jealous God by participating in idolatry. Instead, the Christian should exercise his freedom by taking the way out of temptation that God provides.

The way out is clear, as Topic 4 explores—fleeing from idolatry.

The overriding principle for exercising freedom is stated in Topic 5. Everything must be done for God's glory; avoiding needless offense, forgoing rights, and imitating Christ.

Lesson Outline

Topic 1: Arguments for Freedom to Eat (1 Cor 8:1-6)

We All Have Knowledge (8:1-3)

Only One God (8:4-6)

Topic 2: Principle: Restraint of Love (1 Cor 8:7-13)

Consider the Weak (8:7-10)

Consequences to Brother and Self (8:11-13)

Topic 3: Lessons From Israel's History (1 Cor 10:1-13)

Israel's Baptism and Communion (10:1-4)

Israel's Testing the Lord (10:5-10)

Principle: God's Way Out of Temptation (10:11-13)

Topic 4: Separate From Idolatry (1 Cor 10:14-22)

Communion With Christ and Sacrifices to Demons (10:14-20)

Idolatry and Meat Offered to Idols (10:21-22)

Topic 5: Principle: Do Everything to Glorify God (1 Cor 10:23-11:1)

Principle: The Good of the Other Person (10:23-24)

Application to Eating (10:25-11:1)

Lesson Objectives

Every New Year brings awkwardness. Shan and his mother do special rituals to ask their deceased ancestors for blessings in the coming year. Actually it is a big event for Shan's extended family—something they have been doing for generations. They dress up in traditional clothing, eat special foods, sing special songs, and celebrate. Lotus has no problem with participating in most of the celebrations, but she feels uneasy about going to the town shrine and bowing before the tablet with the ancestors' names. It is especially unsettling because everyone will light incense and make offerings to the ancestors. Lotus explains to Shan that she can no longer do that after she trusted Jesus, because she can only worship and pray to God. At first, he had kept pressuring her, saying that it was only tradition and didn't really mean anything. "If you do it, it keeps the old people happy," he says.

After she trusted Jesus, Lotus also stopped helping her mother-in-law tend to the god shelf in their home every morning. Her mother-in-law is very concerned about keeping the god shelf, changing the fruit and incense sticks, and keeping it clean.

Lotus doesn't know how best to explain all this to her children. Their cousins go every New Year with the rest of the family to the celebrations at the village shrine, but she doesn't want her children to participate. The children are torn in both directions. Even though Shan and his mother don't approve, she keeps them away. After all, she tells Shan, they go with her to church, and church people don't participate in ceremonies at the town shrine.

This year there is another awkward decision to make. The extended family ordered a whole roasted pig to celebrate with at New Year's. Shan has the idea of taking the roasted pig to the shrine to offer it to the ancestors and then bringing it back for a big family dinner. Lotus wonders what to do. She tells him it would be better to cut off a piece of the pig to take to the shrine to offer to the ancestors and leave the rest at their house for everyone to eat. How could she eat it if it has first been offered to the ancestors? She feels it is wrong, and she does not want to give her relatives the impression that she can participate in their religious ceremonies.

She turns to 1 Corinthians 8 and 10 and tries to understand what the Bible says about this issue.

By the end of this lesson, you will be able to:

- Understand the issues relating to eating food sacrificed to idols, and reasons why some advocate freedom in eating
- Reflect on how love limits Christian freedom
- Seek God's way out of temptation
- Reflect on how truth limits Christian freedom
- Consider how your actions affect other believers

Topic 1: Arguments for Freedom to Eat (1 Cor 8:1-6)

Theological arguments can be marshaled in support of improper actions. For example, one possible application to the doctrine of the imminent return of Christ is to quit work, sell everything, and devote oneself to prayer. After all, some might reason, if Christ is coming soon, why spend your time working? The problems with this position are that we don't know when "soon" is, that we need to make money for ourselves and our dependants, and that unbelievers would view quitting work as extreme, fanatical behavior. It is best to live our lives as if Jesus could come at any moment, but to plan our lives as if He will not come for many years.

Similarly, arguments can be marshaled in support of the believer having the freedom to eat anything at any time. Paul referred to these arguments as "knowledge" in 1 Corinthians 8:1, and he compares knowledge to love.

We All Have Knowledge (8:1-3)

Assignment

- Read 1 Corinthians 8:1-3

- Read Constable, "Food Offered to Idols" (refer to the Articles section at the end of this lesson), through the note on 8:3.

- Read "We All Have Knowledge."

We All Have Knowledge

What was the pull or temptation to visit an idol's temple? We find such a temptation hard to understand today, but in ancient Corinth pagan temples had tremendous social importance—not just religious. It might be similar today in some parts of the world, where going to the local church can be primarily a social exercise for many. Perhaps important family events, such as birthdays, weddings, or funerals, would be held at the pagan temples. In other circumstances, attendance at the temple was tantamount to going to a party, eating out with business partners, or just getting together with friends. For a Christian to refuse to attend such gatherings would be viewed as anti-social and might hinder family or business relations.

The ancient city of Corinth had many idols and temples to false gods. Most people in the city did not eat meat as part of their everyday diet. There was no refrigeration and meat was relatively expensive, so it would be eaten mostly on special occasions, frequently with religious significance. Whenever anyone bought a piece of meat, there was a high probability that it had been offered first in worship to a false god.

Generally, there were four situations that a believer faced that could involve eating food offered to idols:

> 1. Eating food bought from the marketplace. Possibly the food had been offered to an idol prior to being sold.

> 2. Eating food in an idol's temple. This meant eating as part of a pagan religious observance.

> 3. Eating food in a restaurant. Choice meat was sold there, but certainly some had already been offered to an idol.

> 4. Eating food at someone's house. If an unbeliever invites you to dinner, there was the possibility that the food had been offered to an idol.

> If love is neglected, knowledge of the truth is counterproductive. People feel proud of having knowledge, but the spiritual person acts based on both knowledge and love.

QUESTION 1

In Corinth, the issue of food sacrificed to idols touched on what areas of life? *(Select all that apply.)*

    A. Social

    B. Family

    C. Business

    D. Religious

QUESTION 2

Correct doctrine does not guarantee that the believer will act according to _____.

Only One God (8:4-6)

Assignment

- Read 1 Corinthians 8:4-6
- Read Constable, "The Content of the Way of Knowledge" (refer to the Articles section at the end of this lesson).
- Read "Only One God."

Only One God

The NET Bible places "we all have knowledge" (1 Cor 8:1), "an idol in this world is nothing" (1 Cor 8:4), and "there is no God but one" (1 Cor 8:4) in quotes, indicating that Paul is repeating the Corinthians' slogans. He agrees with these statements, but not with the Corinthians' applications of them. Knowledge may give freedom to act, but acting from knowledge is not always the same as acting from love. In this case, the Corinthians were using their knowledge to justify eating food offered to idols. Instead of just emphasizing knowledge, valuable though it is, Paul reminds them of the higher value of love.

Christians confidently dismiss idols as false gods, mere blocks of wood, stone, or precious gems. This is consistent with Psalm 115:4-8. Often, however, there are demonic forces behind these blocks of wood. The practical problem is how to deal with social and economic structures built on belief in false gods.

QUESTION 3

The dominant religious view in Corinth when Paul wrote 1 Corinthians was polytheism. *True or False?*

QUESTION 4

Do believers in your church view idols as false gods? If not, how could you explain this to them using Scripture? Open your Life Notebook and record your thoughts.

Topic 2: Principle: Restraint of Love (1 Cor 8:7-13)

Here Paul emphasizes his main reason for avoiding food offered to idols. It is not the food itself nor the idol, but rather the weaker brother. A Christian's authority/freedom must be limited by love: How will my actions affect other believers? If the exercise of my freedom causes a brother to fall into sin, then I am misusing my freedom.

Consider the Weak (8:7-10)

Assignment

- Read 1 Corinthians 8:7-10.
- Read Constable, "The Criterion Care for a Brother" (refer to the Articles section at the end of this lesson), through the note on 8:10.
- Read "Consider the Weak."

> **Consider the Weak**
>
> This is the first time for Paul to use the term "conscience" in this letter, and he uses it seven times in Chapters 8 and 10. Conscience refers to the inner sense of right and wrong. A believer with a "weak" conscience, in this context, has not fully integrated knowledge and emotions. For a new believer who prior to conversion regularly worshipped idols by eating sacrificial foods in a temple, exposure to the same setting after conversion could be a great temptation. Although he knows in his head that "an idol is nothing," still, he lacks the stability of faith to resist the temptation to worship the idol. There is much power in habit, upbringing, culture, and, as Paul will point out later, in demons (1 Cor 10:20). His conscience would be defiled—i.e. his faith would fail to stand up to the temptation, and he would fall back into idolatry.
>
> Paul's position reflects the teaching of Jesus when He said, "But if anyone causes one of these little ones who believe in me to sin, it would be better for him to have a huge millstone hung around his neck and to be drowned in the open sea." (Mt 18:6)

QUESTION 5

The Greek word, "exousia" means "freedom of choice, right, authority, or power." It is translated many different ways in the New Testament. See if you can match the Scriptures below with how *exousia* is translated in the verse."

Reference	Translation
1 Corinthians 6:12	be controlled
1 Corinthians 7:4	this liberty
1 Corinthians 7:37	has the rights to
1 Corinthians 8:9	the right
1 Corinthians 9:4, 5, 6	has control
1 Corinthians 11:10	symbol of authority
1 Corinthians 15:24	authority

QUESTION 6

"Weak" in this context means

    A. Immature and carnal

    B. Unbelieving and rebellious

    C. Confused and wavering

    D. Bound by tradition or prior experience

Consequences to Brother and Self (8:11-13)

Assignment

- Read 1 Corinthians 8:11-13.
- Continue reading Constable, "The Criterion Care for a Brother" (refer to the Articles section at the end of this lesson), through the note on 8:13.
- Read "Consequences to Brother and Self."

Consequences to Brother and Self

The proper application of the principle "love limits freedom" is a willingness to limit one's freedom. To be clear: Paul is not talking about limiting your freedom just because someone disagrees with you, or would be upset with you. He instead refers to situations where a weak believer would be incited to sin, even to the point of denying his faith, because of your example.

Paul does not address the weak brother in his counsel. He writes as if all the readers are "strong," perhaps because that is the position expressed in their letter to him. Nowhere does Paul urge the believers at Corinth to try to change the weak brother, or to alter his convictions.

How does Paul's discussion in 1 Corinthians 8 and 10 relate to the decree of the Jerusalem Council in Acts 15:29? The decree gave certain necessary rules to Gentile believers: "that you abstain from meat that has been sacrificed to idols and from blood and from what has been strangled and from sexual immorality." The Jerusalem Council is dated around AD 49, and 1 Corinthians is dated around six years later. Paul spread news of the decree to the Galatian churches planted during his first missionary journey (Acts 16:4). James considered the decree to be still valid when Paul visited Jerusalem around AD 57, after he had written 1 and 2 Corinthians (Acts 21:25). The decree came on the heels of the clarification of the gospel of salvation by grace through faith. In other words, Gentile believers do not have to be circumcised or keep the law of Moses in order to be saved (neither do Jewish believers).

Why does Paul not mention this decree? One view is that the decree requirements were given for the purpose of fellowship between Jewish background and Gentile background believers. In order for these two groups to not offend each other, Gentiles were asked to keep basic Jewish food laws and to avoid immorality. Probably immorality is mentioned along with these food laws because it was an integral part of worship at temples to false gods. As Dr. Constable says:

> James was not putting Gentile converts under the Mosaic Law by imposing these restrictions. He was urging them to limit their exercise of Christian liberty to make their witness to unsaved Jews more effective and their fellowship with saved Jews more harmonious (cf. 1 Cor. 9:19-23). (*Dr. Constable's Notes on Acts*, 2005 Edition, note on Acts 15:21)

According to this view, since the issue at Corinth was not fellowship between Jewish and Gentile background believers, Paul probably did not think the Jerusalem decree applied in this case.

Another view is that the Jerusalem Council's decree prohibited idolatry, and that the four specific prohibitions of the decree were all connected to pagan temples. (See http://www.torahresource.com/EnglishArticles/NoachideETS2.pdf) Under this view, Paul upheld and elaborated on the decree of the Jerusalem Council in 1 Corinthians 8-10.

The Corinthian believers who advocated continuing to eat in pagan temples appealed to knowledge, but their knowledge was self-centered. They failed to consider the effects of their actions on others.

QUESTION 7

The exercise of our freedom in Christ can be _____ to other believers.

QUESTION 8

Is Paul advising that our freedom be limited to that of the weakest brother? Open your Life Notebook and comment on these situations:

(A) Your church meets for worship in a rented auditorium. Noticing the opportunity for expanded business, the owner of a local bakery sets up a bread stand near the entrance of the auditorium. As you are leaving worship one Sunday, one of the believers says to you, "It's sinful to buy anything on Sunday." How would you respond? Would you buy anything on Sunday?

(B) In many Western countries, Christians disagree as to whether or not drinking alcohol is permissible. What is an issue of disagreement between believers in your culture? How would you approach this issue in light of Paul's admonition?

Topic 3: Lessons From Israel's History (1 Cor 10:1-13)

By continuing to eat at idol feasts, the Corinthian believers were risking God's discipline. One reason to avoid such feasts was already explained—love for the weaker brother. Now Paul outlines a second reason. Drawing on the authoritative record of the Old Testament, Paul warns the church not to follow the example of Israel in the wilderness and suffer the same disastrous results.

Israel's Baptism and Communion (10:1-4)

Assignment

- Read 1 Corinthians 10:1-4.
- Read Constable, "The Sinfulness of Idolatry" (refer to the Articles section at the end of this lesson), through the note on 10:4.
- Read "Israel's Baptism and Communion."

Israel's Baptism and Communion

Paul uses the record of Israel during the exodus and in the wilderness to illustrate the truth that religious rituals and spiritual experiences do not guarantee the inheritance. Neither do such things protect people from falling into sin or from God's judgment on sin.

Paul is countering people who think that baptism, communion, and other spiritual experiences gave them license to sin and to test the Lord—particularly by eating in idol's temples.

Even though the church at Corinth was made up of believers mostly from a Gentile background, Paul reminds them of the experience of God's people in the Old Testament, calling them "our fathers." His point is the analogous situation of experiencing God's blessings as His chosen people.

QUESTION 9

Once a person is baptized, he will not fall into idolatry. *True or False?*

QUESTION 10

Which parallels does Paul draw between Israel in the wilderness and the church at Corinth? *(Select all that apply.)*

- A. Both were baptized.
- B. Both enjoyed spiritual food and drink.
- C. Christ supplied the needs of both.
- D. Both were led by God's appointed leaders.

Israel's Testing the Lord (10:5-10)

Assignment

- Read 1 Corinthians 10:5-10.

- Continue reading Constable, "The Sinfulness of Idolatry" (refer to the Articles section at the end of this lesson), through the note on 10:10.
- Read "Israel's Testing the Lord."

Israel's Testing the Lord

When Israel sinned in the wilderness, the resulting punishment was physical death for many. They died in the wilderness before they gained their inheritance, the land of Canaan. The writer of Hebrews also uses this example to warn the recipients of his letter: the Israelites fell in the desert because of their unbelief (Heb 3:19). Witnessing the amazing miracles of Egypt, the crossing of the Red Sea, water from the rock, God's daily provision of manna, the giving of the law on Mount Sinai, and victory in battle were all insufficient to prevent unbelief. This seems to be the root cause of "putting the Lord to the test"—unbelief.

The history of Israel in the Old Testament is primarily the history of their sin. Concentrating on the example of the generation that God redeemed from Egypt, Paul recounted their repeated heinous sins and God's just judgments.

QUESTION 11

Match the sins Paul warns of in this passage with the Corinthians' behavior

Sins	Behavior
Idolatry	1 Corinthians 11:16
Immorality	1 Corinthians 8:10
Testing the Lord	1 Corinthians 5:1
Grumbling	1 Corinthians 5:2

QUESTION 12

Just as the Israelites were cut down in the wilderness, so the sinning Corinthians risk God's _____.

Principle: God's Way Out of Temptation (10:11-13)

Assignment

- Read 1 Corinthians 10:11-13, and memorize 1 Corinthians 10:13.
- Read "God's Way Out of Temptation."

God's Way Out of Temptation

Different Bibles translate the Greek word in 1 Corinthians 10:13 as either "trial" or "temptation." The word can have either meaning. Probably in this context "temptation" is better, since they were risking idolatry by insisting on their right to eat food offered to idols.

Those who thought they were standing (1 Cor 10:12) probably refers to people who were trusting in their spiritual experiences, like baptism and communion, to protect them. They had a false sense of security.

God always provides the way of escape from temptation, but it takes various forms. Sometimes the way out is simply to say "no" and refuse to do it. God will give us the strength for that.

Sometimes the way out means suffering and even death—you just have to endure and not compromise. Sometimes the way out is to flee the temptation. Sometimes the way out is to choose to trust God and obey Him when you are tempted to doubt.

QUESTION 13

God promises to remove temptation from obedient believers. *True or False?*

QUESTION 14

Paul cautions in this passage against a false sense of security in the Christian life. What things make for a false sense of security for believers today? Open your Life Notebook and list several examples. How would you respond to people who bring up those examples?

Topic 4: Separate From Idolatry (1 Cor 10:14-22)

Having assured them that God gives the way out of temptation, Paul then urges them to utilize that way out: flee idolatry. Not only do they have the power to resist the temptation, but it is the only reasonable course of action for believers who commune with Christ. To fail to flee idolatry risks inciting the jealousy of our holy God.

Communion With Christ and Sacrifices to Demons (10:14-20)

Assignment

- Read 1 Corinthians 10:14-20.
- Read Constable, "The Incompatibility of Christianity and Idolatry" (refer to the Articles section at the end of this lesson), through the note on 10:20.
- Read "Communion With Christ and Sacrifices to Demons."

Communion With Christ and Sacrifices to Demons

"Flee" is seen for the second time in 1 Corinthians. The verb is in the present continuous tense, and indicates continuing or constantly repeated action. Fleeing is God's way out of this temptation to idolatry. In this case, "flee" means to turn your back on idolatry.

Paul draws further analogies between Israel and the Old Testament sacrificial system on the one hand, and believers and the Lord's Supper on the other hand. The issue is not the food itself, nor the idol itself. Food is just food, and an idol is nothing. However, worship of idols is really worship of demons. Demons really do exist and have spiritual power. Paul speaks strongly against believers partnering with false gods. Clearly, it is wrong, a violation of faith in the one true God.

The "knowledge" that gave the Corinthians the right to eat food offered to idols in an idol's temple failed to take into account love and truth. Love for the weaker brother should be sufficient by itself to cause them to refrain. If that were not enough, the truth that there is no fellowship between light and darkness should also cause them to refrain (2 Cor 6:14).

In addition to the parallel between Israel in the wilderness and the church at Corinth, there is also the parallel between offering sacrifices and Communion. Eating at idol feasts means participation with the powers behind those idols, just as eating at Communion means participation with Christ.

QUESTION 15

The spiritual reality associated with idolatry is _____.

QUESTION 16

Paul's warning against idolatry is directed against

    A. Weak believers

    B. Strong believers

    C. Unbelievers

    D. All believers

QUESTION 17

The temptation to idolatry at Corinth fell mainly on weak believers. *True or False?*

Idolatry and Meat Offered to Idols (10:21-22)

Assignment

- Read 1 Corinthians 10:21-22.

Paul forbids believers from participating in idolatry. For him, it is unthinkable and a gross violation of the basics of our faith. To do so brings a believer under God's judgment.

QUESTION 18

In the interests of world peace, Paul would advocate that Christians, Muslims and Buddhists should all participate in each other's worship ceremonies. *True or False?*

Topic 5: Principle: Do Everything to Glorify God (1 Cor 10:23–11:1)

If abstaining from idol feasts is required for believers, what about meat sold in the marketplace or eating at the homes of unbelievers? Are Christians to withdraw from the world, or only eat food they themselves have grown? Here Paul addresses issues of everyday living in a pagan environment.

Principle: The Good of the Other Person (10:23-24)

Assignment

- Read 1 Corinthians 10:23-24.

- Read Constable, "The Issue of the Marketplace Food" (refer to the Articles section at the end of this lesson), through the note on 10:24.

- Read "The Good of the Other Person."

The Good of the Other Person

Paul extends the principle which he previously stated in 1 Corinthians 6:12 with reference to immorality. Here, he applies it in relations not just with fellow believers, but also with the unbelieving community.

Love for others should affect the application of truth. Mature thinking considers the effects of one's actions on others.

QUESTION 19

In 1 Corinthians 10:23-24, Paul advises believers to refrain from exercising their rights

A. For the benefit of others

B. To make others happy

C. Because it's a part of suffering for Christ

D. As a way of subduing one's own body

QUESTION 20

Seeking your own good in this context (1 Cor 10:24) means being selfish. *True or False?*

Application to Eating (10:25–11:1)

Assignment

- Read 1 Corinthians 10:25-33; 11:1.
- Read "Application to Eating."

Application to Eating

In 1 Corinthians 10:25 Paul clarifies his teaching on eating marketplace food. A believer may buy and eat such food freely, regardless of whether or not it has been offered to an idol. He does not have to buy only from a Christian or Jewish meat seller to guarantee its source.

1 Corinthians 10:29-30 are best taken as an aside, or as parenthetical. (Another possibility is to view verses 28 and 29 as parenthetical.) Paul affirms a believer's freedom in Christ, and that freedom includes the freedom not to be judged in disputable matters. Still, that freedom must be tempered by love for the weak brother—a concern not to cause him to fall into sin. Also, though he does not mention it here, that freedom must be tempered by truth—a believer cannot worship both the true God and idols.

Who is the "other person" in 1 Corinthians 10:29? Is he a Christian or a non-believer? Dr. Constable's position is that the other person is an unbeliever who "does not want his Christian guest to be unaware that he is being served food that the Christian might object to and might [want] (*sic*) to abstain from eating."

An alternate view is that Paul is referring to a weak believer who is also eating at the home of the unbeliever. This interpretation makes sense in the broad context where Paul has been concerned about not causing a fellow believer to fall into sin.

Clearly, in 1 Corinthians 10:32, "Do not give offense to Jews or Greeks or to the church of God,"

Paul expands his principle to also include non-believers. It would be insensitive for a Christian to order non-kosher food when dining with an orthodox Jew, or to order pork when eating with a Muslim.

The believer's true freedom is to glorify God, to love others, and to follow the example of Christ. A believer is freed from focusing on himself and his rights, and freed to focus on Christ and others.

Paul and Jesus offended many people, some of whom wanted to kill them. Yet it was never their aim to give offense if it could be avoided while standing for the truth. At Corinth, for a believer to refuse to participate in an idol feast may well have offended some, but such a choice was necessary. Removed from the context of idolatry, eating is an area of Christian freedom, but such freedom may need to be limited for the benefit of others.

QUESTION 21

In 1 Corinthians 10:33, Paul says that he tries "to please everyone in all things." In Galatians 1:10, Paul asserts that he is not trying to please people. Is Paul contradicting himself?

QUESTION 22

Would you visit a mosque, or a Hindu or Buddhist temple? What would you do if asked remove your shoes, or do special washings, or bow, or make a donation as part of the visit?

QUESTION 23

Would you eat meat that has been offered to idols? Under what circumstances would you eat, and under what circumstances would you refrain? How would you counsel Lotus?

Lesson 7 Articles

Notes on 1 Corinthians

Dr. Thomas L. Constable; 2003 Edition

B. FOOD OFFERED TO IDOLS 8:1—11:1

The Corinthians had asked Paul another question, evidently in a combative spirit judging by the apostle's response. It involved a practice common in their culture.

The commentators understand the situation that Paul addressed in two different ways. Some of them believe that the eating of marketplace food that pagans had previously offered to idols was amoral in itself, but it was controversial enough to cause division among the church members. If this was indeed the issue that Paul addressed, it is only one of many similar "doubtful things." Advocates of this view believe that the apostle's directions to his readers here give us guidance in dealing with contemporary doubtful (amoral) matters.

Other interpreters believe that eating food sacrificed to idols involved a specific form of idolatry and was, therefore, not amoral but sinful (cf. 1 Cor 5:10-11). They assume that Paul was responding to the Corinthians' objection to his prohibition of this practice that he had written in his former letter to them. This view sees 1 Cor 8:10 and 1 Cor 10:1-22 as expressing the basic problem to which Paul was responding. I believe the text supports this interpretation of the facts better than the former one.

> "That going to the temples is the real issue is supported by the fact that the eating of cultic meals was a regular part of worship in antiquity. This is true not only of the nations that surrounded Israel, but of Israel itself. In the Corinth of Paul's time, such meals were still the regular practice both at state festivals and private celebrations of various kinds. There were three parts to these meals: the preparation, the sacrifice proper, and the feast. The meat of the sacrifices apparently was divided into three portions: that burned before the god, that apportioned to the worshipers, and that placed on the 'table of the god,' which was tended by cultic ministrants but also eaten by the worshipers. The significance of these meals has been much debated, but most likely they involved a combination of religious and social factors. The gods were thought to be present since the meals were held in their honor and sacrifices were made; nonetheless, they were also intensely social occasions for the participants. For the most part the Gentiles who had become believers in Corinth had probably attended such meals all their lives; this was the basic 'restaurant' in antiquity, and every kind of occasion was celebrated in this fashion.

> "The problem, then, is best reconstructed along the following lines. After their conversion—and most likely after the departure of Paul—some of them returned to the practice of attending the cultic meals. In his earlier letter Paul forbade such 'idolatry'; but they have taken exception to that prohibition and in their letter have made four points:

> "(1) They argue that 'all have knowledge' about idols [i.e., that there are no such things, so participation in these meals is not an issue, cf. vv. 1, 4]. . . .

> "(2) They also have knowledge about food, that it is a matter of indifference to God (8:8) . . .

> "(3) They seem to have a somewhat 'magical' view of the sacraments; those who have had Christian baptism and who partake of the Lord's Table are not in any danger of falling (10:1-4).

> "(4) Besides, there is considerable question in the minds of many whether Paul has the proper apostolic authority to forbid them on this matter. In their minds this has been

substantiated by two factors: first, his failure to accept support while with them; and second, his own apparently compromising stance on idol food sold in the marketplace (he abstained when eating with Jews, but ate when eating with Gentiles; cf. 9:19-23)." (230)

1. The priority of love over knowledge in Christian conduct ch. 8

The amount of corrective instruction concerning knowledge in this epistle makes clear that the Corinthian Christians valued knowledge too highly. Paul wrote that the real aim of the faith should not be knowledge but love.

Knowledge and love compared 8:1-3

Paul began by comparing the way of love and the way of knowledge to show their relative importance.

8:1 The key phrase *peri de* ("now concerning" or "now about") as well as a change in subject matter mark off a new section of this epistle.

Traditional interpreters of this passage have pointed out that in the Greco-Roman world of Paul's day, pagan Gentiles offered sacrificial animals to various pagan gods and goddesses in temples daily. Only a token portion went to the deity and burned up on the altar. The temple priests, attendants, and their families ate most of the meat, but frequently they could not eat all that the worshippers brought. Consequently they sold what remained to the meat market operators in the *agora* (marketplace).

There the general public purchased it. This meat was very desirable and popular because the pagans usually offered only the best animals in sacrifice. However the butchers did not usually identify it as meat that someone had offered to an idol. Traditional interpreters believe that this is the meat in view in the discussion. (231) As mentioned above, I think eating in an idol temple has better support.

In dealing with this issue Paul began as he customarily did in this epistle by identifying common ground of belief with his readers (1 Cor 6:2; 7:1). All the believers knew that there were no other gods beside the true God. This knowledge was leading some in the church to think that eating in an idol temple was insignificant. It probably led others to make no distinction between the kinds of meat they bought in the market. This was perfectly proper, as Paul pointed out later. Nevertheless knowledge of this fact was not the only factor his readers needed to consider in their relationship to eating this food.

The apostle established at the beginning of his discussion of this important subject that knowledge by itself produces arrogance (1 Cor 1:5; 12:8). We have already seen that arrogance was one of the Corinthians' major weaknesses (1 Cor 4:6, 18-19; 5:2). In contrast, love edifies. Knowledge puffs up, but love builds up (1 Cor 13:4). Paul did not mean his readers should abandon the knowledge that was foundational to their correct conduct. He meant that knowledge without love was incomplete and by itself would not lead them to correct conduct.

8:2 - Paul warned that if anyone thinks he or she has fully mastered any subject he or she can count on the fact that he or she has not. The reason for this is that there is always more to any subject than any one person ever appreciates. There is always another facet to it, another point of view that one has not considered when examining it, or more information about it.

This person's knowledge is deficient in another sense. His attitude toward his knowledge is wrong. He arrogantly and unrealistically claims to have exhausted his subject rather than humbly realizing that he has not done so. To think one has fully mastered any subject is the height of arrogance. Paul said what he did here to humble some of his readers. Some claimed that since there are no such things as idols it was perfectly obvious what the Christian's relation to eating meat in an idol's temple should be.

> "True *gnosis* ["knowledge"] consists not in the accumulation of so much data, nor even in the correctness of one's theology, but in the fact that one has learned to live in love toward all." (232)

"The distinction which it seems that these rather cumbersome clauses seek to express is between, on the one hand, the collection of pieces of information (*gnosis*) about God, and, on the other, the state of being personally, and rightly, related to him." (233)

"A famous preacher used to say, 'Some Christians grow; others just swell.'" (234)

8:3 - Paul chose one subject to illustrate the proper view. Accumulating all the facts about God that one can will not result in the most realistic knowledge of Him. One must also love God. If a person loves God, then God knows (recognizes) him in an intimate way and reveals Himself to him (1 Cor 2:10; Matt 11:27). Consequently it is really more important that God knows us than that we know Him. When He knows us intimately, He will enable us to know Him intimately.

." . . If a man loves God, this is a sign that God has taken the initiative." (235)

Logically not only will God enable those who love Him to know Him better, but He will also enable those who love Him to understand other subjects as well. Paul said this to establish the priority of love over knowledge in determining our behavior in various situations.

The content of the way of knowledge 8:4-6

Paul resumed his discussion of knowledge after digressing briefly in verses 2 and 3 to comment on the superiority of love over knowledge.

8:4 - In this verse Paul returned to the original subject of eating meals in idol temples and applied the priority of love over knowledge to it. Unquestionably idols are not spirit beings such as God. There is only one true God (Deut 6:4). Every Christian should know that, and the Corinthians did. "We know that" affirms what they all knew as true.

8:5 - Nevertheless for many people, the pagans and even Christians who do not have a correct concept of deity, there are many beings they regard as gods and lords over various areas of life. The Greeks applied the term "gods" to their traditional deities and the term "lords" to the deities of their mystery cults. (236)

8:6 - For instructed Christians there is only one God and one Lord. Paul did not mean that there are two separate beings, God and Lord. These are two names for the one true God who exists as Father and Son. The Scriptures establish the deity of Jesus Christ elsewhere (e.g., John 1:1, 14; 10:30; Colossians 1:15-19; et al.). Paul did not argue that point here but simply stated the Son's equality with the Father within the Godhead.

The point of difference is this. The Father is the source and goal of all things whereas the Son is the agent th[r]ough whom all things have come from God and will return to God. Since Paul's point was the unity of the Godhead, there was no need to complicate matters by referring to the Holy Spirit here.

The criterion of care for a brother 8:7-13

"He [Paul] develops an airtight case based on a solid theological foundation (8:6). But then comes the *alla* ('however' [v. 7]), and the argument moves in an entirely different direction.

"At issue is the nature of the community. Is it a community where those with a correct theology can ignore others who have an aversion to eating the idol-consecrated food? What must prevail is not the principle of superior knowledge but the realization that those who lack knowledge are those 'for whom Christ died' (8:11). Edification takes precedence over freedom; the other person's advantage takes precedence over one's own (10:23-24). The christological epistemology of 1:18–2:16 applied to the controversy over eating food offered to idols calls for a community of sensitivity and love." (237)

8:7 - The traditional interpretation of this verse is as follows. Whereas every Christian should know that there are no other gods but the one true God, some of the Corinthians, because of their previous belief in idols, had difficulty shaking that belief. They still had needless false guilt about eating meat that someone had previously dedicated to a heathen deity. They thought they were doing something wrong even though they were not. This false guilt created a problem for them in their relationship with God.

A modern equivalent might be a Christian who gets saved out of a pagan background in which he was spending all of his free time and money on recreation of various kinds. He becomes a Christian and realizes that recreation had been his god. As a conscientious Christian he wants to avoid slipping back into that trap so he avoids recreation. He may even become critical of other believers who enjoy the forms of recreation to which he considers himself previously enslaved. He has trouble accepting recreation as a legitimate activity for Christians. When he sees other Christians enjoying recreation, he tends to look down on them as carnal. He has false guilt about participating in recreation.

Probably Paul was describing a Corinthian Christian who would go to a feast in an idol temple, as he or she had done before conversion. That person would have pangs of true guilt because by participating he or she was tacitly approving the worship and consequently the existence of the idol. Paul said the person's conscience was weak because even though he or she *intellectually* believed there was only one God, his or her *emotions* had not fully assimilated that truth. (238)

8:8 - Foods do not make us more or less pleasing to God. In our relationship to Him we are no better or worse if we participate or abstain. However eating food in a pagan temple was something else.

> "It is the clean heart, and not clean food, that will matter; and the weak brother confounds the two." (239)

8:9 - The knowledge that some food is all right in itself is not the only factor that should determine whether we eat it or not. Love for a brother that our participation bothers is also important. The weak brother is weak because his emotions have not caught up to his intellect. In this context, a stumbling block is any barrier to another individual's personal relationship with God. The Corinthian Christians who had returned to the pagan temples for their feasts where disregarding how their participation was affecting their brethren who still viewed participation as worship of the idol.

8:10 - In verses 10-12 Paul proceeded to appeal on behalf of the rights of the weak. Suppose a Corinthian Christian appreciated the fact that eating meat offered to an idol was insignificant in itself. He might accept an invitation from friends to share a meal in a pagan temple at which the cultic leader served that meat if he saw another Corinthian believer there. Undoubtedly some of the believers in Corinth were attending these feasts and were encouraging other Christians to take this "knowledgeable" stand. (240) This verse is one of the clearest evidences that participating in feasts in idol temples was the issue Paul was addressing rather than simply eating marketplace meat.

8:11 - Paul explained what had taken place in such a situation. The knowledgeable Christian had by his knowledge of what he considered legitimate, and by acting on the basis of that knowledge alone, destroyed his brother's relationship with God. "Ruined" seems strong, but Paul evidently foresaw the weaker brother returning to idolatry, the next step after participating in a feast in an idol temple. The apostle stressed the value of the weaker brother by referring to the fact that Christ died for him. Therefore the stronger brother dare not view him and his scruples as insignificant or unimportant.

8:12 - We are not free to damage another person's relationship with God. We sin against God and that person when we put an occasion for stumbling before him or her. This is the very opposite of what God has called us to do, namely, love God and other people (cf. Matt 22:37-39). The ultimate wrong of the person who lives only by his knowledge is not just that he lacks true knowledge or that he causes a brother to stumble. It is that he sins against Christ.

8:13 - Paul drew a conclusion about his own behavior from what he had said on this subject. He would make love for his brethren the governor over his knowledge of what was true and permissible.

The Greek word translated "causes to stumble [or fall]" is *skandalidzo*. A *skandalon*, the noun form of the word, was the trigger on a trap. Paul viewed eating in an idol temple as a kind of trigger that might set off a trap that could snare a fellow believer. It could retard his progress and cause him pain. Paul was willing to forgo all such eating if by doing so he could avoid creating problems for other Christians in their relationships with God (cf. Rom 14:13-23).

The issue in this chapter is not that of offending someone in the church. Paul dealt with that subject in 1 Corinthians 10:31-33; 11:1 and Romans 14. It is, rather, doing something that someone else would emulate to his or her own hurt. Paul dealt with an attitude in the Corinthians. They were arguing for a behavior on the basis of knowledge. Paul said the proper basis was love.

Our culture promotes our personal rights very strongly. This emphasis has permeated the thinking of most Christians. We need to remember that there is something more important than our freedom to do as we please. That something is the spiritual development of other people. As those to whom other Christians look as examples, it is specially important for you and me to recall this principle as we live. Our willingness to accept this standard for ourselves will reveal our true love for God and people. Our failure to do so will reveal our lack of knowledge as well as our lack of love….

3. The sinfulness of idolatry 10:1-22

Paul continued dealing with the subject of going to idol temples to participate in pagan feasts in this section. In it he gave a warning to the believer who considered himself strong, the one who knew there were really no gods but the true God. Such a person felt free to accept the invitation of a pagan neighbor to dine in a pagan temple (1 Cor 8:10). The apostle cautioned this element in the Corinthian church because, even though there are no other gods, the possibility of participating in idolatry is very real. He drew his lesson from the experience of Israel during the wilderness wanderings (cf. Exodus 13; 14; 15; 16; 17; Num 10; 11; 12; 13; 14; 15).

The tragic example of Israel 10:1-5

The point of this example is that God's people can practice idolatry, and persisting in idolatry has dire consequences. Paul stressed the similarity of experience that the church, the Corinthian church particularly, and Israel shared by pointing out that each group had its own "baptism" and "Lord's Supper."

10:1-2 - Paul did not want his readers to overlook a very important possibility as they thought about eating special meals in idol temples. He reminded them that their fathers in the faith, believers in Israel, were also all under the protective influence of God. The Corinthians *knew* these facts from the Old Testament, but they did not appreciate their *significance*. The cloud that led them in their wilderness wanderings symbolized God's loving care. Likewise they all experienced a miraculous deliverance when they crossed the Red Sea. Moreover all of them associated with Moses who was their leader and God's instrument in their redemption.

Baptism is the outward expression of the believer's identification with the object of his or her faith (cf. Rom 6:3; Gal 3:27). Consequently Paul could say the Israelites were baptized into Moses even though they did not undergo literal water baptism in the name of Moses. By following him and submitting to his authority they expressed their identification with him. The parallel with water baptism was most vivid when they went under the cloud and crossed the Red Sea. These experiences constituted a dry baptism for the Israelites.

10:3-4 - Furthermore all the Israelites, not just some of them, ate the manna and drank water from the rock. They ate manna throughout their wilderness sojourn (Deut 8:2-4), and they drank from the rock at the beginning (Ex 17:1-7) and at the end of it (Num 20:2-13). Paul called the manna and water spiritual food and drink because God provided them supernaturally and because they have spiritual significance. Both of them point to Christ, the real sustainer of His people (cf. Jn 6:35, 48-51; 7:37-38). The Israelites thought of God as a rock (Deut 32: 4, 15, 18, 30-31; et al.). He as a rock, not some physical rock, accompanied them in the wilderness. Their eating and drinking of God is similar to and anticipated the Christian Lord's Supper.

Paul's point in these first four verses was that the Israelites were the chosen people of God just as Christians are now the chosen people of God. God accompanied and provided for them faithfully in the past just as He does for all Christians now.

10:5 - In spite of these blessings, similar to those Christians enjoy, God was not happy with His people Israel. He permitted none of the adult generation of military age, 20 years old and older, to enter the Promised Land, except Caleb and Joshua. All but those two individuals from that generation died in the wilderness. How the majority displeased God and lost their privileges follows.

The application of Israel's example 10:6-13

Though idolatry was the cause of Israel's failure and the focus of Paul's warning to this church, four other evil characteristics of Israel also seem to have marked the Corinthians. These characteristics also resulted in the Israelites dying in the wilderness.

10:6 - The experiences of the Israelites provide lessons for us. Their baptism and partaking of spiritual food and drink did not protect them from God's discipline when they craved evil things. Participation in baptism and the Lord's Supper will not protect Christians either. We should never regard participation in these ordinances as immunizing us against God's discipline if we sin against Him.

The Greek word translated "examples" is *typos* from which we get the English word "type." The experiences of the Israelites in the wilderness are types. They were early examples of situations that would recur later in history that God designed to teach His people lessons. (260)

10:7 - In verses 7-10 Paul cited four practices that got the Israelites into trouble with God. All of them were possibilities for the Corinthians as they fraternized with pagans by participating in their feasts. They are all possibilities for us too.

First, the Israelites participated in idolatry when they ate and played in the presence of the golden calf (Ex 32:6). It is possible that their "play" involved sexual immorality (cf. Gen 26:8; Num 25:1-3). The scene on that occasion must have been similar to what happened at the feasts some of the Corinthians attended. There is a danger that we may compromise our commitment to God, as the Israelites did, when we participate in pagan celebrations.

10:8 - Second, the Israelites practiced immorality (lit. fornication) when they participated in one of the Moabites' religious feasts (Num 25:1-9). (261) If this sin is only implicit in the record of the Golden Calf incident, it is explicit in the account of the Baal Peor incident. Clearly this was taking place in the Corinthian church (1 Cor 5:1-5, 10-11; 6:9-10, 12-20). Some Christians have participated in fornication that unbelievers have lured them into.

10:9 - Third, the Israelites tested the Lord by taxing His patience. (262) They continued to complain even though He faithfully provided for them (Num 21:4-9). His provision of manna and water was not adequate from their point of view, and they despised it (Num 21:5). The Corinthians had given evidence of being dissatisfied with God's prohibition of participation in pagan feasts by opposing Paul's teaching on this point.

Likewise Christians are in danger of failing to appreciate God's provisions for them in Christ and despising Him. We can feel dissatisfied rather than thankful and content. Evidence that this attitude existed in the Corinthian church surfaces in 1 Cor 1:12 and 1 Cor 11:17-34. Perhaps the fact that some of the believers were participating in pagan feasts also indicated dissatisfaction with the Christians' special feast, the Lord's Supper.

10:10 - Fourth, the Israelites grumbled frequently against the Lord during the wilderness wanderings. Moses recorded 10 separate instances in Exodus and Numbers. However the occasion Paul had in mind was when God sent fire that consumed some of the people on the edge of the camp (Num 11:1-3). Here Paul added that God executed His wrath by using an angel, a fact that Moses did not mention in Numbers. The Septuagint translators used the same term, "the destroyer" (Gr. *olothreutes*), to describe the angel who executed the Egyptians' first-born on the night of the Exodus (Ex 12:23; cf. Heb 11:28).

Many instances of the Corinthian Christians' dissatisfactions with God's provisions for them come out in this epistle. Not the least of these was their rejection of some of the Lord's servants who had come to minister to them because they preferred some others (1 Cor 1:10-31; 2; 3; 4:1–4:21). They did not appreciate Paul's earlier instruction to break off company with idolaters and the sexually immoral (1 Cor 5:9-11). Another example is the impatience of the "strong" in the church with the "weak" (1 Cor 8:1-3). Grumbling is a telltale sign of selfishness and discontent with what God has given us.

10:11 - Having cited four specific examples of Israelite failure (1 Cor 10:7-10), Paul restated the general principle (cf. 1 Cor 10:6).

The last phrase in this verse refers to the present age as the time of fulfillment about which the Old Testament prophet had spoken. We should be careful that we do not overlook the lessons of history since we live in these times.

10:12 - Paul concluded with a word of warning to those who felt too confident that they were all right with God (cf. 1 Cor 10:1-4; 8:4-6). The "strong" who felt free to participate in pagan feasts seem to be those he had in mind. Self-confidence could lead to a spiritual fall, as it had so often in Israel's history.

10:13 - The apostle did not want his readers to overreact and become paranoid as they considered Israel's record either. Failure was not inevitable. The temptations the Corinthians faced were not unique, and the Lord would give them grace to handle any temptation they might face. (263)

God has promised to enable us to do His will in any and every situation, and He will stand true to His promise (cf. Matt 28:20; et al.). He provides a way of escape with every temptation He allows to touch us. The use of the definite article "the" with both "temptation" and "way of escape" points to a particular way of escape that is available in each temptation. Paul did not mean there is one way of escape that is available regardless of the temptation. If we deliberately put ourselves in the way of temptation and so put God to the test (1 Cor 10:9), we are not taking advantage of the way of escape. We may fall. Therefore we should flee from idolatry (1 Cor 10:14; cf. 1 Jn 5:21).

The Corinthians were putting themselves in danger by continuing to attend cultic meals, which they needed to stop doing. Nevertheless God had made a way of escape open to them, as He had with Israel. The Lord's Supper and the Christian fellowship connected with it was His divine replacement of this idolatrous activity (1 Cor 10:16).

This whole section (1 Cor 10:1-13) deals with the dangers involved in participating in pagan activities. Some of these activities are wrong in themselves because they involve idolatry, and Christians should not participate in them. If we should participate, we need to be aware that in doing so we are walking on the edge of a precipice over which many other believers have fallen, including the Israelites in the wilderness. We dare not underestimate the danger of the situation or overestimate our own ability to handle it. We need to walk closely with God every day.

The incompatibility of Christianity and idolatry 10:14-22

The apostle proceeded to warn his readers of the danger of idolatry further (cf. 1 Cor 10:7). This paragraph concludes the long argument that Paul began in 8:1 concerning going to temple feasts.

10:14 - Formerly Paul urged the Corinthians to flee fornication (1 Cor 6:18; cf. 1 Cor 10:8). Now he concluded all he said in verses 1-13 with the charge to flee idolatry, the worship of idols. He softened his strong command with an affectionate address ("my beloved"). Amoral activities are alright for the Christian, but if they involve or lead to idolatry we should avoid them.

10:15 - This statement prepares for what follows. The apostle was confident that the Corinthians had the wisdom to understand the correctness of what he was about to tell them. He believed they could make correct judgments about what they should do. Still, to follow his logic they would need to use their minds. As we have seen, the Corinthians considered themselves very wise. They should judge for themselves that Paul was right.

10:16 - The apostle employed rhetorical questions again to make his point. He was setting the Corinthians up for what he would say in verses 19-21.

Most New Testament references to the bread and the cup in the Lord's Supper occur in that order. Here Paul reversed the normal order. He probably turned them around because he wanted to give more attention to the bread in the verses that follow. The cup may focus on the vertical dimension of fellowship between the believer and the Lord whereas the bread focuses on the horizontal dimension (cf. 1 Cor 10:17). (264) The pagan feasts also emphasized both dimensions of fellowship, with the god and with the fellow-worshippers.

The "cup of blessing" was a technical term for the third of four cups of wine that the Jews drank in the Passover celebration. At the Last Supper the drinking of this cup preceded the giving of thanks for the bread (cf. Lk 22:17-20). However the Lord's Supper only involved eating bread and drinking one cup (cf. 1 Cor 11:23-29).

Paul described the cup as a cup of blessing, a common Jewish expression for the last cup of wine drunk at many meals. The Jews used it as a kind of toast to God for His goodness. (265) However, Paul turned this around by saying we bless the cup. That is, we give thanks to God for the cup because of what it symbolizes, namely, our sharing in the benefits of Christ's shed blood (cf. 1 Cor 11:25).

Likewise the bread used at the Christian feast, the Lord's Supper, is a symbol of our participation in the effects of Christ's slain body (cf. 1 Cor 11:24). The Greek word here translated "sharing" (NASB) or "participation" (NIV; *koinonia*) in other places reads "fellowship" or "communion." This is why another name for the Lord's Supper is the communion service.

10:17 - When Christians take communion we all eat from one bread symbolic of the physical body of Christ. In the early church believers seem to have used one loaf, the literal meaning of the word translated "bread" in this verse (*artos*). Paul stressed that many people eating from one loaf symbolized the *solidarity* of our relationship as a redeemed community in Christ. (He developed the idea of the *unity* of the body more fully in 1 Cor 12:14-27 in his explanation of the diversity that exists within the unity of the spiritual body of Christ, the church.) The emphasis here is on the solidarity of believers that forbids all other unions.

10:18 - We can see the partnership of those who partake of sacrifices with everything the altar stands for in Judaism (cf. Deut 14:22-27). Paul referred to Israel literally as "Israel according to the flesh." He contrasted all the physical Israelites with those who are Jewish Christians (cf. Phil 3:3). This description lends no support to the idea that the church replaces Israel in the program of God. "Israel" always refers to Jewish people in the New Testament.

Paul's line of reasoning was proceeding as follows. Christians who eat the bread at the Lord's Supper thereby express their solidarity with one another and with Christ. Likewise Jews who ate the meat of animals offered in the sacrifices of Judaism expressed their solidarity with one another and with God. Therefore Christians who eat the meat offered to pagan gods as part of pagan worship express their solidarity with pagans and with the pagan deities.

> "As in the Holy Communion, therefore, so also in the Temple services, participating in sacrificial feasts is sacrificial fellowship with an unseen power, a power that is Divine.

There is something analogous to this in the sacrificial feasts of the heathen; but in that case the unseen power is not Divine." (266)

The "wise" man in Corinth (1 Cor 10:15) could have replied to Paul's conclusion as follows. Yes, but you agreed before that idols have no real existence and there is only one true God.

10:19 - Paul proceeded to clarify what he meant. He was not saying that sacrifices to idols or idols themselves were anything. That is, sacrifices to idols were not in themselves sinful nor were idols genuine entities. On this point he and the Corinthians agreed. Idols were only pieces of wood or stone, not gods with supernatural powers. Nevertheless these idols represented supernatural powers (1 Cor 10:20), and so eating cultic meals had genuine significance.

10:20 - The power behind pagan religion is demonic (cf. Deut 32:17; Ps 106:37). Consequently people who sacrifice to idols express solidarity with demonic powers. Eating the food sacrificed to idols means that the people who participated shared in what had been sacrificed to demons just as the Israelites shared in what had been sacrificed to God. The cultic feasts were really sacrifices to demons, so they involved the worship of demons.

10:21 - It is inconsistent for a Christian to partake in the Lord's Supper and to take part in pagan religious feasts. In the former he eats and drinks in union with Christ, and in the latter he is in union with demons who direct the devotees to worship idols. What the Lord promotes and what the demons promote are opposite. This inconsistency must be obvious to "wise men" (1 Cor 10:15). Christians have a unique relationship with the Lord and with fellow-believers, which the Lord's Supper symbolizes. It is, therefore, inappropriate for us to have a similar association with demons and unbelievers (1 Cor 10:20-21), which participation in cultic events involves.

10:22 The Israelites provoked the Lord to jealousy by doing just such a thing when they joined in Moabite worship (Num 25; cf. Deut 32:17, 21-22). We are to learn from their experiences. It would be folly to provoke the Lord unless we are stronger than He. If we provoke Him and are not, we can count on His chastening since He is a jealous God.

The Corinthians were arguing for the right to attend pagan religious meals. They even viewed attendance as a way of building their "weaker" brethren. Paul responded that attendance was wrong on two counts: it was unloving, and it was incompatible with life in Christ, which their participation in the Lord's Table symbolized. He forbade any relationship with the demonic. The demonic is not as remote as some modern Western Christians would like to believe.

4. The issue of marketplace food 10:23—11:1

As with the issue of marriage, however, Paul granted that there are some matters connected with idolatry that are not wrong. He next gave his readers some help in making the tough choices needed in view of the amoral nature of some practices connected with pagan worship and the immoral nature of others. He suggested applying the test of what is edifying to these decisions. He proceeded to explain that food formerly offered to idols but sold in the marketplace was all right for Christians to eat at home. He himself had eaten such food (1 Cor 9:19-23), and the Corinthians had challenged him for doing so (1 Cor 10:29).

> "But the real issues seem to lie deeper than the mere question of eating food. Both the nature of their argument for eating at the temples (8:1, 4, 8) and their criticism of Paul (9:1-3, 19-23) have revealed a basic confusion between absolutes and *adiaphora* (nonessentials). They had tried to make temple attendance an *adiaphoron*; for Paul it was an absolute because it was idolatry. At the same time they had confused the true basis for Christian behavior. For them it was a question of knowledge and rights (*gnosis* and *exousia*). For Paul it is a question of love and freedom (*agape* and *eleutheria*). (267)

This section's chiastic structure reflects Paul's alternating concern for personal freedom and love for others.

A The criterion stated: the good of others (10:23-24)

    B Personal freedom explained (10:25-27)

        C The criterion illustrated: love governing liberty (10:28-29a)

    B' Personal freedom defended (10:29b-30)

A' The criterion generalized: that all may be saved (10:33—11:1)

10:23 - Earlier Paul had addressed the issue of Christian liberty and had said that all things were lawful for him, but all things were not beneficial (1 Cor 6:12). Now he went further and clarified that beneficial means beneficial for others, not just self. Thus he sought to bring the rights-conscious Corinthians to their knees.

10:24 - The well-being of one's neighbor is of primary importance. The exercise of all one's liberties is of secondary importance (cf. Rom 15:2; Phil 2:4). The Corinthians viewed their freedom as an opportunity to pursue their own interests. Paul viewed it as an opportunity to benefit and build up another person.

10:25-26 - It was not wrong to eat meat that pagans had offered in sacrifice to an idol. Any food for which one thanks God thereby becomes acceptable for human consumption assuming it is wholesome (1 Cor 10:30; cf. 1 Tim 4:3-5). This was a very un-Jewish viewpoint coming from a Jew. As earlier in this epistle and elsewhere in his writings, Paul appealed to Scripture for a supporting summary statement (Ps 24:1; 50:12).

Remember Paul was talking about distinctions based on spiritual issues. In Christianity there is no distinction between kosher and non-kosher food (Mk 7:19; Acts 10:15). Paul was not talking about distinctions in food based on physical factors such as fat content, calories, and nutritional value. The issue was whether certain foods commend us to or condemn us before God. They do not.

10:27 - The invitation in view must be to the home of an unbeliever for a meal rather than to a pagan temple for participation in a religious feast. This seems clear from the next verse. This freedom may have been hard for many Jewish Christians to accept (cf. Acts 10:28; 11:2-3). Nevertheless it belonged to them. It was wise not to ask if someone had offered the meat to an idol. A Christian might pose this question in the home of a pagan host or in the marketplace (1 Cor 10:25). Not inquiring would obviate the possibility of unnecessary guilt arising in the mind of a scrupulous believer.

10:28-29a - A pagan host might warn his Christian guest that the food before him had been offered in an idol temple. (268) The pagan's conscience is not a reference to his convictions about what is right and wrong for himself but his moral consciousness. (269) He does not want his Christian guest to be unaware that he is being served food that the Christian might object to and might what to abstain from eating. (270) Pagans often associated Christians with Jews at this stage of church history, and many pagans would have assumed that Christians observed the same dietary restrictions as the Jews.

We might think that in such a situation Paul would have advocated exercising Christian liberty to eat the meat, but he did not. He advocated abstaining, not because such meat was out of bounds for believers. It was not out of bounds; Christians could eat such meat. He advocated abstaining for the sake of the pagan's moral consciousness. Specifically, if the Christian ate the meat, the pagan might conclude that his guest was doing something Christians should not do. He would be wrong, of course. Yet Paul advocated not violating the pagan's understanding of what Christians should or should not do rather than instructing him about Christian freedom at the table.

> "A present-day analogy may be imagined if someone with strong principles on total abstention from alcohol were the guest of friends who did not share these principles. He would be well advised not to enquire too carefully about the ingredients of some specially

palatable sauce or trifle, but if someone said to him pointedly, 'There is alcohol in this, you know', he might feel that he was being put on the spot and could reasonably ask to be excused from having any of it." (271)

10:29b - This question resumes the thought of verses 26 and 27. Verses 28-29a are somewhat parenthetical being an illustration. We could restate Paul's thought this way. Why should another person's scruples determine my liberty? The answer is, They should because his spiritual welfare is more important than our Christian freedom.

10:30 - Paul brought his own conduct in similar situations into the picture. He had eaten non-kosher food with Gentiles, but in the argument preceding this verse he advocated abstaining from such food when eating with pagans. The key, of course, is that sacrificial meat was only off limits for Paul when it offended the moral consciousness of the pagans he was with, not all the time.

"The blessing offered at one's meal, predicated on God's prior ownership of all things, means that no fellow Christian may condemn another on this question." (272)

The Christian can give thanks to God for whatever he or she eats, but we should limit our own liberty out of consideration for what other people think is proper. We do not need to alter our *convictions* for the sake of others even though they speak evil of us, as the Corinthians did of Paul (cf. 1 Cor 9:19-23). Nevertheless we should be willing to change our *behavior* for the sake of unbelievers.

10:31 - What glorifies God? Consideration for the consciences of other people and promotion of their well-being does. This contrasts with the observance of distinctions between foods, the satisfaction of one's personal preferences, and insistence on one's own rights. What glorifies God is what puts His preferences, plans, and program first (cf. Col 3:17).

." . . God's own glory is the ultimate foundation of Pauline ethics (10:31)." (273)

10:32 - Giving no offense means putting no obstacle in the path of a person be he Jew (cf. 9:20) or Gentile (cf. 1 Cor 9:21) so that he might come to faith in Christ. If he is already a believer, it means putting nothing in his way that would hinder his growth in Christ (cf. 1 Cor 9:22). It is not a matter of simply "hurting someone's feelings."

Paul regarded these three groups as equal in this verse. Therefore he was probably thinking of three religious groups rather than two racial groups and one religious group. If so, he distinguished between Israel and the church in this verse. This distinction is basic to dispensationalism.

10:33 - If we took the first part of this verse out of context, we might conclude that Paul was a "man pleaser" (cf. Gal 1:10). Obviously he meant he did not allow any of his own attitudes or activities in amoral areas to create barriers between himself and those he sought to help spiritually.

He tried to practice what he preached about putting the welfare of others first (cf. 1 Cor 10:24). "Saved" in this context probably includes Christians and means saved in the wide sense of delivered from anything that keeps someone from advancing spiritually (cf. Rom 15:1-3).

"Christian freedom is not given to us for our own sake but for the sake of others." (274)

11:1 - Paul recommended that his readers follow his example of exercising and limiting their Christian liberty, glorifying God, and giving no offense, as well as in other areas of their lives (cf. 1 Cor 4:16). (275)

All of chapters 8, 9, and 10, including 11:1, deal with the subject of the Christian's relationship to food sacrificed to idols. In summary, Paul forbad going to pagan temples for cultic meals. However, he permitted the eating of marketplace meat under normal circumstances. If something is not sinful it is permissible for the believer, but even so it may be wise to avoid it for the sake of the spiritual welfare of others. The Christian should be willing to limit his or her exercise of his or her Christian liberty because of love for others.

The four principles Paul taught were these. Balance your knowledge with love (ch. 8). Balance your authority with discipline (ch. 9). Balance your experience with caution (1 Cor 10:1-22). And balance your freedom with responsibility (1 Cor 10:23-33). (276)

Bibliography

230. Fee, *The First . . .*, pp. 360-62.

231. E.g., Barrett, pp. 188-89; Wiersbe, 1:594.

232. Fee, *The First . . .*, p. 368.

233. Barrett, p. 190.

234. Wiersbe, 1:595.

235. Barrett, p. 190.

236 Fee, *The First . . .*, p. 373.

237. Cousar, "The Theological . . .," p. 99.

238. Compare Peter's compromise in Galatians 2:11-14.

239. Robertson and Plummer, p. 170.

240. Bruce K. Fisk, "Eating Meat Offered to Idols: Corinthian Behavior and Pauline Response in 1 Corinthians 8—10 (A Response to Gordon Fee)," *Trinity Journal* 10 NS:1 (Spring 1989):49-70, argued that the meals here were spiritually harmless temple meals. This seems indefensible to me.

260. For further information on types, see Bernard Ramm, *Protestant Biblical Interpretation,* pp. 196-219; Milton S. Terry, *Biblical Hermeneutics,* pp. 334-46; Patrick Fairbairn, *The Typology of Scripture*; Elliott E. Johnson, *Expository Hermeneutics: An Introduction*, pp. 126, 208-9.

261. Paul said 23,000 Israelites died in one day. Moses in Numbers 25:9 said 24,000 died as a result of the plague God sent to judge the people. There is, therefore, no conflict between the numbers since they describe somewhat different groups of people. Another explanation that has been suggested is that the larger number included Israel's leaders, and the smaller one did not.

262. The best manuscript evidence suggests that "Christ" rather than "Lord" is the correct word here. If so, Paul again stressed that it was Christ that both the Israelites and the Corinthians were testing (cf. v. 4). He made the apostasy in both cases Christological.

263. For other verses dealing with God's part in temptation, see Exod. 16:4; Deut. 8:2; I Chron. 21:1; Job 1:12; 2:6; Matt. 6:13; and James 1:13.

264. Fee, *The First . . .*, p. 467.

265. Bruce, *1 and 2 Corinthians*, p. 94.

266. Robertson and Plummer, p. 215.

267. Fee, *The First . . .*, p. 477.

268. The context (v. 27) and the terminology (Gr. *hierothyton*, "sacrificial meat," rather than *eidolothyton*, "idol meat," the standard Jewish and Christian designation) present a situation in which a Christian is eating privately with a pagan, not in a temple as in 8:10. Only in verse 32 does the broader principle of not giving offense to fellow believers arise.

269. Fee, *The First . . .*, p. 485.

270. Another view is that the pagan host is trying to test his commitment to Christ, but this seems less probable.

271. Bruce, *1 and 2 Corinthians*, p. 100.

272. Fee, *The First . . .*, p. 488.

273. Idem, "Toward a . . .," p. 40.

274. Barclay, *The Letters . . .*, p. 105.

275. See Robert L. Plummer, "Imitation of Paul and the Church's Missionary Role in 1 Corinthians," *Journal of the Evangelical Theological Society* 44:2 (June 2001):219-35.

276. Wiersbe, 1:594.

Lesson 7 Self Check

QUESTION 1

Paul counsels believers to never eat food that has possibly been dedicated to a false god. *True or False?*

QUESTION 2

What is the great damage that may be done to a weak brother in the matter of food offered to idols?

- A. He may not like you
- B. He may revert to idol worship
- C. He may hold a grudge against you
- D. He may complain about your behavior

QUESTION 3

Paul uses the example of Israel in the wilderness to caution against which sins?

- A. Pride
- B. Gluttony
- C. Immorality
- D. Divisiveness

QUESTION 4

According to 1 Corinthians 8, the best way to handle a weak believer is to try to change his conscience. *True or False?*

QUESTION 5

The punishment for Israelite sinners in the wilderness was physical death. *True or False?*

QUESTION 6

A believer exercising his freedom in Christ should consider the effects of his actions on others. *True or False?*

QUESTION 7

Paul knows that believers who do not flee from idolatry risk the Lord's discipline. *True or False?*

QUESTION 8

Christians do not need to alter their convictions for the sake of others, but they may need to alter their behavior. *True or False?*

QUESTION 9

Sacrifices to idols are really sacrifices to demons. *True or False?*

QUESTION 10

What is the way out for the believer when faced with the temptation to idolatry?

- A. To develop a strong conscience
- B. To refuse to participate in it
- C. To trust that God will forgive him no matter what he does
- D. To try not to think about it

Lesson 7 Answers to Questions

QUESTION 1
- A. Social
- B. Family
- C. Business
- D. Religious

QUESTION 2: *Your answer should be one of the following:*
love, Love

QUESTION 3: True

QUESTION 4: *Your answer*

QUESTION 5

Reference	Translation
1 Corinthians 6:12	be controlled
1 Corinthians 7:4	has the rights to
1 Corinthians 7:37	has control
1 Corinthians 8:9	this liberty
1 Corinthians 9:4, 5, 6	the right
1 Corinthians 11:10	symbol of authority
1 Corinthians 15:24	authority

QUESTION 6
- D. Bound by tradition or prior experience

QUESTION 7: *Your answer should be one of the following:*
Dangerous, Destructive

QUESTION 8: *Your answer*

QUESTION 9: False

QUESTION 10
- A. Both were baptized.
- B. Both enjoyed spiritual food and drink.
- C. Christ supplied the needs of both.

QUESTION 11

Sins	Behavior
Idolatry	1 Corinthians 8:10
Immorality	1 Corinthians 5:1
Testing the Lord	1 Corinthians 5:2
Grumbling	1 Corinthians 11:16

QUESTION 12: Discipline

QUESTION 13: False

QUESTION 14: *Your answer*

QUESTION 15: *Your answer should be one of the following:*
Demonic, Demons

QUESTION 16
- D. All believers

QUESTION 17: False

QUESTION 18: False

QUESTION 19
- A. For the benefit of others

QUESTION 20: True

QUESTION 21: *Your answer should be similar to the following:*
No. The contexts are different. In 1 Corinthians 10:33, he means that he avoids anything that will cause a brother to fall into sin or will hinder an unbeliever from coming to faith. In Galatians 1:10, he means that he refuses to submit to legalism and thus compromise the truth of the Gospel, no matter how much he offends people. In both passages Paul's motive is the spread of the Gospel.
QUESTION 22: *Your answer*
QUESTION 23: *Your answer*

Lesson 7 Self Check Answers

QUESTION 1: False

QUESTION 2
    B. He may revert to idol worship

QUESTION 3
    C. Immorality

QUESTION 4: False

QUESTION 5: True

QUESTION 6: True

QUESTION 7: True

QUESTION 8: True

QUESTION 9: True

QUESTION 10
    B. To refuse to participate in it

Lesson 8: Freedom and Ministry
(1 Cor 9:1-27)

Although in many aspects 1 Corinthians 9 is a self-contained unit, it is best to view it as an integral part of Paul's argument in 1 Corinthians 8–11:1 concerning eating food offered to idols. (In the section 1 Cor 12–14, Paul has a similar structure, with the famous "love" chapter sandwiched between extensive discussions of spiritual gifts.) How is chapter 9 integral to its surrounding context? His theme is "exercising freedom in love." Paul had rights that he did not make use of so as to benefit others. Paul uses the example of his own life to stir the church members to give up their "right" to eat food offered to idols.

Topic 1 looks at an apostle's rights, particularly his right to be financially supported by the people he is serving. Paul refuses to use this right (a choice well known to the Corinthians), claiming that he has a reward for doing so.

In Topic 2, Paul elaborates on the principle of forgoing his rights to the extreme of enslaving himself to everyone. His motive is eternal, both for himself and others. Using athletic imagery, he competes for an imperishable crown.

Lesson Outline

Topic 1: Apostles' Rights (1 Cor 9:1-18)

Right to Remuneration (9:1-12)

Refusal to Use This Right (9:12-18)

Topic 2: Paul's Ministry Principle (1 Cor 9:19-27)

Free to Be Everyone's Slave (9:19-23)

Example of Self-discipline (9:24-27)

Lesson Objectives

During the New Year celebration, Lotus wonders many times if it was really worth it to stay away from the village shrine and family celebrations. Not participating has cost her a lot. She has felt on the outside of Shan's extended family ever since she stopped going. Shan's mother seems to always specially ignore her during the New Year holidays, and the frigidity in their relationship does not begin to thaw until a month or so after the celebrations.

For the first two or three years after she became a Christian, one of Shan's sisters would urge her to come along with them to the temple, but Lotus politely refused. Now nobody even bothers to invite her.

Every year she wonders whether or not to give in and attend. This year, feeling rather depressed since many things are not harmonious in the church, she turns to 1 Corinthians 9 for guidance and encouragement.

By the end of this lesson, you will be able to:

- Explain how Paul exercised giving up his own rights for the gospel to be shared
- Understand that freedom in Christ is freedom from sin and freedom to serve God and others, constrained by love and truth

- Apply the concept of making yourself a slave to all for the sake of the gospel, keeping in mind the present and future rewards for doing so

Topic 1: Apostles' Rights (1 Cor 9:1-18)

According to common sense and the teaching of the Bible, the church at Corinth should have paid Paul for his ministry to them. It seems they wanted to, but Paul refused their patronage. This serves as a personal illustration of giving up rights for the sake of the gospel.

Right to Remuneration (9:1-12)

Assignment

- Read 1 Corinthians 9:1-12.
- Read Constable, "Paul's Apostolic Defense" (refer to the Articles section at the end of this lesson), through the note on 1 Corinthians 9:12.
- Read "Right to Remuneration."

Right to Remuneration

1 Corinthians 9, properly understood, fits into Paul's argument from 1 Corinthians 8-11:1. Chapter 9 is both an illustration and an example of personal application of the principle of Christian freedom and its limits. Consequently, "Am I not free?" (1 Cor 9:1) makes sense as a bridge to this illustration.

In this chapter, being free (1 Cor 9:1, 19) and having rights (1 Cor 9:4, 5, 6, 12, 18) are synonymous. The concept expressed is authority. Paul, by virtue of his apostolic office, had authority to receive financial support from those to whom he ministered the gospel. He goes on to argue that this right applies to all those who proclaim the gospel.

Some at Corinth were "examining" Paul (1 Cor 9:3). This is the Greek word *anakrino*, which could also be translated as "judge." In the same way that many Jews rejected Jesus because He did not fit their expectations of a Messiah, so some believers at Corinth were judging Paul because he did not fit their expectations of an apostle. Earlier, we saw that Paul's image fell short in their eyes: he did not measure up in oratory, in means of support, or in his servant-leadership style. Now they were judging Paul for not taking their money and for appearing inconsistent in eating and culture.

"Do not muzzle an ox" 1 Corinthians 9:9, was this written for the sake of oxen? It was written for the sake of the readers of the law, to teach them about treating animals kindly. By extension, if God is so concerned about the welfare of an ox, then we may be sure He is even more concerned about the welfare of His ministers.

In this passage, the benefits/rewards/blessings that Paul refers to are material and in this life—specifically, food and drink for his apostolic labors.

Paul established his apostolic office, and then his right to remuneration as an apostle. He knows that if the believers at Corinth acknowledge that he is an apostle, then he has the same rights as Cephas. This right to financial support is not just a spiritual principle, but it is readily seen in many areas of life.

QUESTION 1

Paul's discussion of apostolic rights is best viewed as a diversion from the subject of food offered to idols. *True or False?*

QUESTION 2

Paul argued for his right to remuneration because the church at Corinth did not want to pay him. *True or False?*

QUESTION 3

Paul seeks to prove his right to financial support by using which arguments? Match the Bible reference to the best answer.

Reference	Argument
1 Corinthians 9:9	Gratitude
1 Corinthians 9:7	Lesser-to-greater
1 Corinthians 9:5	Biblical
1 Corinthians 9:11	Common sense
1 Corinthians 9:12	Examples of other Christian workers

QUESTION 4

Why did some at Corinth doubt Paul's apostolic credentials?

QUESTION 5

Paul quotes Deuteronomy 25:4 in order to do what?

    A. Teach that the Corinthian believers are under the law
    B. Establish part of the law of Christ
    C. Illustrate his point
    D. Clinch his argument

Refusal to Use This Right (9:12-18)

Assignment

- Read 1 Corinthians 9:12-18.
- Continue reading Constable, "Paul's Apostolic Defense" (refer to the Articles section at the end of this lesson), through the note on 1 Corinthians 9:18.
- Read "Refusal to Use This Right."

Refusal to Use This Right

Why did Paul not want to receive money for preaching the gospel? As 2 Corinthians makes more clear, Paul faced a dilemma with respect to receiving money from the Corinthians. If he refused money, he would be criticized—some would say he was not an authentic apostle, for true apostles received money. If he accepted money, he would be criticized—some would say he was just a traveling evangelist for the money! However, these factors do not seem to be the primary motivations when he wrote 1 Corinthians.

Paul faced many issues regarding receiving money from the Corinthians. (1) If he accepted money, then he could devote himself full time to preaching and teaching. From one point of view, laboring as a tentmaker to earn money would hinder the work of the gospel. (2) Entering into a patronage relationship in ancient society entailed obligations. Paul may have wished to avoid "owing" anything to his supporters. (3) Not only are there the time and patronage considerations, but there are also social status considerations. Anyone doing manual labor had a lower status in Greek society. If Paul would just accept Corinthian patronage, then he could rise in society's eyes to the level of a professional philosopher, and perhaps more people would pay attention to his message. (4) There is the factor of consistency between message and manner. Since the gospel is a free offer of grace, how can the messenger charge money to hear that free offer? (5) Finally, there is the factor of Paul's sense of reward. He felt that if he accepted pay from those he ministered to, he would lose his reward for forgoing this right of support.

Does he mean that he would never receive money from believers or churches? In Philippians 4:10-14, he thanks them for sending funds for his support. Probably they sent money while he was at Corinth planting the church, enabling him to stop his tent-making work and preach full time (Acts 18:5). Paul variously accepted or refused financial support depending on the situation, but always with the willingness to forgo his rights for the sake of the gospel.

What does Paul mean by "woe to me if I do not preach" (1 Cor 9:16)? Paul did not view his apostolic commission as volunteer work for the Lord. It was not optional for him. The Lord had commissioned him to preach. If he shirked his responsibility, the Lord would discipline him. Paul may also be referring to an inner sense of compulsion like the one in Jeremiah 20:9—

> Sometimes I think, "I will make no mention of his message.
>
> I will not speak as his messenger anymore."
>
> But then his message becomes like a fire
>
> locked up inside of me, burning in my heart and soul.
>
> I grow weary of trying to hold it in
>
> and I just cannot do it.

Is Paul talking about an eternal reward in 1 Corinthians 9:17, where he says "if I do this voluntarily, I have a reward"? Here he seems to be talking about a reward in this life. This reward could be subjective—a sense of satisfaction or fulfillment over not having made full use of his rights in the gospel. By so doing, he is able to illustrate the free nature of the gospel.

QUESTION 6

Record your response to the following questions in your Life Notebook.

    a. Why did Paul not want to receive money for preaching the gospel?

    b. Does he mean that he would never receive money from believers or churches?

    c. What does Paul mean by "woe to me" if I do not preach (1 Cor 9:16)?

    d. Is Paul talking about an eternal reward in 1 Corinthians 9:17, where he says "if I do this voluntarily, I have a reward"?

Paul readily gave up his right to food as an apostle, which is a sacrifice at least equal to what he is asking the believers to give up in not eating food offered to idols. Paul makes this sacrifice so that he will not hinder the spread of the gospel.

QUESTION 7

Why did Paul refuse to be paid for his gospel ministry? *(Select all that apply.)*

    A. He already had plenty of money.

    B. He wanted more rewards in heaven.

    C. Money was a temptation to him to sin.

    D. Receiving pay would have hindered the gospel.

    E. He wanted the reward of preaching without pay.

QUESTION 8

Did Paul have the right to refuse to preach the gospel?

QUESTION 9

Paul asserts that Jesus confirmed the right of Christian workers to be supported for their work. *True or False?*

QUESTION 10

Open your Life Notebook and record your reflections on the following. Should pastors and missionaries today refuse financial support from the people they minister to? Under what circumstances might they refuse support, and under what circumstances might they want to accept support?

Topic 2: Paul's Ministry Principle (9:19-27)

Freedom must not be exercised as license. For Paul, freedom is freedom from sin and freedom to serve God and others. Constrained by love and truth, Paul limited his own rights, choices and preferences for the sake of the gospel. It is not exclusively a difficult sacrifice, though, because there are present and future rewards for making yourself a slave to all.

Free to Be Everyone's Slave (9:19-23)

Assignment

- Read 1 Corinthians 9:19-23.
- Read Constable, "Apostolic Freedom" (refer to the Articles section at the end of this lesson).
- Read "Free to Be Everyone's Slave."

Free to Be Everyone's Slave

Paul counseled in 1 Corinthians 7 for everyone to remain as they were when called. Here he says that he has become everyone's slave! Paul does not mean that he became a slave in some economic or legal sense. He remained legally a freeman and a Roman citizen. "Slave" is a metaphor for giving up one's rights. What rights did a slave have in the first century? They were someone else's property. They could not decide where they were to live or what job they were to have. Their duty was to please their master, to adjust to his desires, and to serve without pay.

When we see someone who behaves one way in one situation and another way in another situation, we may view him as inconsistent and lacking integrity. Everyone knew that Paul was a Jew, and that pious Jews kept many rules. However, at times Paul ate kosher food and at times he did not. Sometimes he went to the synagogue on the Sabbath, but sometimes he did not. What on the surface appeared to be inconsistent behavior really followed an underlying principle.

This is a great missionary text. Paul says that he is the one who adjusts to the people he is trying to reach with the gospel—not vice versa. Paul is the one who gave up his rights: where he would like to live, the language he preferred to speak, the customs and culture that he felt most comfortable with, and the food he preferred to eat. All these rights he gave up for the sake of the gospel. He did not demand that people come to him, learn his language, or fit in to his customs in order to become Christians.

Of course, Paul did not adapt himself without limits to the people he tried to reach with the gospel. Even though he was not under the Mosaic law regarding rituals, food regulations, and customs, he was morally constrained by the law of Christ. As a believer, he could not violate Christian principles of truth and love.

What does it mean to "be a participant" (1 Cor 9:23) in the gospel? Some translations offer this phrase as "share in its blessings," or be a "partaker" in it. Is he talking about working for his salvation? We know that fundamental Pauline theology is the gospel of salvation by grace through faith alone. He does not mean that he is working for his salvation, but that he is gaining some benefit from his ministry. The present blessings of the gospel that Paul shared in were many: the joy and fulfillment that came to him when people trusted Christ, churches were planted, and people's lives were transformed. "For how can we thank God enough for you, for all the joy we feel because of you before our God?" (1 Thess 3:9) Eternally, he anticipated an imperishable crown.

Paul turns freedom and rights upside down. Reflecting Jesus' teaching in Mark 10:44, "whoever wants to be first among you must be the slave of all," Paul sets the example by enslaving himself to every man. In non-essentials, Paul adapted himself to the people he was trying to reach.

QUESTION 11

In order to reach unbelievers with the gospel, Paul adapted himself in every way. *True or False?*

QUESTION 12

Some people felt Paul was _____ because he constantly adapted himself to others.

QUESTION 13

What does it mean to be a participant in the gospel (1 Cor 9:23)?

QUESTION 14

In Galatians 2:12, Peter could have claimed that he was just adapting to the weak when he withdrew from eating with the Gentiles. In other words, he was applying Paul's own principle from 1 Corinthians 9:19-23. Note how you would respond to such a claim in your Life Notebook.

QUESTION 15

Answer the following questions in your Life Notebook. Which behaviors are consistent with Paul's principle in 1 Corinthians 9:19-23? Why or why not?

- Attending a non-Christian wedding ceremony
- Eating kosher food
- Bowing to honor the dead at a funeral
- Joining an atheist political organization
- Playing a table game that involves small-time gambling
- Going to a night club with dancing with business associates

Example of Self-discipline (9:24-27)

Assignment

- Read 1 Corinthians 9:24-27.

- Read Constable, "Apostolic Exhortation and Example" (refer to the Articles section at the end of this lesson).

- Read "Example of Self-discipline."

Example of Self-discipline

Paul conducted purposeful activity, focused on the prize, and disciplined his body.

In 1 Corinthians 9:27,"disqualified" may be translated as "rejected," "disapproved," or "castaway." In keeping with the athletic metaphor, "disqualified" seems a suitable translation here.

From what would Paul be disqualified? Suggestions are: (A) eternal life, (B) the blessings of the gospel in this life, (C) rewards in heaven, and (D) apostleship. (A) is most unlikely, since he has already taught that if the Christian worker's work is burned up, he will suffer loss, but not loss of eternal life (1 Cor 3:14, 15). The last three suggestions are more likely, and they are naturally linked to each other in Paul's life.

From his first days at Corinth, Paul preached the message of the cross. Christ gave up His rights to sit at the Father's right hand, to enjoy worship and praise from all His creatures, and to be separated from sin. Instead, He took on the form of a servant in a human body and suffered rejection and death. Jesus' life on earth was one of purpose, focus, and discipline. "For the joy set out for Him He endured the cross, disregarding its shame, and has taken His seat at the right hand of the throne of God." (Heb 12:2) Paul was an imitator of Christ, and here he offers his personal example to encourage the Corinthians to return to the way of the cross. They should be willing to yield their right to eat meat offered to idols if it promotes the kingdom of God.

Athletes who are serious competitors live in line with their goals. Self-discipline is a necessary aspect of the contest. Paul urges believers to view the Christian life as an athletic competition.

QUESTION 16

From what would Paul be disqualified? Record your response in your Life Notebook.

QUESTION 17

In order to minister effectively, Paul wants his body to be his _____.

QUESTION 18

What is the point of the athletic imagery here?

- A. To stimulate believers to compete spiritually with others
- B. To praise harsh treatment of one's physical body
- C. To make believers afraid of losing their salvation
- D. To encourage believers to live purposefully

QUESTION 19

According to the illustration of 1 Corinthians 9:24-27, what characteristics are required for athletes to win the prize? List up to six.

QUESTION 20

What are different views as to what Paul might be disqualified from after preaching to others (1 Cor 9:27)? *(Select all that apply.)*

   A. Apostleship

   B. Eternal life

   C. Rewards in heaven

   D. Blessings in this life

QUESTION 21

Take a few moments to pray and assess your life. Record your thoughts on the following in your Life Notebook: In what ways are you living with self-discipline and purpose, and in what ways do you need to improve?

Lesson 8 Articles

Notes on 1 Corinthians

Dr. Thomas L. Constable; 2003 Edition

2. Paul's apostolic defense ch. 9

The absence of the key phrase "now concerning" is the clue that this chapter does not deal with a new subject. It is a continuation of the discussion of eating in idol temples that Paul began in 1 Corinthians 8:1. Subjecting our freedom for the welfare of other people is not something any of us does naturally. Paul knew his readers would profit from more instruction on this subject. He used himself as an illustration of the proper attitude toward one's freedom and responsibility in Christ.

Evidently the Corinthian Christians had misunderstood Paul's policy of limiting the exercise of his activities to help others (1 Cor 8:13). Some in the church had apparently concluded that because he did not exercise his rights he did not have them, for example his right to material support (cf. 2 Cor 12:13). His apparently vacillating conduct also raised questions in their minds about his full apostolic authority. For example, he ate marketplace food with Gentiles but not with Jews. Paul responded to this viewpoint in this chapter. There have been evidences of the Corinthians' unwillingness to yield to Paul's authority throughout this letter (1 Cor 4:1-5; 5; 6; cf. 1 Cor 14:36-37). This was an appropriate place for him to confront the issue.

Apostolic identity 9:1-2

9:1 - The apostle's four rhetorical questions all expect a positive answer, and they become increasingly specific. Certainly he enjoyed the liberty that every other believer had. Furthermore he possessed the rights and privileges of an apostle. The proof of his apostleship was twofold. He had seen the risen Christ (Acts 1:21-22) on the Damascus road (Acts 22:14-15; 26:15-18), and he had founded the church in Corinth, which was apostolic work (cf. Rom 15:15-21). Clearly Paul's apostleship was at stake in Corinth (cf. 1 Cor 1:1, 12; 4:1-5, 8-13, 14-21; 5:1-2).

9:2 - Others might have doubts about Paul's apostleship, but the Corinthians certainly should not in view of his ministry among them. They themselves were the proof that he was an apostle.

Apostolic rights 9:3-14

The issue of Paul's right to their material support underlies this whole pericope.

> "Philosophers and wandering missionaries in the Greco-Roman world were 'supported' by four means: fees, patronage, begging, and working. Each of these had both proponents and detractors, who viewed rival forms as not worthy of philosophy." (243)

Paul did not begin by justifying his renunciation of his apostolic rights but by establishing that he had these rights. He evidently had to begin there because the Corinthians were challenging these rights. They were assuming that Paul had worked with his hands because he lacked apostolic rights, not because he had chosen to forgo them.

9:3 - If anyone challenged his practice of forgoing his rights as an apostle, his response follows.

9:4 - Paul used the series of rhetorical questions that begins here to force the Corinthians to recognize—they should already have known—that he possessed full apostolic rights. In view of the other rights that follow, Paul's reference to eating and drinking here probably means to eat and drink at the expense of others. It means to accept financial support in his ministry.

9:5 - Evidently it was customary for the other apostles and the Lord's physical brothers to take their wives with them when they travelled to minister. The churches they served covered the expenses of these women as well as those of their husbands. Paul may have mentioned Peter in particular because he had a strong following in Corinth (1 Cor 1:12). His references to the Lord's brothers in this verse and to Barnabas in the next do not necessarily mean that these men had visited Corinth. Probably the Corinthians knew about their habits of ministering second-hand.

9:6 - The Corinthians had acknowledged the right of the other apostles to refrain from secular employment. Paul and Barnabas chose to work with their hands at times so their financial support would not burden their converts (1 Cor 4:12; 1 Thess 2:9; 2 Thess 3:7-9; Acts 20:34). Evidently the practice of Barnabas was well known. Paul had stooped to the demeaning work of making tents while he ministered in Corinth (Acts 18:3). Apparently some of the Corinthian Christians took Paul's action as an indication that he did not think of himself as worthy of support because he was not equal with the other apostles.

9:7 - These three illustrations support the fact that Paul as a servant of the Lord had a right to accept support from those to whom he ministered. The Lord's servants are certainly not inferior to field hands, farmers, and animals.

9:8-9 - God made special provision in the Mosaic Law for the oxen that served people by threshing their grain (Deut 25:4). In so doing, Paul said, God was teaching His concern for the maintenance of all who serve others, not just oxen. (244)

> "Keep in mind that, for the most part, the Greeks despised manual labor. They had slaves to do manual labor so that the citizens could enjoy sports, philosophy, and leisure. The Jews, of course, magnified honest labor." (245)

9:10 - God meant to encourage human laborers with His provision for animals that labored. He wanted human laborers to work with the hope of pay. The people who profited from those services should consider those who served them worthy of support.

> "Not muzzling an ox . . . was probably a proverbial expression concerning just remuneration, properly understood and interpreted as such by Paul. A modern parallel would be the adage, 'You can't teach an old dog new tricks,' which is commonly applied in contexts other than canine obedience." (246)

9:11 - Spiritual things are intrinsically more important than physical things. The former will last forever whereas the latter are only temporary. How much more then should those who benefit from spiritual ministry support physically those who minister to them (cf. Gal 6:6). "Is it too much" reveals that Paul was contending with the Corinthians, not just exhorting them.

9:12 - As the planter of the Corinthian church Paul had a right to the support of the Corinthians more than any of their other ministers did. Yet he did not insist on his right. He chose rather to support himself so his work of establishing the church might not suffer from criticism that he was serving for the material benefits he derived from his converts.

9:13 - Paul appealed to the common Jewish practice, that was also prevalent in pagan religions, of allowing those who minister in spiritual matters to gain physical support from those they serve.

9:14 - The Lord Jesus taught the same right (Matt 10:10; Lk 10:7).

> "All too often, one fears, the objective of this text is lost in concerns over 'rights' that reflect bald professionalism rather than a concern for the gospel itself." (247)

Apostolic restraint 9:15-18

Having argued vigorously for his right to the Corinthians' support, Paul now proceeded to argue just as strongly for his right to give up this right, his point from the beginning. He explained why he had deliberately not accepted their patronage. This pericope gives the reader a window into the apostle's soul. We see here what made him tick.

9:15 - Paul had this right, but he chose not to use it. He did not want his readers to interpret what he had said on this subject as a veiled request for support. He had made his decision to support himself while he preached freely; the Lord did not require this of him. Consequently he could take justifiable pride in it, as anyone who makes a sacrifice for the welfare of others can.

9:16 - He could not take justifiable pride in the fact that he preached the gospel, however. Even though it involved sacrificing for the benefit of others, he had made those sacrifices in obedience to the Lord (Acts 26:16-18; cf. Matt 28:19-20). He had no choice about preaching the gospel as he did about how he would live while he did so. Preaching was his divine destiny. Indeed he would be in serious trouble with his Lord if he did not preach the gospel. (And so will we.)

9:17 - If he preached the gospel willingly, he would receive a reward (pay) from the Lord. If he did so unwillingly, he would not receive a reward but would be simply doing his duty as a steward (manager of a household; cf. 1 Cor 4:1-2).

9:18 - Paul's reward for preaching the gospel willingly was the privilege of preaching it without cost to his hearers. His highest pay was the privilege of preaching without pay. (248) This choice may seem as though it was Paul's decision rather than a reward from the Lord, but he viewed it as a privilege that came to him from the Lord (cf. 2 Cor 11:7-12).

Paul had all the rights of an apostle and was free to insist on them if he chose to do so. He also had the freedom not to insist on them. His relinquishing his right to support corresponds to his giving up his right to eat in a pagan temple (1 Cor 8:13). In both cases it was the welfare of others that led him to forgo a legitimate right.

Apostolic freedom 9:19-23

The extent to which the apostle was willing to lay aside his rights comes out in this pericope. Since Paul chose not to receive pay for his ministry in Corinth, he was free from the restrictions that patronage might impose. This left him free to become the slave of all.

9:19 - Paul was a free man, not a slave of any other human being. Nevertheless as the Lord's servant, he had made himself subject to every other human being so he might win some to Christ. Serving people rather than commanding them is the way to win them (cf. Mk 10:45).

9:20 - It was the apostle's custom to follow Jewish ways when he was in the company of Jews. He did so to make them receptive to him and his message rather than antagonistic (cf. Acts 21:20-26). He did not do this because he felt obligated to keep the Mosaic Law. He did not feel obligated to do so (Rom 6:14). The salvation of Jews was his objective in observing Jewish laws and customs many of which dealt with abstaining from certain foods (cf. 1 Cor 8:13). He had circumcised Timothy at Lystra for this purpose (Acts 16:3).

9:21 - Likewise when Paul was with Gentiles he behaved as a Gentile. This would have involved eating what they did, among other things.

The references to law in this verse may be confusing. In describing Gentiles as being without law, Paul did not mean that Gentiles are totally lawless (cf. Rom 2:14). He meant they were not under the Law of Moses as the Jews were (1 Cor 9:20). Paul wanted his readers to understand that even though he did not observe the Mosaic Law when he was with Gentiles (Gr. *anomos*) he was still under God's authority (*ennomos*). As a Christian he was not under the Law of Moses, but he was under the Law of Christ (cf. Gal 6:2). The law of God for Jews before the Cross was the Law of Moses, but His law for Christians in the present age is the Law of Christ. The Law of Christ is the code of responsibilities that Christ and His apostles taught, which the New Testament contains. Some of the same commands are in the Mosaic Law though the codes, the Mosaic Law and the Law of Christ, are not the same. (249)

"This is one of the most difficult sentences in the epistle, and also one of the most important, for in it Paul shows how the new relation to God which he has in Christ expresses his debt of obedience to God." (250)

9:22 - The weak are those who have extremely sensitive consciences in the area of amoral practices (cf. 1 Cor 8:9) such as the Jews. Here the apostle meant unbelievers as is clear from what he said about them. Paul accommodated himself to their scruples. This policy undoubtedly led some people to conclude that Paul was inconsistent. His superficial inconsistency really manifested a more fundamental consistency. He did everything amoral with a view to bringing people to the Savior. (251)

9:23 - The work of the gospel was the great axis around which everything in Paul's life revolved. He made it such so he might share in its blessings. He proceeded to explain what this involves in the following verses.

Apostolic exhortation and example 9:24-27

This passage is transitional concluding Paul's defense of his apostolic authority (1 Cor 9:1-23) and returning to the argument against participating in cultic meals (ch. 8). Metaphors from the athletic games fill the pericope.

9:24 - The Corinthians were familiar with athletic contests. The Isthmian Games took place in a nearby town every two or three years. They were second only to the Olympic Games in importance in Greece. (Morris) The Greek word translated "race" is *stadion*, the word used to describe the standard 600 foot Greek race. (253)

Paul's emphasis in this verse was on the last statement. We should run our race so we will receive a reward from the Judge. In the Christian race we do not compete with one another for the prize. We compete with ourselves. In a foot race only one person is the winner, but in the Christian race all who keep the rules and run hard will receive a reward (cf. Matt 6:19-21; 2 Tim 2:5).

9:25 - "Competes" is a translation of *agonidzomai* from which we get the English word "agonizes." To receive the prize of our Lord's "well done" we need to give all our effort. We also need to exercise self-control. Competitors in the Isthmian Games had to train for 10 months. (254) An athlete in training denies himself or herself many lawful pleasures to gain an extra edge of superiority. Likewise we may need to limit our liberty for a higher goal as spiritual athletes.

Winners in the Isthmian Games received a wreath of parsley, wild celery, or pine. (255) However the victorious Christian's reward is imperishable (cf. 2 Tim 4:8). It also lies in the eschaton. (256) How much more important it is to be willing to forgo our rights for the spiritual advancement of others than it is to train for a physical foot race (cf. 2 Cor 4:17-18)!

9:26 - In view of the comparative value of these rewards, Paul ran the Christian race purposefully, not aimlessly or halfheartedly. He wanted to gain a prize at the judgment seat of Christ. To use a different figure to make the same point, he did not shadowbox but sought to make every punch score. Christian service is not just activity. It is activity focused on a target, namely, the building of the church and the defeat of the enemy who wants to destroy people. It is the work of the gospel.

9:27 - In another sense Paul viewed his flesh as his enemy. He recognized the need to exercise strict self-discipline. Obviously Paul was not speaking of self-discipline in the physical realm alone. He also had in mind moral discipline and discipline in the amoral areas of his life including voluntary curtailment of personal rights and liberties (cf. 1 Tim 4:8). (257)

We must be careful not to confuse the fear of disqualification with the fear of damnation. Paul had no fear that he would lose his salvation (Rom 8:29-39). In the context what he could lose was a reward. (258) How ironic and pathetic it would be for Paul to forfeit a crown through his own lack of self-discipline or by breaking the Judge's rules since He had instructed others concerning how to win one.

This whole chapter is an explanation of the last verse of the preceding chapter. More generally it clarifies the importance of limiting our legitimate liberty as Christians for higher goals, namely, the glory of God and the welfare of other people.

> "Almost in reaction against . . . globalization, many people are responding with increasing nationalism, sometimes with almost frightening ethnocentrism. Christians are not immune to these sweeping currents of thought. They, too, can be caught up in flag-waving nationalism that puts the interests of my nation or my class or my race or my tribe or my heritage above the demands of the kingdom of God. Instead of feeling that their most important citizenship is in heaven, and that they are just passing through down here on their way 'home' to the heavenly Jerusalem (Heb 12:22-23), they become embroiled with petty priorities that constitute an implicit denial of the lordship of Christ." (259)

Bibliography

243. Fee, *The First . . .*, p. 399

244. See Jan L. Verbruggen, "Of Muzzles and Oxen: Deuteronomy 25:4 and 1 Corinthians 9:9," *Journal of the Evangelical Theological Society* 49:4 (December 2006):699-711, for a study of various ways Paul may have understood and used Deut. 25:4.

245. Wiersbe, 1:599

246. Lowery, p. 523.

247. Fee, *The First . . .*, p. 414.

248. Morris, p. 137. See also Barrett, p. 210.

249. Femi Adeyemi, "The New Covenant Law and the Law of Christ," *Bibliotheca Sacra* 163:652 (October-December 2006):438-52, correctly equated the Law of Christ with the New Covenant Law (cf. Jer. 31:31-34).

250. Barrett, p. 212.

251. See H. Chadwick, "'All Things to All Men' (I Cor. IX. 22)," *New Testament Studies* 1 (1954-55):261-75.

252. Morris, p. 139.

253. Bruce, *1 and 2 Corinthians*, p. 89.

254. Morris, p. 139.

255. Bruce, *1 and 2 Corinthians*, p. 89. In the Olympian Games the prize was a wild olive wreath. Robertson,

4:149.

256. See Wall, pp. 79-89.

257. See Jerry M. Hullinger, "The Historical Background of Paul's Athletic Allusions," *Bibliotheca Sacra* 161:643 July-September 2004):343-59.

258. See Smith, "Can Fallen . . .," pp. 466-67.

259. Carson, p. 116.

Lesson 8 Self Check

QUESTION 1

For believers at Corinth, the confirming sign of Paul's apostleship was that he planted their church. *True or False?*

QUESTION 2

Paul knew that if he neglected to proclaim the Gospel, the Lord would discipline him. *True or False?*

QUESTION 3

Paul's intent in using the athletic metaphor in 1 Corinthians 9:24-27 was to spur believers to compete with each other for the prize. *True or False?*

QUESTION 4

Paul adapted his lifestyle to those he tried to reach with the gospel. *True or False?*

QUESTION 5

For Paul, the most important consideration was:

    A. Making full use of his rights

    B. Spreading the gospel

    C. Making a comfortable living

    D. Punishing his body

QUESTION 6

Proper application of the principle "become all things to all people" has limits. *True or False?*

QUESTION 7

How did Paul view serving as an apostle at his own expense?

    A. More spiritual than being paid

    B. His own reward

    C. His punishment for persecuting the church

    D. His special cross to bear

QUESTION 8

Another possible translation for "disqualified" in 1 Corinthians 9:27 is "rejected." *True or False?*

QUESTION 9

In 1 Corinthians 9, what did Paul boast about?

    A. Preaching the gospel

    B. Not taking pay for preaching the gospel

    C. Having seen the Lord

    D. His rights

QUESTION 10

It is wrong for a missionary to receive pay for preaching the gospel. *True or False?*

Unit 3 Exam

QUESTION 1

Paul does distinguish between the authority of Jesus' statements and that of his own apostolic instruction. *True or False?*

QUESTION 2

The impending crisis, mentioned in 1 Corinthians 7:26 most likely refers to the last days prior to the Lord's return. *True or False?*

QUESTION 3

As a general principle, a believer should remain in the situation in life he was in when he was called. *True or False?*

QUESTION 4

Since a married believer is concerned about the things of the world,

    A. He is a carnal Christian

    B. His interests are divided

    C. He can never please God

    D. Marriage is God's second best

QUESTION 5

It is a sin for a believer to marry an unbeliever. *True or False?*

QUESTION 6

According to Paul's teaching in 1 Corinthians 7, one good reason for a believer to marry is

    A. To avoid immorality

    B. For companionship

    C. To make the parents happy

    D. To have children

QUESTION 7

The right to divorce if the unbelieving partner wants to is sometimes called the Pauline Privilege. *True or False?*

QUESTION 8

Marriage and singleness are both spiritual gifts. *True or False?*

QUESTION 9

Paul used the record of the Israelites' sin in the wilderness because the situation of the Corinthian believers was similar. *True or False?*

QUESTION 10

Anyone who sacrifices to an idol is really sacrificing to demons. *True or False?*

QUESTION 11

Believers may eat anything sold in the marketplace:

A. After they have first determined that it was not offered to an idol

B. Without asking questions as to its origin

C. Even if the food is advertized as previously offered to an idol

D. If they are hungry enough

QUESTION 12

Paul cautioned believers in Corinth against a false sense of security. *True or False?*

QUESTION 13

The best way to handle a difference with a believer who has a weak conscience is:

A. Argue with him until he changes his view.

B. Ignore his conscience problem and act with complete freedom.

C. Respect his convictions.

D. Adopt his view as your own.

QUESTION 14

Baptism into Moses means identification with Moses. *True or False?*

QUESTION 15

Which of the following is **not** a reason Paul uses for believers to avoid eating in idol temples?

A. To avoid causing a brother in Christ to fall

B. To avoid the Lord's discipline

C. To avoid sharing with demons

D. To avoid legalism

QUESTION 16

The punishment for Israelite sinners in the wilderness was:

A. Spiritual death

B. Eternal death

C. Physical death

D. Purgatory

QUESTION 17

In humility, Paul never used himself as an example but always pointed to Christ. *True or False?*

QUESTION 18

Proclaiming the gospel was optional for Paul. *True or False?*

QUESTION 19

Why did Paul adapt to those he tried to reach with the gospel?

- A. He was afraid they would not like him if he did not adapt to them.
- B. He wanted to remove any hindrance to the spread of the gospel.
- C. He lacked a stable sense of self-confidence.
- D. He wanted the gospel to seem socially acceptable.

QUESTION 20

In order to win others, Paul made himself the slave of all. *True or False?*

QUESTION 21

Refusing money for his apostolic services made Paul more spiritual than the other apostles. *True or False?*

QUESTION 22

Paul viewed that proclaiming the gospel at his own expense was his reward. *True or False?*

QUESTION 23

The principle "become all things to all people" is

- A. Without limitations
- B. Properly applied in conjunction with the law of Christ
- C. Only for reaching your friends
- D. A sufficient reason to eat food offered to idols

QUESTION 24

Paul usually accepted money from those he was ministering to. *True or False?*

QUESTION 25

The purpose of the athletic metaphor in 1 Corinthians 9:24-27 is to prove that believers can lose their salvation. *True or False?*

Lesson 8 Answers to Questions

QUESTION 1: False
QUESTION 2: False
QUESTION 3

Reference	Argument
1 Corinthians 9:9	Biblical
1 Corinthians 9:7	Common sense
1 Corinthians 9:5	Examples of other Christian workers
1 Corinthians 9:11	Gratitude
1 Corinthians 9:12	Lesser-to-greater

QUESTION 4: *Your answer should be similar to the following:*
Probably some at Corinth reasoned that Paul was not an apostle because he did not exercise all his apostolic rights. His inconsistency in eating marketplace food may have also influenced their view of him.

QUESTION 5
    C. Illustrate his point

QUESTION 6: *Your answer*

QUESTION 7
    D. Receiving pay would have hindered the gospel.
    E. He wanted the reward of preaching without pay.

QUESTION 8: *Your answer should be similar to the following:*
Paul was called and commissioned to preach the gospel. If, like Jonah, he had refused his responsibility, God would surely have disciplined him.

QUESTION 9: True

QUESTION 10: *Your answer*

QUESTION 11: False

QUESTION 12: Inconsistent

QUESTION 13: *Your answer should be similar to the following:*
To share in its blessings

QUESTION 14: *Your answer*

QUESTION 15: *Your answer*

QUESTION 16: *Your answer*

QUESTION 17: Slave

QUESTION 18
    D. To encourage believers to live purposefully

QUESTION 19: *Your answer should be similar to the following:*
Purpose, activity, self-control, endurance, suffering, hope

QUESTION 20
    A. Apostleship
    B. Eternal life
    C. Rewards in heaven
    D. Blessings in this life

QUESTION 21: *Your answer*

Lesson 8 Self Check Answers

QUESTION 1: True
QUESTION 2: True
QUESTION 3: False
QUESTION 4: True
QUESTION 5
    B.   Spreading the gospel
QUESTION 6: True
QUESTION 7
    B.   His own reward
QUESTION 8: True
QUESTION 9
    B.   Not taking pay for preaching the gospel
QUESTION 10: False

Unit 3 Exam Answers

QUESTION 1: False
QUESTION 2: True
QUESTION 3: True
QUESTION 4
    B. His interests are divided
QUESTION 5: True
QUESTION 6
    A. To avoid immorality
QUESTION 7: True
QUESTION 8: True
QUESTION 9: True
QUESTION 10: True
QUESTION 11
    B. Without asking questions as to its origin
QUESTION 12: True
QUESTION 13
    C. Respect his convictions.
QUESTION 14: True
QUESTION 15
    D. To avoid legalism
QUESTION 16
    C. Physical death
QUESTION 17: False
QUESTION 18: False
QUESTION 19
    B. He wanted to remove any hindrance to the spread of the gospel.
QUESTION 20: True
QUESTION 21: False
QUESTION 22: True
QUESTION 23
    B. Properly applied in conjunction with the law of Christ
QUESTION 24: False
QUESTION 25: False

Unit 4: Freedom Has Limits in the Church

Unit Introduction

Freedom indicates the authority, or right, to do something. The Corinthians were misinterpreting and misapplying the idea of freedom. Christian freedom has several facets:

(a) Christians, in principle, can eat anything, but we do not have freedom to eat in an idol's temple. We are not free to participate in idol worship or immorality.

(b) Believers have the right to listen to great Christian teachers and leaders, but we do not have the freedom to idolize them or splinter into factions over a particular leader.

(c) Although believers are new people in Christ, that truth does not mean that our pre-Christian marriages have come to an end.

Paul's point is that freedom is truly available in Christ, but that freedom is not a believer's highest value, nor is it without limits. We cannot think only about ourselves. We have to be guided in our use of freedom by truth and love.

Lessons 9-11 deal with freedom in the worship service in the local church. In each case there is freedom in Christ: for men and women to pray and prophesy (Lesson 9); to celebrate the Lord's Supper (Lesson 10); and to exercise spiritual gifts (Lesson 11). In no case does Paul allow unbridled freedom, for freedom can be abused.

Lesson 12 deals with a fundamental doctrine: resurrection. Paul's concern, and the question of the Corinthians, was not chiefly regarding Christ's resurrection, but the resurrection of believers. Paul is concerned that the believers understand correct doctrine dealing with the importance of the physical body. We do not have freedom to deviate from orthodoxy and deny the resurrection.

Unit Outline

Lesson 9: Freedom in Worship: Headship (1 Cor 11:2-16)

Lesson 10: Freedom in Worship: The Lord's Supper (1 Cor 11:17-34)

Lesson 11: Freedom in Worship: Spiritual Gifts (1 Cor 12:1-14:40)

Lesson 12: Freedom in Doctrine: Resurrection (1 Cor 15:1-58)

Unit Objectives

Lotus is beginning to lose patience with Esther and Sara over their interest in Sister Marie's teachings. But even more seriously, she is considering going to another church.

At church there seems to be one problem after another. The teaching and music are good, but there are so many controversies and the whole sense of unity seems lost. Communion Sunday has lost much of its special appeal since they stopped having the shared dinner after the service. The disciplinary action against Daniel left a number of church members disgruntled, and Ai still has not started coming back to church. Now Sara and Esther are distributing Sister Marie's DVDs, and some church people are saying that their worship service does not follow the practices of the New Testament church closely enough.

Fewer and fewer are attending Sunday worship, although recently a new believer named Quan started attending. He told Lotus about a really great Bible study group that has started in town. Lotus thinks she will try it out. Maybe the relationships there will be more harmonious than in her church.

Lesson 9: Freedom in Worship: Headship (1 Cor 11:2-16)

In 1 Corinthians 11:2-16 many difficult interpretive issues arise, both in understanding Paul's meaning and in a proper application today. The main principle Paul addresses here is headship, and this principle touches on the relationship between men and women and on order in the worship service. The immediate issue at hand in Corinth was head coverings.

Churches vary from paying no attention to the head covering issue to strictly enforcing head coverings for women and none for men. In ancient Corinth it was an issue of sufficient importance for Paul to give detailed instructions and arguments to support his teaching.

Today it is important for Christians to grasp the timeless principles and make appropriate applications in their contexts.

Topic 1 identifies the issue of headship and elucidates possible meanings for the figurative sense of "head." Topic 1 also examines what Paul meant when he talked about men and women in a headship relationship.

Topic 2 looks at head coverings for both men and women in ancient Corinthian society.

Paul makes a number of theological arguments to undergird his instruction. Topic 3 examines arguments from apostolic tradition, creation, and glory.

Cultural arguments—shame and nature—are the subject of Topic 4.

In Topic 5 we suggest steps for applying these principles today.

Lesson Outline

Topic 1: Headship

    Meaning of Head

    Restrictions on Men and Women

Topic 2: Meaning of Head Covering

Topic 3: Theological Arguments

    Headship

    Creation

    Angels

Topic 4: Cultural Arguments

    Shame

    Nature

Topic 5: Application for Today

Lesson Objectives

Now Sisters Esther and Sara, who really love Sister Marie's teachings and hold their own special prayer meeting, have decided to completely stay away from the church. They told Lotus that the church is ungodly because no one enforces the rule that women have to wear head coverings.

In the new DVD from Sister Marie, she is wearing a shawl over her head and a veil over her face, teaching that all the women have to do the same. She even says that women should wear this head covering any time they are out in public, including when they go to work. It has created something of a stir, because until Esther and Sara started doing this, the only women who wore head coverings in town were the Muslims. Several people have asked Lotus if Esther and Sara have become Muslims.

Lotus talks to her church leaders about it, but they say that they do not intend to make a rule that women have to wear head coverings. They feel that women could wear head coverings to come to church if they want to, but that times have changed since the Bible was written, and that head coverings are not a sign of modesty or submission to leaders as they once were. They urge Lotus to talk to Esther and Sara about it and study 1 Corinthians 11:2-16 with them.

By the end of this lesson, you will be able to:

- List several meanings for "head"
- Discuss Paul's theological and cultural arguments for headship
- Explain your application of headship in the church today
- Apply the heart of Paul's teachings on headship and roles to your church or ministry.

Topic 1: Headship

Some people malign Paul, assuming that he hates women. Passages such as 1 Corinthians 11:2-16 may be used as evidence of this view. However, a close reading of this passage reveals that Paul upholds the principle of headship, maintaining distinctions between men and women and also upholding the freedom of both men and women to pray and prophesy in the worship service.

QUESTION 1

Read 1 Corinthians 11:2-16 and then read the following statements. Which statements are closest to your feelings about this passage? Take a few moments to elaborate in your Life Notebook.

- It makes me angry because of what Paul says about women.
- It is irrelevant—either outdated, or concerns such a small issue that it is more trouble than it is worth.
- It is important for male/female relationships. It is part of God's Word, and we ignore its teachings to our peril.
- It is too controversial—no matter what you say, you will be misunderstood!

Meaning of Head

Assignment

- Read 1 Corinthians 11:2-6.

- Read Constable, "Propriety in Worship" (refer to the Articles section at the end of this lesson), through the note on 11:6.

- Read the articles "Specific Issue" and "Figurative Meaning of 'Head.'"

Figurative Meaning of Head

What are the possibilities for the figurative meaning of "head" in 1 Corinthians 11:2-16?

1. Authority (see Eph 1:22; 5:23)

2. Source, origin (some suggest Col 2:19 as an example)

3. Prominent (as in "the head of the line")

4. Oneself (as in Acts 18:6, "Your blood be on your own heads!")

5. Some combination of these meanings

Based on extensive studies, Wayne Grudem concludes:

> Even in the texts where "source" or "prominent part" is alleged as the correct meaning, the person who is called "head" is always a person in leadership or authority. Therefore there is no linguistic basis for proposing that the New Testament texts which speak of Christ as the head of the church or the husband as the head of the wife can rightly be read apart from the attribution of authority to the one designated as "head." (Grudem, Wayne *Recovering Biblical Manhood & Womanhood: A Response to Evangelical Feminism* [Wheaton, IL: Crossway Books], 2006, Kindle edition.)

Paul's concern is that Christian worship should reflect the order of headship in creation, between male and female, and in the Godhead. Paul's teaching in this passage regarding headship emphasizes issues of honor and shame rather than authority and submission.

Specific Issue

What was the specific behavioral issue during the corporate worship at Corinth that Paul was addressing? The specific issue is stated clearly in 1 Corinthians 11:4, 5:

> Any man who prays or prophesies with his head covered disgraces his head. But any woman who prays or prophesies with her head uncovered disgraces her head.

Thus, the specific issue is both men's and women's behavior in corporate worship. Both men and women had freedom to pray and prophesy during worship, but that freedom had limits—women must wear a head covering and men must not. The praying or prophesying in this context meant taking a public role in the worship—not just sitting quietly. From 1 Corinthians 14:26, we know that other public roles during Corinth's congregational worship included sharing a song, giving a message in tongues, interpreting a message in tongues, and giving a lesson.

QUESTION 2

What do you think the issue of headship between men and women means? What does it not mean? Record your response in your Life Notebook.

Paul begins to answer a question from the Corinthians' letter dealing with difficult concepts of headship, the relationship between men and women, shameful behavior, and head coverings. Biblical scholars debate exactly how to interpret what Paul meant in this passage.

Study the fourteen times "head" is used in this passage in the graphic below. Take note of whether "head" in each instance means a physical body part, or has a figurative meaning, or has both meanings.

Scriptural Headship		
Instance	Physical	Spiritual
1 Cor 11:3 But I want you to know that Christ is the **head** of every man, and the man is the **head** of a woman, and God is the **head** of Christ.		X X X
1 Cor 11:4 Any man who prays or prophesies with his **head** covered disgraces his **head**.	X X	X
1 Cor 11:5 But any woman who prays or prophesies with her **head** uncovered disgraces her **head**, for it is one and the same thing as having a shaved **head**.	X X X	X
1 Cor 11:6 For if a woman will not cover her **head**, she should cut off her hair. But if it is disgraceful for a woman to have her hair cut off or her **head** shaved, she should cover her **head**.	X X X	
1 Cor 11:7 For a man should not have his **head** covered, since he is the image and glory of God. But the woman is the glory of the man.	X	
1 Cor 11:10 For this reason a woman should have a symbol of authority on her **head**, because of the angels	X	
1 Cor 11:13 Judge for yourselves: Is it proper for a woman to pray to God with her **head** uncovered?	X	

QUESTION 3

Each of Paul's references to a "head" in Scripture refers to either physical or spiritual headship, but never both simultaneously. *True or False?*

QUESTION 4

The context for Paul's instruction in 1 Corinthians 11:2-16 is a local church worship meeting. *True or False?*

QUESTION 5

Possible figurative meanings for "head" in 1 Corinthians 11:2-16 include *(Select all that apply.)*

    A. Prominent

    B. Source

    C. Authority

    D. Representative

    E. Savior

Restrictions on Men and Women

Assignment

- Read "Meaning of Man and Woman."

Meaning of Man and Woman

What is the meaning of "man" and "woman" in 1 Corinthians 11:2-16? Two positions are advocated:

1. The meaning is man and woman generally, without regard to family relationship.

2. The meaning is man and woman in a family relationship—particularly husband/wife, and possibly father/daughter.

The Greek words are general, but can mean either man or woman or husband and wife. Frequently in Paul's writings, when these words are used together the meaning is "husband and wife." However, if you try to consistently read "husband and wife" as the translation throughout this passage, it seems awkward for 1 Corinthians 11:12. A complicating consideration is that the first man and woman, Adam and Eve, were also husband and wife.

Practically in the church, not every woman was married or had a man as her head, but Paul's statements in 1 Corinthians 11 may be taken generally. Thus, when Paul uses "man" and "woman" in this passage, he is probably referring primarily to husband and wife in the marriage relationship, but with application to male-female relationships in general.

English Bible translations of this passage vary. Some translations (NET, KJV, NIV) use only "man" and "woman" consistently throughout. Some translations (ESV, GNT) use "husband" and "wife" in some places along with "man" and "woman" in other places.

QUESTION 6

According to 1 Corinthians 11:2-16, which of the following statements are true? *(Select all that apply.)*

- A. Every man is the authority over every woman.
- B. There is an order of headship in the Trinity.
- C. A husband is the head of his wife.
- D. Some actions can bring dishonor to one's head.

QUESTION 7

The Greek word that Paul uses for "woman" in 1 Corinthians 11:2-16 can also be translated _____.

Topic 2: Meaning of Head Covering

Today in some churches, women worshippers wear shawls over their heads. In other churches, the women wear a little piece of cloth or lace on their heads. In still other churches, the women come to worship bareheaded. What did Paul mean when he instructed the women at Corinth regarding head coverings?

Assignment

- Read "Meaning of Head Covering."

Meaning of Head Covering

What is the meaning of "head covering"? The three Greek words translated "with his head covered" (1 Cor 11:4) literally mean "having down from the head." Paul does not say "veil," although there is a Greek word for veil, which he uses elsewhere (2 Cor 3:13).

Many interpretive questions arise as to what specifically was meant:

1. Was this a shawl or a veil? Did it cover the face, the top of the head, or both?

2. Since Paul does not use the word "veil," was he just referring to long hair? Some suggest he was referring to the particular style of hair—wearing the hair up or down.

3. Culturally, did all women normally wear head coverings in public? Was this a difference between Greek/Roman and Jewish women?

4. When did men wear head coverings and why?

Many suggestions have been made in attempts to answer these questions, and there seems to be no clear consensus among scholars. Some suggest relationships between wearing, or not wearing, head coverings and sexual immorality, pagan worship, or the obscuring of male/female sexual differences. A few sculptures indicate that Greek/Roman males and females both covered their heads when performing pagan religious acts. There were times when women wore head coverings in public, and many scholars think this was the normal practice for Greek/Roman women. (See Augustus' wife Livia (50 BC-AD 29) wearing a head covering: http://gbgm-umc.org/umw/corinthians/veils.stm.)

The NET Bible has a note at the end of 1 Corinthians 11:15 that argues strongly that a woman's hair is **not** the head covering that Paul specifies:

> No word for veil or head covering occurs in vv. 3-14 (see the note on *authority* in v. 10). That the hair is regarded by Paul as a *covering* in v. 15 is not necessarily an argument that the hair is the same as the head covering that he is describing in the earlier verses (esp. v. 10). Throughout this unit of material, Paul points out the *similarities* of long hair with a head covering. But his doing so seems to suggest that the two are not to be identified with each other. Precisely because they are similar they do not appear to be identical (cf. vv. 5, 6, 7, 10, 13). If head covering = long hair, then what does v. 6 mean ("For if a woman will not cover her head, she should cut off her hair")? This suggests that the covering is not the same as the hair itself.

"Head covering" could possibly refer to the length or style of hair, but evidence may indicate that Greek/Roman women of the time normally wore a cloth head covering in public.

QUESTION 8

Paul does not use the Greek word for _____ when talking about head coverings in 1 Corinthians 11:2-16.

QUESTION 9

Scholars use sculptural evidence from the first century to try to understand what Paul meant by "head coverings." *True or False?*

Topic 3: Theological Arguments

Paul's theological arguments include teaching about headship and creation, as well as a statement about angels.

Headship

Assignment

- Read 1 Corinthians 11:7-12.
- Read Constable, "The Argument From Creation" (refer to the Articles section at the end of this lesson), through the note on 11:9.
- Read "Headship."

Headship

Paul makes a number of theological arguments to underpin his instructions. Included among his theological arguments are statements about apostolic teaching, headship and glory.

When first addressing this subject, Paul refers to maintaining "the traditions just as I passed them on to you." (1 Cor 11:2) He finishes this segment by stating, "If anyone intends to quarrel about this, we have no other practice, nor do the churches of God" (1 Cor 11:16). The point here is that this instruction is from his apostolic authority. It is not something that you can take or leave, depending on your personal feelings. His instruction is not optional.

His argument about headship is first seen in 1 Corinthians 11:3— "But I want you to know that Christ is the head of every man, and the man is the head of a woman, and God is the head of Christ." There is an order to the headship, and this order should be preserved in the public worship of the church.

Closely tied to this headship argument is the idea of glory, which seems to relate to honoring or shaming one's head. Since man is the glory of God, in the context of ancient Corinth a man's physical head should be uncovered in acts of public worship (such as praying and prophesying) to reveal God's glory. Conversely, the woman is the glory of the man, so in the context of ancient Corinth her physical head should be covered in acts of public worship so that only God will be glorified.

The purpose of worship is to reveal God's glory and not man's. Thus, Paul explains culturally appropriate ways to manifest God's headship should be maintained during corporate worship.

QUESTION 10

In 1 Corinthians 11:2, far from just denoting local custom, Paul used the word _____ to mean authoritative apostolic instruction.

QUESTION 11

What is the argument from glory explaining why the woman's head should be covered in ancient Corinth?

Creation

Assignment

- Continue reading Constable, "The Argument From Creation" (refer to the Articles section at the end of this lesson), through 11:12.

- Read "Creation."

> ## Creation
>
> Another supporting theological argument for headship is the relationship of man and woman at creation. Both the priority of man and his interdependence with the woman are established by the creation accounts.
>
> The NET Bible translates the first part of 1 Corinthians 11:10 as "For this reason a woman should have **a symbol of** authority on her head" (emphasis added). The NET Bible footnote states:
>
>> Paul does not use a word specifying what type of "covering" is meant (veil, hat, etc.). The Greek word he uses here (*exousia*; translated *symbol of authority*) could be (1) a figure of speech that may substitute the result (the right to participate in worship) for the appropriate appearance that makes it possible (the covered head). Or (2) it refers to the outward symbol (having the head covered) as representing the inward attitude the woman is to possess (deference to male leadership in the church).
>
> As Constable points out in his note on 11:10, "a symbol of" is not part of the original Greek. If "a symbol of" is not inserted in the translation of 1 Corinthians 11:10, then the phrase may be translated "for this reason a woman should have authority over her head." The sense of this authority could be authority to control how people perceive her head. If it is covered, then she appears decent and avoids shame. (See Robertson and Plummer [1963:232].)

Referring to Genesis 1 and 2, Paul argues that the relationship of man and woman from the beginning should be reflected in Christian worship.

QUESTION 12

What arguments from the creation account does Paul refer to in 1 Corinthians 11:7-12? *(Select all that apply.)*

A. Man was created prior to woman

B. Man named the woman

C. Woman was formed from the man

D. Woman was created for the man

E. It was not good for the man to be alone

QUESTION 13

What are suggested interpretations for the meaning of the authority a woman should have on (or over) her head (1 Cor 11:10)? *(Select all that apply.)*

    A. A head covering is a sign of her submission to male authority.

    B. A head covering is a sign of her freedom in Christ to pray and prophesy in the worship service.

    C. A head covering is a sign both of her freedom to pray and prophesy and of her submission to male authority.

    D. A head covering is authority to control how people perceive her head so as to avoid shame.

Angels

Assignment

- Read "Angels."

Angels

The reference to angels is extremely obscure. The meaning of "because of the angels" is unclear in 1 Corinthians 11:10. See the NET Bible note on this verse:

> Paul does not explain this reference to *the angels*, and its point is not entirely clear. It seems to reflect an awareness that angels are witnesses to church life (cf. Eph 3:10) and would be particularly sensitive to resistance against God's created order.

> Another suggestion is that the word translated "angels" really refers to human messengers sent from other churches to observe the worship service and report back if it is safe to attend.

Even though we are not sure of the precise meaning of Paul's reference to angels (or human messengers), we can catch the thrust of his argument. "Because of the angels" is another argument in support of a woman covering her head.

QUESTION 14

Suggestions for Paul's meaning of the phrase "because of the angels" include: *(Select all that apply.)*

    A. Angels will punish women without head coverings.

    B. Angels wear veils, so women should, too.

    C. Angels observe Christian worship and would be offended by women without head coverings.

    D. Evil angels might lust after women without head coverings.

    E. "Angels" mean church messengers who report back to other churches on the worship service.

Topic 4: Cultural Arguments

Paul's cultural arguments were especially relevant to the church at Corinth almost two thousand years ago. Such arguments may be difficult for today's readers to understand, since the cultural picture has greatly changed. Identifying the cultural aspects of Paul's teaching is important for making proper application of the headship principle today. Arguments from shame and nature may be considered cultural arguments.

Shame

Assignment

- Read 1 Corinthians 11:13-16.

- Read Constable, "The Argument From Propriety (11:13-16)" (refer to the Articles section at the end of this lesson).

- Read "Shame."

Shame

In several places Paul mentions shame as part of his argument (1 Cor 11:4, 5, 6, 13, 14). The shame idea is communicated by consideration of what is disgraceful and proper. Shame concepts vary from culture to culture. For example, Paul and the people of Corinth considered it shameful for a woman to have her head shaved. Today in many places, if a woman came into the worship service with her head shaved, perhaps no one would view it as shameful. Reactions may vary from fashionable to eccentric, with not a few wondering if she had not just been through chemotherapy for cancer.

In the view of the author of the *International Standard Bible Encyclopedia* (ISBE) article "Head," Paul was advocating following the current customs of the Greeks so as to avoid shameful behavior:

> In this connection the Pauline injunction as to the veiling of women in the public gatherings of the Christians (1 Cor 11:5), while men were instructed to appear bareheaded, must be mentioned. This is diametrically opposed to the Jewish custom, according to which men wore the head covered by the Tallith or prayer shawl, while women were considered sufficiently covered by their long hair (1 Cor 11:15). The apostle here simply commends a Greek custom for the congregation residing among Greek populations; in other words, he recommends obedience to local standards of decency and good order. (From ISBE article "Head")

Paul teaches that what society in general views as right and proper must be respected in the church. He does not use only theological arguments to support his case for women wearing head coverings in ancient Corinth.

QUESTION 15

Paul's arguments about shame are based on: *(Select all that apply.)*

- A. Middle Eastern conceptions of shame at the time
- B. Greek/Roman conceptions of shame at the time
- C. Old Testament conceptions of shame and honor
- D. Universal conceptions of shame and honor

Nature

Assignment

- Read "Nature."

> ## Nature
>
> Paul mentions that nature teaches that long hair on a man is disgraceful, but that long hair on a woman is her glory (see 1 Cor 11:14, 15).
>
> Some think Paul means "'the way things are' because of God's design" (NET Bible note on 1 Cor 11:14). If correct, then the argument from nature would be absolute and unchanging.
>
> Others view nature as denoting customs or traditions. If that is the meaning of "nature," then what nature teaches would not be absolute or unchanging. Since Paul's immediate subject is long hair, culture would tend to influence what constitutes long hair for a man and a woman. Undeniably, just in Western history, views as to what constitutes long hair on a man have changed from time to time and place to place. Chinese customs have changed as well—think of the long hair queue on men during the Qing Dynasty.

In ancient Israel it was apparently not always shameful for a man to have long hair. See the examples of Samson (Judg 13:5) and Absalom (2 Sam 14:26), although their examples may not have been considered common or ordinary. People's view of what nature teaches may be conditioned by cultural traditions.

QUESTION 16

In Constable's view, the main theme of Paul's teaching in 1 Corinthians 11:2-16 is:

A. The subjugation of women to men

B. The wearing of head coverings

C. Angelic supervision of the church

D. A woman's acceptance or rejection of her role in God's administrative order

QUESTION 17

Some might argue that if wearing head coverings can be adapted to changing cultural settings, so can acceptance or rejection of homosexual practice. How would you respond?

QUESTION 18

Please open your Life Notebook and list two or three examples of appearances, behaviors, or speech from your culture where society's views of what is proper and improper have changed over the past one hundred years? What is your view of those changes and how do you as a Christian react to them?

Topic 5: Application for Today

An issue like headship must be handled carefully, recognizing its importance and the varying applications of believers in different cultural contexts today.

Assignment

- Read "Application for Today."

Application for Today

A Christian's response to the teaching of this passage should distinguish between unchanging principles and appropriate cultural applications of those principles. The key principle Paul upholds is headship, and he expects the Corinthians to uphold his head coverings instructions as an application of that principle. Today, we should understand the principle of headship and apply it in culturally relevant ways in our churches. In some contexts today, it is still an important application of headship for women to wear head coverings and for men to not wear them. In other contexts, wearing a head covering no longer communicates headship. Other ways of applying the principle of headship in Western churches may include: restricting certain church leadership positions to males, wives not publicly criticizing their husbands, avoiding outrageous or shameful behaviors or appearances in church, etc.

The principle of headship should be applied in culturally appropriate ways today.

QUESTION 19

The issue of head coverings is fundamental to salvation. *True or False?*

QUESTION 20

According to Constable, a woman who _____ her head in ancient Greek/Roman society was trying to appear as a man.

QUESTION 21

Answer the following question in your Life Notebook: In your cultural setting, how do you apply the principle of headship in your local church?

QUESTION 22

Answer the following question in your Life Notebook: In your cultural setting, how do you apply the principle of headship in your home?

Lesson 9 Articles

Notes on 1 Corinthians

Dr. Thomas L. Constable; 2003 Edition

C. PROPRIETY IN WORSHIP 11:2-16

This section and the next (11:17-34) deal with subjects different from meat offered to idols, but Paul did not introduce them with the phrase "now concerning." These were additional subjects about which he wanted to give the Corinthians guidance. He had evidently learned of the Corinthians' need for instruction in these matters either through their letter to him, from the messengers that brought that letter to Paul, or from other sources.

1. The argument from culture 11:2-6

Paul introduced the first of the two subjects he dealt with in this chapter, the Corinthian women's participation in church worship, with praise. He did not introduce the second subject this way (vv. 17, 22). As with the other sections of this epistle, we can see the influence of Corinthian culture and world view in this one, particularly in the behavior of the women in the church.

11:2 - Paul commended his original readers for remembering his teaching and example. This chapter deals with things that were going on in the meetings of the church primarily, as the context shows. The "traditions" (NASB) were "teachings" (NIV; Gr. *paradoseis*) the Corinthians had received from the apostle. Some of these involved divinely inspired revelations and others just prudent advice (cf. 2 Thess 3:6-10). They may have been following his instructions, but not in the proper ways, as his following discussion makes clear.

> "*The traditions* (as the other references show) were the central truths of the Christian faith, handed on at this stage (before the emergence of Christian literature) orally from evangelist and teacher to convert." (244)

11:3 - "But" indicates that things were not quite as Paul thought they should be. He began dealing with his subject by reminding the Corinthians again (cf. 3:23; 8:6) of God's administrative order. This is the order through which He has chosen to conduct His dealings with humans.

Jesus Christ is the head of every male human being (Gr. *aner*). Second, the male is the head of woman (Gr. *gune*). This Greek word for woman is very broad and covers women of any age, virgins, married women, or widows. Paul used it earlier in this epistle of a wife (7:3-4, 10-12, 14, 16). In this chapter it evidently refers to any woman who was in a dependent relationship to a man such as a wife to a husband or a daughter to a father. Paul probably did not mean every woman universally since he said the male is the head of woman, or a woman, but not *the* woman. He was evidently not talking about every relationship involving men and women, for example the relationship between men and women in the workplace. Third, God the Father is the head of God the Son. This shows that headship exists even within the Godhead.

The New Testament uses the term "head" (Gr. *kephale*) to describe headship in two ways. Sometimes it describes origin (source), and other times it describes authority (leader). Some scholars favor one interpretation and others the other. (245) Both meanings are true to reality, so it is difficult to decide what Paul meant here.

In favor of the origin view, it is true that Christ created mankind, Eve came from Adam, and Christ came from the Father in the Incarnation to provide redemption. In favor of the authority view, humanity is under Christ's authority, God created woman under man's authority, and the Son is under the Father's authority. The idea of origin is more fundamental than that of authority. Also "head" occurs later in this passage with the idea of source (vv. 8, 12), so origin may be the preferable idea here too. (246)

11:4 - Here Paul used the word "head" twice. Clearly in the first instance he meant the man's physical skull. What did he mean the second time he referred to the man's head? He could have meant his physical skull again. However, in view of what he just said (v. 3) and would say, he probably meant his spiritual head, Jesus Christ. In Judaism when a man prayed with his physical head covered, as was common, he did not thereby dishonor himself. In Christian worship the men did not wear head coverings.

Paul's reference to praying and prophesying sets his instructions in the context of the church at public worship. (247) Praying involves expressing one's thoughts and feelings to God. Prophesying might involve any of three things. Prophets foretold future events pertaining especially to the kingdom of God (Matt. 11:13; Acts 2:17-18; 21:9). They also declared new revelation from God (Matt. 26:68; Mk 14:65; Lk 22:64; 7:39; Jn 4:19). Third, they could under divine impulse utter some lofty statement or message that would glorify God (Lk 1:67; Acts 9:6; cf. 1 Chron. 25:1), or a word of instruction, refutation, reproof, admonition, or comfort for others (1 Cor. 13:9; 14:1, 3-5, 24, 31, 39). This last type of prophecy did not contain a new revelation or a prediction involving the future. (248) The last activity is what seems to be in view in other references to prophesying in this epistle, and it suits the context here as well. Praying and prophesying were two major features of Christian worship services (cf. Acts 2:42).

11:5a - The opposite condition existed when women prayed or prophesied in the church meetings. Every woman who had her physical skull *uncovered* thereby dishonored her metaphorical head, namely, her husband or father (v. 3).

What did Paul mean when he described a woman's head as "uncovered?" There have been three major explanations. He may have meant that her head lacked some type of external cover, such as a shawl. Second, he could have meant that she had short hair that did not cover her head as completely as long hair. Third, he may have meant that she had let her hair down rather than leaving it piled up on her head. It was customary for women to wear their hair up when they went out in public. Probably he meant that she did not have an external covering on her head (view one). (249) The woman would dishonor her man by participating in public worship as he did, namely, with head uncovered.

Christian women typically wore a head-covering in the church meetings. This was not a stylish hat, skull cap, or inconspicuous doily, as some western women do today, but a shawl that covered her entire head and concealed her hair. (250)

> "Her face was hidden by an arrangement of two head veils, a head-band on the forehead with bands to the chin, and a hairnet [sic] with ribbons and knots, so that her features could not be recognized." (251)

In Paul's culture most women, Christians and non-Christians alike, wore such a covering whenever they went out in public. Conservative Islamic women still veil themselves when they go out in public.

Probably the issue in the Corinthian church that Paul was addressing was that certain "wise," "spiritual," liberated women had stopped wearing this covering in the church meetings. Paul had previously written that in Christ males and females are equal before God (in many respects; Gal. 3:28). This teaching, combined with the Corinthians' carnal tendencies, were evidently the root of the problem.

11:5b-6 - A woman who shaved her head in Greco-Roman culture did so to appear as a man. This resulted in the blurring of the relationship between men and women, particularly the sexual distinctions. Men typically wore their hair short, and women wore theirs long. If a woman cut her hair short, it indicated that she wanted to take the place of a man. Not covering her head made the same statement in that society.

> "The prostitutes wore their hair very short, and they did not wear a head-covering in public. Their hairstyle and manner announced to others just what they were and what they were offering. . . .
>
> "In Jewish law, a woman proved guilty of adultery had her hair cut off (Num. 5:11-31)." (252)

It was a shameful thing for a woman not to cover her head in the early New Testament churches. Such an act made a statement that she was repudiating her position as a woman. It was not so much a repudiation of her submission to her male authority as it was a repudiation of her origin as being a woman who had come from man (v. 3). The issue is origin throughout the passage, not primarily authority. Obviously a woman who repudiated her origin as a woman might also repudiate her authority to function under her male head. However in this passage Paul seems to have been dealing with the more fundamental issue of origin.

Today it is not shameful for a woman to have short hair, but it was in Paul's day. There are many short hair styles that no one regards as disgraceful. However in Paul's culture short hair for a woman represented rebellion, and people considered it shameful. Paul used the common reaction to women's short hair in his day to urge his female readers to wear a head-covering. His point was that since it was shameful for a woman to have short hair it was also shameful for her to have her head uncovered when she prayed or prophesied.

Must a Christian woman cover her head in church meetings today? I think not. Covering the head and wearing short hair do not normally mean the same thing in modern times, at least in the West, as they did in Paul's culture. If he were writing to a western church today, for example, I do not believe Paul would have said it is a shameful thing for a woman to have short hair. Therefore I do not think he would have said she ought to cover her head. Covering the head was a sign of acknowledgement of origin in Paul's day, which implied some acknowledgement of authority, but it is not today typically. Today there is no item of clothing that makes such a statement, nor does the length of a woman's hair. Perhaps her willingness to take her husband's family name when she marries does, or her willingness to wear a wedding ring might. A woman's whole personal demeanor, especially how she views herself as a woman, reveals this about her. (253)

> "Although various Christian groups have fostered the practice of some sort of head covering for women in the assembled church, the difficulties with the practice are obvious. For Paul the issue was directly tied to a cultural shame that scarcely prevails in most cultures today. Furthermore, we simply do not know what the practice was that they were abusing. Thus literal 'obedience' to the text is often merely symbolic. Unfortunately, the symbol that tends to be reinforced is the subordination of women, which is hardly Paul's point. Furthermore, it would seem that in cultures where women's heads are seldom covered, the enforcement of such in the church turns Paul's point on its head." (254)

2. The argument from creation 11:7-12

Paul proceeded with a second supporting argument to correct the Corinthians' perversion regarding women's head-coverings.

11:7 - Men should not cover their heads in Christian worship because they are the glory of God. Whereas Paul referred to man being the image and glory of God, his primary point was that man is the glory of God. His reference to man as the image of God clearly goes back to Genesis 1:26-28, but there "glory" does not appear. "Glory" is Paul's word, his reflection on the creation of man. This is the word that he proceeded to use to contrast man and woman.

Notice that Paul did not say that the woman is to cover her head because she is the glory of man. Instead he proceeded to describe what her being his glory means. A subordinate glorifies the one in authority over him or her just by being in a subordinate position.

> ." . . he [Paul] says that woman is the glory of man—not his image, for she too shares the image of God, and is not (as some commentators have thought) more remote from God than is man." (255)

11:8 - Woman is the glory of man, first, because she came from him in creation. As Adam glorified God by being the product of His creation, so Eve glorified Adam because she came from him. The female sex did not produce the male sex, but the first woman came from the first man. God formed Eve out of a part of Adam whom He created first (Gen. 2:18, 20).

11:9 - Furthermore woman is the glory of man because God created Eve to complete Adam. God did not create the man as a companion for the woman but the woman for man's sake (Gen. 2:21-22). When Adam saw Eve for the first time, he "gloried" in her (Gen. 2:23). Neither of these verses (vv. 8-9) refer to the subordination of woman under man, though many interpreters have read this into the text. Rather they refer to her origin as being from man.

11:10 - Paul drew a conclusion from what he had already said (vv. 7-9) and gave a supporting reason for his conclusion. Unfortunately the NASB translators have added "a symbol of" to the original text thus implying that the head-covering is what women ought to wear on their heads. The Greek text simply says "the woman ought to have authority on her head." In the preceding verses the reason is that she is the man's glory. In light of verse 7, we might have expected Paul to say that because the woman is the glory of the man she should cover her head. Yet that is not what Paul said.

What is this "authority" that women ought to have on their heads? Some interpreters believe it refers to the man in her life who is in authority over her. The covering is the sign that she recognizes him in this role. (256) This view lacks support in the passive use of *exousia* ("authority"). Furthermore the idiom "to have authority over" never refers to an external authority different from the subject of the sentence elsewhere.

Other interpreters view "authority" as a metonym for "veil." (257) This view is unlikely because "authority" is a strange word to use if Paul really meant "veil." It would have been more natural for him to say "veil" or "covering."

A third view is to take "to have authority" as meaning "a sign of authority, namely, as a means of exercising authority." Advocates believe Paul meant that women were to have authority to do things in worship previously forbidden, such as praying and prophesying along with men. Her covering would serve as a sign of her new liberty in Christ. (258) There does not seem to be adequate basis of support for this view in the passage.

The fourth major view takes having "authority" in its usual meaning of having the freedom or right to choose. The meaning in this case would be that the woman has authority over her head (man) to do as she pleases. (259) Obviously this seems to run contrary to what Paul taught in the passage and elsewhere. I think perhaps Paul meant that women have freedom to decide how they will pray and prophesy within the constraint that Paul had imposed, namely, with heads covered. The head-covering, then symbolized both the woman's subordinate position under the man and the authority that she had to pray and prophesy in public. (260)

The other major interpretive problem in this verse is "because of the angels." Why did Paul introduce angels into this discussion? Perhaps the Corinthian women needed to wear a head-covering because angels view what is taking place among God's people (cf. 4:9; Eph. 3:10; 1 Tim. 5:21). Angels are the guardians of God's created order. For other people to see Christian women unveiled was bad enough because it was a sign of insubordination, but for angels to see it would be worse. (261)

There may also be something to the suggestion that these Corinthian women, and some of the men as well, may have been exalting themselves to the position of angels (cf. 7:1; 13:1). (262) Paul may have mentioned the angels to remind them that they were still under angelic scrutiny.

Other less acceptable interpretations of "because of the angels" are these. Women should cover their heads because evil angels lusted after women in the church (cf. Gen. 6:2). If this were the reason, should not all women wear veils at all times since angels apparently view humans in other than church meetings?

They should do so because the word angels (lit. messengers) refers to pastors of the churches who might lust after them. They should wear head-coverings because good angels learn to be submissive to authority from the women's example. They need to cover themselves because good angels are an example of subordination and would take offense if they viewed insubordinate women. Finally they should wear head-coverings because a woman's insubordination would tempt good angels to be insubordinate.

Is observance by angels not a reason Christian women should cover their heads in church meetings today? Again I think not. In that culture a woman's appearance in public unveiled was a declaration of her rejection of her God-given place in creation. The angels would have recognized it as such, and it would have offended them. However today a woman's decision to appear unveiled does not usually make that statement. Consequently her unveiled condition does not offend the angels.

11:11 - Even though the positions of man and woman differ in God's administrative order, this does not mean they can get along without each other. They are mutually dependent on each other. They complement one another. They are interdependent, even as the Son and the Father are. Paul's main point was that woman is not independent of man. This is further evidence that he was countering an illegitimate spirit of independence among some Corinthian women.

In a family, companionship should replace isolation and loneliness. There must be oneness in marriage for a husband and a wife to complete one another. Self-centered individuality destroys unity in marriage. If you are married, you need your husband or wife. Your spouse is necessary for you to be a well-rounded person.

11:12 - Even though God created Eve from Adam, now every male comes from a female. This fact illustrates male female interdependence and balances Paul's emphasis in verse 11. Together verses 11 and 12 form a chiasm structurally. Husbands and wives have equal worth. Still God originates both of them, and both are subordinate to Him.

The apostle's emphasis in this section was on the authority that a woman has in her own right by virtue of creation. She must not leave her divinely appointed place in creation by seeking to function exactly as a man in church worship. Furthermore she should express her submission to this aspect of God's will in a culturally approved way. At the same time she must maintain a healthy appreciation for the opposite sex.

3. The argument from propriety 11:13-16

Paul now returned to the main argument (vv. 4-6), but now he appealed to the Corinthians' own judgment and sense of propriety. He raised two more rhetorical questions. The first (v. 13b) expects a negative answer and the second (vv. 14-15) a positive response. The apostle appealed to the nature of things. His points were that "nature" itself distinguishes between the sexes, and that a woman's naturally longer hair reinforces the propriety of covering her head in worship.

11:13 - In Paul's culture it was not proper for a woman to act as a spokesman for people with God by praying publicly with her head uncovered. To do so would be tantamount to claiming the position of a man in God's order. The apostle did not think it wise for Christian women to exercise their liberty in a way that would go against socially accepted behavior even though they were personally submissive. Today what is socially accepted is different. Again her attitude is crucial.

11:14-15 - Women's hair naturally grows longer than men's hair. Paul reasoned from this fact that God intended for women to have more head-covering than men. People generally regard the reverse of what is natural as dishonorable. In the man's case this would be long hair and in the woman's case short hair. By "nature" Paul evidently meant how his culture felt about what was natural. (263) "Glory" means "honor." This is a very general observation. The fact that some acceptable men's hair styles are longer than some women's does not mean these styles are perversions of the natural order. Men are usually taller than women, but this does not mean that a short man or a tall woman is dishonorable.

11:16 - If any of his readers still did not feel inclined to accept Paul's reasoning, he informed them that the other churches followed what he had just explained. This is one of four similar statements in this epistle that served to inform the Corinthians that they were out of step with the other churches in their conduct (cf. 3:18; 8:2; 14:37). Some women were evidently discarding their head-covering in public worship.

As with the issues of eating in idol temples and meat offered to idols, Paul dealt with a cultural practice when he dealt with head-coverings. As should be clear from his argumentation, he did not feel that this was a major issue. He argued for maintaining a custom, not for obeying God, and he used shame, propriety, and custom to urge the Corinthians to cooperate. However, important issues lay behind the practices. In the case of head-coverings, the issue is women's position in the life of the church, in particular their relationship to the men. Today no item of clothing consistently identifies a woman's acceptance or rejection of her role in God's administrative order. At least none does in western culture. It is usually her speech and her behavior that do. The important thing is her attitude toward her womanhood and how she expresses it, not whether she wears a particular item of clothing. (264) Rather than teaching women to be submissive to men this passage glorifies womanhood.

Bibliography

244. Barrett, p. 247. Of course, there were already a few inspired New Testament documents circulating among the churches.

245. For helpful studies, see Stephen Bedale, "The Meaning of *kephale* in the Pauline Epistles," *Journal of Theological Studies* NS5 (1954):211-15; Paul S. Fiddes, "'Woman's Head Is Man:' A Doctrinal Reflection upon a Pauline Text," *Baptist Quarterly* 31:8 (October 1986):370-83; Wayne Grudem, "Does *kephale* ('Head') Mean 'Source' or 'Authority Over' in Greek Literature? A survey of 2,336 Examples," *Trinity Journal* 6NS (1985):38-59; idem. "The Meaning of *kephale*: A Response to Recent Studies," *Trinity Journal* 11NS (1990):3-72; idem, "The Meaning of *kephale* ('head'): An Evaluation of New Evidence, Real and Alleged," *Journal of the Evangelical Theological Society* 44:1 (March 2001):25-65.

246. Barrett, p. 248.

247. Harold R. Holmyard III, "Does 1 Corinthians 11:2-16 Refer to Women Praying and Prophesying in Church?" *Bibliotheca Sacra* 154:616 (October-December 1997):461-72, argued that 11:2-16 does not address congregational settings. Other commentators who held this view include J. N. Darby, *Notes of Readings on the Epistles to the Corinthians*, pp. 85-87; Olshausen, p. 174; C. T. Ellicott, *St. Paul's First Epistle to the Corinthians*, p. 202; W. E. Vine, *1 Corinthians*, p. 147; J. A. Beet, *A Commentary on St. Paul's Epistles to the Corinthians*, p. 181; Lenski, p. 437; Grosheide, pp. 341-42; and J. MacArthur Jr., *1 Corinthians*, p. 256.

248. *A Greek-English Lexicon of the New Testament*, s.v. "*propheteuo*," p. 553. See also Wayne A. Grudem, "Prophecy—Yes, But Teaching—No: Paul's Consistent Advocacy of Women's Participation Without Governing Authority," *Journal of the Evangelical Theological Society* 30:1 (March 1987):11-23; and idem, "Why Christians Can Still Prophesy," *Christianity Today*, September 16, 1988, pp. 29-31, 34-35. Grudem sought a middle position between the charismatic and non-charismatic interpretations of the gift of prophecy. See his *The Gift of Prophecy in 1 Corinthians* and *The Gift of Prophecy in the New Testament and Today*. Robert L. Thomas, "Prophecy Rediscovered? A Review of *The Gift of Prophecy in the New Testament and Today*," *Bibliotheca Sacra* 149:593 (January-March 1992):83-96, gave a helpful critique of Grudem's views.

249. See Fee, *The First . . .*, pp. 495-97, 509-10.

250. Bruce, *1 and 2 Corinthians*, p. 104.

251. Joachim Jeremias, *Jerusalem in the Time of Jesus*, p. 359.

252. Wiersbe, 1:604.

253. For a defense of the view that women should wear head coverings today in church meetings, see Bruce K. Waltke, "1 Corinthians 11:2-16: An Interpretation," *Bibliotheca Sacra* 135:537 (January-March 1978):46-57.

254. Fee, *The First . . .*, p. 512.

255. Barrett, p. 249.

256. The Living Bible gives this interpretation by paraphrasing the verse, "So a woman should wear a covering on her head as a sign that she is under man's authority." See also F. Godet, *Commentary on the First Epistle of St. Paul to the Corinthians*, 2:122; Charles Hodge, *A Commentary on 1 & 2 Corinthians*, p. 211.

257. A metonym is a figure of speech in which one word appears in place of another associated with or suggested by it (e.g., "the White House says" for "the President says"). The RSV translation gives this interpretation: "That is why a woman ought to have a veil on her head."

258. Bruce, *1 and 2 Corinthians*, p. 106. See also M. D. Hooker, "Authority on Her Head: An Examination of I Cor. XI. 10," *New Testament Studies* 10 (1963-64):410-16.

259. William M. Ramsay, *The Cities of St. Paul*, pp. 202-5; Morris, p. 154.

260. See Barrett, p. 255.

261. Robertson and Plummer, p. 233.

262. Fee, *The First . . .*, p. 522.

263. Barrett, p. 257.

264. See David K. Lowery, "The Head Covering and the Lord's Supper in 1 Corinthians 11:2-34," *Bibliotheca Sacra* 143:570 (April-June 1986):159, who concluded that head coverings are not necessary today. For another exposition of verses 2-16 by a former Dallas Seminary professor, see H. Wayne House, "Should a Woman Prophesy or Preach before Men?" *Bibliotheca Sacra* 145:578 (April-June 1988):141-61. He concluded they should not. See also Kenneth T. Wilson, "Should Women Wear Headcoverings?" *Bibliotheca Sacra* 148:592 (October-December 1991):442-62, who concluded that women need not wear a head covering today, as did Barclay, *The Letters . . .*, p. 110.

Lesson 9 Self Check

QUESTION 1

Paul teaches in 1 Corinthians 11:2-16 that women should always remain silent in the worship service. *True or False?*

QUESTION 2

Perhaps the most obscure argument Paul makes in 1 Corinthians 11:2-16 is the reference to angels. *True or False?*

QUESTION 3

Some scholars believe that Paul's argument about headship in 1 Corinthians 11:3 refers to source rather than authority. *True or False?*

QUESTION 4

A strong argument that head coverings did not mean hair is found in 1 Corinthians 11:6. *True or False?*

QUESTION 5

In 1 Corinthians 11:2-16, Paul makes theological arguments from all **except**

    A. Apostolic authority

    B. Headship

    C. Law

    D. Glory

QUESTION 6

When Paul mentions traditions in 1 Corinthians 11:2, he is referring to cultural standards that vary from place to place. *True or False?*

QUESTION 7

Paul makes cultural arguments from shame in 1 Corinthians 11:2-16. *True or False?*

QUESTION 8

Constable suggests that Paul calls woman the glory of man (1 Cor 11:7) because

    A. The woman reflects man's glory

    B. The woman is not the image of God

    C. A woman with her head covered looks like a man

    D. In creation the woman came from the man

QUESTION 9

Paul advocates church discipline for violators of his instruction about head coverings. *True or False?*

QUESTION 10

Which statement is **not** advised for making application of 1 Corinthians 11:2-16 in today's churches?

    A. Recognize that churches apply the principles of this passage in different ways

    B. Recognize that there are many difficult interpretive issues

    C. Distinguish between unchanging principles and cultural applications of those principles

    D. Avoid the headship issue because it is so sensitive

Lesson 9 Answers to Questions

QUESTION 1: *Your answer*
QUESTION 2: *Your answer*
QUESTION 3: False
QUESTION 4: True
QUESTION 5
    A. Prominent
    B. Source
    C. Authority
QUESTION 6
    B. There is an order of headship in the Trinity.
    C. A husband is the head of his wife.
    D. Some actions can bring dishonor to one's head.
QUESTION 7: Wife
QUESTION 8: Veil
QUESTION 9: True
QUESTION 10: Traditions
QUESTION 11: *Your answer should be similar to the following:*
During corporate worship, when praying or prophesying, a woman's head should be covered so that only God will be glorified. If she does not cover her head, then the glory of man is displayed.
QUESTION 12
    A. Man was created prior to woman
    C. Woman was formed from the man
    D. Woman was created for the man
QUESTION 13
    A. A head covering is a sign of her submission to male authority.
    B. A head covering is a sign of her freedom in Christ to pray and prophesy in the worship service.
    C. A head covering is a sign both of her freedom to pray and prophesy and of her submission to male authority.
    D. A head covering is authority to control how people perceive her head so as to avoid shame.
QUESTION 14
    C. Angels observe Christian worship and would be offended by women without head coverings.
    D. Evil angels might lust after women without head coverings.
    E. "Angels" mean church messengers who report back to other churches on the worship service.
QUESTION 15
    A. Middle Eastern conceptions of shame at the time
    B. Greek/Roman conceptions of shame at the time
QUESTION 16
    D. A woman's acceptance or rejection of her role in God's administrative order
QUESTION 17: *Your answer should be similar to the following:*
The principle of headship in the church remains valid today, even if the cultural expression of that principle changes. Homosexual practice is the violation of God's moral command, and there is no question in Scripture of different cultural practices.
QUESTION 18: *Your answer*
QUESTION 19: False
QUESTION 20: Shaved
QUESTION 21: *Your answer*
QUESTION 22: *Your answer*

Lesson 9 Self Check Answers

QUESTION 1: False
QUESTION 2: True
QUESTION 3: True
QUESTION 4: True
QUESTION 5
    C. Law
QUESTION 6: False
QUESTION 7: True
QUESTION 8
    D. In creation the woman came from the man
QUESTION 9: False
QUESTION 10
    D. Avoid the headship issue because it is so sensitive

Lesson 10: Freedom in Worship: The Lord's Supper (1 Cor 11:17-34)

Depending on the local church, celebration of the Lord's Supper may occur weekly, monthly, or perhaps as seldom as once a quarter. Churches view communion as an important ritual, but the atmosphere for observing this ceremony may range from joyful celebration to sorrowful confession. Almost always are the words of the institution read, many times directly from 1 Corinthians 11.

Few people today would say that their church fails to recognize the importance of communion or fails to conduct it in a holy manner. Unfortunately, that was not the case in ancient Corinth. Paul rebuked a congregation where many viewed themselves as "spiritual" for abusing the Lord's Supper—to the extent that he could not even call it the Lord's Supper! The reason for the abuse was not some theological heresy, or neglect, or malicious debate as to the meaning of the ceremony. Instead, they were abusing communion by drunkenness, selfishness, and unruly conduct. They failed to grasp the holiness of the meal, and as a result the Lord was disciplining them.

In Topic 1, we discuss the problem with communion at Corinth and consider the purposes of the Lord's Supper.

In Topic 2, we consider what preparation is needed to participate in communion so as to avoid the Lord's discipline.

In Topic 3, you are invited to consider any issues and remedies to problems related to communion in your local congregation.

Lesson Outline

Topic 1: False and True Communion (1 Cor 11:17-26)

    Abuse of Communion (11:17-22)

    Institution of the Lord's Supper (11:23-26)

Topic 2: Examining Ourselves (1 Cor 11:27-34)

    Consequences of Eating Unworthily (11:27)

    Avoiding God's Discipline (11:28-34)

Topic 3: Communion in Your Church

Lesson Objectives

Lotus always used to look forward to Communion Sunday, but not now. It used to be the big church celebration of the month. Everybody would bring special dishes of food they had made. After the worship service, tables would be set up for a big meal, which Brother Thomas called a "love feast." There was always plenty to go around with lots left over. As word got around, attendance for Communion Sunday became the largest of any Sunday in the month. Usually there was some type of program after the love feast, with brothers and sisters sharing their testimonies, or special singing, or one of the leaders giving a short evangelistic message. It used to be a time of great fellowship, and wonderful eating.

Now the potluck has changed and everyone brings and eats their own bag lunches. No one is encouraged to share their food any more. Some church members say that the potlucks are attracting a lot of strangers, people who come only once a month, and even homeless or less-desirable people. None of these people contribute food to the potluck, and it has become quite a drain on the church. As a result of this change, attendance on Communion Sunday has dropped, the poor people no longer stay for the meal, if they come at all, and even some of the more wealthy church members no longer stay. They say that they would rather go eat at home.

Lotus is sad because much of the fellowship she used to look forward to has diminished. She feels that the church is missing out on the blessings of sharing together and is also missing an outreach opportunity. She prays to the Lord for help, and turns to 1 Corinthians 11:17-34 for insight.

By the end of this lesson, you will be able to:

- Explain the issues the church at Corinth were having regarding the Lord's Supper
- Recognize the seriousness of the Lord's Supper and the consequences if it is abused
- Understand the importance of preparation for the Lord's Supper
- Delve into issues regarding the observance of communion in your church

Topic 1: False and True Communion (1 Cor 11:17-26)

Every church is a gathering of believers who can be divided according to age, sex, race, educational level, economic standing, citizenship, and other similar issues. The communion service should draw everyone together in unity, focusing on the sacrifice of Jesus on the cross. If the ceremony does not achieve its basic purposes, then something is wrong.

Abuse of Communion (1 Cor 11:17-22)
Assignment

- Read 1 Corinthians 11:17-22.
- Read Constable, "The Abuses" (refer to the Articles section at the end of this lesson), through the note on 11:22.
- Read "Abuse of Communion."

Abuse of Communion

It seems strange that Paul would find a good purpose in the divisions among believers at Corinth. The divisions he refers to in 1 Corinthians 11:18 are socioeconomic and reflect a failure of unity in the church. The thrust of this passage is to get rid of those divisions. Paul's comment that divisions show those who are approved probably warns the believers about the coming judgment.

Was communion linked to a community meal in the early church? It appears that that was the case in Corinth, for some people were able to eat plenty while others went hungry. Why? Perhaps they brought food to a group meal, but some ate as much as they wanted, not waiting for everyone to assemble first. Another possibility is that people brought food but did not share it with others. Believers who were poor, slaves, or arrived later would then go hungry. Instead of promoting peace and unity, the meal promoted disorder and ill feelings. Paul could not properly call it the Lord's Supper, for it did not achieve the purposes of that ceremony.

Although they were going through the motions of celebrating the Lord's Supper, the church at Corinth was making a mockery of the institution. Love and unity were not the result, but instead divisions resulted.

QUESTION 1

The Lord's Supper was associated with a congregational meal in first-century Corinth. *True or False?*

QUESTION 2

What was the problem with the Lord's Supper in Corinth?

    A. Confusion about the theology of the Lord's Supper

    B. Socioeconomic divisions when celebrating the Lord's Supper

    C. Neglect of the ceremony

    D. Women not wearing head coverings when partaking of the elements

QUESTION 3

Taking the Lord's Supper without the right attitude invalidates its meaning. *True or False?*

Institution of the Lord's Supper (11:23-26)

Assignment

- Read 1 Corinthians 11:23-26.
- Read Constable, "Abuse of the Lord—11:23-26" (refer to the Articles section at the end of this lesson).
- Read "Institution of the Lord's Supper."

Institution of the Lord's Supper

This is one of the few places in the writings of Paul where he quotes something Jesus taught. Paul saw communion as an important ritual for believers to participate in, and as something instituted and commanded by Jesus. It is of similar importance to the gospel message itself, as shown by the close association of the wording in 1 Corinthians 15:3 and 1 Corinthians 11:23. In both cases he passed on what he received.

Paul's communion wording is more similar to Luke 22:19, 20 than to the wording in Matthew or Mark. Perhaps this similarity indicates Paul's close association with Luke.

The stated purpose of communion is to remember Jesus—specifically His sacrificial death. Communion is a memorial tradition. Additional purposes are to proclaim the Lord's death and to express the unity of the body of Christ. The unity is seen as believers observe this together with other believers, and in the one bread and one cup from which all partake. Taking communion does not guarantee that one's sins are forgiven any more than being baptized guarantees eternal life. The Lord's Supper is a ceremony for the edification of believers who are saved and forgiven by faith in Christ.

Clearly, when Jesus said, "This is my body," He was using a figure of speech, because during the Last Supper, His physical body was present with the disciples. Only later, on the cross, was it broken and His blood spilled. Paul was continuing this symbolic, memorial tradition.

Jesus instituted the new covenant with His blood on the cross. The new covenant is a reference to Jeremiah 31:31-34. The critical features of this new covenant are:

1. God's law written on hearts and minds

2. Everyone will know the Lord

3. Forgiveness of sins

The actualization of the new covenant can only come by the ministry of the Holy Spirit in human hearts.

Partaking of the Lord's Supper leads believers to focus on the meaning of the cross. Just as every believer shares in the forgiveness of sins, so every believer should share in the Lord's Supper.

QUESTION 4

Please match the theological position with its explanation

Theological Position	*Explanation*
Catholic	Christ is really present, although not physically present, with the elements.
Lutheran	Christ is spiritually present in the elements.
Presbyterian	The elements only represent the body and blood of Christ.
Anabaptist	The elements actually become the body and blood of Christ.

QUESTION 5

Besides the Lord's Supper, communion, and the breaking of bread, another name for this ceremony is _____.

QUESTION 6

Most Christian groups observe two ordinances or sacraments: _____ and the Lord's Supper.

QUESTION 7

How do Christians proclaim the Lord's death every time they celebrate the Lord's Supper?

QUESTION 8

Why is the Lord's Supper considered an ordinance of the church?

QUESTION 9

Taking communion ensures the forgiveness of sins. *True or False?*

QUESTION 10

What are valid reasons for taking communion? *(Select all that apply.)*

    A. To gain right standing with God

    B. To obey Jesus' command

    C. To remember Jesus' sacrifice

    D. To express unity in the body of Christ

QUESTION 11

What are the main aspects of the new covenant from Jeremiah 31:31-34? *(Select all that apply.)*

    A. The law written in the heart

    B. The gifts of the Spirit

    C. The forgiveness of sins

    D. All know the Lord

    E. The resurrection of believers

QUESTION 12

What is your view of the nature of Christ's presence in communion? Why? Record your thoughts in your Life Notebook.

Topic 2: Examining Ourselves (1 Cor 11:27-34)

No one should partake of the Lord's Supper without preparing himself. Believers risk serious consequences if they fail to recognize the sanctity of the ceremony.

Consequences of Eating Unworthily (1 Cor 11:27)

Assignment

- Read 1 Corinthians 11:27.
- Read Constable, "The Correctives" (refer to the Articles section at the end of this lesson), through the note on 11:27.
- Read "Consequences of Eating Unworthily."

Consequences of Eating Unworthily

It is a sin to partake of the Lord's Supper in an unworthy manner. In the context of 1 Corinthians 11, the believers at Corinth were committing this sin by their disorderly and unloving conduct at communion.

Paul assumes that it is possible to partake of the Lord's Supper in a worthy manner. Communion was an ordinance given to the church for regular observance by ordinary believers. Communion is not just for the most spiritual or mature in the congregation.

The sin of partaking of the Lord's Supper in an unworthy manner is a sin not only against the congregation, but also a sin against the Lord. Such a violator is "guilty of the body and blood of the Lord" (1 Cor 11:27). This probably means that the violator is guilty of profaning the sanctity of the ordinance, and thus also guilty of sinning against Christ.

A believer can abuse communion by partaking of it unworthily. This abuse is a serious sin both against the church and the Lord.

QUESTION 13

Since all have sinned, it is impossible to partake of communion in a worthy manner. *True or False?*

QUESTION 14

What does being "guilty of the body and blood of the Lord" (1 Cor 11:27) mean?

    A. Guilty of putting Jesus to death

    B. Guilty of rejecting salvation through Jesus

    C. Guilty of profaning the holiness of the Lord's Supper

    D. Guilty of handling sacred things

QUESTION 15

How can you avoid taking the Lord's Supper as a meaningless ritual? Record your thoughts in your Life Notebook.

Avoiding God's Discipline (11:28-34)

Assignment

- Read 1 Corinthians 11:28-34.
- Read Constable, "Notes on 11:34" (refer to the Articles section at the end of this lesson).
- Read "Avoiding God's Discipline."

Avoiding God's Discipline

The consequences of profaning communion were serious, as 1 Corinthians 11:30 makes clear. Weaknesses, sickness, and death were all aspects of the Lord's discipline. Based purely on the mention of such severe penalties, abuse of communion seems as or more serious than the other sins of that church—divisions, pride, eating meat offered to idols, immorality, etc.

By this clear teaching on the dangers and consequences of abusing communion, Paul has warned all believers and given them the way out. The way out, or the way to avoid God's discipline in this matter, is to partake of communion in a worthy manner.

What should one do if he feels that he is not worthy to partake of communion? Is it an option to not take it? First, recognize that the issue is **not** who is worthy to take communion. Every believer is worthy to take communion based solely on the sacrifice of Christ. Rather, the question is how to partake **in a worthy manner**. No believer should partake in an unworthy manner, but the solution to his problem is not to just avoid it, but rather to recognize the spiritual significance of the observance and change his attitude and actions. Jesus and Paul expect believers to regularly observe communion.

Who should take communion and who should not? It seems clear that communion was not intended for non-believers or for people who are just inquirers about the faith. It is for believers and believers only. There is no stated requirement that a believer be baptized in order to partake of communion. Based on the requirement of self-examination, it seems implied in Paul's teaching that only those who are capable of self-examination should take communion. This would perhaps exclude very small children from participation. Participants in communion need to have a clear understanding of its meaning and how to partake in a worthy manner.

No reference is made as to who is qualified to officiate at communion. The best answer to this question is perhaps 1 Corinthians 14:40, "Do everything in a decent and orderly manner." Each local church should decide how that applies in their context.

The call to self-examination is not fundamentally a call to introspection to try to search out every sin in your own heart. It is more a call to sober recognition of the meaning of the Lord's Supper and the importance of lovingly and reverently observing this tradition in an orderly manner.

Perhaps the most dangerous thing a person can do in church is to abuse the Lord's Supper. God's judgment may be avoided by recognizing the holiness of the ceremony and behaving appropriately.

QUESTION 16

The best way to avoid God's discipline in communion is to refuse to partake. *True or False?*

QUESTION 17

Which of the following are examples of discipline from God for profaning the Lord's Supper? *(Select all that apply.)*

- A. Sickness
- B. Physical death
- C. Weakness
- D. Eternal death
- E. Demon possession

QUESTION 18

Churches should use the communion service as an evangelistic tool to attract unbelievers. *True or False?*

QUESTION 19

In a local church, who may officiate at communion?

QUESTION 20

How do you apply Paul's instruction to partake of communion in a worthy manner? Record your response in your Life Notebook.

Topic 3: Communion in Your Church

Paul placed a high value on the proper practice of communion in the local church. He was concerned that it would achieve the purposes for which it was instituted by our Lord. Paul taught that this intended expression of fellowship and unity could be ruined, ending up doing more harm than good. The consequences of such sinful behavior are extremely serious.

QUESTION 21

Consider the practice of communion in your church. Open your Life Notebook and reflect on the following dangers of misuse or abuse of the institution. Which are problems in your church? What can be done about them? Be prepared to share with others.

- Neglect of observance
- Lack of self-examination
- Has become just a routine
- Flippant attitude
- Divides believers
- Other issues

Lesson 10 Articles

Notes on 1 Corinthians

Dr. Thomas L. Constable; 2003 Edition

D. THE LORD'S SUPPER 11:17-34

Most of the Corinthians had been following Paul's instructions regarding women's headcoverings so he commended them (v. 2), but he could not approve their practice at the Lord's Supper. They needed to make some major changes there. What they were doing cut at the heart of both the gospel and the church. This is the one certain situation in the Corinthian church that Paul addressed in chapters 7-16 that the Corinthians themselves had not asked him about. He wrote that he had heard about it (v. 18).

By way of background, we need to remember that in antiquity meals typically accompanied public worship in the early church, in Judaism, and in the pagan world. The early Christians observed the Lord's Supper as part of such a meal, often called the love feast.

1. The abuses 11:17-26

The first abuse reflects a problem on the horizontal level, between believers in the church. The second more serious abuse was vertical, involving the church and its Lord.

Abuse of the poor 11:17-22

This aspect of the problem involved showing disregard for the poorer members of the church.

11:17 - The Corinthians' behavior at the Lord's Supper was so bad that Paul could say they were worse off for observing it as they did rather than better off. Their failure was not that they failed to observe the Lord's Supper. It was that when they gathered they did not behave as the church, in which there is no distinction between "Jews or Greeks," "slaves or free" (12:13).

11:18 - "In the first place" evidently refers to all that follows in verses 18-34. Paul decided to wait to deal with other similar matters until he arrived in Corinth (v. 34).

The context of the occasion in view was the assembling of the whole church family (cf. 14:23). When Paul later wrote his epistle to the Romans from Corinth, the Corinthian church was meeting in the home of Gaius (Rom. 16:23).

The divisions (Gr. *schismata*) to which Paul referred here were social groupings within the church, not differences involving loyalty to leaders (1:12).

Evidently those who had reported this abuse in the Corinthian church to Paul had given him much detail about what was happening. Paul said he believed enough of this to conclude that there was a serious problem.

11:19 - Divisions or factions (Gr. *haireseis*) of this type have a positive side. They clarify whom God approves as faithful and trustworthy and who are not (cf. Matt. 10:34-37; 18:7; 24:9-13).

11:20 - In the Christian church's early years the Lord's Supper occupied a more central position in the life of local assemblies than it does in most churches today. The early believers often celebrated it daily or weekly (cf. Acts 2:42-46; 20:7). However, it was just as impossible to observe this feast properly in an atmosphere of social discrimination as it was to do so while also attending feasts that honored idols (10:21).

11:21 - The Lord's Supper was usually part of a meal the Christians shared together, the so-called "love feast." In Corinth instead of sharing their food and drinks, each family was bringing its own and eating what it had brought. The result was that the rich had plenty but the poor had little and suffered embarrassment as well. This was hardly the picture of Christian love and unity (cf. Acts 2:44-46; 4:32, 34-35). Furthermore some with plenty of wine to drink were evidently drinking too heavily. They were eating their own private meals rather than sharing a meal consecrated to the Lord.

11:22 - This verse contains some of the apostle's most critical statements in this epistle. If his original readers chose to behave in such a selfish way, they should stay home and eat rather than humiliating their less fortunate brethren. Such conduct showed disrespect for the church as the temple of God (cf. 3:17).

> "The early Church was the one place in all the ancient world where the barriers which divided the world were down. The ancient world was very rigidly divided; there were the free men and the slaves; there were the Greeks and the barbarians—the people who did not speak Greek; there were the Jews and the Gentiles; there were the Roman citizens and the lesser breeds without the law; there were the cultured and the ignorant. The Church was the one place where all men could and did come together. . . . A Church where social and class distinctions exist is no true Church at all. A real Church is a body of men and women united to each other because all are united to Christ.

> "A Church is not true Church where the art of sharing is forgotten." (265)

Abuse of the Lord 11:23-26

There was an even more serious dimension to this problem. The Corinthians were sinning against the Lord as well as one another.

11:23 - What Paul taught here came ultimately from the Lord Jesus Himself. This reminder stresses the importance of this revelation.

> "The verbs 'received' and 'passed on,' which occur again in combination in 15:3, are technical terms from Paul's Jewish heritage for the transmission of religious instruction. His present concern is to establish that the tradition about the Supper they had received from him came from Jesus himself: 'I received [it] from the Lord.'" (266)

The terminology used here does not require us to understand that the Lord Jesus communicated this information to Paul personally. Paul's wording suggests that he may have been repeating exactly what others had taught him. This is not a verbatim quotation from one of the Gospel accounts.

Paul described the night Jesus instituted the Lord's Supper as the night in which He was betrayed. This draws attention to the Savior's great love for His own. The Lord was graciously providing for His disciples when one of them was plotting to do away with Him.

11:24 - The Greek word *eucharisteo*, "to give thanks," accounts for the fact that another name for the Lord's Supper is the Eucharist. Likewise some Christians call it "the breaking of bread" because Jesus broke the bread as Paul stated here.

There have been various interpretations of what Jesus meant when He said, "This is my body." There are four main views. Roman Catholics take it as a literal statement meaning the bread really becomes the body of Christ and the contents of the cup become the blood of Christ. They believe this is true when duly authorized representatives of the church conduct the service properly. This is the transubstantiation view. Adherents believe God transfers the body and blood of Christ into the substance of the elements. The bread and wine really become the physical body and blood of Christ.

A second view is not quite so literal. It is the consubstantiation view and, as the word implies, its advocates see the body and blood of Christ as present "in, with, and under" the elements. Christ is "really" present, though not physically present, in this Lutheran view.

The third major view is the spiritual presence view that Presbyterians and some other followers of Calvin hold. For them the spiritual presence of Christ is in the elements and, as in the former views, God ministers grace to the communicant in a concrete way through participation.

The fourth view is the memorial view. Advocates believe that when Jesus said, "This is my body," he meant, "This represents my body." In other words, they understand His statement as completely metaphorical. They view the elements as pictures or emblems of the body and blood of Christ. In contrast to the preceding views this one does not see Christ present in any special sense in the elements. Ulrich Zwingli, the Swiss reformer, promoted this view. Today most of the churches from the Anabaptist branch of Protestantism (i.e., Baptists, Methodists, independent Bible churches, et al.) follow this interpretation. (267)

> "The identification of the bread with the body is semitic imagery in its heightened form. As in all such identifications, he means 'this signifies/represents my body.' It lies quite beyond both Jesus' intent and the framework within which he and the disciples lived to imagine that some actual change took place, or was intended to take place, in the bread itself. Such a view could only have arisen in the church at a much later stage when Greek modes of thinking had rather thoroughly replaced semitic ones." (268)

Jesus invited his disciples to take the bread that represented His body. He thus gave them a share in His body and invited them to participate in the meaning and benefits of His death. His body was "for" them in a double sense. It was what secured atonement *on their behalf* (cf. 15:3; Rom. 5:6, 8), and it was a body offered *in their place* (e.g., Gal. 3:13; 2 Cor. 5:21).

The Lord's request that His disciples remember Him by partaking of bread and the fruit of the vine is rich with significance. Many followers remember their leaders by erecting stone monuments to their memories and making pilgrimages to these sites. In contrast the Lord Jesus made remembering Him easy yet profound. Eating the elements helps us appreciate the fact that Christ is really within us. Eating together reminds us of our unity with other believers in Christ's body.

Remembering in biblical terminology does not mean just calling to memory. It includes realizing what the event remembered involved (cf. Ex 13:3; 20:8; Deut. 5:15; 7:18; et al.). The Lord's Supper is not just something Christians do to bring the memory of Jesus back into fresh view. It is a memorial of the salvation that He accomplished by His death and resurrection. 1 Corinthians 11:24 contains the Lord's command to observe the Eucharist as do the Gospel accounts of the institution of this ordinance. (269) It is impossible to be an obedient Christian without observing the Lord's Supper.

Some Christian groups refer to the Lord's Supper as one of the "sacraments." They mean the elements minister grace to the participant in a more direct and physical way than those who speak of it as an "ordinance," assuming they are using these terms properly. An ordinance or sacrament is a rite the Lord commanded His followers to observe.

Most Protestants believe there are two ordinances, baptism and the Lord's Supper. A few Protestant groups include foot washing as an ordinance on the basis of John 13:12-17 (e.g., the Grace Brethren, some Mennonites, et al.).

11:25 - As Jesus had taken the bread and given thanks for it, so He also took the cup and gave thanks for it (Matt. 26:28; Mk 14:24; Lk 20:25).

When Jesus shed His blood on Calvary, that blood ratified (gave formal sanction to) the New Covenant that Jeremiah had predicted (Jer. 31:31-34, cf. Ex 24:8). The New Covenant replaced the old Mosaic Covenant (Heb. 8:8-13; 9:18-28). Even though the Jews will be the major beneficiaries of the benefits of this covenant in the Millennium, all believers began to benefit from the death of Christ when He died. (270)

This arrangement resembles one that is possible to set up in a Charitable Lead Unit Trust under the Internal Revenue Code of the United States. Suppose there was a vastly wealthy and generous philanthropist of the magnitude of a Rockefeller or Vanderbilt. As he prepared his will he bequeathed millions of dollars to various charitable causes that would benefit millions of people all over the world when he died. He also wrote into his will that when his only son reached the age of 21 he would inherit billions of dollars. When this man died, his son was only five years old, so for 16 years he did not enter into his father's inheritance. However as soon as the philanthropist died the millions of dollars he had bequeathed to charity went to work immediately to help many people.

This illustration shows how the church enters into the blessings of the New Covenant. When Christ established the Lord's Supper it was as though He notarized His will; it became official then. The will is the New Covenant. When He died His "estate" became available to those He chose to profit from it. Soon many people around the world, Jews and Gentiles in the church, began to benefit from the blessings of His death. However His chosen people, His son Israel, will not enter into their inheritance until the appointed time, namely, the Millennium. Blessings for the church began almost immediately after Christ's death. Blessings for Israel will not begin until Christ's appointed time arrives.

Whenever the Jews celebrated the Passover the father who was conducting the service would explain the significance of each part to the rest of the family (cf. Deut. 16:3). Jesus did the same for His disciples when He instituted the Lord's Supper.

11:26 - Paul continued Jesus' explanation. Participation in the Lord's Supper dramatizes the gospel. The service becomes a visual as well as an audible setting forth of the death of Christ and its significance.

> "The Eucharist is an *acted* sermon, an *acted* proclamation of the death which it commemorates; but it is possible that there is reference to some *expression of belief* in the atoning death of Christ as being a usual element in the service." (271)

Paul may have referred to "the cup" rather than "the wine," which would have been parallel to "the bread," to avoid the direct identification of the wine in the cup with blood. The idea of drinking blood was revolting to most people in the ancient world, particularly the Jews. (272) On the other hand, he may have viewed both elements symbolically, the cup being a symbol of one's lot in life and the bread a symbol of what sustains life.

The Lord's Supper is not only a memorial celebration looking back to Jesus Christ's first advent. It is also an anticipatory celebration looking forward to His second advent. Evidently when the Lord returns to set up His earthly kingdom He will establish a new form of worship that will include the offering of certain animal sacrifices (Ezek. 40; 41; 42; 43; 44; 45; 46; 47; 48). These will be similar to the animal sacrifices the Jews offered under the Old Covenant. However since Jesus Christ has made a final sacrifice these animal offerings will evidently be memorial and entirely for worship, not for the expiation of sin. Another possibility is that they will be for the purpose of restoring fellowship with God then. (273)

> "The Communion is not supposed to be a time of 'spiritual autopsy' and grief, even though confession of sin is important. It should be a time of thanksgiving and joyful anticipation of seeing the Lord!" (274)

In this section Paul reviewed and expounded the significance of the Lord's Supper so his readers would value and celebrate it appropriately.

> "In short, Paul is doing one thing and one thing alone. He is impressing on the Corinthians the tremendous importance of doing just this: eating *this* bread and drinking *this* cup. It is, after all, a matter of celebrating the Lord's *death*." (275)

2. The correctives 11:27-34

Paul proceeded to urge the Corinthians to change their observance of the Lord's Supper and explained what they should do to correct their conduct.

Discerning the body 11:27-32

The Lord's Supper is more than a personal, introspective remembering, Paul went on to explain. It has implications for the church because in His death Jesus Christ laid the foundation for a new community of believers who bear His name. Thus the Lord's Supper should lead us to reflect on our relationship to one another as Christians as well as to recall Calvary.

11:27 - An unworthy manner is any manner that does not reflect proper appreciation for the significance of the body and blood of Christ (e.g., v. 21). This does not mean that every participant must grasp the fullness of this significance. Nevertheless everyone should conduct himself or herself appropriately in view of his or her individual depth of understanding. Even a child is capable of doing this. The Corinthians had lost the point of the memorial, which involves proclaiming salvation through Christ's death portrayed in ritual. The gospel goes out when we observe the Lord's Supper in a worthy manner.

Being guilty of Christ's body and blood means being guilty of treating them in an unworthy manner, of profaning them. It does not mean that such a person is in some special sense responsible for the death of Christ.

11:28 -"The Corinthians neglected to examine themselves, but they were experts at examining everybody else." (276)

The reason for examining oneself is to determine that we are partaking in a worthy manner rather than in an unworthy manner. In the context this would involve behaving in a loving and unselfish way toward our fellow Christians as well as being appreciative of the significance of the Lord's body and blood. We need to examine ourselves so the Lord will not have to examine and judge us for failing to participate worthily (v. 31).

Having conducted this brief self-examination the believer should then proceed to participate. An unusually sensitive Christian might hesitate to participate after thoughtful reflection feeling overwhelmed by his or her personal unworthiness. However no one is ever worthy to partake. If someone thinks he is, he is not. We are only worthy because Christ has made us worthy. We need to partake feeling unworthy to do so. This attitude is part of what it means to partake in a worthy manner.

This simple reflection and participation lie at the very root of motivation for living a life that glorifies God. The church has invented many ways to motivate Christians to put Jesus Christ first in their lives. These include altar calls, "revival" services, campfire dedication services, and many others all of which have values. Unfortunately we have also neglected what the Lord Jesus instructed us to do that will motivate His people to live for Him better than anything else. If this observance has lost its punch, it is because those who lead it have failed to give it the preparation, attention, and priority it deserves in church life. The frequent observance of the Lord's Supper in a way that takes us back to the Cross is one of the most powerful and effective motivators for living the Christian life. If you think a frequent observance of the Lord's Supper tends to become tiresome, remember that your spouse never tires of your frequent expressions of love for him or her.

11:29 - Eating and drinking in an unworthy manner results in divine judgment. Judgment is inevitable at the Lord's Table. We judge ourselves (Gr. *diakrino*) before we partake and then participate in a worthy manner, or God will judge (*krino*) us. The "body" has a double sense: the body of Christ given on the cross, and the mystical body of Christ, the church.

> "The 'unworthy' or 'inappropriate' participation in the Lord's Supper that entails eating and drinking judgment against the participants comes in not 'discerning (*diakrinon*) the body' (11:29). How members of the community view one another, whether they are sensitive to the poor and latecomers or whether the prevailing social customs dictate their behavior, becomes the decisive issue. Does the congregation recognize itself as the distinctive body of Christ?" (277)

11:30 - In Corinth, God was judging with sickness and death. The reasons were the unjudged sin of selfish living (v. 21) and thoughtless participation in the communion service.

11:31 - If God's people do not judge their own sins themselves, God will judge them. This judgment may involve physical illness or even, in extreme cases, premature physical death (cf. Acts 5; 1 Jn 5:16).

11:32 - We should regard God's punishment of Christians as discipline (Gr. *paideia*, lit. child training; cf. Heb. 12:5-11). The condemnation God intends this discipline to spare us from experiencing is not eternal destruction from the presence of the Lord that the unsaved world will suffer (Rom. 8:1). It is premature death and the Lord's disapproval at the judgment seat of Christ (cf. 3:15; 5:5). (278)

Waiting for one another 11:33-34

Practical application now follows theological explanation.

11:33 - Rather than disregarding the members of the congregation who had little or no food to bring to the love feasts, those who had plenty should share what they had. They should also wait to eat until all had been served.

Many churches these days have pot luck suppers periodically that provide a modern counterpart to the first century love feast. A few Christians have felt that we should practice the love feast whenever we observe the Lord's Supper today. Most have concluded that the love feast was just the setting in which the Lord's Supper took place in the early church. Jesus did not specifically command His disciples to observe the love feast as He urged them to eat the Lord's Supper. Therefore most Christians believe the love feast is not an ordinance of the church and we do not need to perpetuate it as the early church practiced it.

11:34 - If some of the Corinthian Christians were too hungry to wait to eat, they should eat something before they came to the service. Otherwise their unloving selfishness might result in the Lord's judgment. It is very important to the Lord that we put the needs of others before our own needs (cf. Mk 10:45; Phil. 2:3; et al.).

Evidently there were other details of how the Corinthians were behaving when they congregated that Paul did not want to comment on in this letter. Perhaps they were of local importance only. He planned to address these issues when he visited Corinth again (cf. 4:18-21; 16:2-3, 5-7).

The selfish attitude that marked the Corinthian church comes through strongly in this section of the epistle. It manifested itself in a particularly ugly display at the Lord's Table. Paul dealt with it severely for the sake of the reputation of the Savior and for the welfare of the saints.

Bibliography

265. Ibid., pp. 112-13.

266. Fee, *The First . . .,* p. 548.

267. For more information on these views, see articles on the Lord's Supper and synonymous terms in Bible encyclopedias.

268. Fee, *The First . . .,* p. 550.

269. For further study of the ordinances, see Charles C. Ryrie, *Basic Theology*, pp. 421-27, or any of the standard theologies.

270. See Rodney J. Decker, "The Church's Relationship to the New Covenant," *Bibliotheca Sacra* 152:607 (July-September 1995):290-305.

271. Robertson and Plummer, p. 249.

272. Barrett, p. 268.

273. See Jerry M. Hullinger, "The Problem of Animal Sacrifices in Ezekiel 40-8," *Bibliotheca Sacra* 152:607 (July-September 1995):279-89.

274. Wiersbe, 1:607.

275. Troels Engberg-Pedersen, "Proclaiming the Lord's Death," in *Pauline Theology. Vol. II: 1 & 2 Corinthians*, p. 116.

276. Wiersbe, 1:606.

277. Cousar, "The Theological . . .," p. 100.

278. This is another instance of wordplay in the Greek text. If we discerned (*diakrino*) ourselves, we would not come under divine judgment (*krino*). When God judges us (krino), it is to correct us so we will not be condemned (*katakrino*) with the world.

Lesson 10 Self Check

QUESTION 1

Paul criticized the church at Corinth for shaming which group of people at communion?

    A. Women

    B. First-time visitors

    C. The poor

    D. The not-yet baptized

QUESTION 2

Communion is an important ritual of the church because the ceremony was instituted and commanded by Jesus. *True or False?*

QUESTION 3

Which one of the following is not a purpose of communion?

    A. Guaranteeing salvation to all who partake

    B. Expressing the unity of the church

    C. Remembering Jesus' sacrifice on the cross

    D. Obeying Jesus' command

QUESTION 4

The transubstantiation view of the nature of Christ's presence in communion is held by Catholics. *True or False?*

QUESTION 5

Taking communion in an unworthy manner is any manner that does not reflect proper appreciation for the significance of the body and blood of Christ. *True or False?*

QUESTION 6

Paul's call to self-examination before communion is mainly a call to search out every sin in your own heart. *True or False?*

QUESTION 7

According to Paul's teaching in 1 Corinthians 11:17-34, which item below is **not** a qualification for partaking of communion?

    A. Already baptized

    B. Has examined himself

    C. Understands the sanctity of communion

    D. Has trusted Christ

QUESTION 8

By partaking of communion in an unworthy manner, believers may incur the Lord's discipline. *True or False?*

QUESTION 9

The new covenant will be ratified when Jesus comes again. *True or False?*

QUESTION 10

What is the best answer to the issue of who is qualified to officiate at communion?

    A. Ordained pastors

    B. Church elders or deacons

    C. Each church decides according to the principle of doing all things decently and in order

    D. Any believer

Lesson 10 Answers to Questions

QUESTION 1: True

QUESTION 2

    B. Socioeconomic divisions when celebrating the Lord's Supper

QUESTION 3: True

QUESTION 4

Theological Position	Explanation
Catholic	The elements actually become the body and blood of Christ.
Lutheran	Christ is really present, although not physically present, with the elements.
Presbyterian	Christ is spiritually present in the elements.
Anabaptist	The elements only represent the body and blood of Christ.

QUESTION 5: Eucharist

QUESTION 6: Baptism

QUESTION 7: *Your answer should be similar to the following:*

Believers proclaim the Lord's death both visually, in partaking of the elements, and audibly, in the words of the ceremony

QUESTION 8: *Your answer should be similar to the following:*

Jesus instituted it and commanded that it be observed.

QUESTION 9: False

QUESTION 10

    B. To obey Jesus' command

    C. To remember Jesus' sacrifice

    D. To express unity in the body of Christ

QUESTION 11

    A. The law written in the heart

    C. The forgiveness of sins

    D. All know the Lord

QUESTION 12: *Your answer*

QUESTION 13: False

QUESTION 14

    C. Guilty of profaning the holiness of the Lord's Supper

QUESTION 15: *Your answer*

QUESTION 16: False

QUESTION 17

    A. Sickness

    B. Physical death

    C. Weakness

QUESTION 18: False

QUESTION 19: *Your answer should be similar to the following:*

The local church may decide under the principle of doing all things in a decent and orderly manner.

QUESTION 20: *Your answer*

Lesson 10 Self Check Answers

QUESTION 1

   C. The poor

QUESTION 2: True

QUESTION 3

   A. Guaranteeing salvation to all who partake

QUESTION 4: True

QUESTION 5: True

QUESTION 6: False

QUESTION 7

   A. Already baptized

QUESTION 8: True

QUESTION 9: False

QUESTION 10

   C. Each church decides according to the principle of doing all things decently and in order

Lesson 11: Freedom in Worship: Spiritual Gifts (1 Cor 12:1–14:40)

Spiritual gifts are one of the most wonderful and controversial aspects of the church. It is typical to distinguish between charismatic and non-charismatic churches and fellowships. Charismatic churches may manifest speaking in tongues, prophetic utterances, and healings. Non-charismatic churches choose to worship exclusively with Scripture, prayer, and music. Significant problems can occur when charismatic worship styles are introduced into non-charismatic churches, sometimes resulting in church splits. Non-charismatic worshippers may believe that the gifts of tongues and prophecy passed away with the end of the apostolic age, and that the modern displays are divisive, fake, or of the devil.

Paul addressed the misuse of spiritual gifts in 1 Corinthians 12–14. Although he highly valued spiritual gifts and urged their expression, there was something that he valued even more highly—love. Spiritual gifts must be used in love, recognizing the needs of the congregation, and are not to be exercised publicly without thought for others.

This lesson will examine Paul's instruction regarding the proper exercise of spiritual gifts in church worship. Although there are different views today, nobody holds that any spiritual gifts had passed away at the time Paul wrote this letter. All of the gifts were in common use at that time. The early church had to face how to handle speakers of tongues, prophets, and women who were speaking during the meetings. He counsels doing all things decently and in order in the context of love.

Topic 1 introduces the variety of spiritual gifts given to Christians.

Concentrating on the need for unity, in Topic 2 we see how Paul uses the metaphor of a body to emphasize that the church needs all of the spiritual gifts.

The famous "love chapter" is sandwiched between Paul's discussions of spiritual gifts. Topic 3 examines the characteristics of love and why Paul talks about this subject here.

Topic 4 hammers home the importance of intelligibility in the worship service, so that all are benefitted. This is an aspect of love.

In addition to intelligibility, Paul wants everything in the worship service done in an orderly manner. Topic 5 outlines his instructions for order with respect to the expression of spiritual gifts and the role of women.

Lesson Outline

Topic 1: Definition of Spiritual Gifts (1 Cor 12:1-11)

Basic Test (12:1-3)

Diversity of Gifts (12:4-11)

Topic 2: Unity and Diversity in One Body (1 Cor 12:12-31)

One Body With Different Parts (12:12-20)

All Are Needed (12:21-26)

Arranged by God (12:27-31)

Topic 3: Priority of Love (1 Cor 13:1-13)

Necessity of Love (13:1-3)

Description of Love (13:4-7)

Permanence of Love (13:8-13)

Meaning of "The Perfect"

Topic 4: Prophecy and Tongues (1 Cor 14:1-25)

Prophecy and the Principle of Intelligibility (14:1-5)

Principle Applied to Tongues (14:6-19)

Impact of Tongues and Prophecy on Unbelievers (14:20-25)

Topic 5: Order in Public Worship (1 Cor 14:26-40)

Order and Gifts (14:26-33)

Order and Women (14:34-35)

Warning and Conclusion (14:36-40)

Lesson Objectives

Thankfully, Lotus made some headway with Esther and Sara about women's head coverings. They were willing to discuss the issue with her, and the three of them had a really good Bible study on 1 Corinthians 11:2-16.

But now there's another reason they do not want to go to the church. Both Esther and Sara say that they have the gift of tongues, and they say there is no opportunity for them to express the gift at church. They complain that only some spiritual gifts are allowed in church, such as teaching, singing, giving, and administration. But no one is allowed to speak in tongues or prophesy. Since these are gifts of the Holy Spirit, why can't they be expressed in church?

Lotus decides that this is a good question for the church leaders. She suggests that the three of them approach the church leaders about this issue, but first they should pray and study through 1 Corinthians 12-14 together. After all, Paul's writings have brought clarity for so many issues already, so maybe the Lord will teach them about speaking in tongues in the church.

By the end of this lesson, you will be able to:

- Compose your own definition of spiritual gifts and consider what gifts you have
- Explain how all gifts are needed to make the body of Christ function well
- Recognize the importance of spiritual gifts being used in love and for the good of the body
- Explain the problem with prophecy and tongues in public worship
- Discuss the important of orderliness in public worship

Topic 1: Definition of Spiritual Gifts (1 Cor 12:1-11)

The exercise of spiritual gifts has split many churches, but that is not God's purpose. Ideally, the varieties of gifts should work together in a congregation to build up the body and to glorify Christ. All who confess Jesus as Lord should benefit from the gifts of the Spirit.

Basic Test (12:1-3)

Assignment

- Read 1 Corinthians 12:1-3.

- Read Constable, "Spiritual Gifts and Spiritual People" (refer to the Articles section at the end of this lesson), through the note on 12:3.

- Read "Basic Test."

Basic Test

As Paul already insisted in 1 Corinthians 2:12, all believers are spiritual. The indwelling of the Holy Spirit marks all Christians as fundamentally different from unbelievers. In 1 Corinthians 12 Paul explains about the many manifestations of spiritual gifts, but as spiritual people all believers confess that Jesus is Lord. This basic confession of faith is not connected to only certain spiritual gifts, but rather is common to all spiritual people.

Paul teaches that the content—rather than the activity—of tongues or prophecy determines whether it is from the Spirit or not. The ultimate purposes of the gifts of the Spirit are the glorification of Jesus and the edification of His church. Consequently, no believer acting under the influence of the Spirit would curse Jesus. In ancient Corinth, perhaps those most likely to say "Jesus is cursed" were the Jews who rejected the gospel.

In introducing spiritual gifts, Paul notes that all believers possess the Spirit and acknowledge that Jesus is Lord. Although the issue of spiritual gifts was divisive at Corinth, Paul wants them to understand that with the diversity of gifts there should be a unity among the believers, not a conflict. Each has his own significant role to play in the growth of the body of Christ. The fundamental difference between people is between believers and non-believers—not between believers with differing gifts.

QUESTION 1

Speaking in tongues proves someone is saved. *True or False?*

QUESTION 2

What does a person who confesses that Jesus is Lord indicate? *(Select all that apply.)*

- A. He is led by the Holy Spirit.
- B. He is a Christian.
- C. He is spiritual.
- D. He has the gift of tongues.

Diversity of Gifts (12:4-11)

Assignment

- Read 1 Corinthians 12:4-11.

- Read Constable, "The Need for Varieties of Spiritual Gifts" (refer to the Articles section at the end of this lesson), through the note on 12:11.

- Read "Diversity of Gifts."

Diversity of Gifts

Paul does not distinguish between classes of spiritual gifts, as is common today: like temporary vs. permanent, or miraculous vs. non-miraculous, etc.

The purpose of spiritual gifts is stated in 1 Corinthians 12:7—for the benefit of all, by which he means the body of Christ.

How do the gifts of the Spirit differ from the fruit of the Spirit? The fruit of the Spirit (Gal 5:22-23) is expressed in character qualities and attitudes, and the fruit of the Spirit is expected in all believers. On the other hand, the gifts of the Spirit differ from believer to believer. All believers should manifest the same fruit of the Spirit as they walk with Christ, but they will manifest different gifts of the Spirit.

Are there any believers without at least one spiritual gift? Are there any believers with all of the spiritual gifts? The answer to both questions is no. In a nutshell, Paul's message about spiritual gifts is this: **All are gifted, and all are needy.** We all have something to offer to the body of Christ, and we all need what other members of the body have to offer.

QUESTION 3

Record your responses to the following in your Life Notebook:

   a. Are there any believers without at least one spiritual gift?

   b. Are there any believers with all of the spiritual gifts?

We see the Spirit's work in believers' lives partly through the special abilities He gives to minister to the church. God works through His people to bless His people. Believers need to serve one another with the gifts they have and benefit from the gifts of others.

QUESTION 4

What is the main purpose of spiritual gifts?

   A. To edify the individual believer

   B. To benefit the body of Christ

   C. To manifest the power of God

   D. To confirm the truth of the gospel

Topic 2: Unity and Diversity in One Body (1 Cor 12:12-31)

To illustrate the concept of unity amongst diversity, Paul could have talked about different roles in the military, or the different parts of a ship. He chose the human body as his metaphor, a choice that every person is intimately familiar with. We value every part of our body, and we know the interconnectedness of the parts. Despite the wide diversity of body parts, together they form a unity.

One Body With Different Parts (12:12-20)

Assignment

- Read 1 Corinthians 12:12-20.
- Read Constable, from "The Body and Its Members" (refer to the Articles section at the end of this lesson), through the note on 12:20.
- Read "One Body With Different Parts."

One Body With Different Parts

The body image here is different from the one Paul used in Ephesians 1:22, 23. In Ephesians, Christ is the head and the church is the body. In 1 Corinthians 12, the church is pictured as a whole body, with one part being the eye, another being the hand, etc. All of these parts are undeniably part of the body, just as each member of the church is part of the body of Christ. Only someone who feels very inferior, unimportant, or unaccepted would ever say that they were not part of the body, but there is no reason that they should! Regardless of the visibility of a person's ministry, their role in the body of Christ is vital to the church's function. We should avoid this kind of exclusive attitude, since it is divisive, harmful, and fails to recognize the importance of the body as a whole as well as one's individual role in that body. To insult part of Christ's body is to insult Him personally.

By God's design, all believers have a role within the unity of Christ's body. Each role is important, having been determined by the Spirit.

QUESTION 5

Paul teaches in 1 Corinthians 12:13 that all believers have been _____ in one Spirit.

QUESTION 6

Which points does Paul make by using the image of the body in 1 Corinthians 12? *(Select all that apply.)*

- A. Christ is the head and believers are the members.
- B. There is diversity in the body.
- C. The different parts of the body are all important.
- D. Some members of the body may not feel important.
- E. The body forms a unity.

All Are Needed (12:21-26)

Assignment

- Read 1 Corinthians 12:21-26.
- Read Constable, "Notes on 12:26" (refer to the Articles section at the end of this lesson).
- Read "All Are Needed."

All Are Needed

If someone told you they didn't need you, how would you feel? The person making this kind of statement would probably feel secure in his role in ministry and feel important. He would fail to see the value of other members of the body of Christ. This kind of attitude is divisive, harmful, and unloving.

Paul contrasts "head" and "eye" versus "hand" and "foot." The latter two come not only physically lower on the body, but symbolize manual rather than mental labors. This may be a reference to the socioeconomic divisions in the congregation as well as to differences in spiritual gifts.

Which parts of the body seem to be "weaker, less honorable, unpresentable, or lesser"? He seems to refer to those parts that we cover up. Yet, Paul also describes these same parts as "essential, clothed with greater honor, and clothed with dignity." In the physical body, God has arranged the parts so as to give "greater honor to the lesser member." This is how it should be also in the body of Christ.

Many people have remarked that in local churches 20 percent of the people do 80 percent of the work! If this is true, then many people are left sitting in the congregation without real ministries. People without ministries may feel unimportant to the local body, wonder what gifts they have, and consider that they have little to offer. On the other hand, people with high visibility ministries may feel that everything depends on them. Paul calls for a proper understanding of the whole body of Christ and each individual's role in it.

QUESTION 7

List three ideas of how you can do to promote "mutual concern for one another" in your local church.

Arranged by God (12:27-31)

Assignment

- Read 1 Corinthians 12:27-31.
- Read Constable, "The Fact of Diversity Restated—12:27-31" (refer to the Articles section at the end of this lesson).
- Read "Arranged by God."

Arranged by God

The ranking of gifts by Paul has provoked much debate. The major interpretive positions are:

A. The ranking reflects importance in the church (See Eph 2:20).

B. The ranking has no special meaning. Paul is just making a list. Supporters of this position say that the overall context argues strongly for equality rather than hierarchy of gifts. Paul is working for unity.

C. The ranking shows chronological priority.

Since Paul goes on to talk about the "greater gifts," position A seems best. Among the greater gifts is prophecy, which is superior to tongues for public use in the church. Prophecy is useful for edifying the church, but tongues are not, unless they are interpreted.

Paul teaches that "you should be eager for the greater gifts." (1 Cor 12:31) The NIV translates, "eagerly desire the greater gifts." Does Paul mean that individuals should seek the greater spiritual gifts for themselves? If so, how does someone seek a spiritual gift? Perhaps a better suggestion for Paul's meaning is this: The Corinthians had been eagerly desiring the lesser gifts, such as tongues, and elevating their importance. Instead, Paul urges them to eagerly desire the exercise of the greater gifts in their assemblies, such as prophecy and teaching. Paul is not encouraging individuals to seek any particular gifts as much as he is urging them to properly value the greater gifts that already exist among them. After all, they "do not lack any spiritual gift." (1 Cor 1:7)

QUESTION 8

Why did Paul order the gifts mentioned? Record your answer in your Life Notebook.

Even though we are all one body in Christ with gifts that the body needs, there are some gifts that are more critical to the building up of the body than others. Since all of the gifts come from God's grace, there is no place for pride. Instead, all gifts should be exercised in love for the benefit of all.

QUESTION 9

Order the following gifts the way Paul ordered them.

Order	Gift
First	Teachers
Second	All other gifts
Third	Prophets
Then	Apostles

QUESTION 10

Love is one of the spiritual gifts. *True or False?*

QUESTION 11

What does Paul mean by the "way that is beyond comparison" (1 Cor 12:31)?

Topic 3: Priority of Love (1 Cor 13:1-13)

Perhaps one of the most familiar and quoted section of the Bible is 1 Corinthians 13. Removed from its context, it stands as a beautiful anthem to love. Within its context, it is a call to temper the abuse of spiritual gifts at Corinth.

Necessity of Love (13:1-3)

Assignment

- Read 1 Corinthians 13:1-3.
- Read Constable "The Supremacy of Love" (refer to the Articles section at the end of this lesson) through the note on 13:3.
- Read "Necessity of Love.

Necessity of Love

Although 1 Corinthians 13 is often read out of its context, Paul intended this discussion of love to strengthen his arguments about the proper use of spiritual gifts. Love was what the Corinthian congregation was lacking in their use of spiritual gifts.

Paul refers in 1 Corinthians 13:1-3 to speaking abilities, spiritual gifts, and self-sacrifice. All these things are easily observable and are often praised by men. If these activities are done without love, then they are of no value in God's eyes, and of no lasting value to the person who does them.

How is it possible to prophesy, speak in tongues, or to give everything away without love? If someone does even such good acts without love and from motives of selfish ambition or competition, then they acts are not praiseworthy. Only the presence of love determines whether a particular action is spiritual and pleasing to God. Thus, love must be defined by proper motive and not just by action alone.

Is love a spiritual gift? Since love is from God, in some sense it is proper to think of it as a gift of God's grace. However, in this context, Paul does not identify it as a spiritual gift, because spiritual gifts are possessed by some but not all. Love is expected of all believers.

Spiritual gifts can be spectacular and greatly admired, but they are not the measuring stick of spirituality. One great misuse of spiritual gifts is to focus attention on the person with the gift. The result is counterfeit spirituality that is divisive.

QUESTION 12

What does Paul teach about the relationship of love to spiritual gifts?

A. Love is a spiritual gift.

B. Love substitutes for spiritual gifts.

C. Without love, the exercise of spiritual gifts is valueless.

D. Love is important but spiritual gifts are unimportant.

Description of Love (13:4-7)

Assignment

- Read 1 Corinthians 13:4-7.
- Read Constable, "The Character of Love" (refer to the Articles section at the end of this lesson).
- Read "Description of Love."

Description of Love

It is better to view 1 Corinthians 13:4-7 as a description of the qualities of love rather than a definition of love. Of course, all these characteristics of love are also qualities of God and of the Spirit-filled life.

The *International Standard Bible Encyclopedia* gives this definition of love: "Love, whether used of God or man, is an earnest and anxious desire for and an active and beneficent interest in the well-being of the one loved." This definition implies that love is exhibited within the context of relationship. Paul is not talking about an abstract quality, but about relationship dynamics.

The negative characteristics that Paul identifies as not love—impatience, unkindness, envy, pride, rudeness, anger, etc.—are characteristics of self-centeredness. Christian love is directed toward others, not the self.

Finally, love endures. It does not evaporate in the face of evils done against it. Christ is the perfect example. He died for those who put Him to death.

QUESTION 13

Reflect on the following questions and record your response in your Life Notebook. How have I not demonstrated love in my ministry and relationships? What changes need to be made in my ministry and in my church in order to better reflect God's value of love?

Paul's description of love is crafted for the situation at Corinth. He wants to show that the church has missed the mark of love in many specific ways.

QUESTION 14

Match the Corinthians' contrasting behavior with the characteristic of love Paul described.

Corinthian church's contrasting behavior	Characteristic of love
"There is still jealousy and dissension among you" (1 Cor 3:3).	Not envious
"Puffed up in favor of the one against the other" (1 Cor 4:6).	Not easily angered or resentful, not glad about injustice.
"For when it is time to eat, everyone proceeds with his own supper. One is hungry and another becomes drunk" (1 Cor 11:21).	Not bragging, not puffed up
"Do not seek your own good, but the good of the other person" (1 Cor 10:24).	Not self-serving.
"The fact that you have lawsuits among yourselves demonstrates that you have already been defeated. Why not rather be wronged? Why not rather be cheated?" (1 Cor 6:7).	Not rude

QUESTION 15

Paul commanded the church to "remove the evil person from among you" (1 Cor 5:13). According to 1 Corinthians 13:4-7, is such strong church discipline loving? Why?

Permanence of Love (13:8-13)

Assignment

- Read 1 Corinthians 13:8-13.
- Read Constable, "The Permanence of Love—13:8-13" (refer to the Articles section at the end of this lesson).
- Read "Permanence of Love."

Permanence of Love

Here Paul draws a clear distinction between love and all spiritual gifts. Love is permanent; spiritual gifts are temporary and partial.

How is love greater than faith and hope? One suggestion is that only love is eternal. But are not faith and hope also eternal? Clearly, this triad of virtues does not belong to the spiritual gifts that Paul asserts will eventually pass away, although there is a sense in which our faith and hope will be actualized at the Second Coming. Another suggestion is that love is the greatest because it most clearly describes God (see 1 Jn 4:8). The Scriptures does not say that God is faith or hope.

QUESTION 16

How is love greater than faith and hope? Record your answer in your Life Notebook.

Spiritual gifts were given to the church until the Lord's return, but love will endure eternally. Wonderful though they are, spiritual gifts are signs of the imperfection of this age rather than of the perfection of the age to come.

QUESTION 17

Spiritual gifts are a mark of the final, eternal state of believers. *True or False?*

Meaning of the Perfect

Assignment

- Read "Meaning of the Perfect."

Meaning of the Perfect

The argument that tongues will cease of themselves is based largely Greek grammar. This verb is in the middle voice, which often carries a reflexive concept, implying that tongues will cease of themselves at some time. Critics disagree, seeing the change of the verb to the middle voice as for a mark of variety of expression in the context: "if there are prophecies, they will be set aside; if there are tongues, they will cease; if there is knowledge, it will be set aside." Critics also point out that the same verb and voice are used in Luke 8:24 to refer to the storm, which certainly did not stop of itself.

What is "the perfect" and when will it come with respect to the "partial"? Three other contrasts serve to explain Paul's meaning: (1) "child" versus "adult," (2) "indirect" versus "face to face," and (3) "in part" versus "fully." Paul's argument asserts that perfection is in the future.

Major options for the meaning of "the perfect" are:

A. Paul is referring to growth as a believer. Someday, when spiritual growth reaches perfection, the spiritual gifts will be set aside. The problem with this view is that Paul never seems to claim perfection in this life (Phil 3:12).

B. Another view is that "the perfect" refers to the completion of the canon of Scripture, specifically the New Testament. Critics say that this view seems foreign to the context: Would the original readers have understood this meaning? Furthermore, even with the completion of the canon, believers' knowledge still remains indirect and partial.

C. The best view is that "the perfect" refers to the second coming of Christ. The church age is like childhood compared to the age after Christ's return. After He returns, there will be no more spiritual gifts, indirect knowledge of Christ, or spiritual immaturity among believers.

When Christ returns, "we shall be like him, because we shall see him as he is" (1 Jn 3:2).

QUESTION 18

What are the major options for the meaning of "the perfect" in 1 Corinthians 13? *(Select all that apply.)*

    A. The second coming

    B. The completion of the canon of Scripture

    C. Spiritual maturity

    D. Love

Topic 4: Prophecy and Tongues (1 Cor 14:1-25)

For the edification of the church, some gifts are more important than others. When the local church is gathered, one critical measuring stick for the exercise of gifts is intelligibility. Comparing prophecy with uninterpreted tongues, only the former is intelligible and can benefit the church.

Prophecy and the Principle of Intelligibility (14:1-5)

Assignment

- Read 1 Corinthians 14:1-5.
- Read Constable, "The Need for Intelligibility" (in the Articles section at the end of this lesson), through the note on 14:5.
- Read "Tongues, Prophecy, and the Principle of Intelligibility."

Tongues, Prophecy, and the Principle of Intelligibility

Were tongues at Corinth identical to tongues at Pentecost (Acts 2)? Comparing the phenomena of tongues at Pentecost and at Corinth, there are many differences:

> 1. At Corinth, the context was a worship service. At Pentecost, the context began as a prayer service and became an evangelistic event.

> 2. No interpreters were needed at Pentecost, but interpreters were needed at Corinth.

> 3. Every believer spoke in tongues at Pentecost, but only some at Corinth had the gift.

> 4. At Pentecost, the gift of tongues was accompanied by the sound of rushing wind and tongues of fire resting on each one. There is no mention of such phenomena at Corinth.

> 5. At Pentecost, tongues had a positive evangelistic effect. At Corinth, the evangelistic effect seems negative (1 Cor 14:23).

The phenomena of tongues in Acts can be understood as visible evidence of the giving of the Holy Spirit to the church. He was given to Jewish believers in Acts 2, to Samaritan believers in Acts 8, and to Gentiles, represented by Cornelius, in Acts 10. Given such evidence, the entire early church could unify around faith in Jesus apart from observance of the Mosaic law. If you are interested in further explanation of this position, please see the article Ryrie Basic Theology: Chapter 62, "The Spirit Indwelling" (placed in the Articles section at the end of this lesson). The function of the gift of tongues at Corinth seems quite different. The gift appears to be primarily used for the personal edification for those who have it (1 Cor 14:4).

Paul advocates the gift of prophecy, and today many scholars question exactly what he meant by prophecy. The simplest definition is that prophecy is speaking God's message. This message could be about the future, the past or the present. It is conveyed in language intelligible to the hearers. Such a definition is broad and begs the question of how to distinguish prophecy from teaching, preaching, or evangelism, which Paul seems to do elsewhere (Eph 4:11; 1 Cor 12:28-29). Typically these functions are distinguished as follows: Most understand teaching and preaching to refer to explaining Scripture. Evangelism refers to proclaiming the message of salvation to unbelievers. Prophecy is usually understood as relating a message from God received directly from the Spirit. Constable defines non-predictive prophecy as preaching, but believes that in this context prophecy refers to an impromptu word that someone would share in a worship service.

How was the early church to understand the authority of prophecy? Paul assumes the validity of the gift and the value of the prophetic messages for the strengthening, encouragement and consolation of the congregation at Corinth. Nowhere in 1 Corinthians does he distinguish the authority of prophecy delivered by an apostle from the authority of prophecy delivered by prophets. Nor does he distinguish between predictive and non-predictive prophecy. He does direct that all prophecies be evaluated (1 Cor 14:29; 1 Thess 5:20, 21).

Prophecy is one of the greater gifts because it is useful for building up the church—not just the individual who has the gift.

Speaking in tongues is a gift of the Holy Spirit that Paul wishes everyone had. Yet, compared to the intelligible speaking gifts, the gift of tongues is not useful for building up the congregation unless it is accompanied by interpretation.

QUESTION 19

Tongues without interpretation are unsuitable for expression in a church service because no one can understand what is being said. *True or False?*

QUESTION 20

How do the tongues at Pentecost differ from tongues at Corinth? *(Select all that apply.)*

  A. There was no need for an interpreter at Pentecost as there was at Corinth.

  B. Only men spoke in tongues at Pentecost, but both men and women spoke in tongues at Corinth.

  C. All believers spoke in tongues at Pentecost, but only some had the gift at Corinth.

  D. Tongues had a positive evangelistic effect at Pentecost, but a negative evangelistic effect at Corinth.

Principle Applied to Tongues (14:6-19)

Assignment

- Read 1 Corinthians 14:6-19.

- Read Constable, "Supporting Analogies" and "Application in View of Believers" (refer to the Articles section at the end of this lesson), through the note on 14:19.
- Read "Principle Applied to Tongues."

Principle Applied to Tongues

Paul illustrates the principle of intelligibility by using examples of musical instruments, clear speech and foreign languages.

The private use of tongues without interpretation is not condemned. Such an expression of the gift is useful for the individual. In the church, though, interpretation is required so that others may profit from the otherwise unintelligible words.

Paul contrasts the spirit with the mind in 1 Corinthians 14:14, 15. Whereas the mind denotes the rational part of man that communes with God, the spirit must denote the non-rational part which is able to commune with God.

Paul forbade the use of the gift of tongues in the worship service unless there was an interpretation. With proper interpretation, he expected tongues to be an accepted part of worship.

The key to using spiritual gifts in the local church is that they benefit, or build up, others. In order for the gift of tongues to be useful in this way, the message spoken must be intelligible.

QUESTION 21

Paul can see no value to the gift of tongues. *True or False?*

QUESTION 22

Suppose someone in your church told you that he had received the gift of tongues. How would you help him to evaluate whether this was the case or not? How would you explain the biblical use of the gift? Open your Life Notebook and record your thoughts.

Impact of Tongues and Prophecy on Unbelievers (14:20-25)

Assignment

- Read 1 Corinthians 14:20-25.
- Read Constable, "Application in View of Unbelievers 14:20-25" (refer to the Articles section at the end of this lesson).
- Read "The Impact of Tongues and Prophecy on Unbelievers."

Impact of Tongues and Prophecy on Unbelievers

In this section, it is difficult to understand Paul's argument. He says that tongues are a sign for unbelievers, but if unbelievers encounter people in the church speaking in tongues, they will view the tongue-speakers as crazy. How, then, are tongues a sign for unbelievers? Conversely, according to Paul, prophecy is a sign for believers. Yet, when unbelievers encounter prophecy, their reaction is conviction of sin and worship of God. As Dr. Constable pointed out, prophecy benefitted everybody, but uninterpreted tongues were of no benefit to the assembly.

Perhaps the best explanation of these difficult statements is to look at the Old Testament. Paul quotes Isaiah 28:11, 12 referring to God's judgment of the Northern Kingdom of Israel when He sent the Assyrian army—a people who spoke a foreign language. Thus, tongues (foreign languages) are a sign of God's judgment on unbelievers, in this case, Israel. This does not imply that the unbelievers recognized that sign or its meaning. On the other hand, prophecy is a sign for believers—not of judgment but of God's blessing (See Joel 2:28). Unbelievers, however, can benefit from hearing prophecy, even though the sign is not intended for them.

When the gift of tongues without interpretation is used in the worship service, no one benefits. Prophecy benefits all, both believers and unbelievers.

QUESTION 23

Prophecy in the church service has positive evangelistic value, but uninterpreted tongues do not. *True or False?*

QUESTION 24

What does Paul's quote of Isaiah 28:11-12 in 1 Corinthians 14:21 show?

    A. Tongues are a sign for believers.

    B. God sometimes communicates in strange ways.

    C. Tongues are of the devil.

    D. Tongues are a sign of God's judgment on unbelievers.

Topic 5: Order in Public Worship (1 Cor 14:26-40)

In addition to intelligibility, the second major principle Paul gives for the exercise of spiritual gifts in the worship service is orderliness. Any unruly, disrespectful, or disgraceful behavior is improper. In the worship service, each believer should consider the needs of the whole group.

Order and Gifts (14:26-33)

Assignment

- Read 1 Corinthians 14:26-33.

- Read Constable, "The Need for Order" (refer to the Articles section at the end of this lesson), through the note on 14:33.

- Read "Order and Gifts."

Order and Gifts

Worship at Corinth was congregational, participatory, and an occasion for displaying spiritual gifts. Paul encouraged such worship, provided that intelligibility and order also prevailed.

Who evaluates the message of the prophets? What is meant by "evaluate" (1 Cor 14:29)? Does the call to "evaluate" mean to evaluate the content of the prophet's statements, determining if it is true or false? Does it mean to evaluate how to respond to or apply his statements? (Acts 11:29; 21:12, 13) Or does it mean to judge whether the speaker is a true or false prophet? Consider, for example, what the early church did with Agabus' statement in Acts 11:28-30. The Scripture identifies Agabus as a true prophet, and he was accepted as a prophet by the early church, including Luke and Paul. After he gave his prophecy predicting a severe famine, the disciples considered how to respond.

The prophecy here is what is commonly called New Testament prophecy. Is New Testament prophecy different from Old Testament or apostolic prophecy in truthfulness? Some say the gift of prophecy, when exercised by an apostle, was infallible, but when an ordinary member of the body exercised the gift, the result was fallible. Advocates of this view base their argument heavily on the account of Agabus in Acts 21:11. "The Holy Spirit says this: 'This is the way the Jews in Jerusalem will tie up the man whose belt this is, and will hand him over to the Gentiles." The record of what happened is in Acts 21:27-33. Some claim that there are two errors in this prophecy:

1. The Romans bound Paul—not the Jews. (Response: This is an argument from silence. Perhaps the Jews bound Paul but Luke did not record it.)

2. The Jews did not hand Paul over to the Gentiles. (Response: This is also an argument from silence—perhaps the crowd did hand Paul over to the Romans. Certainly, the result of the Jews' seizure of Paul was his being delivered over to the Romans.

It is better to view these differences as a question of harmonizing passages than to assert that Luke thought Agabus gave an error-filled prophecy. Harmonization is an issue throughout Scripture (such as with Jesus' resurrection narratives), but difficulties in harmonization do not overthrow the complete truthfulness of Scripture. Elsewhere in Acts we see another harmonization issue of a similar nature. See Acts 5:30. Peter and the apostles accused the Jewish leaders of seizing and killing Jesus, but they did not actually do so. It was the Romans who put Jesus to death. Nevertheless, the Jewish leaders were also morally responsible for killing Jesus.

Thus it is best to consider that the same standard of truthfulness expected of prophets in the Old Testament applied in the New. False prophets abounded in both Testaments. It was the responsibility of the local church to discern true from false prophecy as well as to consider how to respond to true prophecy.

In addition to intelligibility, Paul insists on orderliness in the worship service. Order means limits on behavior, taking turns, yielding to others, and evaluating what is prophesied.

QUESTION 25

How do you see love in Paul's regulations for the worship service?

QUESTION 26

How would you share in worship services in your local church if they were like those described in 1 Corinthians 14:26-33? Are there ways to exercise those gifts in your local church? Record your answers in your Life Notebook.

Order and Women (14:34-35)

Assignment

- Read 1 Corinthians 14:34-35.
- Read Constable, "The Ordering of the Women—14:34-35" (refer to the Articles section at the end of this lesson).
- Read "Order and Women."

Order and Women

The Greek word for "silent" in 1 Corinthians 14:34 is the same word used in 1 Corinthians 14:28. If there is no interpreter, then those with the gift of tongues should be silent in the church service. That person should not speak in tongues during the service, but, if he has other gifts to bless the congregation that are intelligible—such as a song, a lesson, or a revelation—then he may speak. The silence Paul commands is not absolute, but rather a silence springing from love and from doing things decently and in order.

Similar to the arguments he made about women's head coverings in 1 Corinthians 11:2-16, Paul again uses theological argument ("the law says") and cultural argument ("it is disgraceful for a woman to speak in church").

The notes in the NET Bible are enlightening for this passage:

> "The word for "woman" and "wife" is the same in Greek. Because of the reference to husbands in v. 35, the word may be translated "wives" here. But in passages governing conduct in church meetings like this (cf. 11:2-16; 1 Tim 2:9-15) the general meaning "women" is more likely."

> "*For they are not permitted to speak.* In light of 11:2-16, which gives permission for women to pray or prophesy in the church meetings, the silence commanded here seems not to involve the absolute prohibition of a woman addressing the assembly. Therefore (1) some take *be silent* to mean not taking an authoritative teaching role as 1 Tim 2 indicates, but (2) the better suggestion is to relate it to the preceding regulations about evaluating the prophets (v. 29). Here Paul would be indicating that the women should not speak up during such an evaluation, since such questioning would be in violation of the submission to male leadership that the OT calls for (*the law*, e.g., Gen 2:18)."

The issue of women's role in the local church is much debated by Biblical scholars. There are many passages of Scripture to consider, including 1 Corinthians 11:5, 1 Corinthians 14:34, 35, and 1 Timothy 2:11-15. For insight into the 1 Timothy 2 passage, please refer to Dr. Constable's notes (http://www.soniclight.com/constable/notes/pdf/1timothy.pdf).

Paul mentions women both at the beginning and near the end of his extended discussion about proper behavior during the worship service, starting in 1 Corinthians 11:2. The behavior of women was causing problems, and Paul does not allow disgraceful behavior during worship.

QUESTION 27

Which of the following are arguments for why Paul did not mean absolute silence for women during the worship service? *(Select all that apply.)*

    A. He allowed women to pray and prophesy in 1 Corinthians 11:5.

    B. The same Greek word for "silence" (1 Cor 14:34) is also used in 1 Corinthians 14:28 and does not mean absolute silence for the person.

    C. In the context, silence for women may refer to evaluating prophets.

    D. Paul's main point is a wife's submission to male leadership.

Warning and Conclusion (14:36-40)

Assignment

- Read 1 Corinthians 14:36-40.

- Read Constable, "Concluding Confrontation—14:36-40" (refer to the Articles section at the end of this lesson).

- Read "Warning and Conclusion."

Warning and Conclusion

Paul asserts his apostolic authority, claiming that his written instructions are God's command. Spiritual people will recognize his authority and submit to it. Warning that those who reject his authority will not be recognized means that those people have no standing before the Lord or in His church.

Note that in 1 Corinthians 14:37, 38, Paul places his authority above the prophets in the church at Corinth. In the Old Testament, the highest spiritual authority resided with the true prophets of the Lord who spoke and/or wrote His Word. Many have observed that in the New Testament the highest spiritual authority resides with the Apostles, and their authority exceeds New Testament prophets. However, this principle does not imply that messages from the Lord spoken by New Testament prophets were subject to error.

The general principle governing all affairs of the local church is to do all things "in a decent and orderly manner." Each local church must decide its own affairs before the Lord, taking into account local customs, biblical principles, and the needs of the congregation, always seeking wisdom from God.

Paul admonishes the church to listen to his instruction as from God or face rejection by God. Spiritual gifts are to be valued and exercised according to love.

QUESTION 28

In the New Testament church, with whom did the highest spiritual authority reside?

    A. Prophets

    B. Teachers

    C. Apostles

    D. Those with the gift of tongues

Lesson 11 Articles

Notes on 1 Corinthians

Dr. Thomas L. Constable; 2003 Edition

E. SPIRITUAL GIFTS AND SPIRITUAL PEOPLE CHS. 12-14

Paul had been dealing with matters related to worship since 8:1. He had forbidden the Corinthians from participating in temple meals but had allowed eating marketplace meat under certain circumstances (8:1-11:1). Then he dealt with two issues involving their own gatherings for worship: head-coverings and the Lord's Supper (11:2-34). The issue of spiritual gifts (chs. 12-14) was the third issue involving their own gatherings for worship. This is the most important of the three as evidenced by the amount of text Paul devoted to it and by the issue itself. Paul explained that being "spiritual" at present, for the perfect state has not yet come (13:8-13), means to edify the church in worship.

> "More than any other issue, the Corinthians and Paul are at odds over the role of the Spirit. For them 'Spirit' has been their entrée to life in the realm of *sophia* ('wisdom') and *gnosis* ('knowledge'), with their consequent rejection of the material order, both now (7:1-7) and for the future (15:12), as well as their rejection of the Christian life as modeled by Paul's imitation of Christ (4:15-21). Their experience of tongues as the language(s) of angels had allowed them to assume heavenly existence now (4:8), thought of primarily in terms of nonmaterial existence, rather than ethical-moral life in the present. Thus Paul tries to disabuse them of their singular and overly enthusiastic emphasis on tongues (the point of chaps. 12-14); but in so doing, he tries to retool their understanding of the Spirit so as to bring it into line with the gospel." (279)

Paul wanted to correct the Corinthians in this section, not just provide more teaching, as he did throughout this epistle. This becomes clear in chapter 14. They were abusing the gift of tongues. The whole section divides into three parts and structurally follows an A-B-A chiastic pattern, as do other parts of this letter (i.e., chs. 1-3; 7:25-40; chs. 8-10). First there is general instruction (ch. 12), then a theological interlude (ch. 13), and finally specific correction (ch. 14).

> ." . . there is not a single suggestion in Paul's response that they were themselves divided on this issue or that they were politely asking his advice. More likely, the crucial issue is their decided position over against him as to what it means to be *pneumatikos* ('spiritual'). Their view apparently not only denied the material/physical side of Christian existence (hence the reason why chap. 15 follows hard on the heels of this section), but had an element of 'spiritualized (or overrealized) eschatology' as well.

> "The key probably lies with 13:1, where tongues is associated with angels. As noted elsewhere (7:1-7; 11:2-16), the Corinthians seem to have considered themselves to be already like the angels, thus truly 'spiritual,' needing neither sex in the present (7:1-7) nor a body in the future (15:1-58). Speaking angelic dialects by the Spirit was evidence enough for them of their participation in the new spirituality, hence their singular enthusiasm for this gift." (280)

1. The test of Spirit control 12:1-3

The apostle began his discussion by clarifying the indicators that a person is under the control of the indwelling Spirit of God. With this approach, he set the Corinthians' former experience as idolaters in contrast to their present experience as Christians. "Inspired utterance" in itself does not identify what is truly "spiritual." The intelligible content of such an utterance does when the content is the basic confession that Jesus Christ is Lord.

12:1 - The presence of the phrase *peri de* ("Now concerning" or "Now about") plus the change in subject mark another matter about which the Corinthians had written Paul with a question (cf. 7:1; 8:1). It had to do with the gifts or abilities the Holy Spirit gives those believers He indwells. (281) This subject is the focus of all that Paul wrote in chapters 12-14 including the famous thirteenth chapter on love.

As in 10:1, Paul implied that what followed was instruction his readers needed. "Spiritual gifts" is literally "the spirituals" (Gr. *ton pneumatikon*). (282) This is a broader term than the gifts themselves, though it includes them. It appears to refer primarily to the people who are spiritual (cf. 2:15; 3:1). Evidently the Corinthians' question dealt with the marks of a spiritual Christian. A spiritual Christian is a believer under the control of the Holy Spirit compared with one under the control of his or her flesh (Gal. 5:16) or a demonic spirit (10:20-21). (283)

12:2 - Many of the Corinthian believers had been pagans. Various influences had led them away from worship of the true God and into idolatry.

> "Corinth was experience-oriented and self-oriented. Mystery religions and other pagan cults were in great abundance, from which cults many of the members at the Corinthian church received their initial religious instruction. After being converted they had failed to free themselves from pagan attitudes and they confused the true work of the Spirit of God with the former pneumatic and ecstatic experiences of the pagan religions, especially the Dionysian mystery or the religion of Apollo." (284)

Dumb idols are idols that do not speak in contrast with the living God who does speak. Paul previously said that demons are behind the worship of idols (10:20). He did not say that the prophecy or glossolalia (speaking in tongues) being spoken in the Corinthian church proceeded from demonic sources. He only reminded his readers that there are "inspired" utterances that come from sources other than the Holy Spirit. Probably some of them had spoken in tongues when they were pagans.

> "In classical [Greek] literature, Apollo was particularly renowned as the source of ecstatic utterances, as on the lips of Cassandra of Troy, the priestess of Delphi or the Sibyl of Cumae (whose frenzy as she prophesied under the god's control is vividly described by Virgil); at a humbler level the fortune-telling slave-girl of Ac. 16.16 was dominated by the same kind of 'pythonic' spirit." (285)

12:3 - Enthusiasm or ecstasy or "inspired" utterance do not necessarily indicate spirituality. (286) Paul's original readers needed to pay attention to what the person speaking in such a state said.

> "Not the manner but the content of ecstatic speech determines its authenticity." (287)

What the person said about Jesus Christ was specially important. No one the Holy Spirit motivated would curse Jesus Christ. Probably no one in the Corinthian church had. Likewise no one would sincerely acknowledge that Jesus is Lord, Savior and or Sovereign, unless the Holy Spirit had some influence over him or her. This was true regardless of whether the person was speaking in an ecstatic condition or in plain speech. Paul was not enabling his readers to test the spirits to see if they were of God (cf. 1 Jn 4:1-3). His point was that "inspired" utterance as such does not indicate that the Holy Spirit is leading a person.

The Holy Spirit leads those under His control to glorify Jesus Christ, not dumb idols, with their speech (cf. 2:10-13).

> "The ultimate criterion of the Spirit's activity is the exaltation of Jesus as Lord. Whatever takes away from that, even if they be legitimate expressions of the Spirit, begins to move away from Christ to a more pagan fascination with spiritual activity as an end in itself." (288)

2. The need for varieties of spiritual gifts 12:4-31

Paul planned to return to the subject of glossolalia (ch. 14), but first he wanted to talk more generally about spiritual gifts. In the verses that follow he dealt with differences in gifts in the church.

> "Having given the negative and positive criterion of genuine spiritual endowments as manifested in speech, the Apostle goes on to point out the essential oneness of these very varied gifts." (289)

Diversity, not uniformity, is necessary for a healthy church, and God has seen to it that diversity exists (vv. 6, 7, 11, 18, 24, 28). Notice that the Corinthians were doing in the area of spiritual gifts essentially what they were doing in relation to their teachers (3:4-23). They were preferring one over others and thereby failing to benefit from them all. This section of Paul's argument puts the subject of gifts into proper theological perspective whereas the previous pericope put it into its proper Christological perspective.

Diversity in the Godhead and the gifts 12:4-11

12:4 - Although there is only one Holy Spirit He gives many different abilities to different people. Everything in this pericope revolves around these two ideas. "Gifts" (Gr. *charismata*, from *charis* meaning "grace") are abilities that enable a person to glorify and serve God. God gives them freely and graciously. That they are abilities is clear from how Paul described them here and elsewhere (Rom. 12).

12:5 - Likewise there are different ministries or services (Gr. *diakonia*; opportunities for service) that the one Lord over the church gives.

12:6 - Furthermore there are different effects or workings (Gr. *energemata*; manifestations of the Spirit's power at work) that the one God who is responsible for all of them bestows. Just as Spirit, Lord, and God are distinct yet closely related in verses 4-6, so are gifts, ministries, and effects. We should probably not view these words as representing entirely separate ideas but as facets of God's work in and through the believer. It is God who is responsible for our abilities, our opportunities for service, and the individual ways in which we minister including the results.

12:7 - Each believer regardless of his or her gifts, ministries, and the manner and extent of God's blessing demonstrates the Holy Spirit through his or her life. (290) All three of these things manifest the Spirit's presence, not just the more spectacular ones in each category. Believers who have spectacular gifts, ministries, or effectiveness are not more spiritual than Christians who do not. Each believer makes a unique contribution to the common good, not just certain believers (cf. vv. 12-27; 3:4-10). Several examples of this fact follow in verses 8-10.

12:8 - Paul mentioned nine ways in which the Spirit manifests Himself through believers. The list is representative rather than exhaustive as is clear when we compare this list with other similar ones (cf. vv. 28, 29-30; 7:7; 13:1-3, 8; 14:6, 26; Rom. 12:4-8; Eph. 4:11).

In this verse there is no definite article before the word "word" in either of its uses. This probably points to Paul's referring to an utterance of wisdom or knowledge, namely, a wise or knowledgeable utterance (cf. 1:17–2:16). (291) The difference in the utterances probably lies in wisdom representing a mature perception of what is true to reality (cf. 1:24; 2:6-13; 14:6) and knowledge standing for understanding of God's mysteries (revelations) in particular (cf. 13:2; 14:6).

> "It is the discourse, not the wisdom or knowledge behind it, that is the spiritual gift, for it is this that is of direct service to the church . . ." (292)

12:9 - Faith is trust in God. Every Christian has some faith just as every Christian has some wisdom and knowledge. However some believers have more God-given ability to trust God than others just as some have more God-given wisdom or knowledge than others. All believers should seek to cultivate wisdom, knowledge, and faith, but some have a larger God-given capacity for one or another of them than other Christians do.

The "gifts of healings" (literally) by definition refer to abilities to cause healing to take place. Evidently there were various types of healings that those so gifted could produce, for example physical, psychological, and spiritual healings. Counselors and medical doctors have a degree of ability to produce healing today. However most Christians believe God has not given the ability to restore people to health instantaneously today as He did in the early church. (293)

12:10 - Miracles are mighty works (Gr. *dynameis*) that alter the natural course of events. Probably all types of miracles beside healings are in view. God gave the ability to do miracles to His Son and to some Christians in the early church to signify that He was with them and empowering them (cf. Lk 4:14-36; 5; 6; 7; 8; 9-9:50; Gal. 3:5; Heb. 2:4). (294)

Prophecy has a three-fold meaning in the New Testament. Prophets foretold future events. They also declared things known only by special new revelation from God. Third, they uttered under the Spirit's prompting some lofty statement or message in praise of God, or a word of instruction, refutation, reproof, admonition, or comfort for others (cf. 11:4; 13:9; 14:1, 3-5, 24, 31, 39). Evidently the first and second of these abilities passed out of existence with the composition of the New Testament books. (295)

> "First, although prophecy was an especially widespread phenomenon in the religions of antiquity, Paul's understanding—as well as that of the other NT writers—was thoroughly conditioned by his own history in Judaism. The prophet was a person who spoke to God's people under the inspiration of the Spirit. The 'inspired utterance' came by revelation and announced judgment (usually) or salvation. Although the prophets often performed symbolic acts, which they then interpreted, the mainstream of prophetic activity, at least as it came to be canonized, had very little to do with 'ecstasy,' especially 'frenzy' or 'mania.' For the most part the prophets were understood only too well! Often the word spoken had a futuristic element, so in that sense they also came to be seen as 'predicters'; but that was only one element, and not necessarily the crucial one." (296)

The ability to distinguish between spirits (i.e., the spirit of the prophet through whom a higher spirit or the Holy Spirit spoke) was apparently a gift of discernment. It enabled a person to tell whether a propounded prophecy was genuine or counterfeit, from the Holy Spirit or a false spirit (cf. 14:29; 1 Thess. 5:20-21).

The gift of tongues, about which Paul would say much more in chapter 14, was the ability to speak in one or more languages that the speaker had not learned. However the languages do not seem limited to human languages (cf. 13:1). Nevertheless they were intelligible with interpretation (14:10-14). They were not just gibberish.

> It should be noted . . . that only tongues is included in every list of 'gifts' in these three chapters [12:8-10, 28, 29-30; 13:1-3, 8; 14:6, 26]. Its place at the *conclusion* of each list in chap. 12, but at the beginning in 13:1 and 14:6, suggests that the problem lies here. It is listed last not because it is 'least,' but because it is the problem. He always includes it, but at the end, after the greater concern for diversity has been heard." (297)

The person with the ability to interpret tongues could translate what a tongues-speaker said accurately so that others present could know the meaning of what he or she said. Presumably some Christians with the gift of tongues also had the gift of interpreting tongues so they could explain what they had said.

12:11 - This section concludes with another reminder that though these manifestations of the Spirit vary they all indicate the presence and working of the Spirit of God. Paul also stressed again the Spirit's sovereignty in distributing the gifts (cf. John 3:8). The Corinthians should not try to manipulate the Spirit but accept and submit to His distribution of the gifts as He saw fit.

There is a general progression in this list from the more common to the more uncommon and esoteric gifts (cf. v. 28). The more unusual gifts that appear toward the end of this list attracted the Corinthians. Some gifts were probably more common at one place and in one church than were others depending on the Spirit's sovereign distribution (cf. 1:4-5). Some were probably more common at some times than at others, too, as the Spirit bestowed them.

The body and its members 12:12-14

Paul now compared the body of Christ, the universal church, though by extension the local church as well, to a human body. Again his point was not that the church needs to have unity but that it needs to have diversity.

12:12 - The apostle spoke of this comparison in other epistles as well (Rom. 12:4-5; Eph. 4:11-13; Col. 1:18; 2:19). He probably adapted the idea of the body politic, an essentially secular but commonly understood concept, to illustrate the church. There can be unity in a body without uniformity. Here the apostle stressed the fact that diversity among the members is an essential part of a unified body. Evidently the Corinthians were striving for unanimity and did not appreciate that there can and must be diversity in a "spiritual" church.

> "One of the marks of an individual's maturity is a growing understanding of, and appreciation for, his own body. There is a parallel in the spiritual life: as we mature in Christ, we gain a better understanding of the church, which is Christ's body. The emphasis in recent years on 'body life' has been a good one. It has helped to counteract the wrong emphasis on 'individual Christianity' that can lead to isolation from the local church." (298)

12:13 - The baptism of the Spirit took place initially on the day of Pentecost (Acts 1:5; 2:33; 11:16). Subsequently individual believers experienced Spirit baptism when they personally trusted Christ as their Savior (Acts 11:15-17).

In Spirit baptism the Holy Spirit baptizes (Gr. *baptidzo*, lit. submerges) the believer into the body of Christ. He makes us a part of it. Water baptism illustrates this. Every believer experiences Spirit baptism regardless of his or her race or social status. We are now on equal footing in the sense that we are all members of the body of Christ.

The figure of drinking of one Spirit recalls John 7:37-39 where Jesus invited the thirsty to come and drink of Him to find refreshment. Baptism and drinking are both initiation experiences and take place at the same time. In the first figure the Spirit places the believer into Christ, and in the second the Spirit comes into the Christian. This is probably a case of Semitic parallelism in which both clauses make essentially the same point.

> ." . . the Spirit not only surrounds us, but is within us." (299)

12:14 - Both bodies, the physical human body and the spiritual body of Christ, consist of many members. This fact helps us realize our limited contribution to the larger organism. A body composed of only one organ would be a monstrosity.

The modern church often uses this pericope to stress the importance of unity, which is a great need today. However, Paul's emphasis originally was on the importance of diversity.

The application of the figure 12:15-26

Paul proceeded to elaborate his analogy.

12:15-16 - Perhaps Paul chose the feet, hands, ears, and eyes as examples because of their prominence in the body. Even though they are prominent and important they cannot stand alone. They need each other.

." . . Chrysostom remarks that the foot contrasts itself with the hand rather than with the ear, because we do not envy those who are very much higher than ourselves so much as those who have got a little above us . . ." (300)

12:17 - Different functions as well as different members are necessary in the body (cf. v. 4). Paul's point was not the inferiority of some members but the need for all members.

12:18 - Paul again stressed God's sovereignty in placing each member in the body as He has chosen in this verse. We need to discover how God has gifted us and to become as effective as possible where He has placed us. We should concentrate on using the abilities we have received rather than longing to be different or insisting on doing things that God has not gifted us to do (cf. 7:26-27).

> "Whenever we begin to think about our own importance in the Christian Church, the possibility of really Christian work is gone." (301)

12:19 - If all the members of the human body were the same, it would not be able to function as a body. It would be incapable of getting anything accomplished. For example, if all had the gift of tongues, the gift that the Corinthians valued so highly, the body would not function.

12:20 - This is not the case in the human body, however. It has a variety of members, but it is one unified organism.

12:21 - It is interesting that Paul used the head and the feet as examples, the top of the body and the bottom. He was reminding those who felt superior that those whom they regarded as inferior were also necessary (cf. 11:17-34). Too often because we differ *from* each other we also differ *with* each other.

12:22 - Rather than regarding themselves as superior, the "haves" in the church needed to remember that the "have nots" were important for the effective operation of the whole organism. Even the little toe, or the rarely appreciated pancreas, plays a crucial role in the physical body.

12:23-24a - When dealing with our human bodies we bestow more honor on our less honorable parts by covering them up. This makes our unseemly members more seemly. Paul may have been referring to the sexual organs. (302) On the other hand, the more honorable parts, such as our face, do not require special covering. The point is that we take special pains to honor our less esteemed physical members, and we should do the same in the church rather than neglecting or despising them. When is the last time your church gave public recognition to the nursery workers or the clean up crew?

12:24b-25 - God has constructed bodies, both human and spiritual, so the different members can care for one another. He does not ignore any member but makes provision for each one. We do not always see this in the human body, but it is true. Likewise God's honoring the less prominent members in the church may not be apparent now, but it will be at the judgment seat of Christ if not before then.

God does not want dissension (Gr. *schisma*) in His body. There was some in the Corinthian church (1:10; 11:18). Rather (strong contrast in the Greek, *alla*) the members should have anxious care for one another. Paul illustrated this attitude with what follows.

12:26 - The suffering of one means the suffering of all, and the well-being of one means the well-being of all.

> "Plato had pointed out that we do not say, 'My finger has a pain,' we say, 'I have a pain.'" (303)

In view of this we can and should honestly rejoice with those who rejoice and weep with those who weep (Rom. 12:15).

Paul's preceding comments about the body (vv. 12-26) are applicable to both the physical body and the spiritual body of Christ. However, he was speaking about the human body primarily, as an illustration of the spiritual body.

The fact of diversity restated 12:27-31

Next, the apostle spoke more specifically about the members of the body of Christ again (cf. vv. 1-11).

12:27 - "You" is emphatic in the Greek text and is plural. The Corinthian Christians are in view, but what Paul said of them applies to all groups of Christians. Together we make up the body of Christ, and each of us is an individual member in it. Again, what Paul said of the church is true of it in its macro and in its micro forms, the universal church and the local church.

12:28 - Paul listed eight kinds of members with special functions. This list differs somewhat from the one in verses 8-10 where he identified nine manifestations of the Spirit's working. This list, as the former one, is selective rather than exhaustive.

The ranking of these gifted individuals is evidently in the order of the importance of their ministries. When Paul said all the members were essential earlier (v. 21) he did not mean some did not have a more crucial function to perform than others. He did not mention this distinction there because he wanted each member to appreciate the essential necessity of every other member. In another sense, however, some gifts are more important than others (v. 31; 14:1).

God called and gifted the apostles to plant and to establish the church in places the gospel had not yet gone. *Apostello* means to send out, so it is proper to think of apostles as missionaries. Prophets were the channels through whom God sent His revelations to His people (cf. Eph. 2:20). They wrote the books of the New Testament. Teachers gave believers instruction in the Scriptures. Teachers were more important in the church than the prophets who simply gave words of edification, exhortation, and consolation (14:3), but they were less important than the prophets who gave new authoritative revelation. The latter type of prophet is in view in this verse.

> ." . . a scholar will learn more from a good teacher than he will from any book. We have books in plenty nowadays, but it is still true that it is through people that we really learn of Christ." (304)

Workers of miracles and healers gave dramatic proof that the power of God was working in the church so others would trust Christ. They may have ministered especially to the Jews since the Jews looked for such indications of God's presence and blessing (cf. 1:22). Helpers seem to have provided assistance of various kinds for people in need.

Administrators managed and directed the affairs of the churches. Tongues-speakers bring up the rear in this list as being the least important of those mentioned. Paul said more about their relative importance in chapter 14.

> "The shortness of the list of charismata in Eph. iv. II as compared with the list here is perhaps an indication that the regular exercise of extraordinary gifts in public worship was already dying out." (305)

12:29-30 - These two verses contain a third list of gifts in a descending order of priority. Each of Paul's seven questions expects a negative answer. The apostle's point was that it would be ridiculous for everyone to have the same gift. Variety is essential. It is wrong to equate one gift, particularly speaking in tongues, with spirituality.

> "*All* of the believers in the Corinthian assembly had been baptized by the Spirit [v. 13], but not all of them spoke in tongues (1 Cor. 12:30)." (306)

12:31 - Paul advised the Corinthians to seek some gifts more than others because some are more significant in the functioning of the body than others. While the bestowal of gifts is the sovereign prerogative of the Spirit (vv. 8-11, 18), human desire plays a part in His bestowal (cf. Jas 4:2). This seems to indicate that the Spirit does not give all His gifts to us at the moment of our salvation. I see nothing in Scripture that prohibits our viewing the abilities God gives us at birth as part of His spiritual gifts.

Likewise a believer can receive a gift or an opportunity for service or the Spirit's blessing on his ministry years after his conversion. Everything we have or ever will have is a gift from God. (307)

God did not give the gift of apostleship in the technical sense to any other than those whom Christ Himself selected who had seen the risen Lord. It went to a small group in the first generation of the church's history. Apostleship in the general sense of one sent out with a message continues today. Normally we refer to these gifted people as missionaries to distinguish them from Paul and the 12 apostles.

Likewise we use the term prophet in a technical and in a general sense today. Usually we think of prophets as people who gave new revelation from God or predicted the future. As I have pointed out, prophets also spoke forth a word from the Lord by exhorting or encouraging the church. The Greek word *prophetes* means "one who speaks forth." In the first technical sense prophets have ceased in the church. In the second general sense they are still with us. (308) We usually refer to them as preachers to distinguish them from first century prophets who gave new revelation and predicted the future.

Today some people who desire to sharpen their ability to preach and teach the Scriptures enroll in seminary to do so. This is one example of zealously desiring the greater gifts.

However, Paul said there is an even more important discipline that a believer should cultivate to reach the goal of being maximally effective. That way involves valuing and cultivating love (ch. 13). The apostle did not mean, of course, that one should disregard the most important gifts but seek love. We should give attention to cultivating love and cultivating abilities that are strategically important in Christ's body. Nevertheless as important as sharpening abilities is, it is even more important that we excel in loving.

> "'The most excellent way' which Paul will now show his friends at Corinth is not one more gift among many, but 'a way beyond all this.' That extraordinary way is, of course, the way of *agape*, that fruit of the Spirit which is of primary importance to every believer and to the body of Christ." (309)

> "What Paul is about to embark on is a description of what he calls 'a way that is beyond comparison.' The way they are going is basically destructive to the church as a community; the way they are being called to is one that seeks the good of others before oneself. It is the way of edifying the church 914:1-5), of seeking the common good (12:7). In that context one will still earnestly desire the things of the Spirit (14:1), but precisely so that others will be edified. Thus it is not 'love versus gifts' that Paul has in mind, but 'love as the only context for gifts'; for without the former, the latter have no usefulness at all—but then neither does much of anything else in the Christian life." (310)

Chapter 12 is a chapter that stresses balance. On the one hand each Christian is only a part of a larger organism, but each is an indispensable part. In one sense we are equally important because we all serve an essential function, but in another sense some are more crucial than others. God determines our gifts, ministries, and individual differences, yet our desire and initiative do have something to do with our service as well. Ability, ministry opportunity, and individuality are very important, but love is even more important. A good measure of our personal maturity as Christians will be how well we can keep these paradoxes in balance in our personal lives and ministries. The Corinthians needed help in this area.

> "The Church is neither a dead mass of similar particles, like a heap of sand, nor a living swarm of antagonistic individuals, like a cage of wild beasts: it has the unity of a living organism, in which no two parts are exactly alike, but all discharge different functions for the good of the whole. All men are not equal, and no individual can be independent of the rest: everywhere there is subordination and dependence. Some have special gifts, some have none; some have several gifts, some only one; some have higher gifts, some have lower: but every individual has some function to discharge, and all must work together for the common good. This is the all-important point—unity in loving service." (311)

	Unity	Diversity	Maturity
1 Corinthians	12:1-13	12:14-31	13:1-13
Romans	12:1-5	12:6-8	12:9-21
Ephesians	4:1-6	4:7-12	4:13-16 (321)

3. The supremacy of love ch. 13

Paul now proceeded to elaborate on the fact that love surpasses the most important spiritual gifts. Some of the Corinthian Christians may not have possessed any of the gifts mentioned in the previous three lists in chapter 12, but all of them could practice love. Clearly all of them needed to practice love more fully. The fruit of the Spirit (Gal. 5:22-23) is a more obvious demonstration of the Spirit's presence in a life and His control over a life than the gifts of the Spirit.

Love is the most fundamental and prominent of these graces. The love in view is God's love that He has placed in the believer in the indwelling Spirit that should overflow to God and others. It is the love that only the indwelling Holy Spirit can produce in a believer and manifest through a believer. Fortunately we do not have to produce it. We just need to cooperate with God by doing His will so the Spirit can produce it.

> "A Christian community can make shift somehow if the 'gifts' of chapter 12 be lacking: it will die if love is absent. The most lavish exercise of spiritual gifts cannot compensate for lack of love." (313)

This chapter is something of a digression in Paul's argument concerning keeping the gift of tongues in its proper perspective (cf. 14:1), but it strengthens his argument considerably.

The necessity of love 13:1-3

In these first three verses Paul showed that love is superior to the spiritual gifts he listed in chapter 12.

> "It is hard to escape the implication that what is involved here are two opposing views as to what it means to be 'spiritual.' For the Corinthians it meant 'tongues, wisdom, knowledge' (and pride), but without a commensurate concern for truly Christian behavior. For Paul it meant first of all to be full of the Spirit, the *Holy* Spirit, which therefore meant to behave as those 'sanctified in Christ Jesus, called to be his holy people' (1:2), of which the ultimate expression always is to 'walk in love.' Thus, even though these sentences reflect the immediate context, Paul's concern is not simply with their over-enthusiasm about tongues but with the larger issue of the letter as a whole, where their view of spirituality has caused them to miss rather widely both the gospel and its ethics." (314)

> "All four classes of gifts (xii. 28) are included here: the ecstatic in v. 1; the teaching (*propheteia*) and the wonder-working (*pistis*) gifts in v. 2; and the administrative in v. 3." (315)

> "It has well been said that love is the 'circulatory system' of the body of Christ." (316)

13:1 - Probably Paul began with tongues because of the Corinthians' fascination with this gift (cf. ch. 14). That is where the problem lay. He also built to a climax in verses 1-3 moving from the less to the more difficult actions. Evidently Paul used the first person because the Corinthians believed that they did speak with the tongues of men and of angels (cf. 14:14-15).

Speaking with the tongues of men and angels does not refer to simple eloquence, as the context makes clear (cf. 12:10, 28, 30). The tongues of men probably refer to languages humans speak. The tongues of angels probably refer to the more exalted and expressive language with which angels communicate with one another. They may refer to languages unknown to humans, namely, ecstatic utterance. However throughout this whole discussion of the gift of tongues there is no evidence that Paul regarded tongues as anything but languages. Throughout the New Testament, "tongues" means languages.

Of course humans do not know the language of the angels, but it is an exalted language because angels are superior beings. The Corinthians evidently believed that they could speak in angelic languages. Paul's point was that even if one could speak in this exalted language and did not have love (i.e., act lovingly) his or her speech would be hollow and empty. (317) Gongs and cymbals were common in some of the popular pagan cults of the time. (318) They made much noise but no sense.

13:2 - Prophecy was a higher gift than glossolalia but was still inferior to love (cf. 14:1-5). Earlier Paul wrote of the importance of understanding life from God's perspective and grasping the truths previously not revealed but now made known by His apostles (2:6-13). Nevertheless the truth without love is like food without drink. Possession of spiritual gifts is not the sign of the Spirit, but loving behavior is.

Even faith great enough to move mountains is not as important as love (12:9; cf. Matt. 17:20; Mk 11:23; Lk 17:6). A mountain is a universal symbol of something immovable.

13:3 - Even what passed for charity, self-sacrifice for less fortunate individuals, is not the same as real love (Gr. *agape*). It is inferior to it. It might profit the receiver, but it did not profit the giver.

Paul's personal sufferings for the salvation of others were also worthless without love (cf. 2 Cor. 11:23-29; 12:10). Even one's acceptance of martyrdom might spring from love. Notwithstanding if it did not it was valueless in the sight of God and would bring no divine reward to the one who submitted to it (cf. Dan. 3:28; Rom. 5:2-3; 2 Cor. 1:14).

Paul was not setting love in contrast to gifts in this pericope. He was arguing for the necessity and supremacy of love if one is to behave as a true Christian.

> "Love is the indispensable addition which alone gives worth to all other Christian gifts." (319)

The character of love 13:4-7

The apostle next pointed out the qualities of love that make it so important. He described these in relationship to a person's character that love rules. We see them most clearly in God and in Christ but also in the life of anyone in whose heart God's love reigns.

13:4a - Patience and kindness like love are aspects of the fruit of the Spirit (Gal. 5:22). The first characteristic is love's passive response and the second its active initiative. Patience and kindness mark God, Christ, and truly Christian behavior.

13:4b-5 - Paul followed the two positive expressions of love with seven verbs that indicate how it does not behave. The first five of these marked the Corinthians, as we have seen. They were envious (cf. 3:3; 4:18), boastful (ostentatious; 3:18; 8:2; 14:37), proud (4:6, 18-19; 5:2; 8:1), rude (7:36; 11:2-16) and self-seeking (10:24, 33). Their behavior was not loving. Love does not deal with other people in a way that injures their dignity. It does not insist on having its own way, nor does it put its own interests before the needs of others (cf. Phil 2:4). It is not irritable or touchy, but it absorbs offenses, insults, and inconveniences for the sake of others' welfare. It does not keep a record of offenses received to pay them back (cf. Lk 23:34; Rom 12:17-21; 2 Cor 5:19).

> "One of the great arts in life is to learn what to forget." (320)

> "One of the most miserable men I ever met was a professed Christian who actually kept in a notebook a list of the wrongs he felt others had committed against him. Forgiveness means that we wipe the record clean and never hold things against people (Eph 4:26, 32)." (321)

In the last two characteristics Paul moved beyond what this letter reveals marked the Corinthians.

13:6 - Love takes no delight in evil or the misfortunes of others, but it takes great pleasure in what is right.

> "Love cannot share the glee of the successful transgressor." (322)

> "Love absolutely rejects that most pernicious form of rejoicing over evil, gossiping about the misdeeds of others; it is not gladdened when someone else falls. Love stands on the side of the gospel and looks for mercy and justice for all, including those with whom one disagrees." (323)

> "Christian love has no wish to veil the truth; it is brave enough to face the truth; it has nothing to conceal and so is glad when the truth prevails." (324)

13:7 - Love covers unworthy things rather than bringing them to the light and magnifying them (cf. 1 Pet 4:8). It puts up with everything. It is always eager to believe the best and to "put the most favorable construction on ambiguous actions." (325)

> "This does not mean . . . that a Christian is to allow himself to be fooled by every rogue, or to pretend that he believes that white is black. But in doubtful cases he will prefer being too generous in his conclusions to suspecting another unjustly." (326)

It is hopeful that those who have failed will not fail again rather than concluding that failure is inevitable (cf. Matt 18:22). It does not allow itself to become overwhelmed but perseveres steadfastly through difficult trials.

The permanence of love 13:8-13

Paul moved on to point out that Christian love (*agape*) characterizes our existence now and forever, but gifts (*charismata*) are only for the present. The Corinthians were apparently viewing the gifts as one evidence that they were already in the eschatological stage of their salvation.

13:8 - Love never fails in the sense of falling away when the physical temporal things on which affection rests pass away; it outlasts temporal things. Gifts of the Spirit will pass away because they are temporary provisions, but the fruit of the Spirit will abide.

Prophecies are messages from God, but when we stand before Him and hear His voice there will be no more need for prophets to relay His words to us. Likewise when we stand before God there will be no need to speak in other languages since we will all understand God when He speaks. The knowledge that is so important to us now will be irrelevant then because when we are in God's presence we will know perfectly (v. 12; cf. 1:5; 8:1; 12:8). The knowledge in view seems to be knowledge of God's ways in the present age. As will become clearer in chapter 14, Paul's preference regarding the gifts was prophecy, but the Corinthians favored tongues and knowledge.

The verb Paul used to describe what will happen to prophecy and knowledge is in the passive voice in Greek and means "shall be terminated" (from *katargeo*; cf. 2:6). The verb he used to describe what will happen to tongues is in the middle voice and means "automatically cease of themselves" (from *pauo*). (327) The passive voice points to God terminating prophecy and knowledge when we see Him. The middle voice suggests that tongues will peter out before we see God. (328) Church history testifies that this is what happened to the gift of tongues shortly after the apostolic age. (329) Paul's dropping tongues from his discussion at this point supports the fact that the gift of tongues would not last as long as knowledge and prophecy. He continued to speak of knowledge and prophecy in the next verses.

13:9 - In the meantime, before we see the Lord, our knowledge and prophecy are imperfect in contrast with what they will be when we see Him. Prophecy is imperfect in the sense that revelations of His mind are only partial, incomplete.

13:10 - In the light of the context, what is perfect (Gr. *teleion*, mature, whole, complete) probably refers to the whole truth about God. (330) Another possibility is that it is our state when we stand in the Lord's presence. (331) When we reach that point in history the Lord will remove (*katargeo*, cf. v. 8) what is partial, the limits on our knowledge and the other limitations we suffer in our present condition. Variations on this second view are that the perfect refers to the Rapture, (332) to the Lord's return, (333) or to the maturing of Christ's body through the course of the church age. (334)

Another view is that the perfect refers to the completion of the New Testament canon and the partial to the incomplete canon and the Corinthians' partial knowledge. (335) They were incomplete because God had not yet given all the prophecy He would give to complete the New Testament. However this view puts too much weight on prophecy and knowledge and not enough on our other temporary limitations to which Paul also referred (v. 12).

A third possibility is that the perfect refers to the new heavens and new earth. (336) However the New Testament does not reveal that God will remove Christians' limitations to any greater extent sometime *after* we see the Lord Jesus than He will *when* we see Him (cf. Rom 8:32).

13:11 - Paul compared our present phase of maturity to childhood and that of our later phase, when we are with the Lord, to adulthood. It is characteristic of children to preoccupy themselves with things of very temporary value. Likewise the Corinthians took great interest in the things that would pass away soon, namely, knowledge, tongues, and prophecy. A sign of spiritual maturity is occupation with things of eternal value such as love. Again Paul was stressing the difference between the present and the future.

13:12 - Another illustration of the difference between our present and future states as Christians is the mirror. In Paul's day, craftsmen made mirrors out of metal.

> ." . . Corinth was famous as the producer of some of the finest bronze mirrors in antiquity." (337)

Consequently the apostle's point was not that our present perception of reality is somewhat distorted, but in the future it will be completely realistic. (338) Rather it was that now we see indirectly, but then we will see directly, face to face. Today we might say that we presently look at a photograph, but in the future we will see what the photograph pictures.

Now we know (Gr. *ginosko*) only partially. When the Lord has resurrected or "raptured" us and we stand in His presence, we will know fully (Gr. *epignosko*), as fully as God now knows us. (339) Now He knows us directly, but then we will also know Him directly.

13:13 - "Now" resumes Paul's original thought about the supremacy of love. It does not carry on the contrast between what is now and what will be later. In contrast to what will pass away—namely, knowledge, tongues, and prophecy—faith, hope, and love will endure (cf. Rom 5:1-5; Gal. 5:5-6;

Eph. 4:2-5; 1 Thess. 1:3; 5:8; Heb. 6:10-12; 10:22-24; 1 Pet. 1:3-8, 21-22). Faith here is not the gift of faith (v. 2; cf. 12:9) but the trust in God that characterizes all His children.

Among the enduring virtues love is the greatest because it will only increase when we see the Lord rather than decreasing in us, as faith and hope will. In the future we will continue to trust God and hope in Him, but the reality of His presence will make it easier for us to do so then than it is now.

Apparently Paul introduced faith and hope at this point to show that love is not only superior to the gifts, but it is superior even to other virtues. Faith and hope are gifts, and they are also Christian virtues of the same type as love. Yet love even outstrips the other major Christian virtues because it will outlast them.

> "Love is a property of God himself. . . . But God does not himself trust (in the sense of placing his whole confidence in and committing himself to some other being); if he did, he would not be God. . . . If God hoped he would not be God. But if God did not love he would not be God. Love is an activity, the essential activity, of God himself, and when

men love either him or their fellow-men they are doing (however imperfectly) what God does." (340)

The point of this beautiful classic exposition of love is this. We should value and give attention to the cultivation and practice of love even more than to that of the spiritual gifts (cf. 12:31). The gifts, as important as they are, are only partial and temporary. As love is the greatest of the virtues that will endure forever, so the gift of tongues is the least of the gifts. It will last only a short time.

4. The need for intelligibility 14:1-25

"Paul had discussed the gift of the Spirit, the gifts of the Spirit, and the graces of the Spirit; and now he concluded this section by explaining the government of the Spirit in the public worship services of the church. Apparently there was a tendency for some of the Corinthians to lose control of themselves as they exercised their gifts, and Paul had to remind them of the fundamental principles that ought to govern the public meetings of the church. There are three principles: edification, understanding, and order." (341)

Paul went on to elaborate on the inferiority of the gift of tongues that the Corinthians elevated so they would pursue more important gifts. His point was that *intelligible* inspired speech (i.e., prophecy) is superior to *unintelligible* inspired speech (i.e., tongues) in the assembly. He argued first for intelligible speech for the sake of the believers gathered to worship (vv. 1-25). In this whole comparison Paul was dealing with the gift of tongues without the gift of the interpretation of tongues.

The superiority of prophecy to tongues 14:1-5

The apostle began this discussion of tongues by comparing it to the gift of prophecy that the Corinthians also appreciated (cf. 12:10, 28; 13:8). He urged the Corinthians to value prophecy above tongues because it can edify and lead to conversion since it involves **intelligible** "inspired" speech.

14:1 - This verse sums up what Paul had just written about love, and it resumes the thought in 12:31 by restating that exhortation. In contrast to some of the milder advice he gave in this epistle, Paul urged his readers strongly to follow the way of love. This imperative then advances the thought by urging the readers to seek the gift of prophesying in particular.

"At the end of chap. 12, where he had been speaking specifically of the *gifts* themselves as gracious endowments, he told them, 'eagerly desire the greater *charismata*.' Now in a context where the emphasis will be on the activity of the Spirit in the community at worship, he says, 'eagerly desire the things of the Spirit [*tapneumatika*].'" (342)

14:2 - Glossolalia by itself is not edifying to other people, but prophecy is. This statement again raises a question about what speaking in tongues involved.

On the day of Pentecost people spoke in tongues and other people who knew the languages spoken received edification because they heard of God's mighty deeds in their native languages (Acts 2:1-11). Interpreters were unnecessary on that occasion (cf. Acts 10:46; 19:6). Evidently what was taking place in the Corinthian church was different from what took place on the day of Pentecost. In Corinth, and perhaps in other early churches, people spoke in tongues among people who did not understand the languages. An interpreter was necessary for those present to understand and benefit from what the tongues-speaker was saying in a strange language (vv. 5, 13). Paul used "tongues" and "languages" interchangeably in this passage (cf. vv. 2, 10, 11, 13, et al.). This is an important proof that tongues were languages.

Some Christians have suggested another distinction. They have claimed that the tongues in Acts were foreign languages but the tongues in Corinthians were ecstatic utterances, not languages but unintelligible speech. (343) There is no basis for this distinction in the biblical text, however. The terminology used is the same, and the passages make good sense if we take tongues as languages wherever they occur. (344)

If someone spoke in an unknown language and no one could interpret what he was saying, the person speaking was not speaking to men. God knew what he was saying even though no one else did including the person doing the speaking. In his human spirit the speaker was uttering mysteries (Gr. *mysteria*, things hidden or secret from the understanding of those in the church listening). Obviously Paul's concern was the edification of the church. He did not disparage the gift of tongues itself, but he put it in its rightful place.

Note, too, that Paul described the spirit as distinct from the mind (cf. vv. 14-19).

> "Contrary to the opinion of many, spiritual edification can take place in ways other than through the cortex of the brain. Paul believed in an immediate communing with God by means of the S/spirit that sometimes bypassed the mind; and in vv. 14-15 he argues that for his own edification he will have both. But *in church* he will have only what can also communicate to other believers through their minds." (345)

14:3 - In contrast to the foreign speech uttered by tongues-speakers, those present could understand what a prophet spoke in the language of his audience. It benefited the hearers by building them up, encouraging them, and consoling them. "Edification," "exhortation," and "consolation" set forth the primary ways in which prophecy (preaching) builds up the church. Its main purpose as a gift was not to predict events in the future but to build up believers in the present.

Official Apostles	The Twelve and the Apostle Paul
Functional (unofficial) apostles	Church planters and missionaries
Official prophets	Communicated new revelation
Functional (unofficial) prophets	Communicated edification, exhortation, and consolation

4:4 - The person who spoke in tongues in church edified himself or herself. He or she praised God and prayed to God while speaking in a tongue. He or she also benefited from realizing that the Holy Spirit was enabling him or her to speak a language that he or she had not studied. This would have encouraged the tongues-speaker, but that one did not edify himself or herself in the sense of profiting from the message the Holy Spirit had given. He did not know what his words meant unless he also had the gift of interpretation, but in this discussion Paul left that gift out of the picture almost entirely (cf. v. 5). Had he known what he was saying he could have communicated this to those present in their language. That is what a prophet did. (346) Paul's point was that edifying the church is more valuable than edifying oneself. He did not deny that speaking in tongues does edify the tongues-speaker (cf. vv. 14-15, 18-19).

14:5 - Paul acknowledged the value of the gift of tongues even though it also required an interpreter. Nevertheless he made it clear that the ability to prophesy was more important. The issue, again, is private versus public benefit. Since Paul depreciated speaking in tongues without interpretation so strongly, it seems very likely that this is what the Corinthians were doing in their meetings. The real issue was not a conflict between tongues and prophecy but between unintelligible and intelligible utterance.

In this whole discussion "prophecy" does not refer primarily to a prepared sermon but to an impromptu word that someone would share in a service in which congregational participation was possible.

Supporting analogies 14:6-12

Paul illustrated his point that hearers do not benefit at all from what they do not understand. He used musical instruments as examples and clarified more about foreign languages.

14:6 - This verse sets the scene for what follows in this pericope. "Revelation," "knowledge," "prophecy," and "teaching" are all intelligible utterances. These words probably refer to a new revelation (cf. 12:8), an insight into truth, a word of edification, exhortation, or consolation from the Lord (v. 3), or instruction in the faith.

14:7-8 - Even the sounds people make using inanimate musical instruments need to be intelligible to profit anyone. This is especially obvious in the case of a call to battle. If the bugler blows a confused tune, the army will not know whether to attack or retreat. The harp and the flute, as well as the bugle, were commonplace in the Greco-Roman world.

14:9 - Incomprehensible speech may be personally satisfying to the one talking, but it profits only a little those who are listening. The only profit would be entertainment. For example, when an international student sings a song in his or her native language in chapel, almost everyone enjoys the song but does not receive edification from it.

14:10-11 - Clearly Paul was speaking about languages, not gibberish, even though the Greek word translated "languages" (*phone*) means "sounds" or "voices." The context shows he had languages in mind, either human or angelic. A non-Greek was a foreigner (Gr. *barbaros*, barbarian) to a Greek. The word *barbaros* is onomatopoetic, meaning the foreigner's language sounded like so much "bar bar bar" to the Greek. Paul's point was that for communicating, the tongues-speaker who did not have an interpreter was no better than an incomprehensible barbarian. Even though his speech had meaning to the speaker, it had none to the hearers.

I enjoy watching and listening to an opera occasionally. I like to listen to the music for its own beauty even if I cannot understand the words. However, when the foreign words being sung are translated into English with captions above the stage or on the screen, I enjoy it even more. I also profit from learning from the story, which I cannot do if all I take away from the performance is the memory of beautiful sounds.

14:12 - In view of this the Corinthians who were zealous for spiritual gifts would be better off pursuing the gifts that would enable them to build up the church. They should value these rather than the gifts that gave them some personal satisfaction when they exercised them but did not edify others. The Corinthians were zealots when it came to spirits (Gr. *pneumaton*). The translators interpreted this word as synonymous with *pneumatikon* (spiritual gifts, v. 1), but it is different. Probably Paul meant that they were zealous over a particular manifestation of the Spirit, what they considered the mark of a "spiritual" Christian, namely, the gift of tongues (cf. vv. 14-15, 32).

> "Utterances that are not understood, even if they come from the Spirit, are of no benefit, that is, edification, to the hearer. Thus, since they have such zeal for the manifestation of the Spirit, they should direct that zeal in corporate worship away from being 'foreigners' to one another toward the edification of one another in Christ." (347)

Application in view of believers 14:13-19

Paul continued his argument by clarifying the effect that unintelligible speech has on believers gathered for worship.

14:13 - The Corinthian who already had the gift of tongues should ask the Lord for the ability to interpret his or her utterances so the whole church could benefit from them (cf. v. 5). Note that Paul never said they should abandon this gift, but their practice of it needed correcting.

14:14 - Public prayer is in view here, as it is in this whole chapter (v. 16), but some may have been praying in tongues privately as well. While praying in a tongue might give the person doing so a certain sense of exultation in his spirit, his mind would not benefit. He would not know what he was saying. The "spirit" (Gr. *pneuma*) seems to refer to that part of the person that exercises this spiritual gift. It is separate from the mind obviously (cf. v. 4). The person's spirit prays as the Holy Spirit gives him or her utterance.

14:15 - Paul advocated praising and praying to God with both the spirit (emotions) and the mind (understanding). (348) One reason tongues is an inferior gift is that in it the reason has no control.

Sometimes modern Christians who believe they have the gift of tongues wonder if they should speak in tongues in private even though they do not know what they are saying. Some of them claim that doing so edifies them (v. 4). Let us assume they are speaking some language that they have not studied, which is what the tongues-speakers in the early church were speaking. This, by the way, eliminates most modern tongues-speakers since most modern tongues-speakers simply repeat gibberish. (349) Paul did not discourage speaking unknown languages in private. Nonetheless the relative value and profitability of such an experience are so minimal that its practice seems almost foolish in view of the more edifying options that are open to Christians. Perhaps the current preoccupation with feeling good, in contrast to having to work hard with one's mind to edify the church, is what makes this practice so attractive to many today.

> "It is, of course, impossible for anyone to prove experimentally that speaking in tongues cannot occur today. It may be demonstrated, however, that speaking in tongues is not essential to God's purpose now, and that there are good reasons to believe that most if not all the phenomena which are advanced as proof of modern speaking in tongues is either psychological or demonic activity." (350)

14:16-17 - Paul used the word "bless" for pray here. When we praise God in prayer we say a benediction on Him, a word of blessing. Those believers (Gr. *idiotes*) who do not understand what the person praying in tongues is saying are unable to add their affirmation at the end of the prayer. "Amen" means "so be it." Whenever we lead in public prayer we should do it so the other people praying can join us and affirm our words. It is clear in verse 16 that Paul was speaking about a public worship situation. Giving thanks in public worship is important even if no one else joins in, but it is even more important that other believers can join in.

14:18-19 - Corinthian tongues-enthusiasts could not reject Paul's instruction because he did not have the gift himself and so failed to appreciate its value. He believed in the validity of the gift but did not value it highly. (351) He almost deprecated it. Edifying instruction was 10,000 times more important than personal private exultation for the building up of the church gathered for worship. The edification of the body is, of course, God's great purpose for Christians today (Matt 16:18).

Paul affirmed the gift that the Corinthians apparently regarded as the sign of genuine spirituality, but he did so by correcting their thinking about what was really important in their meetings. Worship should never be selfish, but it should always be intelligible. (352)

Application in view of unbelievers 14:20-25

Uninterpreted tongues did not benefit visiting unbelievers any more than they edified the believers in church meetings. Prophecy, on the other hand, benefited both groups.

14:20 - Thinking that tongues-speaking demonstrates spirituality evidences immaturity.

> "Children prefer what glitters and makes a show to what is much more valuable; and it was childish to prefer ecstatic utterance to other and far more useful gifts." (353)

"Some people have the idea that speaking in a tongue is an evidence of spiritual maturity, but Paul taught that it is possible to exercise the gift in an unspiritual and immature manner." (354)

There is a sense in which it is good for Christians to be childlike, namely, in our innocence regarding evil. Still in understanding, we need to be mature (cf. 3:1-2). The Corinthians were not innocent in their behavior any more than they were mature in their thinking.

14:21 - The Law refers to the Old Testament here since the passage Paul cited is Isaiah 28:11-12. The context of this passage is the Israelites' refusal to accept Isaiah's warnings concerning the coming Assyrian invasion. God said because they refused to listen to the prophet's words He would "teach" them by using their foreign-speaking invading enemy. Nevertheless even then, God said, they would not repent. Isaiah preached repentance to the Israelites in their own language, but they did not repent. Then God brought the invading Assyrians into Israel. Still His people did not repent even though God "spoke" to them of their need to repent by allowing them to hear the foreign language of this enemy.

14:22 - The "then" in this verse anticipates what is to come rather than drawing a conclusion from what has preceded.

Tongues-speaking in the church signified to visiting unbelievers that the Christians were mad (v. 23). (355) Prophecy signified to the believers that God was present and speaking.

14:23 - Paul painted a picture of the Corinthian church assembled and engaged in a frenzy of unintelligible tongues-speaking. Two types of individuals walk in. One is a believer untaught in the matter of spiritual gifts and the other is an unbeliever. To both of them the worshippers appear to be insane rather than soberly engaged in worship and instruction. The church meeting would resemble the meetings of a mystery cult in which such mania was common.

> "It was strange that what the Corinthians specially prided themselves on was a gift which, if exercised in public, would excite the derision of unbelievers." (356)

14:24-25 - If, on the other hand, the church was practicing prophesying and was receiving instruction, both visitors would gain a positive impression from the conduct of the believers. More importantly, what the prophets said would also convict them (cf. 2:14-15). Paul's description of their response came from Isaiah 45:14 (cf. Zech. 8:23) and contrasts with the unresponsiveness of the Israelites to messages God sent them in foreign languages. Prophecy would result in the repentance of visiting unbelievers, but tongues-speaking would not. These verses summarize the effects of good Christian preaching on unbelievers.

> "The gift of prophesying, however successful, is no glory to the possessor of it. It is the Spirit of God, not the preacher's own power, that works the wonderful effect." (357)

Paul did not mean that every individual in the church would either speak in tongues or prophesy (cf. v. 23). He meant that if one of those gifts dominated to the exclusion of the other the stated results would normally follow.

"The Corinthians tend to shut their ears to prophecy because they gain more satisfaction from listening to tongues than from hearing their faults exposed and their duties pointed out in plain rational language." (358)

Paul permitted only intelligible utterances when the church gathered for worship because they edify believers and bring the lost to conviction of their need for salvation.

5. The need for order 14:26-40

The Corinthians' public worship practices not only failed to be edifying and convicting, but they also involved disorderly conduct. Paul proceeded to deal with this additional need to help his readers value these qualities over the pseudo spirituality that they associated with glossolalia.

The ordering of these gifts 14:26-33

The apostle now began to regulate the use of tongues with interpretation, and he urged the use of discernment with prophecy.

> "St Paul has here completed his treatment (xii.—xiv.) of *pneumatika*. He now gives detailed directions as to their use." (359)

14:26 - The apostle did not want any one gift to dominate the meetings of this richly gifted church. Again his list of utterance gifts was limited and selective. Many Christians could make a variety of contributions to the general spiritual welfare of the congregation. He permitted the use of tongues but not their exclusive use and only if someone provided an interpretation (v. 27).

> "That many in Corinth exercised their gifts in the interests of self-development and even of self-display can hardly be doubted; this was contrary to the law of love which regulates all Christian behaviour." (360)

14:27-28 - Paul laid down three guidelines for the use of tongues in public worship. First, the believers should permit only two or at the most three interpreted tongues messages. This is in harmony with the inferior contribution that tongues make compared with prophecy. Second, the speakers should give them consecutively rather than concurrently to minimize confusion. The Spirit does not overpower the speaker but is subject to the speaker, and the Spirit leads speakers to contribute in appropriate times and ways. The Spirit's leading of the Old Testament prophets to speak at appropriate times and settings illustrates this. Third, the Christians should not allow tongues without interpretation in the church services, though Paul did permit private tongues-speaking (vv. 2, 4, 27). However remember that tongues were languages, and Paul valued private tongues-speaking quite low (vv. 2, 10, 11, 13, 14, et al.).

14:29 - Likewise the prophets should minister in an orderly fashion and limit themselves to two or three messages at a service. The others in the congregation (not just other prophets) should pay attention to what they said. The Greek word *diakrino* means "pass judgment"" (NASB) or "weigh carefully" (NIV). In 12:10 it reads "distinguish." Here it probably means to evaluate carefully and, if need be, to reject if the ministry was not in harmony with Scripture.

> "The apostle does *not* instruct the churches to sort out the true and false *elements in any particular prophecy*. Rather, he instructs them to sort out the true and false *prophecies among the many they would hear*." (361)

14:30-31 - Here we seem to have an example of two of the different kinds of prophesying that took place in the early church conflicting with each other. What Paul seems to have envisioned was one person— men and women could prophesy in this sense (11:4-5)—sharing a word from the Lord. This type of prophesying was open to almost anyone in the church. While this person was speaking, another prophet received a revelation from the Lord. This appears to be a more direct revelation than just the desire to address the congregation that had moved the first speaker to minister. In such a case the first speaker was to give preference to the person making the new revelation. Presumable the first speaker would finish what he was saying later.

> "There was obviously a flexibility about the order of service in the early Church which is now totally lacking. . . . Everything was informal enough to allow any man who felt that he had a message to give to give it.

14:32-33 - Prophets were to control themselves when speaking, even when giving new revelation (cf. vv. 27-28). The nature of this gift was that it did not sweep the prophet into a mindless frenzy. Pagans who received demonic revelations frequently lost control of themselves. Inability to control oneself was no evidence that the prophet spoke from God. On the contrary, it indicated that he was not submitting to God's control because God produces peace, not confusion.

> "The theological point is crucial: the character of one's deity is reflected in the character of one's worship. The Corinthians must therefore cease worship that reflects the pagan deities more than the God whom they have come to know through the Lord Jesus Christ (cf. 12:2-3). God is neither characterized by disorder nor the cause of it in the assembly." (362)

Again the apostle reminded his readers that what he was commanding was standard policy in the other churches (cf. 1:2; 4:17; 7:17; 11:16; 14:36). This reminds us again that this church had some serious underlying problems.

Confusion and disorder in church services are not in keeping with the character of God and so dishonor Him.

The ordering of the women 14:34-35

Paul had formerly acknowledged that women could share a word from the Lord in the church meetings (11:4-16). Now he clarified one point about their participation in this context of prophesying.

14:34 - The word translated "silent" (Gr. *sige*) means just that, namely, to keep silent or to hold one's peace. However in 11:5 Paul spoke as though women prophesying in the church was a common and acceptable practice. I think the best explanation of this apparent contradiction comes out of the context, as is usually true. Paul had just permitted others in the congregation to evaluate the comments that a prophet made (v. 29). Now he qualified this by saying the women should not to do so vocally in the church meetings as the men could. The teaching of the Law on this subject appears to be a reference to woman's subordination to the authoritative man in her family (Gen 3:16). The "Law" then would refer to the Old Testament, as in verse 21.

14:35 - Rather than calling out a question in the middle of some male or female prophet's message, a woman was to wait and ask her husband about it at home after the service. Presumably unmarried women would ask their fathers or some other man in the church after the service. Men could raise questions or make comments, but too much of this could ruin the order of the service and the edifying value of the message. Consequently Paul asked the women, evidently because of their natural position of subordination, to refrain. It is improper for a woman to speak in church meetings in the situation Paul addressed in the context. That situation is the questioning and perhaps challenging of what a prophet said who was sharing something he or she believed God had given him or her to pass on to the church. (363)

There have been many other explanations of this apparent contradiction. Richard Lenski assumed that all of what Paul said in 14:26-32 applies only to men and that he added verses 33-36 as an appendix to deal with women's participation. (364) However this does not harmonize with 11:4-5. William Barclay believed at this point Paul was not able to rise above the spirit of his age that said women should not participate in intellectual activities on a par with men. (365) This view fails to appreciate the implications of Paul's inspiration by the Spirit as he wrote as well as his high regard for women that he expressed elsewhere in his writings. G. Campbell Morgan seems to have regarded Paul's prohibition as necessary in view of conditions unique in Corinth. (366) C. K. Barrett believed Paul did not write verses 34-35. He presumed some other person added them to the text later when Christians thought good order was more important than the freedom of the Spirit. (367) Gordon Fee also argued that these verses are inauthentic. (368) Harry Ironside believed the occasions at which women could speak were different from the official meetings of the church at which they were to be silent. (369) David Lowery wrote that Paul wanted the married women whose husbands were present in the meeting to be silent, but that other women could speak if properly covered. (370) S. Lewis Johnson, Jr., seems to have felt women could never speak in the church meetings except when they prayed or prophesied. (371) H. Wayne House concluded women could not speak if others considered what they said was authoritative. (372) Anne Blampied said Paul told the women to keep silent because they were violating the principle of order in the church, not because they were women. (373)

The most common view is that Paul forbade some form of inappropriate speech, not all speech. (374) The second most popular interpretation is that Paul forbade some form of "inspired" speech other than prophecy, perhaps contradicting the prophets or speaking in tongues.

> "Paul's long response to the Corinthians' enthusiasm for tongues is now finished. The basic issue is over what it means to be *pneumatikos* ('spiritual'); and on this issue Paul

and they are deeply divided. They think it has to do with speaking in tongues, the language(s) of the angels, the sure evidence that they are already living in the pneumatic existence of the future. For this reason they have great zeal for this gift (cf. v. 12), including an insistence on its practice in the gathered assembly. Apparently in their letter they have not only defended this practice, but by the same criterion have called Paul into question for his lack of 'spirituality.' Hence the undercurrent of apologetic for his own speaking in tongues in vv. 6, 15, and 18.

"Paul's response to all this has been twofold. First, they are to broaden their perspective to recognize that being Spirit people by its very nature means a great variety of gifts and ministries in the church (chap. 12). Second, the whole point of the gathered people of God is edification, the true expression of love for the saints. Whatever they do in the assembly must be both intelligible and orderly so that the whole community may be edified; thus it must reflect the character of God, which is how it is (or is to be) in all the churches of the saints (v. 33)." (375)

Concluding confrontation 14:36-40

Paul concluded his answer to the Corinthians' question concerning spiritual gifts (chs. 12—14) and his teaching on tongues (ch. 14) with a strong call to cooperation. He zeroed in on their individualism (v. 36; cf. v. 33) and confronted them on the issue of who indeed was spiritual (v. 37). As a prophet of old he warned anyone who disagreed with his instructions (v. 38) and finally summarized his argument (vv. 39-40; cf. 4:18-21).

14:36 - In this verse Paul reminded the Corinthians that they did not set the standard for how the church meetings should proceed. Their arrogance evidently drew this warning. The Corinthian church was not the mother church nor was it the only church to which the gospel had come (cf. 11:16; 14:33b). Therefore the Corinthian readers should submit to the apostle's direction (cf. 9:1-23).

14:37 - Anyone could easily validate a Corinthian's claim to being a prophet or spiritual. He could do so by seeing if he or she acknowledged that what Paul had written was authoritative because he was an apostle of the Lord. Submission to apostolic authority was the test, not speaking in tongues. Submissiveness to the apostles and their teaching was an expression of submission to the Lord Himself (cf. 7:10, 25). It still is.

14:38 - The Corinthians should not recognize as a prophet or as a person under the control of the Holy Spirit anyone who refused to acknowledge the apostle's authority. Failure to recognize the Lord as the source of Paul's teaching would lead to that person's failure to be recognized (i.e., acknowledged with approval) by the Lord (cf. 8:2-3)

14:39 - "Therefore" signals a summation of the entire argument on spiritual gifts. "My brethren" sounds a loving note at the end of this very stern discussion (cf. 1:10). "Desire earnestly to prophesy" repeats the imperative with which Paul began (v. 1). "Do not forbid to speak in tongues" concedes the legitimacy of their favorite gift. Paul heartily encouraged the exercise of the gift of prophecy, but he only permitted the gift of speaking in tongues with certain qualifiers.

As time passed, God no longer gave prophets revelations concerning the future. The apostle John was evidently the last person to function as a prophet in this sense (cf. Rev 22:18). They also no longer received new revelation from the Lord. We can see this passing away even during the history of the church that Luke recorded in Acts. Much of the revelation contained in the books of the New Testament was of this type. In this sense the gift of prophecy was foundational to the establishment of the church and has ceased (Eph 2:20). Nevertheless people continued to speak forth messages from the Lord, the basic meaning of the Greek word *propheteuo* (to prophesy). In the more general sense this gift is still with us today (cf. v. 3).

Paul said his readers were not to forbid speaking in tongues. He meant they were not to do so provided they followed the rules he had just explained for the exercise of the gift. Certainly if someone has the New Testament gift of tongues, he or she should observe these rules today as well. However, many Christians seriously doubt that anyone has this gift today. Christians involved in the charismatic movement believe the gift does exist today. Nevertheless the differences between tongues-speaking as practiced today and what took place in first century churches has led most believers to conclude that these are very different experiences.

14:40 - The foundational principles that should underlie what takes place in church meetings are these. Christians should do everything in a decent and orderly manner, everything should be edifying (v. 26), and a spirit of peace should prevail (v. 33).

This chapter on speaking in tongues is extremely relevant because of current interest in the charismatic gifts of the Spirit. If believers followed the teaching in this chapter alone, even in charismatic churches, there would be far less confusion in the church over this subject.

> "In these three chapters (xii.-xiv.) the Apostle has been contending with the danger of *spiritual anarchy*, which would be the result if every Christian who believed that he had a charisma were allowed to exercise it without consideration for others." (376)

Bibliography

279. Fee, "Toward a . . .," p. 45.

280. Idem, *The First* . . ., pp. 572-73.

281. For defense of the view that spiritual gifts are ministries rather than abilities, see Kenneth Berding, "Confusing Word and Concept in 'Spiritual Gifts': Have We Forgotten James Barr's Exhortations?" *Journal of the Evangelical Theological Society* 43:1 (March 200):37-51.

282. Paul used *pneumatika* when he wanted to emphasize the Spirit, and he used charismata when he wanted to stress the gift.

283. In 2:15 Paul described all Christians as "spiritual" (Gr. *pneumatikos*, having the Spirit) in contrast to "natural" (i.e., unsaved). However, he proceeded immediately to clarify that it is not only *possession of* the Spirit but also *control by* the Spirit that marks one as truly spiritual (3:3).

284. H. Wayne House, "Tongues and the Mystery Religions of Corinth," *Bibliotheca Sacra* 140:558 (April-June 1983):147-48.

285. Bruce, *1 and 2 Corinthians*, p. 117.

286. By "inspired" utterance I mean any utterance that the speaker claimed came from God, not necessarily a truly inspired new revelation from God.

287. Barrett, p. 279. Cf. Deut. 13:2-6; 18:21-22.

290. Paul's point was not that each believer has a gift, though that is true (cf. 1 Pet. 4:10). His point was that the Spirit manifests Himself in a great variety of ways.

291. Morris, p. 170.

292. Barrett, pp. 284-85.

293. For a discussion of the temporary nature of some of the gifts, namely, that they were in use in the early church but not thereafter, see Thomas R. Edgar, "The Cessation of the Sign Gifts," *Bibliotheca Sacra* 145:580 (October-December 1988):371-86; and John F. Walvoord, "Contemporary Issues in the Doctrine of the Holy Spirit. Part IV: Spiritual Gifts Today," *Bibliotheca Sacra* 130:520 (October-December 1973):315-28. This article was reprinted under the title "The Holy Spirit and Spiritual Gifts" in *Bibliotheca Sacra* 143:570 (April-June 1986):109-21. See also Vern S. Poythress, "Modern Spiritual

Gifts as Analogous to Apostolic Gifts: Affirming Extraordinary Works of the Spirit within Cessationist Theology," *Journal of the Evangelical Theological Society* 39:1 (March 1996):71-101.

294. Luke's Gospel, in particular, presents Jesus as teaching and then validating His teaching by doing miracles. Acts shows the apostles doing the same thing.

295. The last of the New Testament books that God inspired was probably Revelation, which dates from about A.D. 95.

296. Fee, *The First . . .*, p. 595.

298. Wiersbe, 1:607.

299. Barrett, p. 289.

300. Robertson and Plummer, p. 273.

301. Barclay, *The Letters . . .*, p. 127.

302. Fee, *The First . . .*, pp. 613-14.

303. Barclay, *The Letters . . .*, p. 126.

304. Ibid., p. 129.

305. Robertson and Plummer, p. 281, n. Cf. *A Dictionary of the Bible*, "Lord's Day," 3:141, by N. J. D. White.

306. Wiersbe, 1:609.

307. See Barclay, *The Letters . . .*, p. 120.

308. See John E. Johnson, "The Old Testament Offices as Paradigm for Pastoral Identity," *Bibliotheca Sacra* 152:606 (April-June 1995):182-200.

309. Thomas A. Jackson, "Concerning Spiritual Gifts: A Study of I Corinthians 12," *Faith and Mission* 7:1 (Fall 1989):68.

310. Fee, *The First . . .*, p. 625.

311. Robertson and Plummer, pp. 269-70.

312. Wiersbe, 1:607.

313. Bruce, *1 and 2 Corinthians*, p. 124.

314. Fee, *The First . . .*, p. 630.

315. Robertson and Plummer, p. 288.

316. Wiersbe, 1:610.

317. To act lovingly, of course, means to seek actively the benefit of someone else.

318. Bruce, *1 and 2 Corinthians*, p. 125; Barclay, *The Letters . . .*, p. 131; Robertson and Plummer, p. 289.

319. Barrett, p. 303.

320. Barclay, *The Letters . . .*, p. 136.

321. Wiersbe, 1:611.

322. Robertson and Plummer, p. 294.

323. Fee, *The First . . .*, p. 639.

324. Barclay, *The Letters . . .*, p. 137.

325. Bruce, *1 and 2 Corinthians*, p. 127.

326. Robertson and Plummer, p. 295.

327. A. T. Robertson, *Word Pictures in the New Testament*, 4:179.

328. See Stanley D. Toussaint, "First Corinthians Thirteen and The Tongues Question," *Bibliotheca Sacra* 120:480 (October-December 1963):311-16.

329. Philip Schaff, *History of the Christian Church*, 1:236-37. See also George W. Dollar, "Church History and the Tongues Movement," *Bibliotheca Sacra* 120:480 (October-December 1963):316-21. See also the series of four articles by F. David Farnell, "Is the Gift of Prophecy for Today?" *Bibliotheca Sacra* 149:595 (July-September 1992):277-303; 596 (October-December 1992):387-410; 150:597 (January-March 1993):62-88; and 598 (April-June 1993):171-202.

330. Barrett, p. 306.

331. Fee, *The First . . .*, p. 645; Thomas R. Edgar, *Miraculous Gifts: Are They for Today?* pp. 333-34.

332. Toussaint, "First Corinthians . . .," pp. 312-14.

333. Charles C. Ryrie, *The Ryrie Study Bible*, p. 1744; Robertson and Plummer, p. 297.

334. Robert L. Thomas, *Understanding Spiritual Gifts: An exegetical study of 1 Corinthians 12-14*, pp. 10613; idem, "'Tongues . . . Will Cease,'" *Journal of the Evangelical Theological Society* 17:2 (Spring 1974):81-89; and idem, "1 Cor 13:11 Revisited: an Exegetical Update," *Master's Seminary Journal* 4:2 (Fall 1993):187-201. See also Farnell, 150:598:191-93.

335. Merrill F. Unger, *New Testament Teaching on Tongues*, p. 95; Myron J. Houghton, "A Reexamination of 1 Corinthians 13:8-13," *Bibliotheca Sacra* 153:611 (July-September 1996):344-56.

336. John F. MacArthur Jr., *Charismatic Chaos*, p. 231.

337. Fee, *The First . . .*, pp. 647-48. Cf. Robertson and Plummer, p. 298.

338. Michael Fishbane believed a midrashic interpretation of Numbers 12:8 and Ezekiel 43:3 influenced Paul's writing of this verse. See "Through the Looking Glass: Reflections on Ezek 43:3, Num 12:8 and 1 Cor 13:8," *Hebrew Annual Review* 10 (1986):63-74.

339. I do not mean that we will be omniscient; we will not be. We will be fully aware.

340. Barrett, p. 311.

341. Wiersbe, 1:612.

342. Fee, *The First . . .*, p. 655

343. E.g., Robertson and Plummer, pp. 301, 306.

344. In 13:1 Paul wrote "of the tongues of men and of angels," evidently two types of languages. See also S. Lewis Johnson Jr., "The Gift of Tongues and the Book of Acts," *Bibliotheca Sacra* 120:480 (October-December 1963):310-11.

345. Fee, *The First . . .*, p. 657.

346. Remember that prophets did not just foretell the future or announce new special revelation from God. They also delivered statements or messages in praise of God, or a word of instruction, refutation, reproof, admonition, or comfort for others. See my note on 11:4.

347. Ibid., p. 666.

348. The spirit and the mind are both receptors as well as expressers of impressions. Music without words makes a real impression on us even though that impression is not intellectual.

349. A pastor friend of mine who used to "speak in tongues" said he had taught many Christians to "speak in tongues" and could teach anyone to do so. According to him it just requires learning a few phrases, getting oneself into the proper emotional state, and releasing one's inhibitions.

350. John F. Walvoord, *The Holy Spirit*, pp. 185-86. Most of the books on the modern tongues movement listed in the bibliography of these notes deal with this issue in more detail.

351. See Chadwick, p. 269.

352. Barclay, *The Letters . . .*, p. 145.

353. Robertson and Plummer, p. 315.

354. Wiersbe, 1:614.

355. See Zane C. Hodges, "The Purpose of Tongues," *Bibliotheca Sacra* 120:479 (July-September 1963):226-33; J. Lanier Burns, "A Reemphasis on the Purpose of Tongues," *Bibliotheca Sacra* 132:527 (July-September 1975):242-49; and Harold W. Hoehner, "The Purpose of Tongues in 1 Corinthians 14:2025," in *Walvoord: A Tribute*, pp. 53-66.

356. Robertson and Plummer, p. 317.

357. Ibid., p. 318.

358. Barrett, p. 324.

359. Robertson and Plummer, p. 319.

360. Barrett, p. 327.

361. R. Fowler White, "Does God Speak Today Apart from the Bible?" in *The Coming Evangelical Crisis*, p. 84. This essay is a rebuttal of the teaching of Jack Deere, *Surprised by the Power of the Spirit*, pp. 133-43, 209-15; and Grudem, *The Gift . . .*; idem, *Systematic Theology*, pp. 1049-61, on this subject.

362. Fee, *The First . . .*, p. 697.

363. This is the view of Bruce, *1 and 2 Corinthians*, pp. 136-37; Morris, pp. 201-2; Robertson and Plummer, p. 325; James B. Hurley, *Man and Woman In Biblical Perspective*, pp. 188, 190; and others including myself.

364. Lenski, p. 614.

365. Barclay, *The Letters . . .*, p. 151.

366. Morgan, pp. 180-81.

367. Barrett, pp. 332-33.

368. Fee, *The First . . .*, pp. 699-702.

369. Harry A. Ironside, *Addresses on the First Epistle to the Corinthians*, pp. 454-55. Cf. Wiersbe, 1:616.

370. Lowery, "1 Corinthians," p. 541.

371. S. Lewis Johnson Jr., "1 Corinthians," in *The Wycliffe Bible Commentary*, p. 1255.

372. H. Wayne House, "Caught in the Middle," *Kindred Spirit* 13:2 (Summer 1989):14; idem, "The Speaking of Women and the Prohibition of the Law," *Bibliotheca Sacra* 145:579 (July-September 1988):301-18.

373. Anne B. Blampied, "Paul and Silence for 'The Women' in I Corinthians 14:34-35," *Studia Biblica et Theologica* 18:2 (October 1983):143-65.

374. E.g., Bruce, *1 and 2 Corinthians*, p. 135.

375. Fee, *The First . . .*, p. 709.

376. Robertson and Plummer, p. 328.

Basic Theology
Charles C. Ryrie

Chapter 62: The Spirit Indwelling

As we noted in the preceding chapter in discussing John 14:17, the Spirit does certain new and special things since His "coming" on the Day of Pentecost. At the heart of these distinctive ministries lies the ministry of dwelling in believers, for it is foundational to all His ministries to Christians in this age.

I. THE PEOPLE INDWELT

To express indwelling Paul not only used the preposition en but also the verb *oikeo*, to dwell (Rom. 8:9; 1 Cor. 3:16; though, of course, sometimes he used only the preposition as in 1 Cor. 6:19). He related this ministry of the Spirit to all believers.

A. The Indwelling Spirit Is a Gift From God to All Believers

A number of passages clearly teach that the Spirit is given to all believers rather than selectively to some (John 7:37–39; Acts 11:16–17; Rom. 5:5; 1 Cor. 2:12; 2 Cor. 5:5). One would expect this to be so since a gift is not a reward and no merit is involved in receiving this gift.

B. Not to Possess the Indwelling Spirit Indicates an Unsaved Condition

Not to have the Spirit is the same as not belonging to Christ, Paul declared (Rom. 8:9). Jude also described apostates as those who did not have the Spirit (Jude 19) and who were "natural" (niv). This is the same word used in 1 Corinthians 2:14, another verse that describes an unsaved individual. To be natural is to be unsaved and not to have the Spirit. Therefore having the Spirit characterizes all born again people.

C. Sinning Believers Are Indwelt by the Spirit

The acid test of whether or not the Spirit indwells all believers is whether or not He lives in sinning Christians. Clearly He does. 1 Corinthians 6:19 was written to a very spiritually mixed group, some fine, spiritual believers, but many who were carnal and worldly; yet Paul did not say that only the spiritual group were indwelt by the Spirit. One brother, who in Paul's judgment was a believer (1 Cor. 5:5) was living in gross sin. Others were at legal swords' points with each other (chap. 6). Still Paul said that the Spirit was "in" all of them (1 Cor. 6:19). Not only did he make no exceptions to his statement, but he made the indwelling of the Spirit the ground for his exhortation to holy living. Clearly then, all believers, but only believers, have the Spirit living in them.

II. THE PERMANENCE OF INDWELLING

Some who agree that the Spirit is given to all believers feel that He may withdraw from those who commit certain sins. Thus they acknowledge His indwelling but deny its permanence.

Whatever sins could cause His departure would have to be more grievous than the fornication of chapter 5 or the legal disputes of chapter 6, for Paul did not exclude these believers from his statement that the Spirit dwelt in them (v. 19).

Furthermore, if the Spirit leaves sinning Christians, then they are no longer Christians according to Romans 8:9. The Spirit cannot leave a believer without throwing that believer back into a lost, unsaved condition. Disindwelling has to mean loss of salvation, and loss of salvation must include disindwelling. The security of the believer and the permanent indwelling of the Spirit are inseparable doctrines.

But we also have the positive promise of the Savior that He would pray to the Father who would give another Helper in order "that He may be with you forever" (John 14:16). To be sure, sin affects the effectiveness of the Spirit in the believer's life, but it does not remove His presence from believers.

III. SOME PROBLEMS CONCERNING THE INDWELLING OF THE SPIRIT

A. Is Not Obedience a Condition for Indwelling?

Peter spoke of the Holy Spirit "whom God has given to those who obey Him" (Acts 5:32). Does this mean that obedience is a condition for the giving of the Spirit and thus only certain (i.e., obedient) believers have the Spirit? Yes, if obedience is understood in the way Peter used it. He was addressing the unbelieving Sanhedrin and concluded by pressing the matter of their obedience. Obedience to what? Certainly the obedience of the Sanhedrin had nothing to do with obedience to matters in the Christian life, for they were not Christians. The obedience Peter called them to was to obey (believe) the truth that Jesus was their Messiah. Shortly after, some of the priests in Jerusalem did believe and Luke said "a great many of the priests were becoming obedient to the faith" (Acts 6:7).

Two other references use obedience as a synonym for receiving Christ's salvation. Paul described the purpose of his mission as "for obedience to the faith among all nations for his name" (Rom. 1:5). The writer to the Hebrews said that Christ became the Source of eternal salvation to all who obey Him (Heb. 5:9). Therefore, if obedience is understood correctly (as obeying the Gospel), it is a condition for receiving the gift of the Spirit.

B. Are There Not Illustrations of the Temporariness of Indwelling?

Yes, there are, but they are all before the Day of Pentecost (1 Sam. 16:14; perhaps Ps. 51:11; Luke 11:13; John 20:22). But there are no such examples after the coming of the Spirit on the Day of Pentecost. Since those before Pentecost relate to a different economy of the Spirit, they cannot be used to prove that the same thing happens after Pentecost when the Holy Spirit came to indwell believers permanently.

C. Does Not the Delay in Giving the Spirit to the Samaritans Show That It Is Subsequent to Salvation and Thus Selective?

That there was a delay in giving the Spirit to the Samaritans is clear; the question is, Why? Some say it shows that indwelling comes subsequent to salvation and not necessarily to all believers. Others equate this giving of the Spirit with the filling of the Spirit. Still others say the procedure was different in this instance because the Samaritans were the first non-Jewish group to be taken into the church. The latter is partly true: Samaritans were part Jewish and part Gentile. The purely Gentile pattern for the giving of the Spirit is found in Acts 10:44, where the Spirit was given to the Gentiles in Cornelius's house at the moment they believed.

The best explanation of this delay in the case of the Samaritans lies in the schismatic nature of Samaritan religion. Their worship rivaled Jewish worship in Jerusalem; therefore, God needed to prove to them that their new Christian faith was not also to rival the Christian church in Jerusalem. The best way to show beyond doubt that the Samaritan Christians belonged to the same group as the Jerusalem Christians (and vice versa, to show the Jerusalem leaders that Samaritans were genuinely saved) was to delay the giving of the Spirit until Peter and John came from Jerusalem to Samaria. This delay and God's use of Peter and John in conveying the gift of the Spirit saved the early church from having two rival mother churches.

D. Does Not Acts 19:1–6 Show That Indwelling Is Subsequent to Salvation?

To answer yes to this question requires understanding that the twelve disciples of John the Baptist were already Christian believers before they met Paul at Ephesus. But this is not the correct understanding. They did not become believers in Jesus by believing John's message and receiving his baptism; they became Christian believers only after Paul explained to them the difference between John and Jesus. In fact, it does not appear from the text that they even understood much about John's message. But when they understood and believed what Paul explained to them, they immediately received the Spirit through Paul's laying on of hands. There was no delay.

The normal Gentile pattern for receiving the Spirit was established in the house of Cornelius, where the Spirit was given when the people believed, which was while Peter was preaching and before they were baptized in water (Acts 10:44; Acts 10:47).

E. What Is the Relation of Indwelling to Anointing?

Anointing in the Old Testament, a very solemn matter, made a person or thing holy and sacrosanct (Exod. 40:9–15). It was associated with the Holy Spirit and with equipping for service (1 Sam. 10:1, 9; Zech. 4:1–14). In the New Testament Christ was anointed (Luke 4:18; Acts 4:27; 10:38; Heb. 1:9) and all believers are anointed (2 Cor. 1:21; 1 John 2:20, 27). As far as the anointing of believers is concerned, these passages teach that it is not something repeated but something that abides. Although Old Testament anointing was related more to service (as also was Christ's anointing), New Testament believers' anointing concerns a relationship that enables us to understand truth. Old Testament anointing seems closer to the idea of the filling of the Spirit, whereas believers' anointing is akin to the indwelling of the Spirit. Not every believer experienced it in the Old Testament; all do today. It may have been repeated in the Old Testament; it abides on all believers today.

The New Testament clearly teaches that all believers are permanently indwelt. Let not our familiarity with this blunt the significance of it. This universal and permanent ministry to believers stands in sharp contrast with the indwelling ministry of the Spirit in the Old Testament (John 14:17). It means that whether or not we feel it, God the Holy Spirit lives within our beings constantly. This ought to give us (a) a sense of security in our relationship with God, (b) a motivation to practice that presence of God, and (c) a sensitivity to sins against God.

Lesson 11 Self Check

QUESTION 1

Paul diverts to discuss the unrelated topic of love in the middle of his instruction about spiritual gifts. *True or False?*

QUESTION 2

"Tongues" in 1 Corinthians 12-14 can be translated as "languages." *True or False?*

QUESTION 3

In Paul's use of the body metaphor in 1 Corinthians 12, Christ is the head. *True or False?*

QUESTION 4

What does Paul use the body metaphor to illustrate?

    A. Unity amidst diversity

    B. The greater importance of the eye compared to other members of the body

    C. The fact that the body can function even if certain members are missing

    D. The principle of grafting members into the body

QUESTION 5

Spiritual gifts will pass away. *True or False?*

QUESTION 6

Which one of the following adjectives does not describe the kind of worship service that Paul encourages?

    A. Participatory

    B. Orderly

    C. Displaying spiritual gifts

    D. Following a liturgy

QUESTION 7

True prophets in the New Testament era would recognize Paul's apostolic authority. *True or False?*

QUESTION 8

According to which principle are uninterpreted tongues prohibited in the worship service?

    A. Silence for women

    B. Intelligibility

    C. Respect for the weaker brother

    D. Modesty

QUESTION 9

To promote evangelism, Paul advocates speaking in tongues during the worship service. *True or False?*

QUESTION 10

Paul instructed that prophecies should be evaluated. *True or False?*

Lesson 11 Answers to Questions

QUESTION 1: False

QUESTION 2

    A. He is led by the Holy Spirit.

    B. He is a Christian.

    C. He is spiritual.

QUESTION 3: *Your answer*

QUESTION 4

    B. To benefit the body of Christ

QUESTION 5: Baptized

QUESTION 6

    B. There is diversity in the body.

    C. The different parts of the body are all important.

    D. Some members of the body may not feel important.

    E. The body forms a unity.

QUESTION 7: *Your answer*

QUESTION 8: *Your answer*

QUESTION 9

Order	Gift
First	Apostles
Second	Prophets
Third	Teachers
Then	All other gifts

QUESTION 10: False

QUESTION 11: *Your answer should be similar to the following:*

He refers to the way of love, which is the proper context for using the spiritual gifts.

QUESTION 12

    C. Without love, the exercise of spiritual gifts is valueless.

QUESTION 13: *Your answer*

QUESTION 14

Corinthian church's contrasting behavior	Characteristic of love
"There is still jealousy and dissension among you" (1 Cor 3:3).	Not envious
"Puffed up in favor of the one against the other" (1 Cor 4:6).	Not bragging, not puffed up
"For when it is time to eat, everyone proceeds with his own supper. One is hungry and another becomes drunk" (1 Cor 11:21).	Not rude
"Do not seek your own good, but the good of the other person" (1 Cor 10:24).	Not self-serving
"The fact that you have lawsuits among yourselves demonstrates that you have already been defeated. Why not rather be wronged? Why not rather be cheated?" (1 Cor 6:7).	Not easily angered or resentful, not glad about injustice

QUESTION 15: *Your answer should be similar to the following:*

Yes. Paul hoped that church discipline would bring the sinner to repentance. The church's love for God, the church, and the sinner motivated the discipline. Love promotes relationships characterized by truth and godliness.

QUESTION 16: *Your answer*

QUESTION 17: False

QUESTION 18

    A. The second coming

    B. The completion of the canon of Scripture

    C. Spiritual maturity

QUESTION 19: True

QUESTION 20

    A. There was no need for an interpreter at Pentecost as there was at Corinth.

    C. All believers spoke in tongues at Pentecost, but only some had the gift at Corinth.

    D. Tongues had a positive evangelistic effect at Pentecost, but a negative evangelistic effect at Corinth.

QUESTION 21: False

QUESTION 22: *Your answer*

QUESTION 23: True

QUESTION 24

    D. Tongues are a sign of God's judgment on unbelievers.

QUESTION 25: *Your answer should be similar to the following:*

Love is seen in that every believer can participate and contribute, so no one is ignored. Love rules when the believers respect and listen to each other, make sure that everyone can understand, honor the truth, and yield to each other.

QUESTION 26: *Your answer*

QUESTION 27

    A. He allowed women to pray and prophesy in 1 Corinthians 11:5.

    B. The same Greek word for "silence" (1 Cor 14:34) is also used in 1 Corinthians 14:28 and does not mean absolute silence for the person.

    C. In the context, silence for women may refer to evaluating prophets.

    D. Paul's main point is a wife's submission to male leadership.

QUESTION 27: False

QUESTION 28:

    C. Apostles

Lesson 11 Self Check Answers

QUESTION 1: False
QUESTION 2: True
QUESTION 3: False
QUESTION 4
    A. Unity amidst diversity
QUESTION 5: True
QUESTION 6
    D. Following a liturgy
QUESTION 7: True
QUESTION 8
    B. Intelligibility
QUESTION 9: False
QUESTION 10: True

Lesson 12: Freedom in Doctrine: Resurrection (1 Cor 15:1-58)

Confusion about the resurrection of believers, the rapture, and the second coming came up repeatedly in Paul's writings around this time. Apparently, when Paul first preached the gospel in Greece, either he was not clear enough or not well enough understood about the things related to the second coming. This problem came out at Thessalonica and at Corinth—see 1 Thessalonians 4; 5 and 2 Thessalonians. The Thessalonian epistles were probably written while Paul was in Corinth, so he must have realized the problem and made an effort to clarify the issue at Corinth. How then could the Corinthians have missed out on Paul's teaching about the resurrection of believers? Their error is probably related to the low importance they placed on the physical world. They believed that true spirituality is only a matter of the spirit and not the body. If the final state of people is non-material, then the physical body ultimately does not matter. Paul is resolutely opposed to such a concept. He affirms that those who inherit the kingdom will do so in glorified bodies.

How would we view people today who deny the resurrection of the body? Today we would view such people as unorthodox, even heretical, because of the clear teaching of 1 Corinthians 15. Prior to Paul's writings, denial of the bodily resurrection for believers may have been viewed as deviant, but less serious than outright heresy.

Lesson Outline

Topic 1: Christ's Resurrection (1 Cor 15:1-11)

    Basis of the Gospel (15:1-4)

    Many Witnesses (15:5-11)

Topic 2: Resurrection of Believers (1 Cor 15:12-34)

    Consequences of No Resurrection (15:12-19)

    Consequences of the Resurrection (15:20-28)

    Arguments From Behavior (15:29-34)

Topic 3: Nature of the Resurrection Body (1 Cor 15:35-49)

    Analogies (15:35-41)

    Characteristics (15:42-49)

Topic 4: Victory Over Death (1 Cor 15:50-58)

    Putting on Immortality (15:50-57)

    Application (15:58)

Lesson Objectives

A new group has come to town, claiming to be Christians, so Lotus goes to one of their meetings. She met one of them when he came to the church a couple of Sundays ago. He sat quietly, tried to meet some people, and seemed friendly enough. He said his name was Quan. Nobody had seen him before, and he obviously isn't from this area because of his accent. As he was leaving the service, he told Lotus that there was a really good Christian meeting across town on Thursday nights, and that they studied mysteries in the Bible. Quan invited her to come.

Lotus certainly feels that there are many mysteries in the Bible that she wants to understand, so she thinks she will visit Quan's meeting. When she shows up, she is warmly greeted, and she finds herself in a group of about seven people. Quan is the leader, and there are three others who are his "co-workers," as he introduced them, plus Lotus and two women from a nearby village. The meeting goes pretty normally at first, as they sing several familiar hymns and pray. Then they are all ushered into another room with lots of sumptuous delicacies laid out on a big table. It is a time for talking and eating and getting to know each other. One of Quan's co-workers, a very nice looking young lady, comes around to get each person's name, address and phone number.

When they go back to sit down for the teaching time, that's when Lotus begins to feel uncomfortable. First, that same lady who got everybody's name comes around again to collect everybody's cell phone. Quan explains that he didn't want any interruptions during the teaching time. Then he starts talking about mysteries in the Bible—things that are really hard to understand. He says that one of these mysteries is that believers are right now seated in heaven with Jesus. Already we are heavenly men and women. He says that most believers don't understand this truth, and they go around not claiming their inheritance. There is no reason not to wield all of heaven's power except for lack of faith. If you have enough faith, he said, you will realize that right now you have everything you need in Christ. Since you are already a new person in Christ with all of God's resources, you don't need to worry at all about money, or health, or education, or anything else. You are already in heaven. At the end of his teaching, Quan passed around an offering bag and said everyone should put all their cash in it. After all, you already have all the riches of heaven.

Lotus left the meeting confused and shaken. They did give her cell phone back, and over the next several days she got repeated calls, text messages and visits from Quan and his co-workers. Lotus is so unsure about all of this that she calls Brother Thomas to talk about what Quan said. It sounded so good, but so different from what she had been taught by Brother Thomas and at the church. Brother Thomas says to watch out for groups like that who erroneously interpret the Bible. He directs her to 1 Corinthians 15 and urges her to go to her church leaders, because the whole church needs to be warned about Quan and his group.

By the end of this lesson, you will be able to:

- Understand the legitimacy and importance of Christ's resurrection
- Understand how Christ's resurrection guarantees believers' resurrection
- List aspects of the resurrection body
- Apply your hope of resurrection to your daily walk with Christ

Topic 1: Christ's Resurrection (1 Cor 15:1-11)

The kernel of the gospel is the message about the atoning death and resurrection of Christ. This message was proclaimed by all the apostles and apparently was not in question at Corinth.

Basis of the Gospel (15:1-4)

Assignment

- Read 1 Corinthians 15:1-4.
- Read Constable, "The Resurrection of Believers Ch. 15" (refer to the Articles section at the end of this lesson), through the note on 15:4.

- Read "Basis of the Gospel."

Basis of the Gospel

What is the gospel? Paul has used this term several times already in this letter, but here he defines clearly what he means. It is the message about the person and work of Jesus Christ, by which a person is saved. Paul's gospel message has not changed over time—it is the same as he first proclaimed to them. Paul did not invent the gospel or determine what it meant; it came to him by revelation, so he passed on only what he had received.

What does it mean to believe "in vain" (1 Cor 15:2)? The Greek word *eike* ("in vain") is used only by Paul in the New Testament: Rom 13:4; Gal 3:4 (twice); Gal 4:11; Col 2:18. However, Paul uses synonyms several times in this chapter: 1 Cor 15:10 (*kenos*); 1 Cor 15:14 (*kenos*—used twice); 1 Cor 15:17 (*mataios*); and 1 Cor 15:58 (*kenos*). The main options for interpreting believing "in vain" are:

1. It refers to a type of believing that falls short of saving faith. [Comment: Such a suggestion is better refined by pointing out in what way the believing falls short, as in numbers 2 or 3 below.]

2. It refers to those who believe for a time but do not persevere in faith. [Comment: This suggestion draws support from the immediate context. Paul used the present tense "are being saved," suggesting that their salvation is not completed, and he emphasizes holding firmly to the gospel.]

3. It refers to ineffective, valueless or useless belief. In this case it refers to those who deny the resurrection of the body, since they have believed a lie. [Comment: This suggestion draws support from the broader context, and is supported by further statements in 1 Corinthians 15:14 and 15:17.]

4. Paul uses the phrase ironically, referring to what would be the case if Christ had not been raised. [Comment: Paul is speaking seriously in this passage about the gospel, so this suggestion is far from obvious.]

In the context, the best options are numbers 2 and 3.

It is difficult to pinpoint an Old Testament passage that prophecies that Christ would be raised on the third day. Sometimes scholars point to Hosea 6:2, but that verse is not a clear reference to the resurrection of the Messiah. Jesus referred to the sign of Jonah in Matthew 12:40, "For just as Jonah was three days and three nights in the belly of the great fish, so will the Son of Man be three days and three nights in the heart of the earth." Perhaps this is the best Old Testament reference to His resurrection on the third day.

QUESTION 1

What does Paul say about the gospel in this passage? What does it mean to believe in vain? Record your response in your Life Notebook.

The gospel focuses on Christ—His substitutionary death, burial, and resurrection. Thus the gospel message includes certain non-negotiable content·which it is necessary to believe in order to be saved.

QUESTION 2

Believers in Corinth had never been taught that Jesus was raised from the dead. *True or False?*

QUESTION 3

What are the best possibilities in this context for what "unless you believed in vain" means? *(Select all that apply.)*

    A. Faith that does not persevere

    B. The useless faith of those who deny the resurrection

    C. Tiny faith

    D. Faith without works

Many Witnesses (15:5-11)

Assignment

- Read 1 Corinthians 15:5-11.

- Read Constable "notes on 15:11" (refer to the Articles section at the end of this lesson).

- Read "Many Witnesses."

Many Witnesses

The testimony of many witnesses that Paul lists here is testimony to Jesus' resurrection. The truth of Jesus' resurrection is a fundamental tenet of their faith, and it implies the resurrection of believers, as Paul will go on to show.

Why does Paul say he worked harder than the rest of the apostles? Is he being proud? His purpose is not to magnify himself, but to magnify the grace of God, which was at work through him. As he stated earlier, "so neither the one who plants counts for anything, nor the one who waters, but God who causes the growth." (1 Cor 3:7)

QUESTION 4

Why does Paul say he worked harder than the rest of the apostles? Record your response in your Life Notebook.

The post-resurrection appearances of Jesus to His followers clearly demonstrate that He rose bodily from the dead. All the apostles saw Him and bear witness to the same truth.

QUESTION 5

By listing Jesus' post-resurrection appearances, what does Paul demonstrate? *(Select all that apply.)*

    A. Many witnesses saw Jesus after He was bodily resurrected.

    B. In this aspect, Paul is just as qualified to be an apostle as the Twelve.

    C. Most who saw Jesus after He was resurrected are still alive.

    D. Jesus' post-resurrection appearances stopped with His ascension to heaven.

QUESTION 6

Match the order of Jesus' post-resurrection appearances as listed by Paul in 1 Corinthians 15:5-8.

Appearance to	Order
Cephas	First
The Twelve	Second
Five hundred believers at once	Fifth
James	Third
All the apostles	Sixth
Paul	Fourth

Topic 2: Resurrection of Believers (1 Cor 15:12-34)

Paul attacks the position of those who deny the resurrection by pointing out how illogical it is. People who deny the resurrection of believers actually deny one of the fundamentals of the gospel—the resurrection of Christ. If Christ is still in His grave, then there is no salvation. But since Christ has been raised, the resurrection of believers is guaranteed, and death will finally be eliminated when God reigns supreme. Even some in Corinth show that they believe in the resurrection by their unorthodox practice of being baptized for the dead. Paul can face death daily bolstered by his hope in the resurrection. Departing from orthodox doctrine can only bring disastrous results.

Consequences of No Resurrection (15:12-19)

Assignment

- Read 1 Corinthians 15:12-19.

- Read Constable, "The Certainty of Resurrection 15:12-34" (refer to the Articles section at the end of this lesson), through the note on 15:19.

- Read "Consequences of No Resurrection."

Consequences of No Resurrection

Christians believe in the "intermediate state"—believers' spirits are in God's presence after death, awaiting their glorified bodies. In some churches so little is taught about possessing glorified bodies at the second coming that many believers expect only a spiritual existence in heaven after death. Going to heaven at death is an important truth for believers, but it is not the consummation of a believer's hope. After all, Jesus has His glorified body in heaven, and believers will also possess glorified bodies.

Paul lists eight negative conclusions if there is no resurrection:

1. Christ has not been raised.

2. The gospel is false.

3. Christian faith is useless.

4. The apostles have lied.

5. Believers are not forgiven.

6. Believers who have physically died are lost forever.

7. Christian hope is false.

8. Believers are the most pitiful of all people.

Throughout this discussion of the resurrection, Paul's concern is only with the resurrection of believers. He does not discuss the resurrection of unbelievers.

If there is no resurrection of the dead, as some of the Corinthians are asserting, then Paul draws many logical conclusions that completely overthrow the Christian faith.

QUESTION 7

Which of the following are true if Christ has not been raised from the dead? *(Select all that apply.)*

A. His apostles are false witnesses.

B. The Christian faith is useless.

C. Believers who have died have perished.

D. There is no forgiveness for sins.

QUESTION 8

Paul adapted his teaching about the resurrection of the body to fit in with Greek thought. *True or False?*

QUESTION 9

How does the doctrine of the resurrection of the body affect your faith personally? Day to day, how much of a bearing does it have on your life? Record your thoughts in your Life Notebook.

Consequences of the Resurrection (15:20-28)

Assignment

- Read 1 Corinthians 15:20-28.
- Read Constable, "The Positive Reality—15:20-28" (refer to the Articles section at the end of this lesson).
- Read "Consequences of the Resurrection."

Consequences of the Resurrection

Christ's own resurrection is the prototype for believers' resurrection. Believers' resurrection will occur at the rapture. Later, death itself will be destroyed.

"That God may be all in all" is unusual language. It almost sounds pantheistic, but Paul's meaning in context is dominion. In the eternal state, there is no rival to God's authority—neither Satan, or death, nor sin, nor principality, nor power. God alone is sovereign.

There is an order to the resurrection from the dead, culminating in the supremacy of God. First, Christ was raised; second, believers will be raised at His coming; and third, at the end, Christ will deliver the earthly kingdom over which He has been reigning to the Father.

QUESTION 10

What does "so that God may be all in all" (1 Cor 15:28) mean in the eternal state?

A. Everything is God

B. There is no distinction between good and evil

C. God alone is sovereign

D. There is no material existence

QUESTION 11

What agricultural metaphor did Paul use to explain that the resurrection of believers is guaranteed by Christ's resurrection?

QUESTION 12

Does 1 Corinthians 15:28 teach that the Son is not God? Why?

Arguments From Behavior (15:29-34)

Assignment

- Read 1 Corinthians 15:29-34.
- Read Constable, "Other Arguments for Resurrection—15:29-34" (refer to the Articles section at the end of this lesson).
- Read "Arguments From Behavior."

Arguments From Behavior

Paul's arguments are:

1. The practice of baptism for the dead makes no sense if the dead are not raised.

2. Risking death for one's faith makes no sense if there is no hope of resurrection.

3. False teaching (i.e. denying the resurrection) corrupts good behavior.

4. Some have no knowledge of God, and this is shameful for the whole church. Paul could be referring to pagan outsiders, or even to those in their midst who deny the resurrection.

The practice of baptism for the dead directly relates to doctrine. Paul does not come down hard against this practice; in fact, you cannot tell whether he supports it or not from his statements. Yet, today, most Christians would view such a practice as either fringe, cultish, or heretical.

These arguments link doctrine and practice in the Christian life. Good doctrine does affect behavior; likewise, bad doctrine also affects behavior.

Some of the Corinthians demonstrate by their own baptismal practice that they believe in the bodily resurrection. Paul certainly demonstrates his faith when he daily risks his life for the Lord. Paul warns the Corinthians about the consequences of consorting with evil.

QUESTION 13

From 1 Corinthians 15:20-34, what is Paul's view of the relationship between doctrine and practice?

QUESTION 14

Paul agrees with the adage, "Bad company corrupts good morals" (1 Cor 15:33). How do you apply this principle in your life? How does this principle affect your witnessing for the Lord? Record your thoughts in your Life Notebook.

Topic 3: Nature of the Resurrection Body (1 Cor 15:35-49)

In God's future plan, believers will possess glorified bodies suitable for eternal existence. These new bodies will be in many aspects wonderfully different from what we possess now. We need bodies able to bear "an eternal weight of glory far beyond all comparison" (2 Cor 4:17). Paul gives us a glimpse of what these new bodies will be like, using analogies and comparisons.

Analogies (15:35-41)

Assignment

- Read 1 Corinthians 15:35-41.
- Read Constable, "Analogies From Nature" (refer to the Articles section at the end of this lesson), through the note on 15:41.
- Read "Analogies."

Analogies

Paul uses analogies from plant life, from the animal world, and from astronomy to make a point about the resurrection body. He knows that no one can really grasp the meaning of the resurrection body, for its glory is so different and so much higher than what we experience with our earthly bodies. Thus he uses verbal illustrations to attempt an explanation.

Fundamentally, Paul is arguing that the resurrection body is markedly different from the mortal body.

Using the rhetorical device of arguing against an imaginary questioner, Paul illustrates with examples from nature that there are many different kinds of bodies. God will make our glorified bodies suitable for eternal existence, and they will be quite different from our mortal bodies.

QUESTION 15

What will be true of our glorified bodies according to Paul's teaching?

  A. They will be exactly the same as our earthly bodies.

  B. They will be immaterial.

  C. They will be of a different type than our earthly bodies.

  D. They will no longer be human.

Characteristics (15:42-49)

Assignment

- Read 1 Corinthians 15:42-49.

- Read Constable, "Notes on 15:49" (refer to the Articles section at the end of this lesson).

- Read "Characteristics."

Characteristics

In this section, Paul again picks up on the theme of order. There is a definite sequence to possessing our glorified bodies. First came the mortal (Adam); then the "last Adam" (Jesus) with His resurrection; finally, believers will possess their glorified bodies. We have not reached the last stage yet.

Paul's best effort to clarify what he means by the glory of the resurrection body is to list contrasts:

Contrasts

Earthly Body	Resurrection Body
Perishable	Imperishable
Dishonor	Glory
Weakness	Power
Natural	Spiritual
First Adam	Last Adam
Living Person	Life-giving Spirit
From the earth	Heaven

Considering Jesus' resurrected body from the gospel accounts, although it was glorified and in many ways different from ours, He could still be recognized by the disciples. Later, when Paul on the Damascus road saw Jesus, he testified that he "saw a light from heaven, brighter than the sun" (Acts 26:13). Alternately, the apostle John on Patmos saw a glorious Jesus with a head white as snow, fiery eyes, and feet like polished bronze (Rev 1:14, 15). From these Scriptural accounts, it is difficult to describe what our resurrected bodies will be like other than in the broad categories Paul lists in 1 Corinthians 15:42-49. There will be points of continuity with our mortal bodies, but also many points of discontinuity. See Ryrie's discussion below in Basic Theology, Ch. 46, "The

Resurrection and Ascension of Christ," under "A new prototype body."

> "With the resurrection of Christ there appeared for the first time in history a new kind of resurrection body, for He rose with an eternal body, never to die again. Before that event, all resurrections were restorations to the former earthly bodies.
>
> Christ's resurrection body had links with His unresurrected earthly body. People recognized Him (Jn 20:20), the wounds inflicted by crucifixion were retained (Jn 20:25-29; Rev 5:6), He had the capacity (though not the need) to eat (Lk 24:30-33, 41-43), He breathed on the disciples (Jn 20:22), and that body had flesh and bones proving that He was not merely a spirit showing itself (Lk 24:39-40).
>
> But His resurrection body was different. He could enter closed rooms without opening doors (Lk 24:36; Jn 20:19), He could appear and disappear at will (Lk 24:15; Jn 20:19), and apparently He was never limited by physical needs such as sleep or food.
>
> The most detailed description of Christ risen and ascended is found in Rev 1:12-16. Here John recorded his vision of the glorified Christ. He was like a son of man, which links Him to His former earthly appearance, but He also radiated glory from His eyes, feet, voice, and face. This is the way we shall see Him someday.
>
> His resurrection also serves as a prototype of the resurrection of believers. Twice Christ is referred to as the firstborn from the dead (Col 1:18; Rev 1:5). This means that He was the first to have an eternally resurrected body. Our resurrection bodies, like His, will be different from our earthly bodies. When answering the question, "What will believers' resurrection bodies be like?" Paul said that they will not be the same bodies that were laid in the grave simply reconstituted; but they will be new yet related to the former ones (1 Cor 15:35-41)."
>
> Believers in the eternal state will be "like Him" (1 Jn 3:2). What does this mean? John explained in the following verses. To be like Him means to be pure (1 Jn 3:3), to be without sin (1 Jn 3:5), and to be righteous (1 Jn 3:7). Our entire beings, including our bodies, will be characterized these ways.

Our glorified bodies will be made in the likeness of Christ's resurrected body. Just as our mortal bodies are fashioned after Adam's, so our new bodies will be fashioned after Christ's.

QUESTION 16

For humans, spirituality is related to physical existence. *True or False?*

QUESTION 17

Match the similar but contrasting descriptions of Adam and Christ:

Adam	*Christ*
First man	Last Adam
Living person	Spiritual
Natural	From heaven
From the earth	Life-giving Spirit

Topic 4: Victory Over Death (1 Cor 15:50-58)

For believers, death is only a temporary separation from the physical body. When Christ returns, believers who have died will be raised immortal, and believers who are still alive will be transformed. Armed with such a hope, believers can persevere in faith and obedience.

Putting on Immortality (15:50-57)

Assignment

*Read 1 Corinthians 15:50-57.

- Read Constable, "The Assurance of Victory Over Death" (refer to the Articles section at the end of this lesson), through the note on 15:57.
- Read "Putting on Immortality."

Putting on Immortality

Paul is not teaching here that the rapture will be instantaneous (although that may be true)—just that the changing of our bodies will be instantaneous.

What does it mean to inherit the kingdom of God? The word inherit here implies future benefits, not yet fully realized. "Flesh and blood" is parallel to "the perishable" (1 Cor 15:50) and refers to mortal human bodies. The kingdom of God in this verse is parallel to "the imperishable." Paul's emphasizes the glorified bodies that believers will receive when Christ comes again. Who will inherit the kingdom of God? Clearly, Paul means all believers, and all believers will receive glorified bodies. Once we have our glorified bodies, death is ended. The elimination of death implies the elimination of sin through the work of Christ.

QUESTION 18

What does it mean to inherit the kingdom of God in this passage? Record your answer in your Life Notebook.

At the rapture, believers are instantly transformed, inheriting immortality and complete victory over sin and death. What a glorious hope!

QUESTION 19

"Flesh and blood" in 1 Corinthians 15:50 means the mortal body. *True or False?*

QUESTION 20

Why is it impossible for our mortal bodies to enter into eternity?

Application (15:58)

Assignment

- Read 1 Corinthians 15:58.
- Read Constable, "Note on 15:58" (refer to the Articles section at the end of this lesson), through the end.
- Read "Application."

Application

If all believers will experience the rapture and inherit a resurrection body, then what is the motivation to persevere in laboring for the Lord? The motivations are love for the Lord, gratitude for what He has done, and hope of future inheritance. The assurance of the resurrection gives believers the courage to go on, to stand firm, and to labor for the Lord despite their sufferings on earth. Our confidence in the resurrection assures us that everything we suffer for the Lord is worth it. Eventually, we will inherit the kingdom. The rewards and the glory of the kingdom are incomparably greater than our present "light, momentary suffering" (see 2 Cor 4:17). Therefore, no labor for the Lord is in vain.

In view of the future grace awaiting believers that Paul has just outlined, he urges the Corinthians to stand firm in doctrine and practice. Believers' future hope should have direct application in day-to-day living.

QUESTION 21

In your Life Notebook, evaluate yourself according to 1 Corinthians 15:58. Over the past six months, list three ways in which you have been firm, unmoved, and outstanding (or abounding) in the work of the Lord. Thank the Lord for His grace. Also, list three ways in which you have fallen short of this exhortation, and ask for the Lord's forgiveness. How can you improve?

Lesson 12 Articles

Notes on 1 Corinthians

Dr. Thomas L. Constable; 2003 Edition

F. THE RESURRECTION OF BELIEVERS CH. 15

The Apostle Paul did not introduce the instruction on the resurrection that follows with the formula that identifies it as a response to a specific question from the Corinthians (i.e., *peri de*). From what he said in this chapter he apparently knew that some in the church had adopted a belief concerning the resurrection that was contrary to apostolic teaching. They believed that there is no resurrection of the dead (cf. vv. 12, 16, 29, 32; Acts 17:32). Apparently he included this teaching to correct this error and to reaffirm the central importance of the doctrine of the resurrection in the Christian faith.

> ." . . the letter itself is not finished. Lying behind their view of spirituality is not simply a false view of spiritual gifts, but a false theology of spiritual existence as such. Since their view of 'spirituality' had also brought them to deny a future resurrection of the body, it is fitting that this matter be taken up next. The result is the grand climax of the letter as a whole, at least in terms of its argument." (377)

> "This chapter has been called 'the earliest Christian doctrinal essay,' and it is the only part of the letter which deals directly with doctrine." (378)

Evidently the Corinthians believed in the resurrection of Jesus Christ, but belief in His resurrection did not necessarily involve believing that God would raise all believers in Christ. Christ's resurrection gave hope to believers about the future, but that hope did not necessarily involve the believer's resurrection. This seems to have been the viewpoint of the early Christians until Paul taught them that their bodily resurrection was part of their hope, which he did here. Thus this chapter has great theological value to the church.

> ." . . apparently soon after Paul's departure from Corinth things took a turn for the worse in this church. A false theology began to gain ground, rooted in a radical pneumatism that denied the value/significance of the body and expressed in a somewhat 'overrealized,' or 'spiritualized,' eschatology. Along with this there arose a decided movement against Paul. These two matters climax in this letter in their pneumatic behavior (chaps. 12—14) and their denial of a resurrection of the dead (chap. 15), which included their questioning of his status as *pneumatikos* ([spiritual] 14:36-38) and perhaps their calling him an 'abortion' or a 'freak' (15:8). Thus, as elsewhere, Paul sets out not only to correct some bad theology but at the same time to remind them of his right to do so." (379)

l. The resurrection of Jesus Christ 15:1-11

Paul began by reaffirming their commonly held belief: Jesus Christ was raised from the dead. In this section the apostle stressed the objective reality of both Jesus Christ's death and resurrection.

15:1 - The Corinthians and all Christians have their standing in Christ as a result of the gospel message.

15:2 - Paul did not entertain the possibility that his readers could lose their salvation by abandoning the gospel he had preached to them. The NIV translation captures his thought well. Their denial of the Resurrection might indicate that some of them had not really believed the gospel.

15:3 - As with the events of the Lord's Supper (11:23) Paul had heard of the Lord Jesus' death, burial, resurrection, and post-resurrection appearances and had then passed this information along to others. Elsewhere he wrote that he had not received the gospel from other people but directly from the Lord (Gal.

1:11). Probably some aspects of it came to him one way and others another. He apparently received the essence of the gospel on the Damascus road and learned more details from other sources.

> "He received the facts from the Apostles and others; the import of the facts was made known to him by Christ (Gal. i. 12)." (380)

Three facts are primary concerning Jesus' death. He died, He died for people's sins, and He died as the Scriptures revealed He would. These facts received constant reaffirmation in the early preaching of the church (cf. Acts 3:13-18; 8:32-35).

> "People are wicked and sinful; they do not know God. But Christ died 'for our sins,' not only to forgive but also *to free people from their sins.* Hence Paul's extreme agitation at the Corinthians' sinfulness, because they are thereby persisting in the very sins from which God in Christ has saved them. This, after all, is what most of the letter is about." (380)

> "Since Judaism did not interpret this passage messianically, at least not in terms of a personal Messiah, and since there is no immediate connection between the death of Jesus and the idea that his death was 'for our sins,' it is fair to say that whoever made that connection is the 'founder of Christianity.' All the evidence points to Jesus himself, especially at the Last Supper with his interpretation of his death in the language of Isa. 53 as 'for you' (see on 11:23-25)." (382)

15:4 - Burial emphasizes the finality of the Messiah's death (cf. Acts 2:29) and attests the reality of His resurrection (cf. Acts 13:29-30).

The perfect tense and passive voice of the Greek verb translated "was raised" implies that since God raised Him He is still alive. The third day was Sunday. Friday, the day of the crucifixion, was the first day, and Saturday was the second. The phrase "according to the Scriptures" probably describes the Resurrection alone in view of the structure of the sentence (cf. Lev. 23:10-14; Ps. 16:10-11; 17:15-24; Isa. 53:10b; Hos. 6:2; Matt. 12:38-41).

> "Though the resurrection is part of the gospel message, it is not part of the saving work of Christ on the cross. The resurrection is stated as proof of the efficacy of Christ's death. Having accomplished redemption by His death, Jesus Christ was 'raised because of our justification' (Rom. 4:25). The fact that Jesus Christ is alive is part of the Christian's good news, but individuals are saved by His death, not by His resurrection." (383)

15:5 - Peter was, of course, the leader of the disciples. Perhaps Paul referred to the Lord's special appearance to Peter (Lk 24:34) because some in the Corinthian church revered Peter (1:12) as well as because he was the key disciple. "The twelve" refers to the 12 disciples even though only 11 of them were alive when the Lord appeared to them. This was a way of referring to that particular group of Jesus' followers during His earthly ministry (Mt. 10:1).

15:6 - This is the only record of this particular appearance in the New Testament. That Jesus appeared to so many people at one time is evidence that His resurrection body was not a spirit. Many people testified that they had seen Him on this single occasion. Since the Resurrection took place about 23 years before Paul wrote this epistle, it is reasonable that the majority of this group of witnesses was still alive. Any skeptical Corinthians could check with them.

15:7 - This James was most likely the half-brother of Jesus. He became the leader of the Jerusalem church.

The apostles as a group included Matthias who was not one of the 12 original disciples. This probably refers to a collective appearance to all the apostles.

15:8 - Paul regarded the Lord's appearance to him on the Damascus road as an equivalent post-resurrection appearance and the Lord's last one. The apostle may have referred to himself as he did (lit. as if to an abortion) not because his apostleship came to him prematurely. The Lord appointed him some time after the others. He probably did so because compared with the backgrounds and appointments of the other apostles Paul's were unusual.

> "Since this is such an unusual term of deprecation, and since it occurs with the article, *the* 'abortion,' it has often been suggested that the Corinthians themselves have used the term to describe Paul, as one who because of his personal weaknesses is something of a 'freak' in comparison with other apostles, especially Apollos and Peter. Others have suggested that the term is a play on Paul's name—*Paulus*, 'the little one.' Hence they dismissed him as a 'dwarf.' This has the advantage of helping to explain the unusual 'digression' in vv. 9-10, where he in fact allows that he is 'least' of all the apostles; nonetheless God's grace worked the more abundantly in his behalf.

> "In any case, whether it originated with them, which seems altogether likely, or with Paul himself in a sudden outburst of self-disparagement, it seems hardly possible to understand this usage except as a term that describes him vis-à-vis the Corinthians' own view of apostleship." (384)

Paul stressed the appearances of the risen Christ (vv. 5-9) because they prove that His resurrection was not to a form of "spiritual" (i.e., noncorporeal) existence. Just as His body died and was buried so it was raised and many witnesses saw it, often many witnesses at one time.

15:9 - The apostle probably used their view of him as a "freak" to comment on his view of himself in this verse and the next one. Evidently Paul felt himself the least worthy to be an apostle. He did not regard his apostleship inferior to that of the other apostles, however. The reason for his feeling this way was the fact that while the other apostles were building up the church he was tearing it down.

15:10 - Paul's apostolic calling was a gracious gift from God. The giving of God's grace proves vein when it does not elicit the appropriate response of loving service. Paul responded to God's unusually great grace to him by offering back unusually great service to God. However, he did not view his service as self-generated but the product of God's continual supply of grace to him. God saved Paul by grace, and Paul served God by God's grace.

15:11 - Paul and the other apostles all believed and preached the same gospel. Paul did not proclaim a different message from what Peter, James, and the others did. This commonly agreed on message is what the Corinthians had believed when those who had ministered in Corinth had preached to them. By denying the resurrection the Corinthians were following neither Apollos, nor Cephas, nor Christ. They were pursuing a theology of their own.

The point of this section of verses was to present the gospel message, including the account of Jesus Christ's resurrection, as what many reliable eyewitnesses saw and all the apostles preached. Paul did this to stress that Jesus Christ's resurrection, which most of the Corinthians accepted, had objective reality, not to prove that He rose from the dead. Even though Paul had a different background from the other apostles, he heralded the same message they did. Consequently his original readers did not need to fear that what they had heard from him was some cultic perversion of the truth. It was the true gospel, and they should continue to believe it.

2. The certainty of resurrection 15:12-34

In the preceding paragraph Paul firmly established that the gospel the Corinthians had believed contained the fact that God had raised Jesus Christ bodily, along with other equally crucial facts. Next he proceeded to show the consequences of rejecting belief in the resurrection of the body.

The negative alternative 15:12-19

Paul first appealed to the Corinthians' logic. (385) Here it becomes clear for the first time in the chapter that some of them were saying that there is no resurrection of the dead. If they were correct, they had neither a past nor a future.

15:12 - Belief in the resurrection of the body seems to have been difficult for Greeks to have accepted in other places as well as in Corinth (cf. Acts 17:32; 2 Tim. 2:17). Evidently some of the Corinthian Christians were having second thoughts about this doctrine.

> "These deniers apparently believe that those who are truly 'spiritual' (in the Corinthians' sense) are already 'reigning with Christ' in glory (see 4:8)." (386)

> "On the whole the Greek did believe in the immortality of the soul, but the Greek would never have dreamed of believing in the resurrection of the body." (387)

15:13-14 - Belief in bodily resurrection is foundational to the Christian faith. If the resurrection of the body is impossible, then the resurrection of Jesus Christ is a fiction. If He did not rise, the apostles' preaching rested on a lie, and consequently the Corinthians' faith would have been valueless as well as misplaced.

This is the first in a series of conditional statements that run through verse 19. They are first class conditions in the Greek text, which express the assumption of reality for the sake of the argument. In verse 13 Paul did not express disbelief in the resurrection from the dead. He assumed there is none to make a point. This was also his tactic in verses 14, 16, 17, and 19.

15:15 - Moreover the apostles would not just be in error, they would be false witnesses against God. They would be saying something untrue about God, namely, that He raised Jesus Christ when He really had not. This would be a serious charge to make against the man who had founded their church and claimed to represent God. Really by denying the resurrection the unbelieving Corinthians were the false witnesses.

15:16-18 - Paul repeated his line of thought contained in verses 12-14 in different terms. If Christ was still dead and in the grave, then confidence in Him for salvation is futile. (388) This means the believer is still dead in his or her sins. He or she is without any hope of forgiveness or eternal life. Christians who had already died would be lost forever, eternally separated from God.

> "The denial of their future, that they are destined for resurrection on the basis of Christ's resurrection, has the net effect of a denial of their past, that they have received forgiveness of sins on the basis of Christ's death." (389)

Paul evidently meant that given the Corinthians' position the believer has no future of any kind. "Perished" probably has this meaning since even though they denied the resurrection they were baptizing for the dead (v. 29). It seems unlikely that they would have done this if they believed that death ended all.

15:19 - If the Christian's hope in Christ is just what he or she can expect this side of the grave, that one deserves pity. Of course there are some benefits to trusting Christ as we live here and now (cf. 1 Tim. 4:8). However, we have to place these things in the balance with what we lose in this life for taking a stand for Him (cf. Phil. 3:8; 1 Cor. 4:4-5; 9:25). If we have nothing to hope for the other side of the grave, the Christian life would not be worth living.

To summarize his argument, Paul claimed that if believers have no future, specifically resurrected bodies like Christ's, we have no past or present as well. That is, we have no forgiveness of our sins in the past, and we have no advantage over unbelievers in the present.

> "It is a point of very great importance to remember that the Corinthians were not denying the Resurrection of Jesus Christ; what they were denying is the resurrection of the body; and what Paul is insistent upon is that if a man denies the possibility of the resurrection of the body he has thereby denied the possibility of the Resurrection of Jesus Christ, and has

therefore emptied the Christian message of its truth and the Christian life of its reality." (390)

The positive reality 15:20-28

Paul turned next to show that the resurrection of Christ makes the resurrection of believers both necessary and inevitable. The consequences of this fact are as glorious as the effects of His not being raised are dismal. Those "in Christ" must arise since Christ arose. His resurrection was in the present, but ours will be in the future (i.e., in the eschaton). Christ's resurrection set in motion the defeat of all God's enemies including death. His resurrection demands our resurrection since otherwise death would remain undefeated.

15:20 - The argument advances here by connecting the believer with Christ. Christ was the firstfruits of the larger group of those whom God has chosen for salvation. This is the last mention of Christ's resurrection in the argument, but all that follows rests on this fact.

The Jews celebrated Passover on the fourteenth day of the first month on their sacred calendar. Jesus died on the day Jewish fathers slew the Passover lamb, which was a Friday that year. The Jews offered a sacrifice of firstfruits the day after the Sabbath (Saturday) following the Passover (Lev. 23:10-11), namely, Sunday. This was the day Jesus arose. Fifty days later on Pentecost they presented another offering of new grain that they also called an offering of firstfruits (Lev. 23:15-17). The firstfruits they offered following the Passover were only the first of the crops that they offered later. Paul saw in this comparison the fact that other believers would rise from the dead just as Jesus Christ did. He used the firstfruits metaphor to assert that the resurrection of believers is absolutely inevitable. God Himself has guaranteed it.

15:21-22 - The apostle also drew a lesson from two uniquely representative men, Adam and Christ. Adam was the first man in the old creation, and, like him, all of his sons die physically. Christ is the first man in the new creation, and, like Him, all of His sons will live physically (cf. Rom. 5:12-19). Obviously Paul was referring to believers only as sons of Christ. Both Adam and Jesus were men. Therefore our resurrection will be a human resurrection, not some "spiritual" type of resurrection. Physical resurrection is as inevitable for the son of Jesus Christ as physical death is for the son of Adam.

15:23 - The word translated "order" or "turn" is a military one used of ranks of soldiers (*tagma*). Paul's idea was that Christ was the first rank and experienced resurrection. Christians are in a different rank and will experience resurrection together at a different time, namely, at the Lord's coming (Gr. *parousia*, lit. appearing, i.e., at the Rapture). The apostle did not go on to give a complete explanation of the various resurrections here. There will be other ranks of people who will rise at other times: Tribulation saints, Old Testament believers, the unsaved, etc.

> "Passages like John 5:25-29 and Revelation 20 indicate that there is no such thing taught in Scripture as a 'general resurrection.'" (391)

Paul's point here was that the resurrection of Christians is just as certain to take place as the fact that Christ's already took place. He did not mean that our resurrection will be of a different type than Christ's (i.e., "spiritual" rather than physical).

15:24-26 - The end refers to the end of the present heavens and earth in view of what Paul said about it here. This will come more than 1,000 years after the Rapture. Then Christ, who will have been reigning over His earthly millennial kingdom, will turn over that reign to His Father. Christ's abolishing all other rule, authority, and power will take place when He subdues the rebels that rise up against Him at the end of the Millennium (Rev. 20:7-10). He will also defeat death, and from then on no one will die. The saved will enter the new heavens and new earth to enjoy bliss with God forever while the lost will suffer everlasting torment (Matt. 25:46; Rev. 20:11-15; Rev. 21:1).

"Many see evidence of the millennium in Paul's discourse on resurrection (1 Cor 15, esp. vv. 20-28)." (392)

."... it is not only possible but probable that Paul understood this final triumph to take place during the millennial reign of Christ. To sum up the principal evidence, Paul's use of *epeita* ('after that') and *eita* ('then') in 1 Corinthians 15:23-24, the syntax of 15:24-25, and the parallel use of Psalms 8 and 110 in 1 Corinthians 15 and Hebrews 1 and 2 all point to the understanding that when Paul mentioned a kingdom and reign in 15:24-25, he referred to the reign of Christ on this earth following His return and prior to the eternal state, a time that Revelation 20:4-6 calls 'the thousand years.'" (393)

Even though Jesus triumphed over death in his resurrection, believers still die. Therefore we *must* experience resurrection because we are in Christ and because only then will the final enemy, death, be subdued. Only then will God become all in all.

15:27 - Paul saw Jesus Christ as the person who fulfilled the prophecy recorded in Psalm 8:7. (394) In the psalm the ruler in view is man, but He will be the Man who regained for humanity all that Adam lost (cf. Ps. 110:1). Of course, God Himself will not be under the rule of the Son of God. He is the One who will finally bring all things into subjection to Christ.

15:28 - Finally God will be the head of everything (cf. Rom. 11:36). The earthly millennial kingdom will end and everything will merge into the eternal kingdom of God (cf. Isa. 9:7; Luke 1:33). (395) Christ will be submissive to His Father forever. This is the central passage that affirms the eternal functional (not ontological) subordination of the Son to the Father (cf. 3:22-23; 11:3; John 17:24; Eph. 3:21; Phil. 2:9-11). (396) The Resurrection set in motion a chain of events that will ultimately culminate in the death of death. Then God will resume being what He was before creation, "all in all."

"The meaning seems to be that there will no longer be need of a Mediator: all relations between Creator and creatures, between Father and offspring, will be direct." (397)

In this pericope Paul traced the career of Christ from His resurrection to His final exaltation, which will occur at the end of the present heavens and earth. Undoubtedly he intended his readers to identify with the Savior since he had taught them that believers reproduce the experiences of their Lord as they reproduce His attitudes and actions. In view of what lies ahead, how foolish it would be to deny the resurrection of the body. This passage clarifies the true significance of Easter.

Other arguments for resurrection 15:29-34

Paul turned from Christ's career to the Christian's experience to argue *ad hominem* for the resurrection. (398) The Corinthians' actions, and his, bordered on absurdity if the dead will not rise. This paragraph is something of a digression, and the main argument resumes in verse 35.

15:29 - This verse probably refers to proxy baptism, the custom of undergoing baptism for someone who died before he or she could experience baptism. (399) Evidently the Corinthians were practicing this for people who became Christians on their deathbeds or under other conditions that made it difficult or impossible for them to undergo baptism in water. Paul's mention of the custom is not necessarily an endorsement of it. On the other hand, he did not specifically condemn it either.

Whether he approved of it or not, the Corinthian believers were evidently doing it. Paul used this practice to argue for the reality of resurrection. His point was that if there is no physical resurrection it is foolish to undergo baptism for someone who had died because in that case they are dead and gone forever. (400) Suppose, on the other hand, there is a resurrection. When God will raise those baptized by proxy, they would not suffer shame for failure to undergo baptism while they were alive. Those who had not benefited from proxy baptism would suffer embarrassment.

The Corinthians may have carried proxy baptism over into the church from pagan religions. That is a distinct possibility since we have seen that they had done this with other pagan practices. There is nothing in Scripture that encourages this practice, though some have interpreted this verse as an encouragement. Some Christian groups that believe water baptism contributes to a person's salvation advocate it. Today the Mormons do. However the mention of a practice in Scripture does not always constitute endorsement of it. We have seen this in chapters 8-11 especially.

15:30 - If there is no resurrection, why did Paul endure so many hardships and dangers in his ministry? The apostle's sacrifices do not prove there will be a resurrection, but they do show that he believed there would be one. He willingly faced death daily because he believed God would raise him and that his resurrected body would continue beyond the grave.

15:31 Paul backed up this assertion with a kind of oath. He said he faced death daily just as he boasted about the Corinthians. In this epistle Paul was quite critical of his readers. Probably he meant that he boasted in their very existence as Christians rather than that he boasted to other churches about their behavior.

15:32 - One example of facing death occurred in Ephesus where Paul was when he wrote this epistle. His fight with "wild beasts" was not with wild animals. This expression describes his conflict with very hostile human adversaries. The phrase *kata anthropon* ("from human motives" or "for . . . human reasons," lit. according to man) identifies Paul's words as figurative language. Furthermore Roman citizens did not participate in hand to hand combat with animals in the arenas. (401) Perhaps Demetrius and or Alexander were Paul's antagonists (Acts 19:24-41; 2 Tim. 4:14).

Paul quoted Isaiah 22:13 to prove his point (cf. Ecclesiastes 2:24; 9:7-10). If there is no resurrection we may as well live only for the present.

15:33 - This quotation, contained in a comedy by Menander titled *Thais*, but perhaps dating back to Euripides, (402) had become proverbial. The Greeks generally recognized it as encapsulating a wise thought. Therefore Paul used it to warn his readers that if they kept company with people who denied the resurrection their character would eventually suffer.

15:34 - The Corinthians needed to think correctly. Rather than living for the present, as their pagan neighbors were undoubtedly encouraging them to do, they needed to stop sinning and fulfill their present purpose, namely, propagating the gospel. It was a shame that they had neighbors who still had no knowledge of God since they had much knowledge of God (1:5; 8:1).

> "Since salvation finally has to do with being known by and knowing God (13:12), what makes the Corinthians' persisting in sin so culpable is that it keeps others from the knowledge of God (15:34). (403)

It may be that Paul was also using irony to refer to the "spiritual" viewpoint of the Corinthians. The appearance of "knowledge" here again raises that possibility since, as we have seen, "knowledge" was a Corinthian fascination. Paul had also spoken something to their "shame" earlier (cf. 6:5). If he meant to be ironic, the apostle was probably putting down those responsible for taking the church in the dangerous direction that it had gone. He would have meant that his readers should sober up and stop sinning because some of them did not have the truth, which was to their shame.

These *ad hominem* arguments do not prove beyond doubt that God will raise the bodies of people from the dead, but they support Paul's stronger logical arguments in the preceding section (vv. 12-34). They show that Christians generally and the apostle in particular believed in the Resurrection deeply. It affected the way they lived, as it should. (404)

3. The resurrection body 15:35-49

Paul next addressed the objection that the resurrection of the body is impossible because when a person dies his or her body decomposes and no one can reassemble it. The Corinthians seem to have wanted to avoid thinking that the material body was essentially good. Hellenistic dualism seems to have influenced their thinking about the human body and, therefore, the resurrection. (405) They did not, and most people do not, view very positively a resurrection that involves simply resuscitating human corpses. Paul proceeded to show that the resurrection of believers was not that but a resurrection of *glorified* bodies. Paul taught a more glorious future for believers than the present "spiritual" existence that some in Corinth lauded.

> "The Corinthians are convinced that by the gift of the Spirit, and especially the manifestation of tongues, they have already entered into the spiritual, 'heavenly' existence that is to be. Only the body, to be sloughed off at death, lies between them and their ultimate spirituality. Thus they have denied the body in the present, and have no use for it in the future." (406)

A key word in this section of Paul's argument is "body" (Gr. *soma*), which occurs 10 times compared to no times in the first 34 verses. (407)

Analogies from nature 15:35-44

The apostle proceeded to offer two sets of analogies (seeds, vv. 36-38; and types of bodies, vv. 39-41) that he then applied to the resurrection of the dead (vv. 42-44).

15:35 - This objection to the resurrection has to do with the reconstruction of the body out of the same elements that it formerly possessed. Obviously it would be impossible to reassemble the same cells to reconstruct a person after he or she had been dead for some time. This is the primary problem that Paul solved in the rest of this pericope.

For example, if someone died at sea and sailors buried him, a fish might eat his body. The atoms and molecules of his body would become part of the fish. If a fisherman caught and ate the fish, its body would become part of the fisherman's body. If the fisherman died and an undertaker buried him in the ground and someone eventually sowed wheat over his grave, the fisherman's atoms and molecules would go into the wheat. A third person would eat the wheat and so on. How could the first person's body ever come together again?

15:36-38 - Such an objection sounds very reasonable on the surface, but it is really foolish, and it drew a sharp rebuke from Paul. The "wise" Corinthians were "fools!" The body that God resurrects will not be the same *type* of body that died even though it is the body of the same person. Paul proceeded to illustrate with a seed of grain. A new form of life springs forth from death. The body surrounding the life is different before and after death. Likewise human life exists in one form of body before death, and after death it exists in a different type of body. God does this with grain, so He can do it with humans too. This is so obvious in nature that we can understand Paul's sharp retort in verse 36. (408)

15:39-41 - This passage begins and ends by stressing the differences within kinds of bodies.

> "(Pet lovers take note: Paul did not teach here that animals will be resurrected. He only used them as an example.)" (409)

The second and fifth sentences stress the differences within genus while contrasting the earthly with the heavenly. The central elements state the realities of earthly and heavenly "bodies." Structurally the passage is a chiasm. (410)

A Not all *flesh* is the same (i.e., earthly bodies).

   B Examples of different kinds of flesh: people, animals, birds, fish.

      C There are heavenly and earthly kinds of bodies.

      C' The splendor of heavenly bodies is of one kind and the splendor of earthly bodies is of another kind.

   B' Examples of different kinds of splendor: sun, moon, stars

A' Not all stars (i.e., heavenly bodies) have the same *splendor*.

In verse 39 Paul used animal life to point out the different types (substance) of flesh: human, land animals, birds, and fish. This anticipates what he said later about the earthly and heavenly existence of believers. A body can be genuinely fleshly and still subsist in different forms for different environments. The fact that there are different kinds of bodies among animals should help us understand that there can also be different kinds of human bodies. Some human bodies are mortal and some are immortal. Some are corruptible and others incorruptible.

Likewise the fact that celestial bodies differ in glory (brightness) should help us realize that human bodies can also differ in glory. The glory of a perishable mortal human body is much less than that of an imperishable immortal human body. Also the differing glory of the heavenly bodies argues for differences among glorified believers.

15:42-43 - The human body goes into the ground perishable, as a seed. However, God raises it imperishable, as grain. It goes into the ground in a lowly condition (in "dishonor"), but it arises with honor ("glory"). It is weak when it dies, but it is powerful when it arises.

15:44 - It is natural (Gr. *psychikon*, soulish), belonging to the present age; but it becomes spiritual (*pneumatikos*, i.e., supernatural), belonging to the future age. The Corinthians had not entered into their eschatological states yet. This would come with their resurrections. Their *bodies* would become spiritual, namely, fitted for their future existence.

The analogy from Scripture 15:45-49

Paul now returned to his analogy between Adam and Christ (cf. vv. 21-22) to reinforce his argument, which he had brought to a head in verse 44.

15:45 - The natural body is physical, the product of Adam who received life from God (Gen. 2:7). That life resides in a body characterized as "soulish" (i.e., alive with material and immaterial components). It eventually dies. However the resurrection body is spiritual, the product of Jesus Christ, the second Adam, who gives new life. That life will inhabit a body that will never die. Paul called it spiritual because it is ready for the spiritual rather than the physical realm. Moreover it comes to us from a spirit being, Jesus Christ, rather than a physical being, Adam. One can assume full "spiritual" existence, including a spiritual body, only as Christ did, namely, by resurrection. (411)

15:46 - Even though God breathed life into Adam at Creation, that gift constituted Adam a natural person fitted for the present order. The breathing of new life into believers at resurrection, so to speak, will make us spiritual persons fitted for the eschaton. We have the physical body until the eschaton, not before it begins.

Paul may have included this word of clarification to refute the Platonic idea that the ideal precedes the real. Plato taught that the ultimate realities are spiritual, and physical things only represent them. This is probably a view that some in Corinth held. Paul said the physical body precedes the spiritual body, which is the ultimate body.

15:47-48 - God formed Adam out of dust to live on this planet (Gen. 2:7). Jesus Christ had a heavenly origin. However, Paul seems to have meant more than this since he compared two human beings, "the first Adam" and "the last Adam." His emphasis seems to have been that the first Adam was fitted for life in this age with natural life whereas the last Adam was fitted for life in the age to come with spiritual life. God equipped both to live in the realm that they would occupy. Similarly the bodies we inherit from Adam are for earthly existence. The bodies we will receive from Christ at our resurrection will be for living in the spiritual realm. Paul was not speaking of heavenly existence as distinct from life in hell but as spiritual in contrast with earthly.

> "Each race has the attributes of its Head. As a consequence of this law . . ., we who once wore the likeness of the earthly Adam shall hereafter wear that of the glorified Christ.

What Adam was, made of dust to be dissolved into dust again, such are all who share his life; and what Christ is, risen and eternally glorified, such will be all those who share His life." (412)

15:49 - Those born only of the first Adam, whom God equipped to live in the natural world, likewise exist in that world. However those born also of the last Adam, whom God equipped to live in the supernatural world by resurrection, also will exist in that world. Paul concluded this pericope by reminding them that their bearing the image of the heavenly Adam was still future, and it is certain.

God's intent to make man in His own image (Gen. 1:26) will finally reach fulfillment when believers eventually receive bodies that enable us to live in the spiritual sphere as He does. God's forming man out of the dust of the ground and breathing into his nostrils the breath of life was only the first step toward God's realization of His goal. His creation of resurrection bodies for us will be the second and final step.

> "The problem is that the Corinthians believed that they had already assumed the heavenly existence that was to be, an existence in the Spirit that discounted earthly existence both in its physical and in its behavioral expressions. What Paul appears to be doing once again is refuting both notions. They have indeed borne—and still bear—the likeness of the man of earth. Because of that they are destined to die. But in Christ's resurrection and their being 'in him' they have also begun to bear the likeness of the man of heaven. The urgency is that they truly do so now as they await the consummation when they shall do so fully." (413)

4. The assurance of victory over death 15:50-58

Paul brought his revelation of the resurrection to a climax in this paragraph by clarifying what all this means for the believer in Christ. Here he also dealt with the exceptional case of living believers' transformation at the Rapture. Transformation is absolutely necessary to enter the spiritual mode of future existence. This transformation will happen when Christ returns.

15:50 - The apostle's introductory words indicate a new departure in his thought. The phrase "flesh and blood" refers to the mortal body and living mortals in particular. It is impossible for us in our present physical forms to enter into, as an inheritance, the heavenly place in the kingdom of God that Christ said He was going to prepare for us (John 14:2-3). It is of the spiritual order. "The perishable" also describes us now but looks at the destruction of our present bodies through death.

15:51 - "Behold" or "Listen" grabs the reader's attention and announces something important. Paul was about to explain something never before revealed, a mystery (Gr. *mysterion*; cf. Mt. 13:11; Rom. 11:25; 16:25; 1 Cor. 2:7; 4:1; 13:2; 14:2; Eph. 1:9; 3:3-4, 9; 5:32; 6:19; et al.). He had previously written that at the Rapture dead Christians would rise before God will catch living Christians up to meet the Lord in the air (1 Thess. 4:15-17). (414) He had just revealed that resurrection bodies will be different from our present bodies, spiritual rather than natural (vv. 35-39). Now he revealed that living believers translated at the Rapture would also receive spiritual bodies.

Not every Christian will die before he or she receives a new body, but every one must experience this change, even the "spiritual" Corinthians. Whether we are alive or dead when the Rapture takes place we will all receive spiritual bodies at that moment.

15:52 - This transformation will not be a gradual process but instantaneous. The Greek word translated "moment" or "flash" (*atomos*) refers to an indivisible fragment of time. The blinking of an eye takes only a fraction of a second.

This trumpet blast will summon Christians home to heaven (cf. 1 Thess. 4:16). It is the last trumpet that connects with *our* destiny, the one that signals the end of our present existence and the beginning of our future existence. (415)

> "We need not suppose that St Paul believed that an actual trumpet would awaken and summon the dead. The language is symbolical in accordance with the apocalyptic ideas of the time. The point is that the resurrection of the dead and the transformation of the living will be simultaneous, as of two companies obeying the same signal." (416)

Some posttribulationists equate this trumpet with the seventh or last trumpet of Revelation 11:15-18. (417) This does not seem to me to be valid. Other trumpets will sound announcing various other events in the future (cf. Matt. 24:31; Rev. 8:2, 6, 13; 9:14; et al.). However, Christians, believers living in the church age, will not be on the earth, and those trumpets will not affect us. (418) The fact that Paul included himself in the group living at the time of the Rapture shows he expected that event to take place imminently (cf. 1 Thess. 4:15, 17). If he had believed the Tribulation precedes the Rapture, it would have been natural for him to mention that here. (419)

> "Christ's return is always imminent; we must never cease to watch for it. The first Christians thought it so near that they faced the possibility of Jesus' return in their lifetime. Paul thinks he too may perhaps be alive when it happens." (420)

> "The simple fact is that Paul did not know when Christ would return. He was in the exact position in which we are. All that he knew, and all that we know, is that Christ may come at any time." (421)

Paul did not answer the interesting questions of who will blow or who will hear this trumpet.

Throughout Israel's history God announced His working for the nation and He summoned His people to Himself with the blowing of trumpets (Exod. 19:16, 19; 20:18; Lev. 25:9; Num. 10:2, 8-10; et al.). He will use a trumpet for this purpose at the Rapture as well.

15:53 - The dead will rise in bodies that are not subject to corruption, and the living will receive immortal bodies too. Paul may have wanted to contrast the dead and the living by the terms he chose for each in the first and second parts of this verse respectively. (422) Still the distinction is not strong enough to be significant. Both the dead and the living will receive imperishable immortal bodies.

15:54 - This transformation will fulfill the prophecy in Isaiah 25:8. What Paul just revealed harmonizes with prophetic Scripture. God will overcome death (cf. vv. 23-28).

15:55 - Paul modified for his own purposes Hosea's defiant challenge for death to do its worst (Hos. 13:14) and used the passage to taunt death himself. Death is man's last enemy (cf. v. 25). God will defeat it when He raises His people to life.

15:56 - The fatal sting of death touches humans through sin (Rom. 6:23). What makes sin sinful is the law of God (Rom. 7:7-11). Because Jesus Christ overcame sin and fulfilled the law, death cannot hold its prey (Rom. 5:12, 20). Death is still an enemy in the sense that it robs us of mortal life. Notwithstanding it is not a terror to the believer because it is the doorway into an immortal life of bliss.

15:57 - The victory over the condemnation of the law, sin, and death comes to us through Jesus Christ (cf. Rom. 8:2). For this Paul was very grateful to God, as every believer should be.

15:58 - Paul concluded his discussion of the resurrection with an exhortation to be faithful in the present (cf. 4:16-17; 5:13; 6:20; 7:40; 10:31-33; 11:33-34; 12:31; 14:39-40).

> "Despite the magnificent crescendo with which Paul brings the argument of chap. 15 to its climax, the last word is not the sure word of future hope and triumph of vv. 50-57; rather, in light of such realities, the last word is an exhortation to Christian living (v. 58). Thus, eschatological salvation, the great concern of the epistle, includes proper behavior or it simply is not the gospel Paul preaches." (423)

Specifically Paul's exhortation does not just call for ethical behavior (cf. vv. 33-34) but for continued involvement in fulfilling the Great Commission, the work of the gospel.

This chapter began with a review of the gospel message from which some in the church were in danger of departing by denying the resurrection. The charge to remain steadfast therefore probably means to remain steadfast in the gospel as the Lord and the apostles had handed it down to them. Paul's readers should not move away from it but should remain immovable in it. They should also increase their efforts to serve the Lord even as Paul had done (v. 10). Rather than living *for* the present (v. 32) believers should live *in* the present with the future clearly in view (cf. 1:9; 9:26). One day we will have to give an account of our stewardship (3:12-15).

No one except Jesus Christ has come back from the dead to tell us what is on the other side. However, His testimony through His apostles is sufficient to give us confidence that there is life and bodily resurrection after death. We will live that life in a changed body that will be incapable of perishing. It is therefore imperative that we make sure we and all around us enter that phase of our existence with our sins covered by the sacrifice of Christ.

Bibliography

378. Robertson and Plummer, p. 329.

379. Fee, *The First . . .*, p. 716.

380. Robertson and Plummer, p. 333.

381. Fee, "Toward a . . .," p. 49.

383. Idem, *The First . . .*, p. 724.

383. Thomas L. Constable, "The Gospel Message," in *Walvoord: A Tribute*, p. 203.

384. Fee, *The First . . .*, p. 733.

385. In this form of logic, called *modus tollens*, Paul's argument was that since Christ was raised there is a resurrection of believers. That Paul had believers in view, rather than all people, seems clear in that he was discussing the hope of believers. Other passages teach the resurrection of other groups of people, even all others (e.g., Dan. 12:2; Rev. 20:4-5, 12; et al.).

386. Furnish, p. 74.

387. Barclay, *The Letter . . .*, p. 156.

388 See Norman L. Geisler, "The Significance of Christ's Physical Resurrection," *Bibliotheca Sacra* 146:582 (April-June 1989):148-70.

389. Fee, *The First . . .*, p. 743.

390. Barclay, *The Letter . . .*, p. 153.

391. Wiersbe, 1:618.

392. Robert L. Saucy, *The Case for Progressive Dispensationalism*, p. 280.

393. D. Edmond Hiebert, "Evidence from 1 Corinthians 15," in *A Case for Premillennialism: A New Consensus*, p. 234.

394. See Donald R. Glenn, "Psalm 8 and Hebrews 2: A Case Study in Biblical Hermeneutics and Biblical Theology," in *Walvoord: A Tribute*, pp. 44-45.

395. Cf. Saucy, *The Case . . .*, pp. 321-22. Some interpreters believe the kingdom Paul referred to is Christ's present cosmic lordship that he exercises from heaven, e.g., C. E. Hill, "Paul's Understanding of Christ's Kingdom in I Corinthians 15:20-28," *Novum Testamentum* 30:4 (October 1988):297-320. But this view does not harmonize well with biblical eschatology.

396. John V. Dahms, "The Subordination of the Son," *Journal of the Evangelical Theological Society* 37:3 (September 1994):351-64. See also Mark 13:32; 14:62; John 1:1; 14:28; 1 Cor. 8:6; Phil. 4:19-20.

397. Robertson and Plummer, p. 358.

398. An *ad hominem* argument is one that appeals to self-interest rather than to logic.

399. Morris, p. 219, wrote that there are 30 to 40 different explanations of this verse. See the commentaries for other views and John D. Reaume, "Another Look at 1 Corinthians 15:29, 'Baptized for the Dead'," *Bibliotheca Sacra* 152:608 (October-December 1995):457-75. Joel R. White, "Baptized on Account of the Dead": The Meaning of 1 Corinthians 15:29 in its Context," *Journal of Biblical Literature* 116:3 (1997):487-99, believed the first reference to "the dead" in this verse refers to the apostles who had died metaphorically (cf. v. 31).

400. See Barrett, pp. 362-63; Robertson and Plummer, p. 360.

401. Bruce, *1 and 2 Corinthians*, p. 149; Robertson and Plummer, p. 362.

402. Morris, p. 221.

403. Fee, "Toward a . . .," p. 40.

404. For an introduction to reincarnation, which denies resurrection, see H. Wayne House, "Resurrection, Reincarnation, and Humanness," *Bibliotheca Sacra* 148:590 (April-June 1991):131-50.

405. Dualism is the philosophy, so common in pagan Greek thought, that the body is only the husk of the real "person" who dwells within. The more one can live without the constraints that the body imposes the better. The biblical view, on the other hand, is that the body is essentially good and just as much a part of the real "person" as the immaterial part (cf. Gen. 2:7).

406. Fee, *The First . . .*, p. 778.

407. "Dead" (Gr. *nekros*), on the other hand, appears 11 times in verses 1-34 but only three times after verse 34. These facts illustrate the shift in Paul's argument.

408. A fool in biblical literature is someone who excludes God from consideration. That is exactly what the Corinthians were doing when they failed to observe what God did in the seed that they sowed in their fields.

409. Wiersbe, 1:620.

410. Fee, *The First . . .*, p. 783.

411. For further discussion, see Richard B. Gaffin Jr., "'Life-Giving Spirit': Probing the Center of Paul's Pneumatology," *Journal of the Evangelical Theological Society* 41:4 (December 1998):573-89.

412. Robertson and Plummer, p. 374.

413. Fee, *The First . . .*, p. 795.

414. The three key New Testament passages that deal with the Rapture are John 14:1-3; 1 Corinthians 15:51-53; and 1 Thessalonians 4:13-18.

415. See Barnabas Lindars, "The Sound of the Trumpet: Paul and Eschatology," *Bulletin of the John Rylands University Library of Manchester* 67:2 (Spring 1985):766-82.

416. Robertson and Plummer, p. 377.

417. E.g., Alexander Reese, *The Approaching Advent of Christ*, p. 73.

418. Renald E. Showers, *Maranatha: Our Lord, Come! A Definitive Study of the Rapture of the Church*, pp. 259-69, showed that this "last trump" is not the very last one.

419. For more evidence that the Rapture takes place before the Tribulation, see J. Dwight Pentecost, *Things to Come*, pp. 193-218; John F. Walvoord, *The Rapture Question*; idem, *The Blessed Hope and the Tribulation*; and Ryrie, *Basic Theology*, pp. 482-87.

420. Gaston Deluz, *A Companion to I Corinthians*, p. 248. See also Gerald B. Stanton, *Kept from the Hour*, ch. 6: "The Imminency of the Coming of Christ for the Church," pp. 108-37.

421. Lenski, p. 737.

422. Joachim Jeremias, "Flesh and Blood Cannot Inherit the Kingdom of God," *New Testament Studies* 2 (1955-56):152.

Lesson 12 Self Check

QUESTION 1

Paul wrote 1 Corinthians 15 because some believers at Corinth did not believe that Jesus had been raised from the dead. *True or False?*

QUESTION 2

Jesus' resurrection took place about twenty-three years before Paul wrote 1 Corinthians. *True or False?*

QUESTION 3

Paul argued that Christ's resurrection was the firstfruits, guaranteeing believers' resurrection. *True or False?*

QUESTION 4

What does 1 Corinthians 15:28 teach?

    A. The Son is not God.

    B. In eternity everything is God.

    C. The Son is functionally subordinate to the Father.

    D. Jesus is no different from the angels.

QUESTION 5

Believers' glorified bodies will no longer be human. *True or False?*

QUESTION 6

If Christ has not been raised from the dead, all of the following are true **except** which one?

    A. The apostles are spreading lies.

    B. Believers in Christ are still in their sins.

    C. Preaching the gospel is futile.

    D. The sacrifices of believers are still worthwhile.

QUESTION 7

To whom is putting on imperishable bodies promised?

    A. Only believers who have died

    B. Only believers who are alive at the rapture

    C. All believers

    D. All mankind

QUESTION 8

Paul supports the practice of baptism for the dead. *True or False?*

QUESTION 9

When Paul wrote that he "fought with wild beasts at Ephesus" (1 Cor 15:32), what did he mean that he fought with?

    A. Wild animals

    B. Human adversaries

    C. Demons

    D. His sin nature

QUESTION 10

A person's beliefs directly influence their behavior. *True or False?*

Unit 4 Exam

QUESTION 1

Paul made arguments from theology and culture when he advocated women's head coverings in worship services. *True or False?*

QUESTION 2

In 1 Corinthians 11:2-17 Paul's main point is male dominance in human society. *True or False?*

QUESTION 3

Many scholars believe that Paul's argument about headship in 1 Corinthians 11:3 refers to source rather than authority. *True or False?*

QUESTION 4

Love involves motives as well as actions. *True or False?*

QUESTION 5

Which of the following is true about a believer's freedom in Christ?

    A. Is without restrictions

    B. Must be limited by truth and love

    C. Makes sin unimportant for the believer

    D. Guarantees his bodily resurrection

QUESTION 6

Which group holds the transubstantiation view of the nature of Christ's presence in communion?

    A. Lutherans

    B. Baptists

    C. Catholics

    D. Presbyterians

QUESTION 7

Prophecy was encouraged at Corinth, under which of the following conditions?

    A. It was only done by men

    B. It was evaluated

    C. The prophet wrote down what he said

    D. It contained future predictions

QUESTION 8

In 1 Corinthians 11:17-34, Paul instructed that only baptized believers should take communion. *True or False?*

QUESTION 9

The new covenant was prophesied in the Old Testament by whom?

   A. Moses

   B. David

   C. Daniel

   D. Jeremiah

QUESTION 10

Paul instructs believers to examine themselves before partaking of communion. What did he mean?

   A. Go to confession with the pastor before taking communion

   B. Don't take communion unless you are absolutely sure you have confessed every sin

   C. Make sure you don't take communion with dirty hands

   D. Examine your heart and manner to be sure they reflect the holiness of the Lord's Supper

QUESTION 11

What is the best indication that someone is spiritual?

   A. He performs miracles.

   B. He predicts the future.

   C. He speaks in tongues.

   D. He confesses Jesus as Lord.

QUESTION 12

Spiritual gifts are eternal. *True or False?*

QUESTION 13

Paul's extended metaphor in 1 Corinthians 12 to illustrate unity amidst diversity is the body. *True or False?*

QUESTION 14

In the body of Christ, no one person has all the spiritual gifts. *True or False?*

QUESTION 15

Paul mentions God's discipline for believers in 1 Corinthians 11-15 with regard to which sin?

   A. Violation of the women's head covering standard

   B. Profaning the holiness of communion

   C. Speaking in tongues during the worship service without an interpreter

   D. Teaching that there is no resurrection of believers' bodies

QUESTION 16

Many scholars believe that 1 Corinthians 15:23-24 supports the concept of the millennium. *True or False?*

QUESTION 17

Paul encouraged worship services at Corinth that were orderly, displayed spiritual gifts, and allowed the congregation to participate. *True or False?*

QUESTION 18

Speaking in tongues in the worship service without interpretation violates the principle of intelligibility. *True or False?*

QUESTION 19

Speaking in tongues is a sure sign that someone is a Christian. *True or False?*

QUESTION 20

When Paul wrote that he "fought with wild beasts at Ephesus" (1 Cor 15:32), he meant that he fought with human adversaries. *True or False?*

QUESTION 21

All believers will receive resurrected bodies. *True or False?*

QUESTION 22

A person's beliefs have no relationship to his behavior. *True or False?*

QUESTION 23

Why did Paul write 1 Corinthians 15?

    A. Some believers at Corinth had never heard the gospel.

    B. Some believers at Corinth were saying there is no bodily resurrection for believers.

    C. The church wrote to ask him if they should expect a bodily resurrection.

    D. Some in Corinth believed that only baptized believers would be resurrected.

QUESTION 24

Paul brings up baptism for the dead for what reason?

    A. To show that those who practice it must believe in the bodily resurrection

    B. To condemn the practice

    C. To advocate the practice

    D. To support the principle of doctrinal freedom for believers

QUESTION 25

All of the following are true of believers' glorified bodies **except** which one?

    A. They are not human.

    B. They are not mortal.

    C. They are spiritual.

    D. They are glorious.

Lesson 12 Answers to Questions

QUESTION 1: *Your answer*
QUESTION 2: False
QUESTION 3
    A. Faith that does not persevere
    B. The useless faith of those who deny the resurrection
QUESTION 4: *Your answer*
QUESTION 5
    A. Many witnesses saw Jesus after He was bodily resurrected.
    B. In this aspect, Paul is just as qualified to be an apostle as the Twelve.
    C. Most who saw Jesus after He was resurrected are still alive.
QUESTION 6

Appearance to	Order
Cephas	First
The Twelve	Second
Five hundred believers at once	Third
James	Fourth
All the apostles	Fifth
Paul	Sixth

QUESTION 7
    A. His apostles are false witnesses.
    B. The Christian faith is useless.
    C. Believers who have died have perished.
    D. There is no forgiveness for sins.
QUESTION 8: False
QUESTION 9: *Your answer*
QUESTION 10
    C. God alone is sovereign
QUESTION 11: *Your answer should be one of the following:*
    Firstfruits, First fruits
QUESTION 12: *Your answer should be similar to the following:*
No. In this verse, God refers to the Father. The verse teaches the functional subordination of the Son to the Father.
QUESTION 13: *Your answer should be similar to the following:*
Doctrine and practice are directly related. People act according to what they believe.
QUESTION 14: *Your answer*
QUESTION 15
    C. They will be of a different type than our earthly bodies.
QUESTION 16: True
QUESTION 17

Adam	Christ
First man	Last Adam
Living person	Life-giving Spirit
Natural	Spiritual
From the earth	From heaven

QUESTION 18: *Your answer*
QUESTION 19: True
QUESTION 20: *Your answer should be similar to the following:*
Our mortal bodies are perishable, corrupted by sin, and unsuitable for eternal existence.

QUESTION 21: *Your answer*

Lesson 12 Self Check Answers

QUESTION 1: False
QUESTION 2: True
QUESTION 3: True
QUESTION 4
    C. The Son is functionally subordinate to the Father.
QUESTION 5: False
QUESTION 6
    D. The sacrifices of believers are still worthwhile.
QUESTION 7
    C. All believers
QUESTION 8: False
QUESTION 9
    B. Human adversaries
QUESTION 10: True

Unit 4 Exam Answers

QUESTION 1: True
QUESTION 2: False
QUESTION 3: True
QUESTION 4: True
QUESTION 5
    B. Must be limited by truth and love
QUESTION 6
    C. Catholics
QUESTION 7
    B. It was evaluated
QUESTION 8: False
QUESTION 9
    D. Jeremiah
QUESTION 10
    D. Examine your heart and manner to be sure they reflect the holiness of the Lord's Supper
QUESTION 11
    D. He confesses Jesus as Lord.
QUESTION 12: False
QUESTION 13: True
QUESTION 14: True
QUESTION 15
    B. Profaning the holiness of communion
QUESTION 16: True
QUESTION 17: True
QUESTION 18: True
QUESTION 19: False
QUESTION 20: True
QUESTION 21: True
QUESTION 22: False
QUESTION 23
    B. Some believers at Corinth were saying there is no bodily resurrection for believers.
QUESTION 24
    A. To show that those who practice it must believe in the bodily resurrection
QUESTION 25
    A. They are not human.